ANNIHILATOR

GRANT MORRISON
writer

FRAZER IRVING
illustrator

JARED K. FLETCHER
letterer

JOHN J. HILL
book & logo designer

COMICRAFT/TYLER SMITH
new collected edition

GREG TUMBARELLO
associate editor

BOB SCHRECK
editor

LEGENDARY

© 2020 Legendary Comics, LLC and Grant Morrison. All Rights Reserved. Published by Legendary Comics, 2900 W Alameda Ave, Suite 1500, Burbank CA 91505. No portion of this publication may be reproduced or transmitted in any form or by any means, whether now known or hereafter invented, without the express written permission of the copyright owners, except where permitted by law. No similarity between any of the names, characters, persons and/or institutions in this publication and those of any existing or pre-existing person or institution is intended, and any similarity that may exist is purely coincidental. Legendary Comics and the Knot Logo are the trademarks of Legend Pictures, LLC. Printed in Canada. Printed at Transcontinental Inc. First Printing: November 2020. 10 9 8 7 6 5 4 3 2 1

Thanks to Antonio Solinas and Paolo Accolti Gil for the Italian translations in chapter 3.

INTRODUCTION:
I first met Grant Morrison in
Brooklyn. I was there to be Nick Sax, to bring
to life the character Grant had created in his comic
book series, *HAPPY!*, he was there to see how we would be
treating his creation…it was an unnerving situation for all. I have
to admit I did not fully understand Grant's standing in the Pantheon Of
Graphic Novel Greatness. But there he was on that Brooklyn soundstage:
dressed in black, shaved head, maniacal grin, mischievous glint in his eyes…yup,
that's what I expected. When we were introduced to each other he immediately said,
"I bloody need sex", which I thought was too much info on a first meeting….or, it could
have been "Yur, bloody Nick Sax", but he has a very thick Scottish brogue and I'm never
quite sure of anything he's saying. So anyway, even though Grant said very little I was
strangely drawn…to his whole…"thing". And over time, whether it was on set, in a bar with
a drink in hand, or in the writers room the "thing" I came to realize was his relentless mind
that always saw the World from angles I did not have the capacity to see, let alone dream
up and codify into frameworks of reality and belief. The "thing" was his spirit of anarchy, his
desperation to create HIS way.

In Annihilator I see everything Grant is- a poet, rebel, tortured artist in search of truth, fighter
drawn to the darkness so that he may kick its ass and find the light, or redemption, or
truth…or life….or whatever the hell it is that we're all looking for. Here is the master
story teller exercising (exorcising?) his restless mind, his demanding imagination and
bringing gothic horror sci fi present day futuristic mind bend time bend anti-hero
saga…and I know I left a half dozen descriptors out. Annihilator is what you
get when you let a creative madman alone in a room with himself and
allow him to run free.

"SEND ME TO THE ABYSS.
I'LL SHOW YOU THE SOURCE OF ALL ART"
MAX NOMAX

CHRISTOPHER MELONI

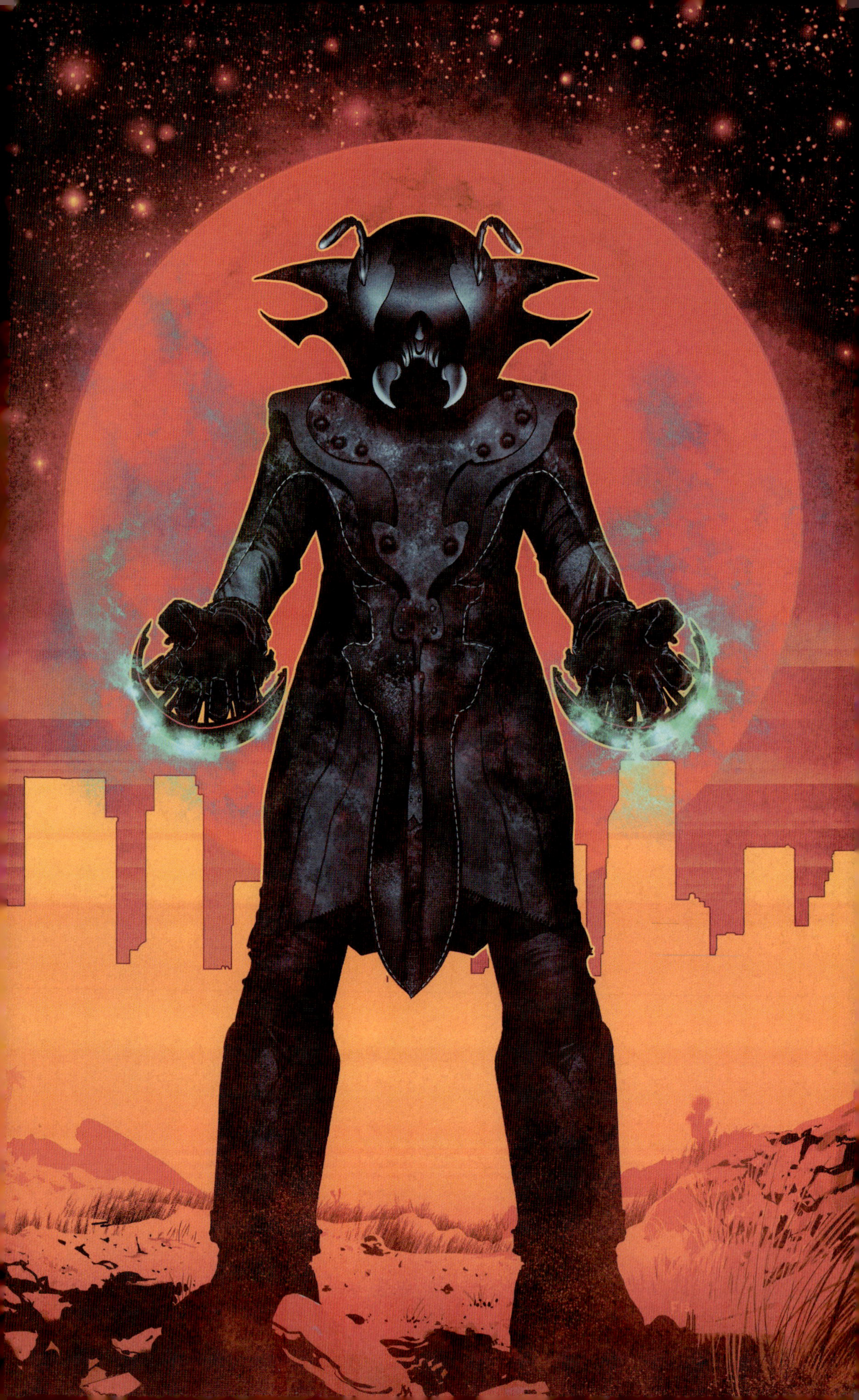

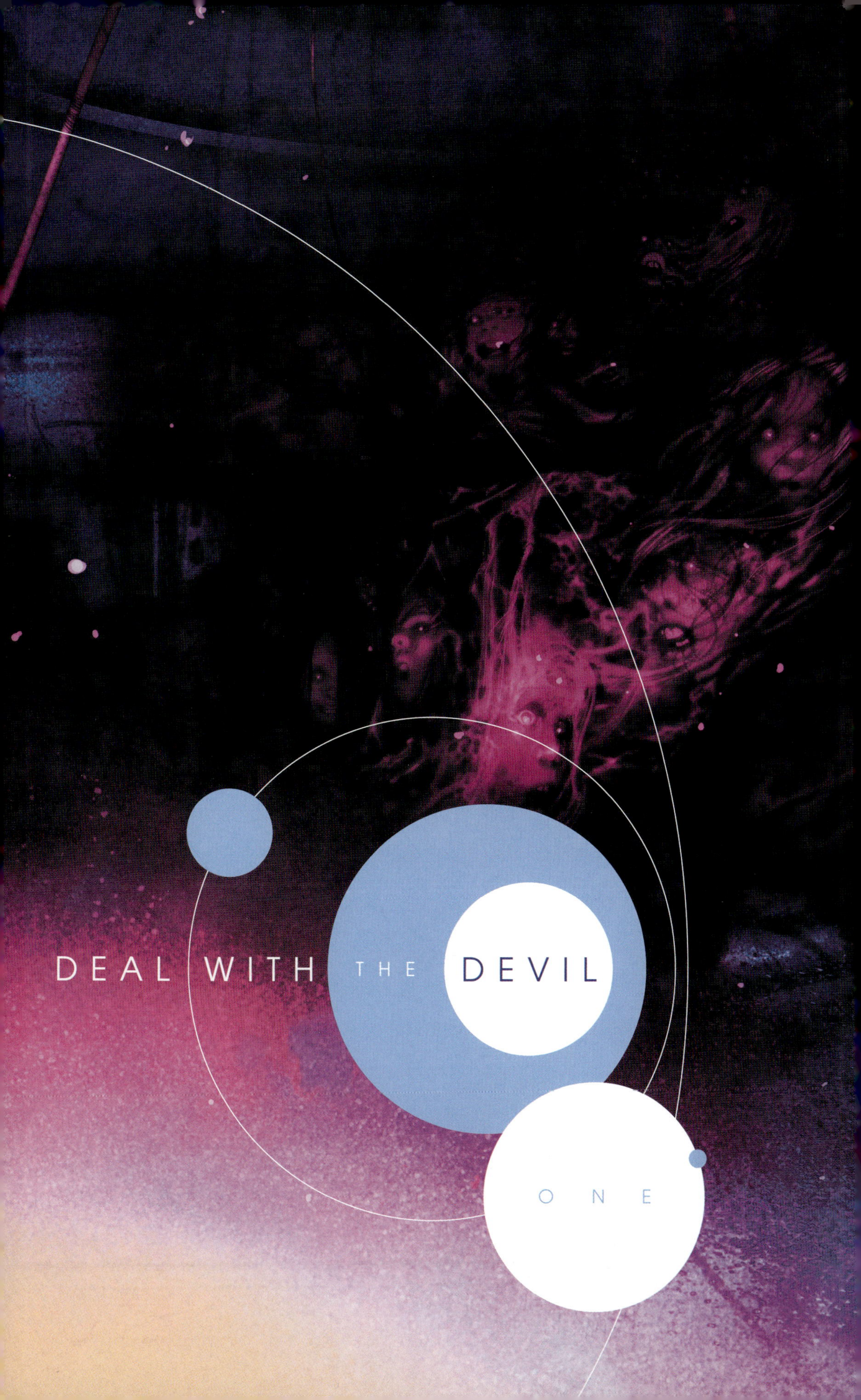
DEAL WITH THE DEVIL
ONE

EXT. SPACE — GALACTIC SPIRAL

At the center of our lives, is a gravity that
nothing can escape. In the hollow heart of
existence waits a yearning, hungry void.

Like a spider squatting in a web of 200 billion lights-
at the rotten core of the galaxy we call home—
there broods a supermassive black hole.

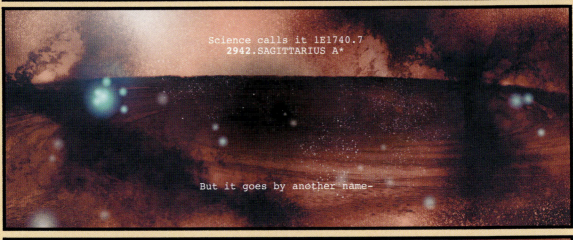

Science calls it 1E1740.7
2942.SAGITTARIUS A*

But it goes by another name-

Welcome to the Great Annihilator.

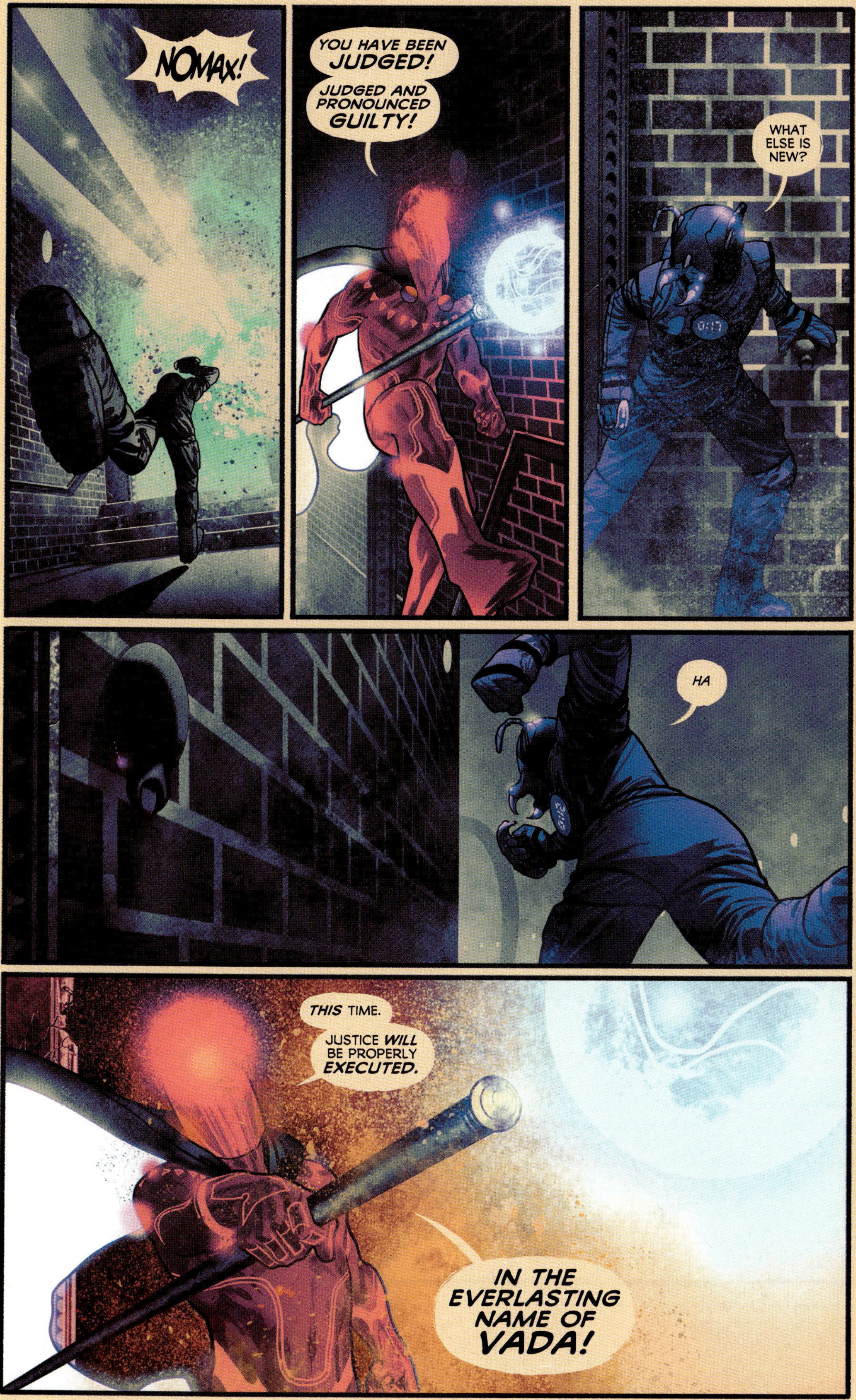
NOMAX!
YOU HAVE BEEN JUDGED!
JUDGED AND PRONOUNCED GUILTY!
WHAT ELSE IS NEW?
HA
THIS TIME.
JUSTICE WILL BE PROPERLY EXECUTED.
IN THE EVERLASTING NAME OF VADA!

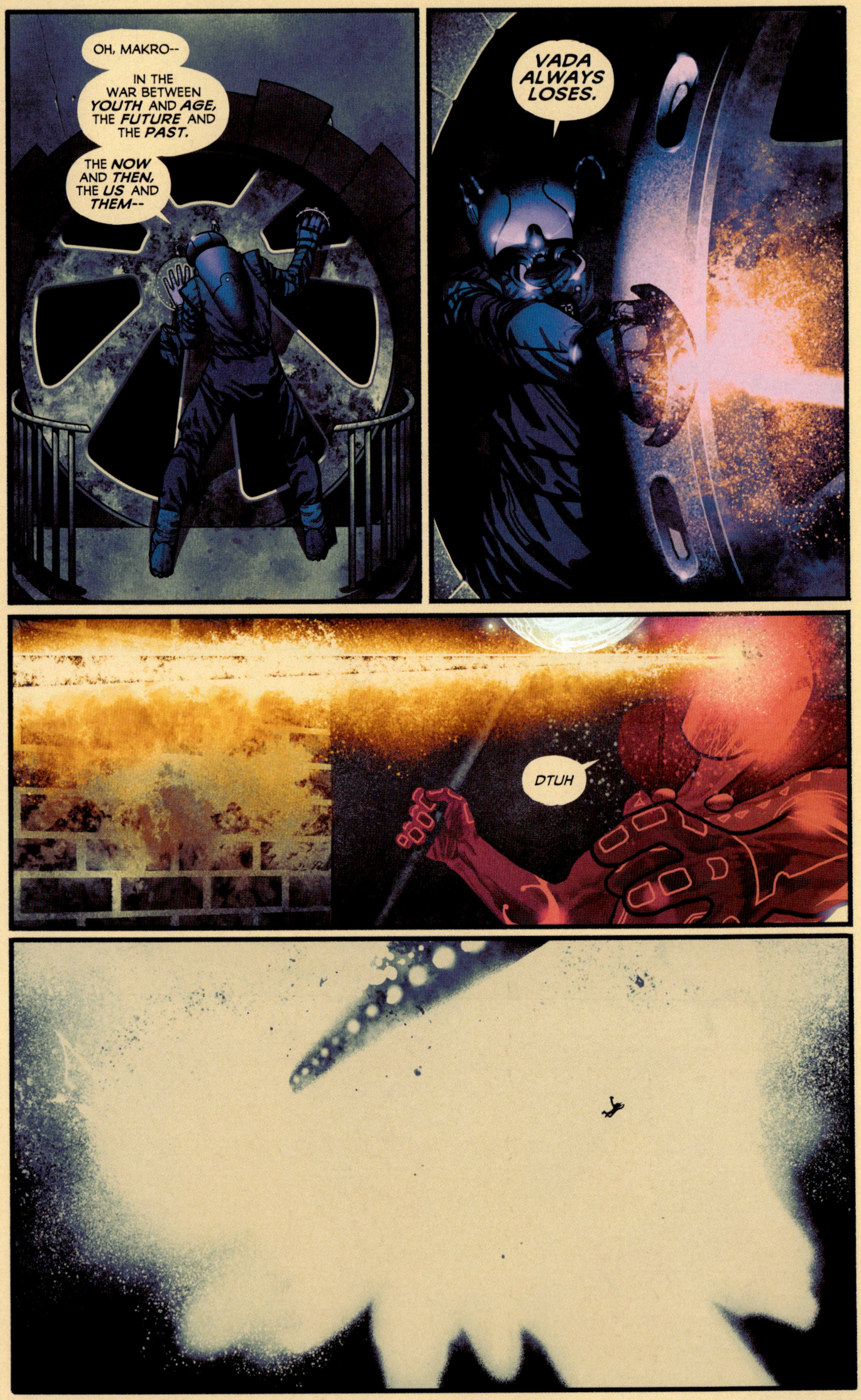
OH, MAKRO--
IN THE WAR BETWEEN YOUTH AND AGE, THE FUTURE AND THE PAST.
THE NOW AND THEN, THE US AND THEM--
VADA ALWAYS LOSES.
DTUH

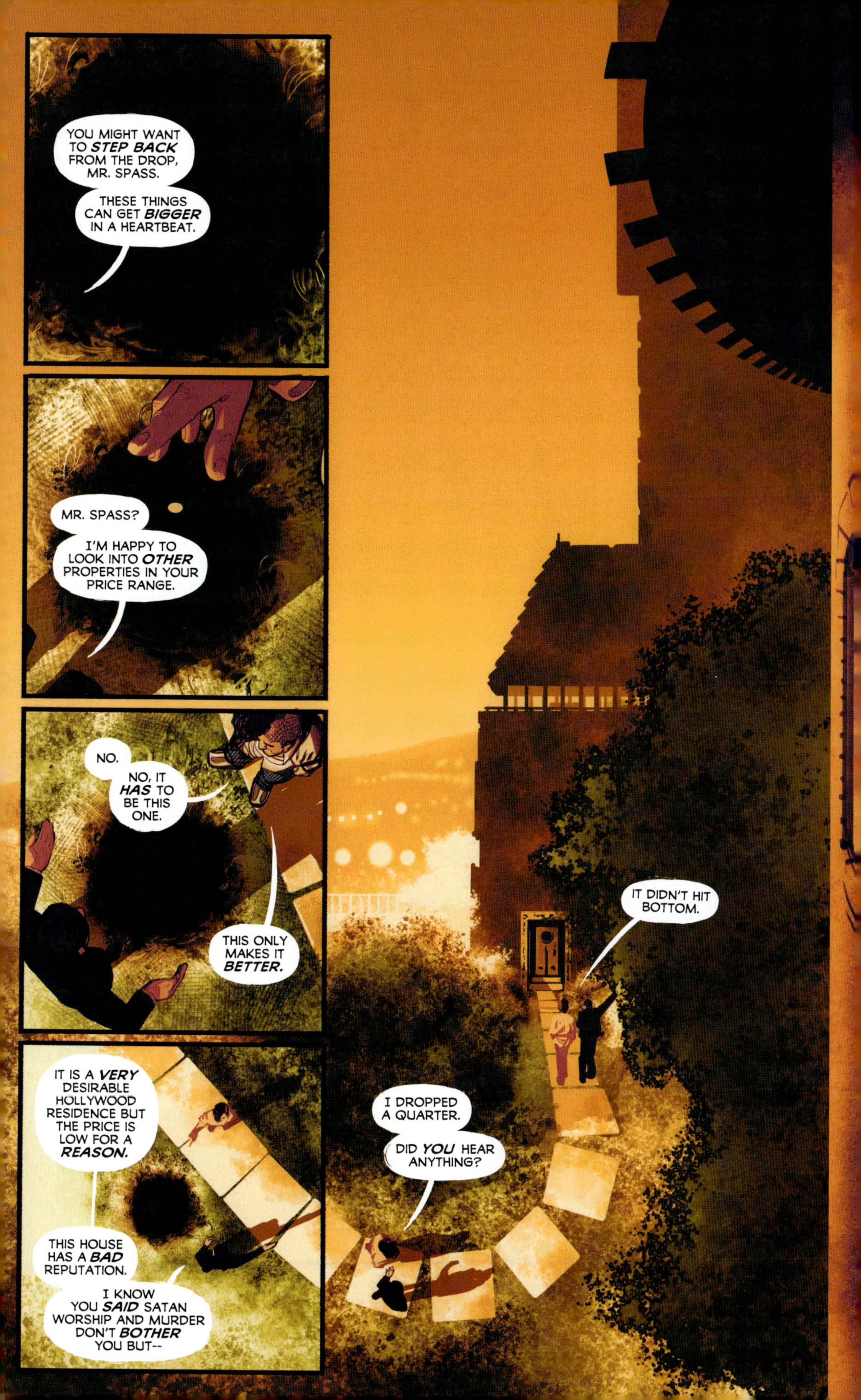
YOU MIGHT WANT TO STEP BACK FROM THE DROP, MR. SPASS.
THESE THINGS CAN GET BIGGER IN A HEARTBEAT.
MR. SPASS?
I'M HAPPY TO LOOK INTO OTHER PROPERTIES IN YOUR PRICE RANGE.
NO.
NO, IT HAS TO BE THIS ONE.
THIS ONLY MAKES IT BETTER.
IT IS A VERY DESIRABLE HOLLYWOOD RESIDENCE BUT THE PRICE IS LOW FOR A REASON.
THIS HOUSE HAS A BAD REPUTATION.
I KNOW YOU SAID SATAN WORSHIP AND MURDER DON'T BOTHER YOU BUT--
I DROPPED A QUARTER.
DID YOU HEAR ANYTHING?
IT DIDN'T HIT BOTTOM.

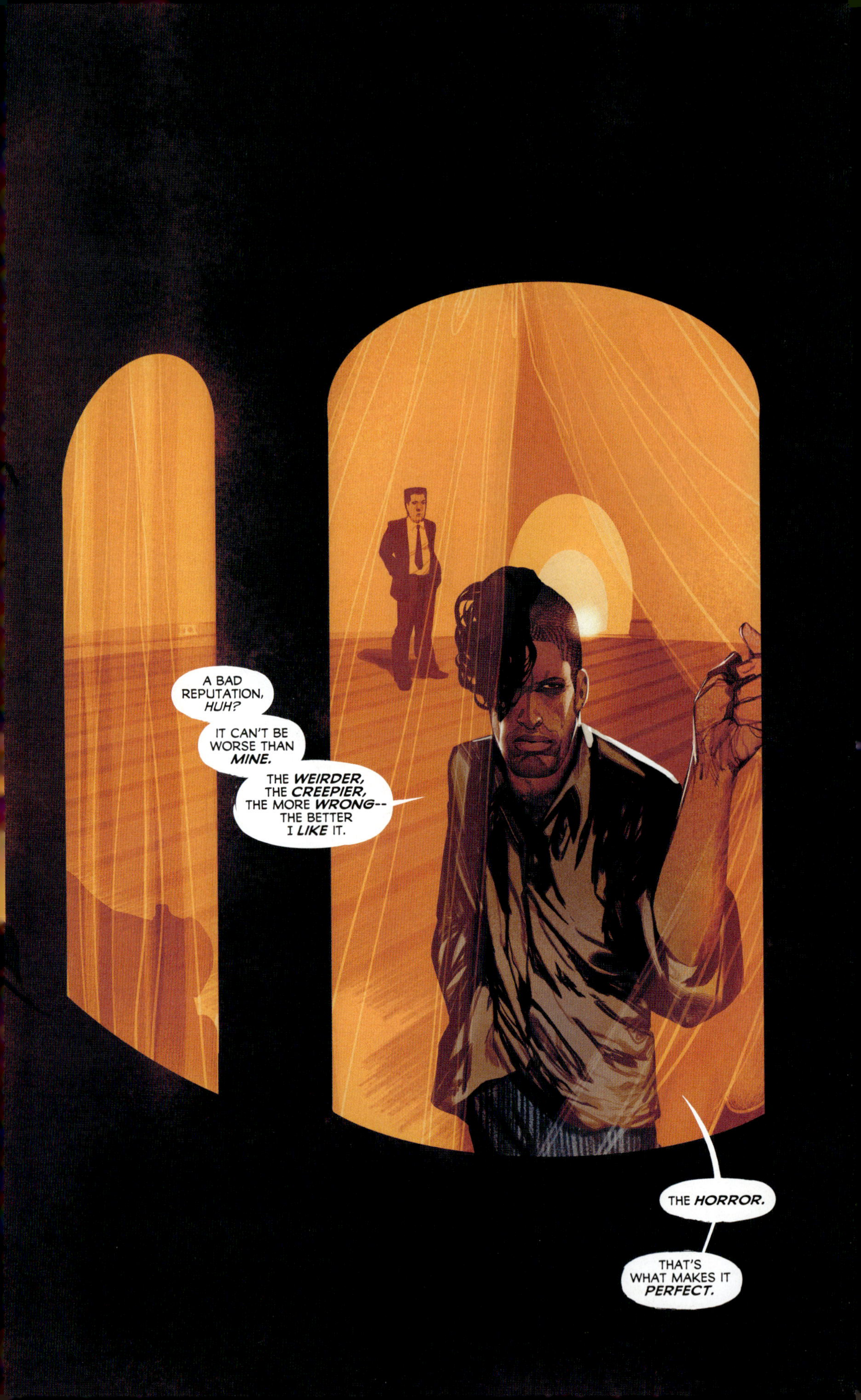
A BAD REPUTATION, *HUH?*
IT CAN'T BE WORSE THAN ***MINE.***
THE ***WEIRDER,*** THE ***CREEPIER,*** THE MORE ***WRONG***-- THE BETTER I ***LIKE*** IT.
THE ***HORROR.***
THAT'S WHAT MAKES IT ***PERFECT.***

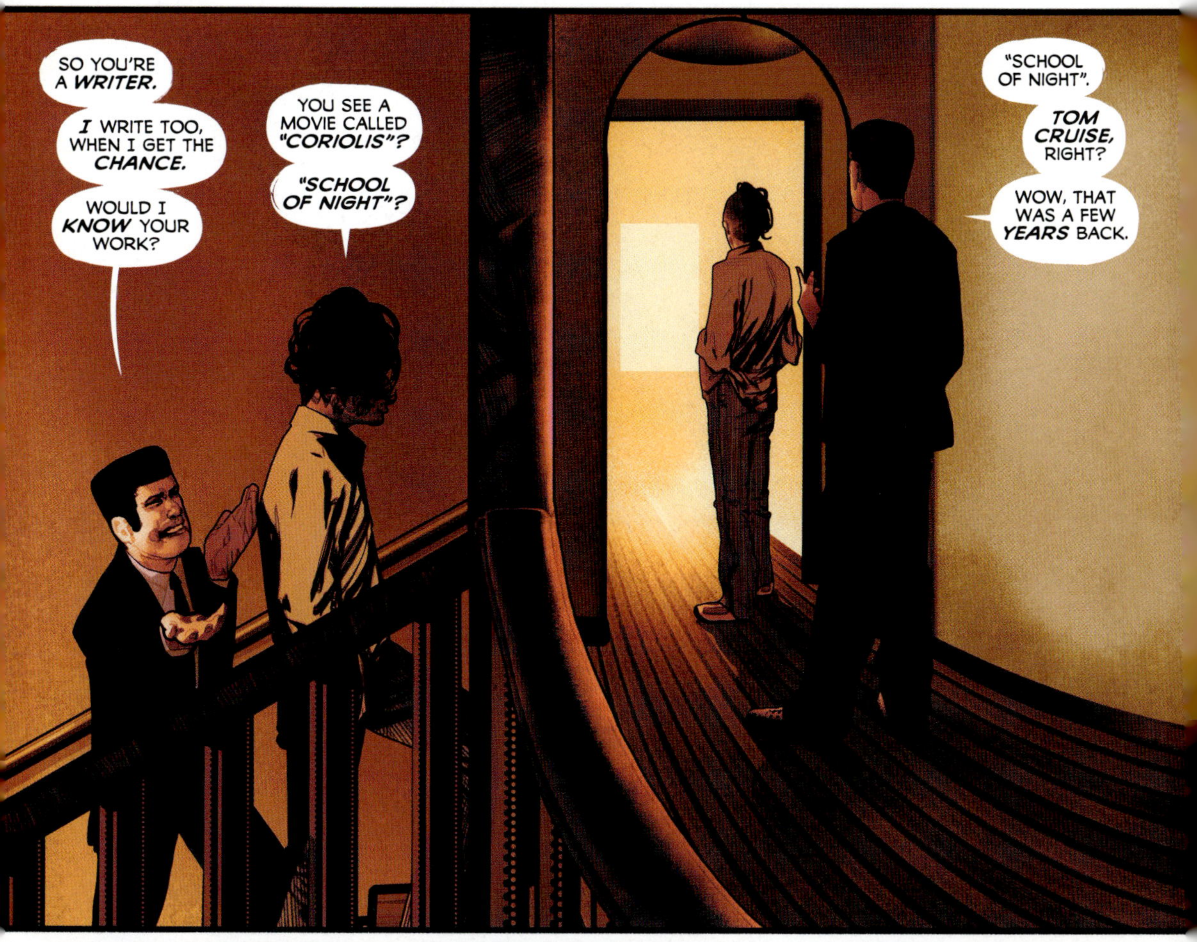
SO YOU'RE A WRITER.
I WRITE TOO, WHEN I GET THE CHANCE.
WOULD I KNOW YOUR WORK?
YOU SEE A MOVIE CALLED "CORIOLIS"?
"SCHOOL OF NIGHT"?
"SCHOOL OF NIGHT".
TOM CRUISE, RIGHT?
WOW, THAT WAS A FEW YEARS BACK.

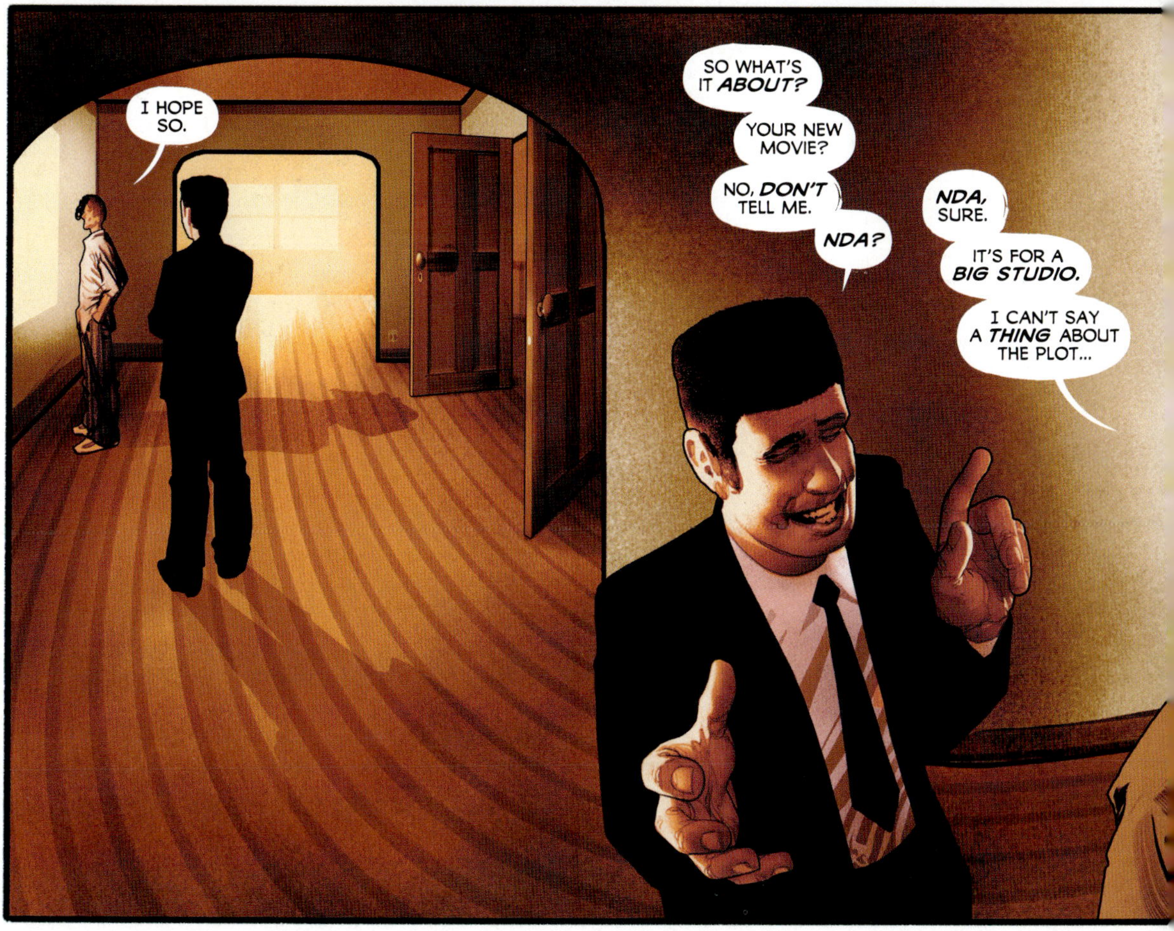
I HOPE SO.
SO WHAT'S IT ABOUT?
YOUR NEW MOVIE?
NO, DON'T TELL ME.
NDA?
NDA, SURE.
IT'S FOR A BIG STUDIO.
I CAN'T SAY A THING ABOUT THE PLOT...

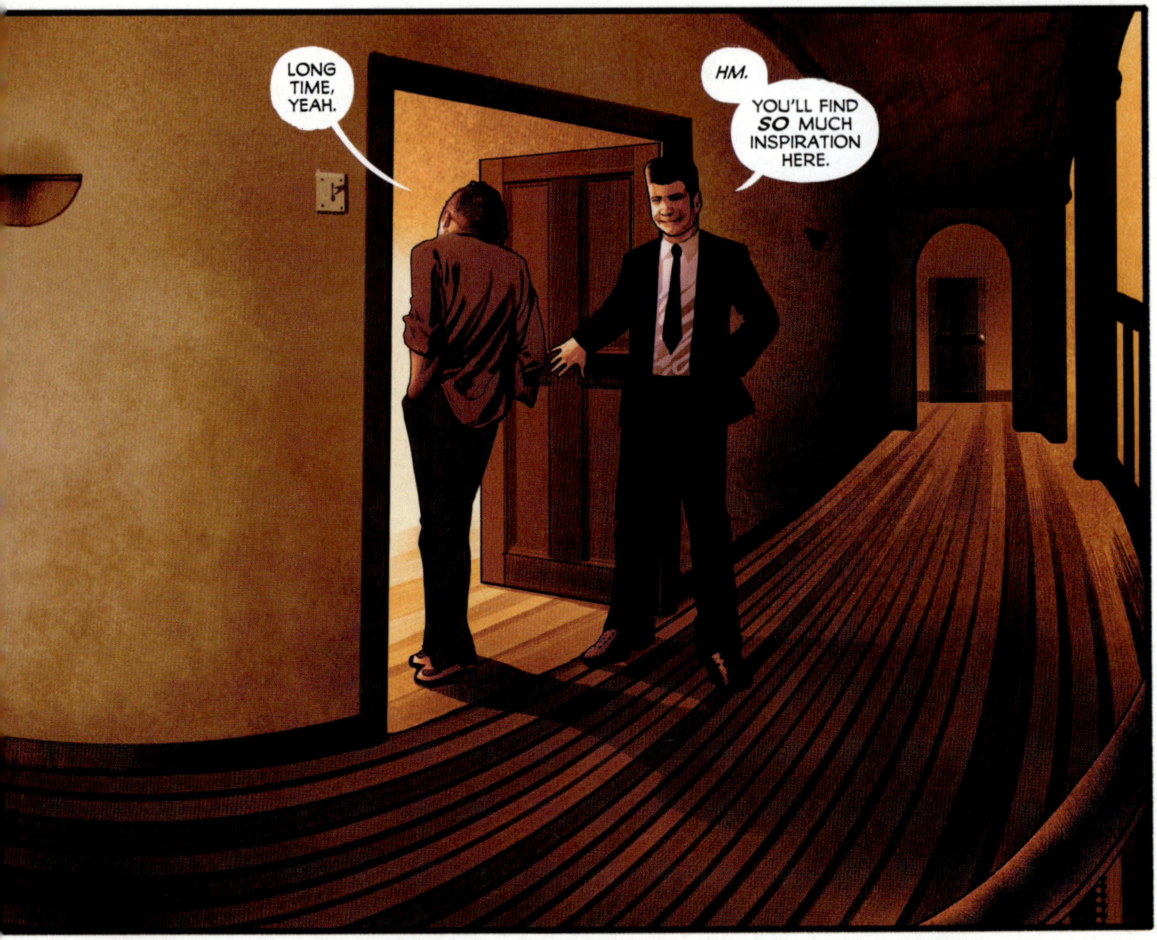
LONG TIME, YEAH.
HM.
YOU'LL FIND ***SO*** MUCH INSPIRATION HERE.

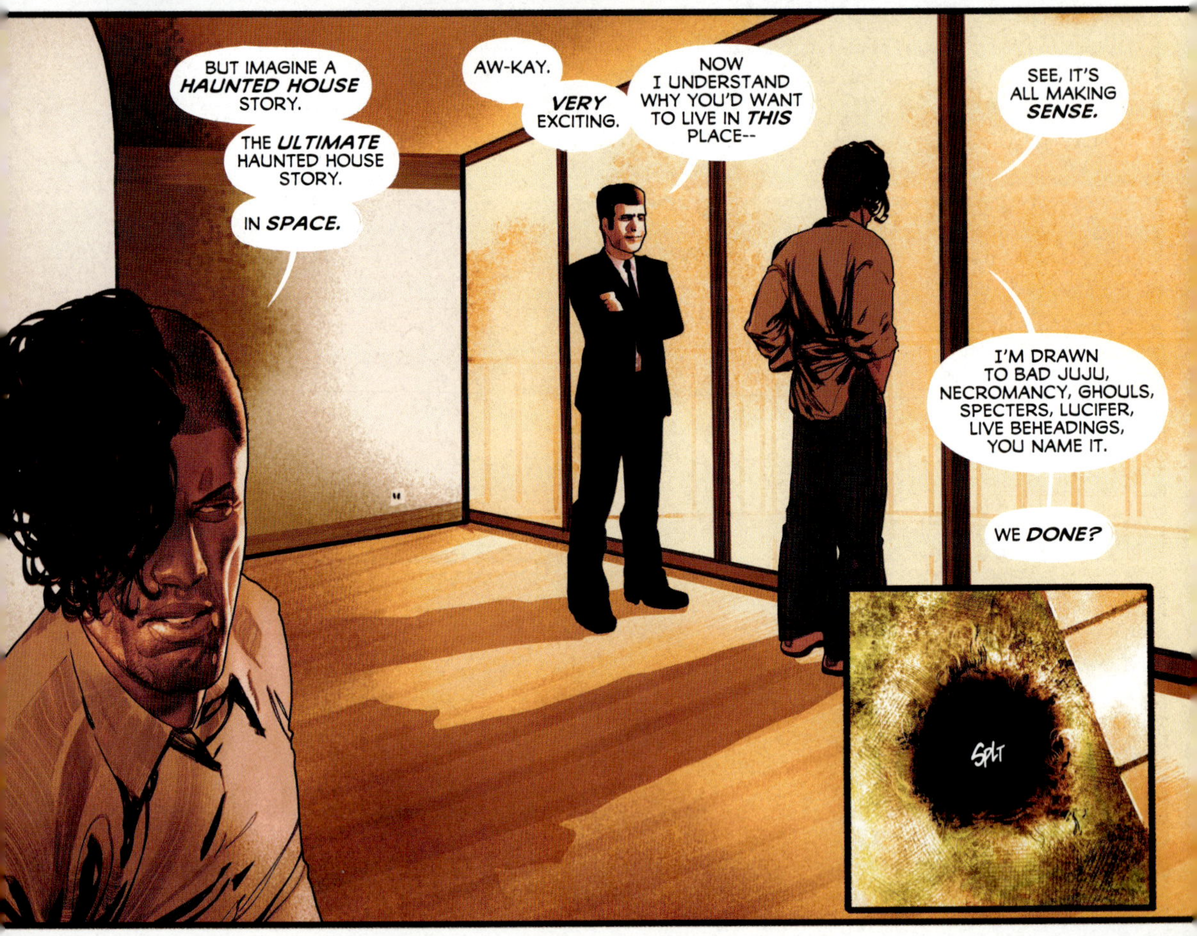
BUT IMAGINE A ***HAUNTED HOUSE*** STORY.
THE ***ULTIMATE*** HAUNTED HOUSE STORY.
IN ***SPACE.***
AW-KAY.
VERY EXCITING.
NOW I UNDERSTAND WHY YOU'D WANT TO LIVE IN ***THIS*** PLACE--
SEE, IT'S ALL MAKING ***SENSE.***
I'M DRAWN TO BAD JUJU, NECROMANCY, GHOULS, SPECTERS, LUCIFER, LIVE BEHEADINGS, YOU NAME IT.
WE ***DONE?***
SPLT

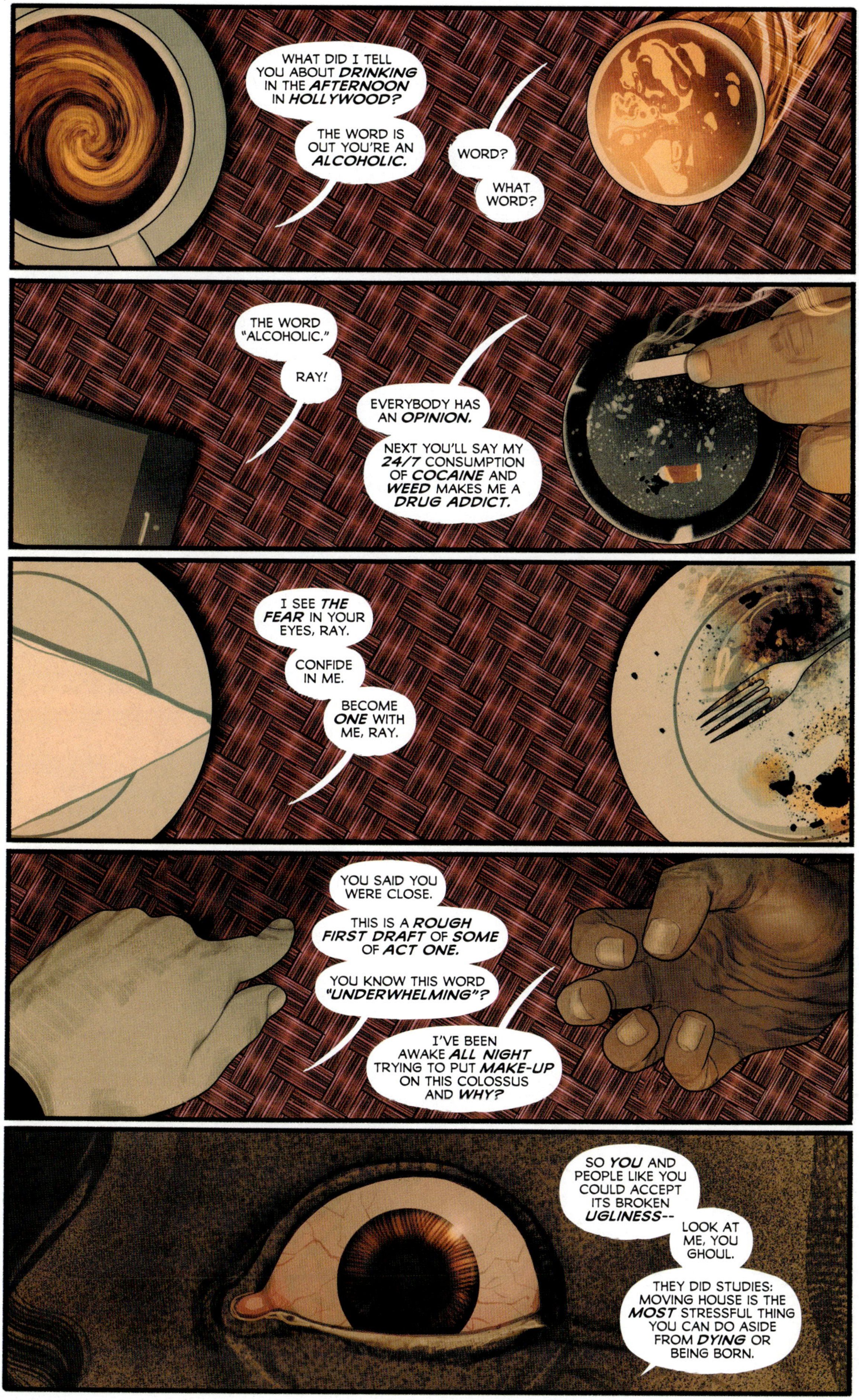
WHAT DID I TELL YOU ABOUT DRINKING IN THE AFTERNOON IN HOLLYWOOD?
THE WORD IS OUT YOU'RE AN ALCOHOLIC.
WORD?
WHAT WORD?
THE WORD "ALCOHOLIC."
RAY!
EVERYBODY HAS AN OPINION.
NEXT YOU'LL SAY MY 24/7 CONSUMPTION OF COCAINE AND WEED MAKES ME A DRUG ADDICT.
I SEE THE FEAR IN YOUR EYES, RAY.
CONFIDE IN ME.
BECOME ONE WITH ME, RAY.
YOU SAID YOU WERE CLOSE.
THIS IS A ROUGH FIRST DRAFT OF SOME OF ACT ONE.
YOU KNOW THIS WORD "UNDERWHELMING"?
I'VE BEEN AWAKE ALL NIGHT TRYING TO PUT MAKE-UP ON THIS COLOSSUS AND WHY?
SO YOU AND PEOPLE LIKE YOU COULD ACCEPT ITS BROKEN UGLINESS--
LOOK AT ME, YOU GHOUL.
THEY DID STUDIES: MOVING HOUSE IS THE MOST STRESSFUL THING YOU CAN DO ASIDE FROM DYING OR BEING BORN.

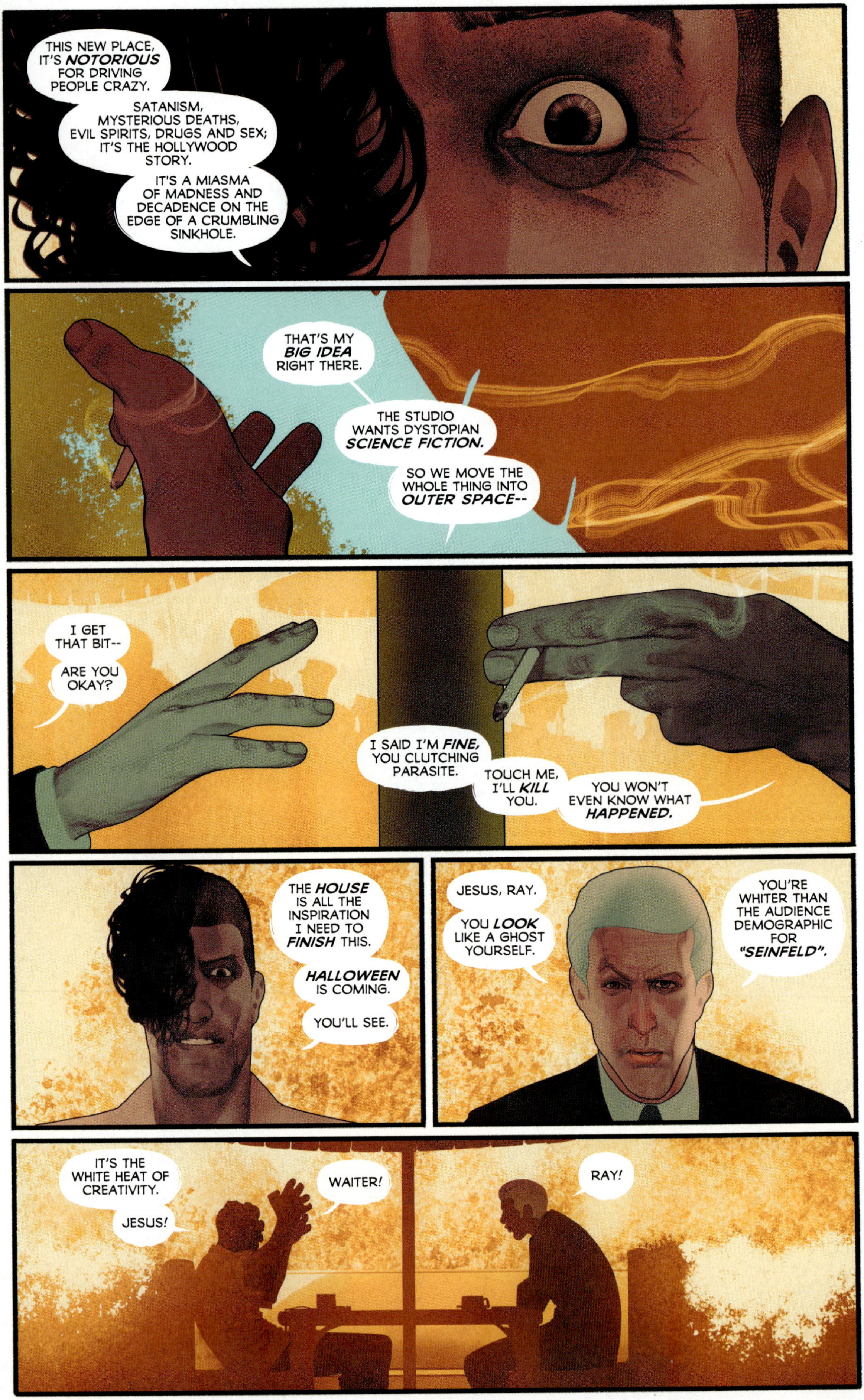
THIS NEW PLACE, IT'S ***NOTORIOUS*** FOR DRIVING PEOPLE CRAZY.
SATANISM, MYSTERIOUS DEATHS, EVIL SPIRITS, DRUGS AND SEX; IT'S THE HOLLYWOOD STORY.
IT'S A MIASMA OF MADNESS AND DECADENCE ON THE EDGE OF A CRUMBLING SINKHOLE.
THAT'S MY ***BIG IDEA*** RIGHT THERE.
THE STUDIO WANTS DYSTOPIAN ***SCIENCE FICTION.***
SO WE MOVE THE WHOLE THING INTO ***OUTER SPACE--***
I GET THAT BIT--
ARE YOU OKAY?
I SAID I'M ***FINE,*** YOU CLUTCHING PARASITE.
TOUCH ME, I'LL ***KILL*** YOU.
YOU WON'T EVEN KNOW WHAT ***HAPPENED.***
THE ***HOUSE*** IS ALL THE INSPIRATION I NEED TO ***FINISH*** THIS.
HALLOWEEN IS COMING.
YOU'LL SEE.
JESUS, RAY.
YOU ***LOOK*** LIKE A GHOST YOURSELF.
YOU'RE WHITER THAN THE AUDIENCE DEMOGRAPHIC FOR ***"SEINFELD".***
IT'S THE WHITE HEAT OF CREATIVITY.
JESUS!
WAITER!
RAY!

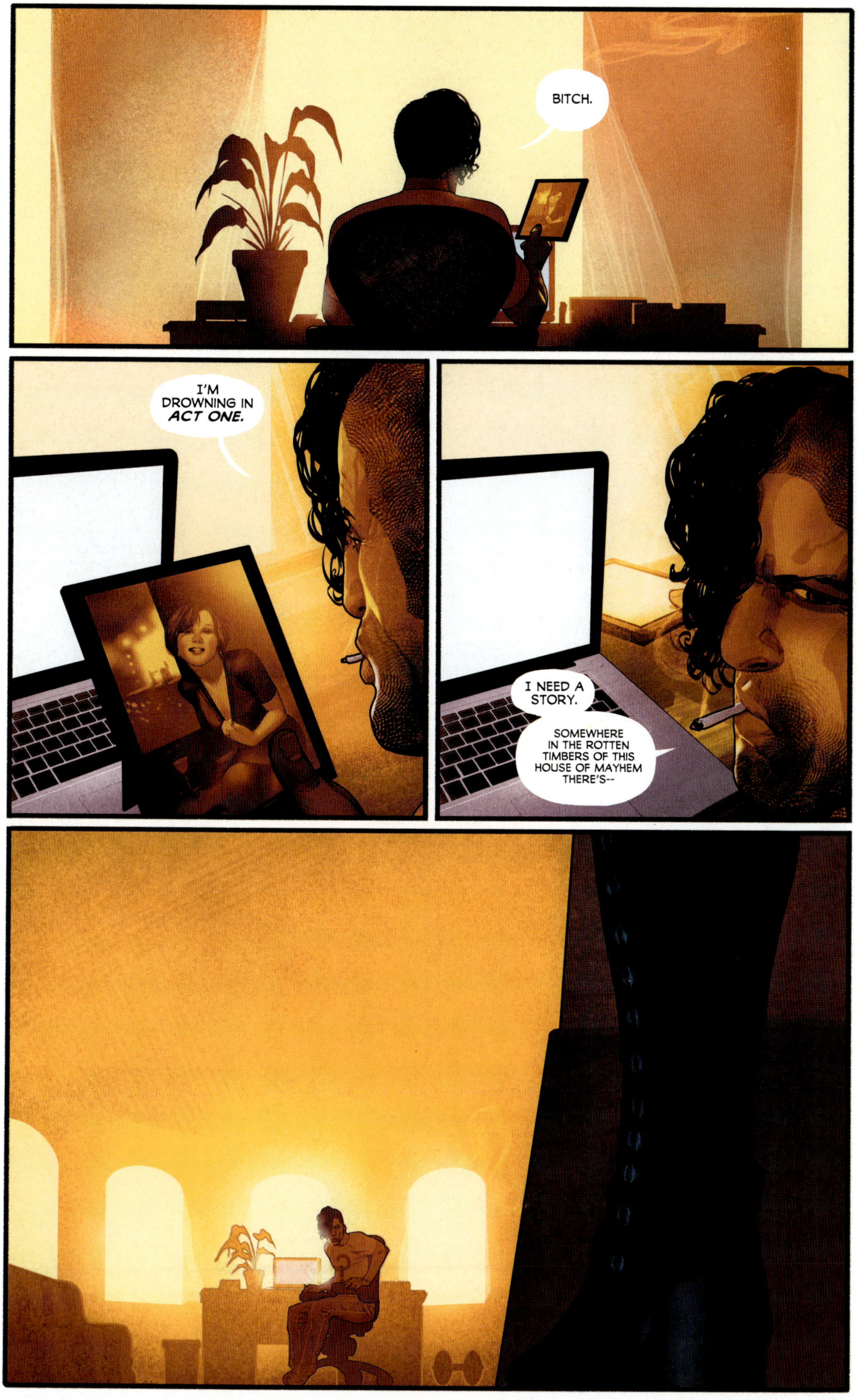
BITCH.
I'M DROWNING IN *ACT ONE.*
I NEED A STORY.
SOMEWHERE IN THE ROTTEN TIMBERS OF THIS HOUSE OF MAYHEM THERE'S--

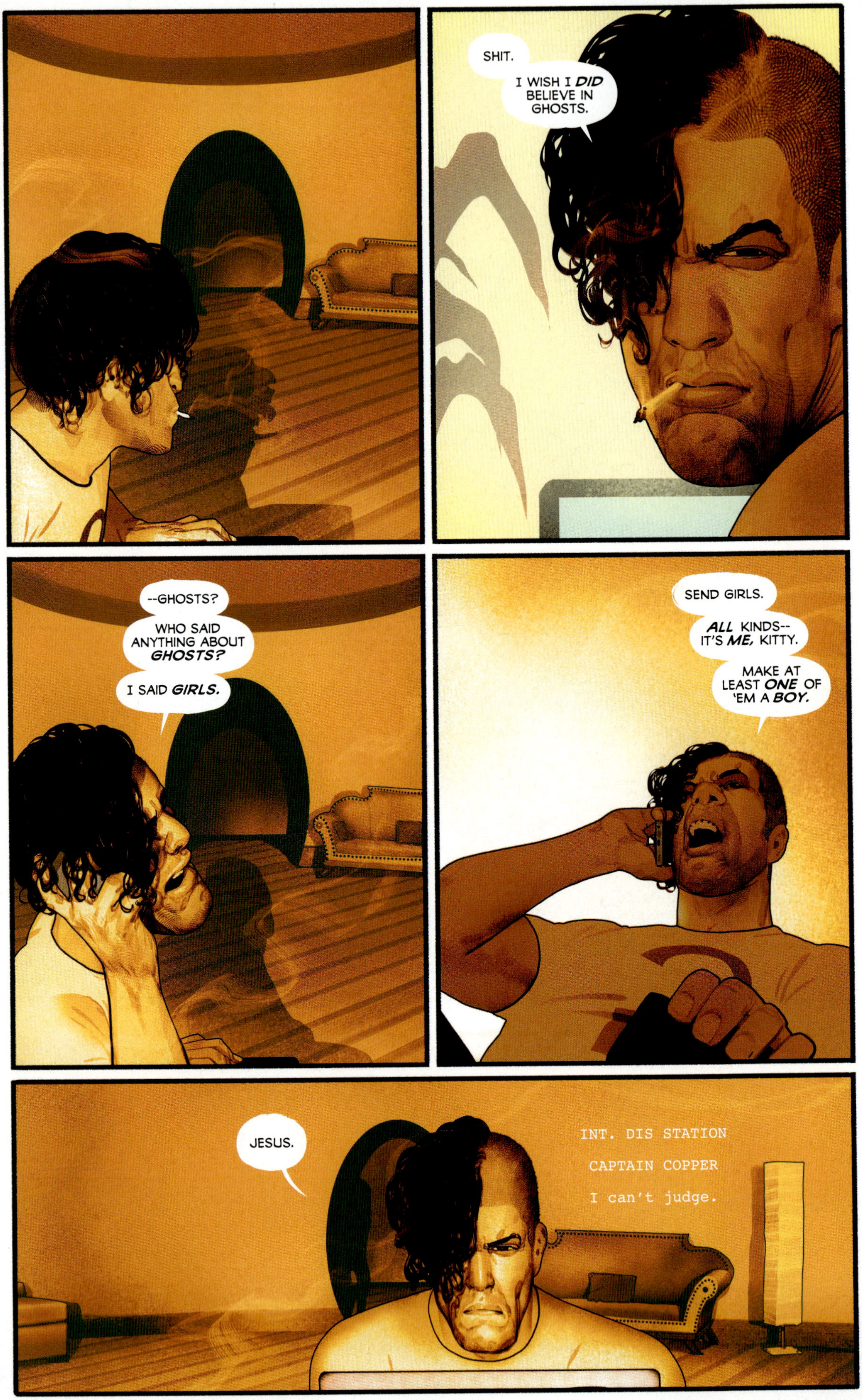
SHIT.
I WISH I *DID* BELIEVE IN GHOSTS.
--GHOSTS?
WHO SAID ANYTHING ABOUT *GHOSTS?*
I SAID *GIRLS.*
SEND GIRLS.
ALL KINDS-- IT'S *ME,* KITTY.
MAKE AT LEAST *ONE* OF 'EM A *BOY.*
JESUS.
INT. DIS STATION
CAPTAIN COPPER
I can't judge.

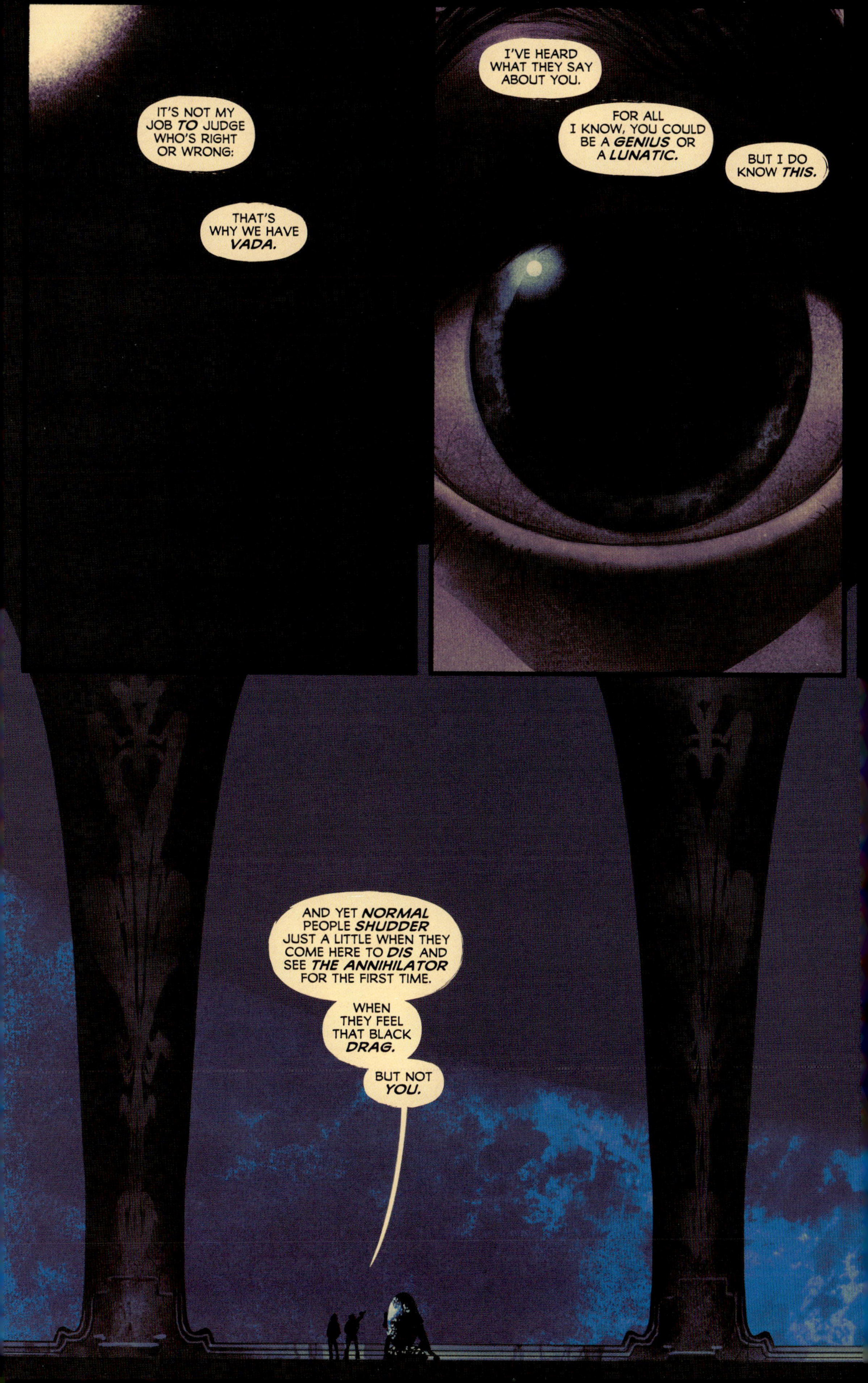
IT'S NOT MY JOB TO JUDGE WHO'S RIGHT OR WRONG:
THAT'S WHY WE HAVE VADA.
I'VE HEARD WHAT THEY SAY ABOUT YOU.
FOR ALL I KNOW, YOU COULD BE A GENIUS OR A LUNATIC.
BUT I DO KNOW THIS.
AND YET NORMAL PEOPLE SHUDDER JUST A LITTLE WHEN THEY COME HERE TO DIS AND SEE THE ANNIHILATOR FOR THE FIRST TIME.
WHEN THEY FEEL THAT BLACK DRAG.
BUT NOT YOU.

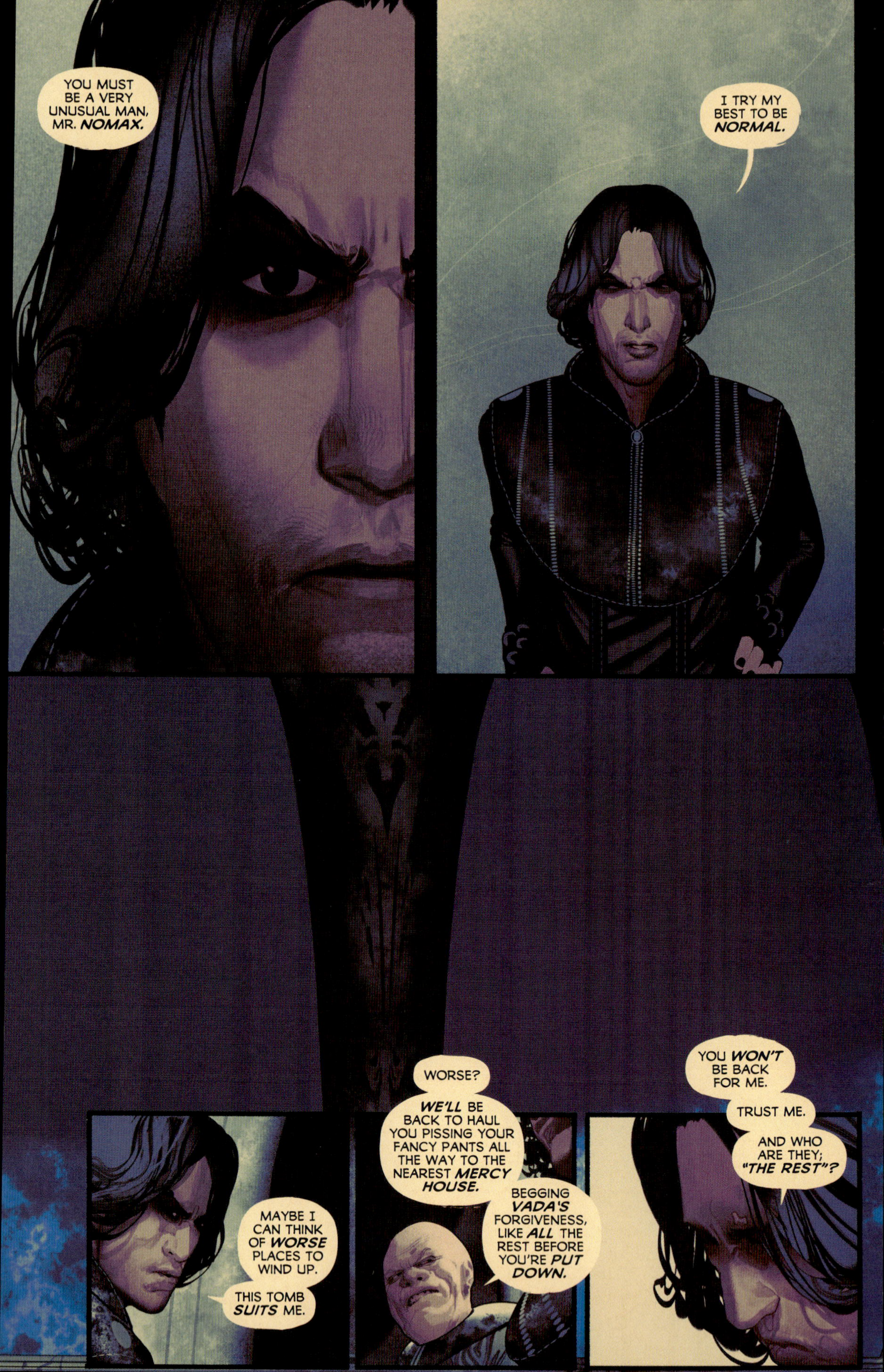
YOU MUST BE A VERY UNUSUAL MAN, MR. ***NOMAX.***
I TRY MY BEST TO BE ***NORMAL.***
MAYBE I CAN THINK OF ***WORSE*** PLACES TO WIND UP.
THIS TOMB ***SUITS*** ME.
WORSE?
WE'LL BE BACK TO HAUL YOU PISSING YOUR FANCY PANTS ALL THE WAY TO THE NEAREST ***MERCY HOUSE.***
BEGGING ***VADA'S*** FORGIVENESS, LIKE ***ALL*** THE REST BEFORE YOU'RE ***PUT DOWN.***
YOU ***WON'T*** BE BACK FOR ME.
TRUST ME.
AND WHO ARE THEY; ***"THE REST"?***

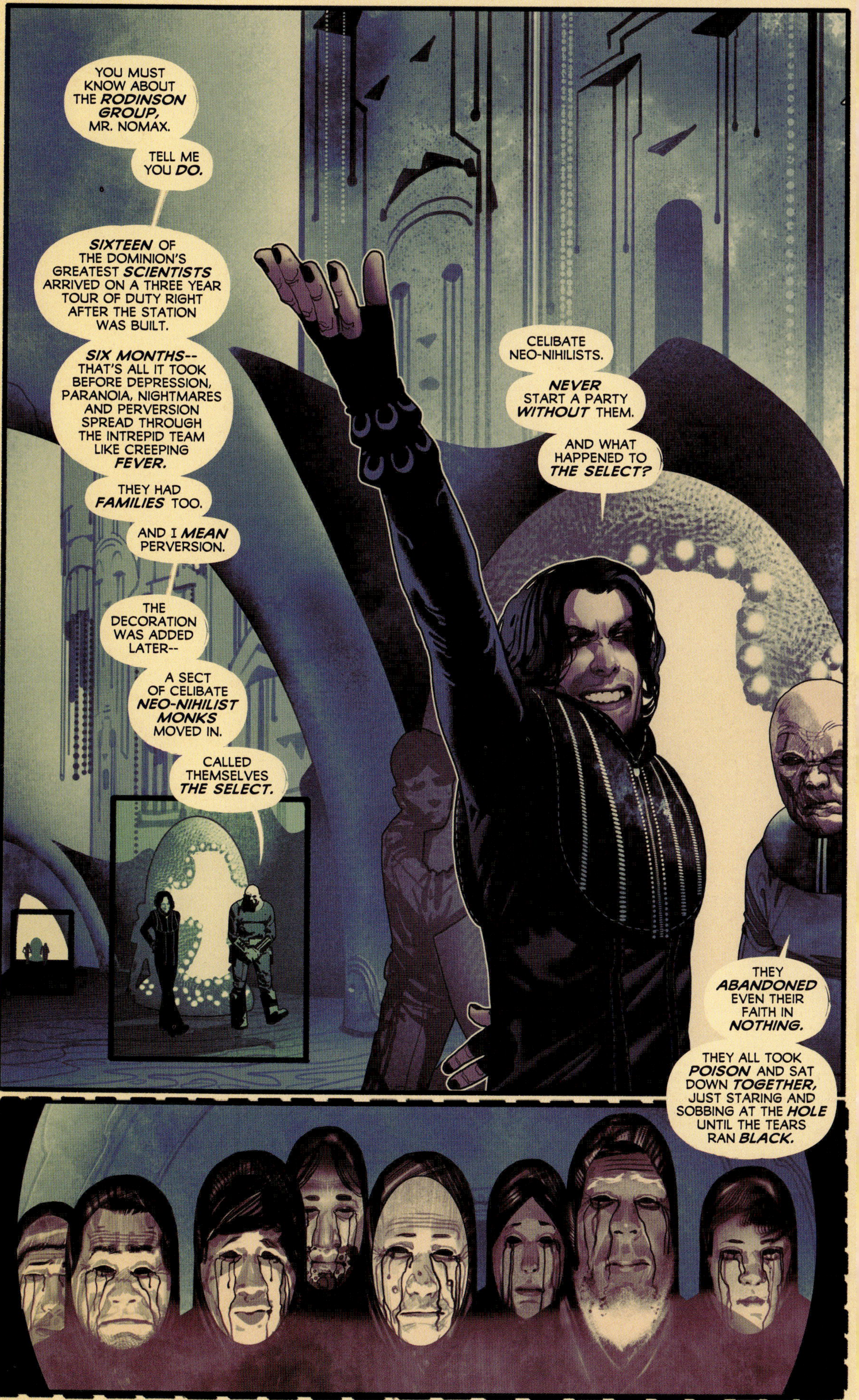

YOU MUST KNOW ABOUT THE RODINSON GROUP, MR. NOMAX.
TELL ME YOU DO.
SIXTEEN OF THE DOMINION'S GREATEST SCIENTISTS ARRIVED ON A THREE YEAR TOUR OF DUTY RIGHT AFTER THE STATION WAS BUILT.
SIX MONTHS-- THAT'S ALL IT TOOK BEFORE DEPRESSION, PARANOIA, NIGHTMARES AND PERVERSION SPREAD THROUGH THE INTREPID TEAM LIKE CREEPING FEVER.
THEY HAD FAMILIES TOO.
AND I MEAN PERVERSION.
THE DECORATION WAS ADDED LATER--
A SECT OF CELIBATE NEO-NIHILIST MONKS MOVED IN.
CALLED THEMSELVES THE SELECT.
CELIBATE NEO-NIHILISTS.
NEVER START A PARTY WITHOUT THEM.
AND WHAT HAPPENED TO THE SELECT?
THEY ABANDONED EVEN THEIR FAITH IN NOTHING.
THEY ALL TOOK POISON AND SAT DOWN TOGETHER, JUST STARING AND SOBBING AT THE HOLE UNTIL THE TEARS RAN BLACK.

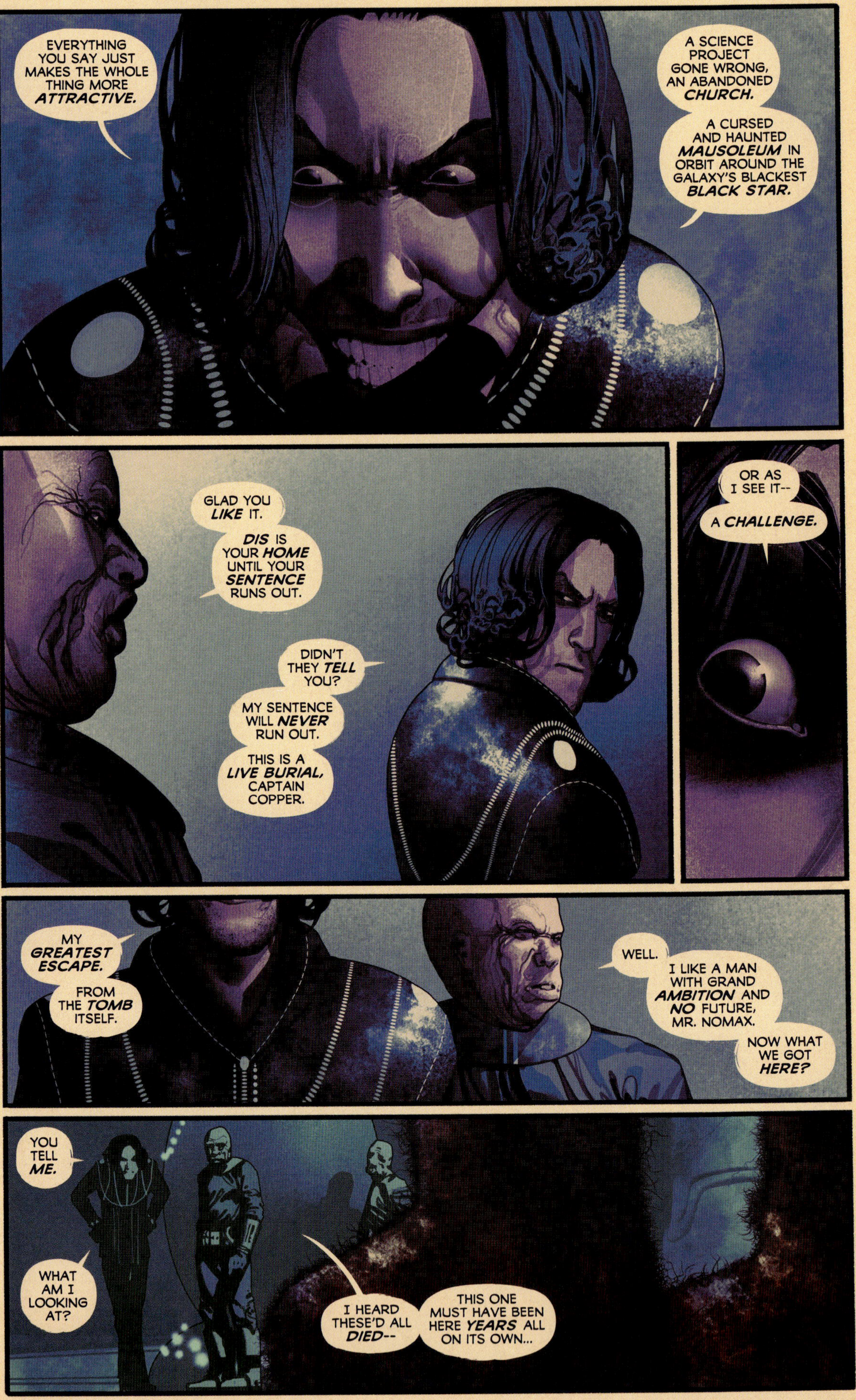
EVERYTHING YOU SAY JUST MAKES THE WHOLE THING MORE ATTRACTIVE.
A SCIENCE PROJECT GONE WRONG, AN ABANDONED CHURCH.
A CURSED AND HAUNTED MAUSOLEUM IN ORBIT AROUND THE GALAXY'S BLACKEST BLACK STAR.
GLAD YOU LIKE IT.
DIS IS YOUR HOME UNTIL YOUR SENTENCE RUNS OUT.
DIDN'T THEY TELL YOU?
MY SENTENCE WILL NEVER RUN OUT.
THIS IS A LIVE BURIAL, CAPTAIN COPPER.
OR AS I SEE IT--
A CHALLENGE.
MY GREATEST ESCAPE.
FROM THE TOMB ITSELF.
WELL.
I LIKE A MAN WITH GRAND AMBITION AND NO FUTURE, MR. NOMAX.
NOW WHAT WE GOT HERE?
YOU TELL ME.
WHAT AM I LOOKING AT?
I HEARD THESE'D ALL DIED--
THIS ONE MUST HAVE BEEN HERE YEARS ALL ON ITS OWN...

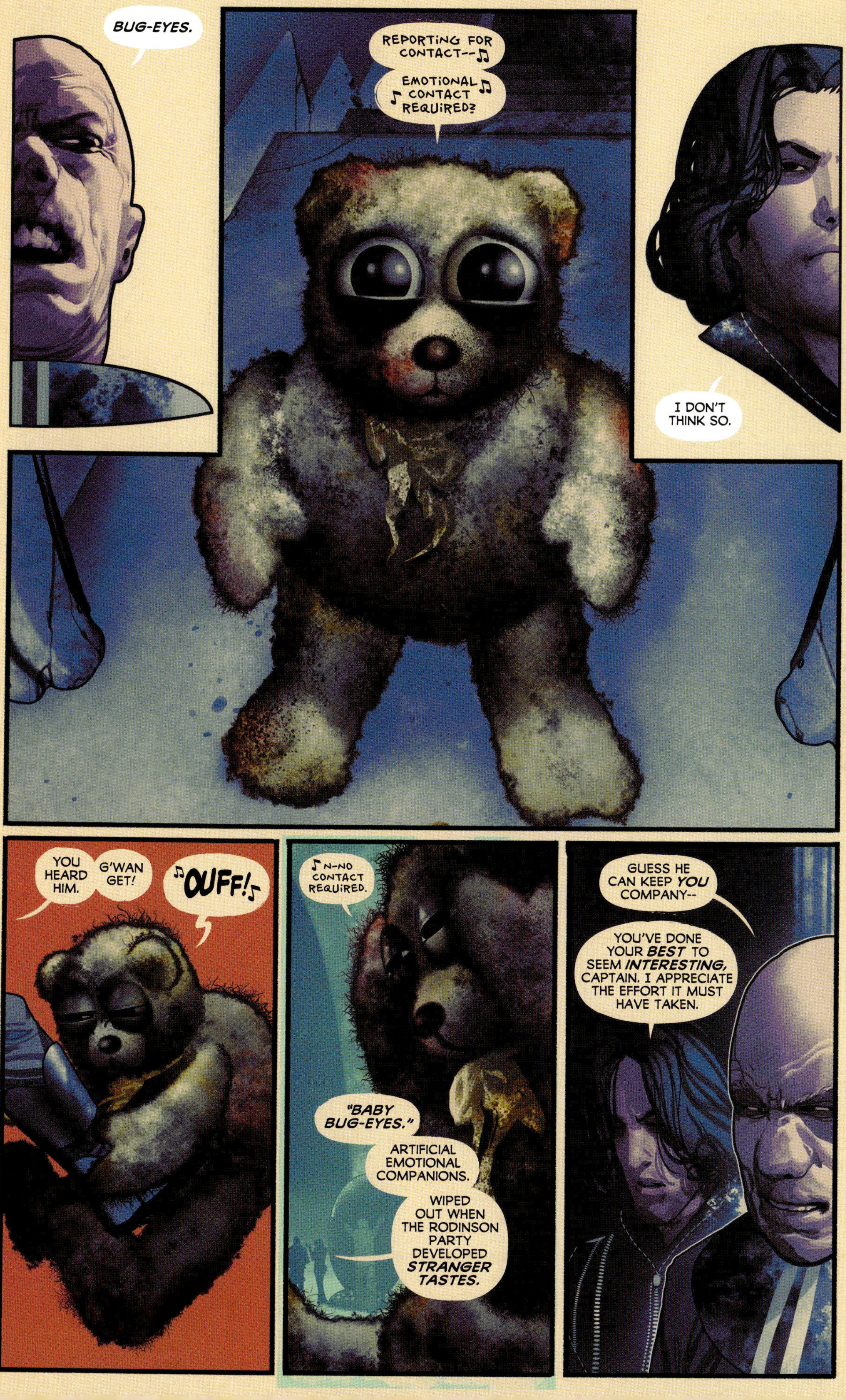
BUG-EYES.
REPORTING FOR CONTACT--♫
EMOTIONAL CONTACT REQUIRED?
I DON'T THINK SO.
YOU HEARD HIM.
G'WAN GET!
OUFF!
N-NO CONTACT REQUIRED.
"BABY BUG-EYES."
ARTIFICIAL EMOTIONAL COMPANIONS.
WIPED OUT WHEN THE RODINSON PARTY DEVELOPED STRANGER TASTES.
GUESS HE CAN KEEP YOU COMPANY--
YOU'VE DONE YOUR BEST TO SEEM INTERESTING, CAPTAIN. I APPRECIATE THE EFFORT IT MUST HAVE TAKEN.

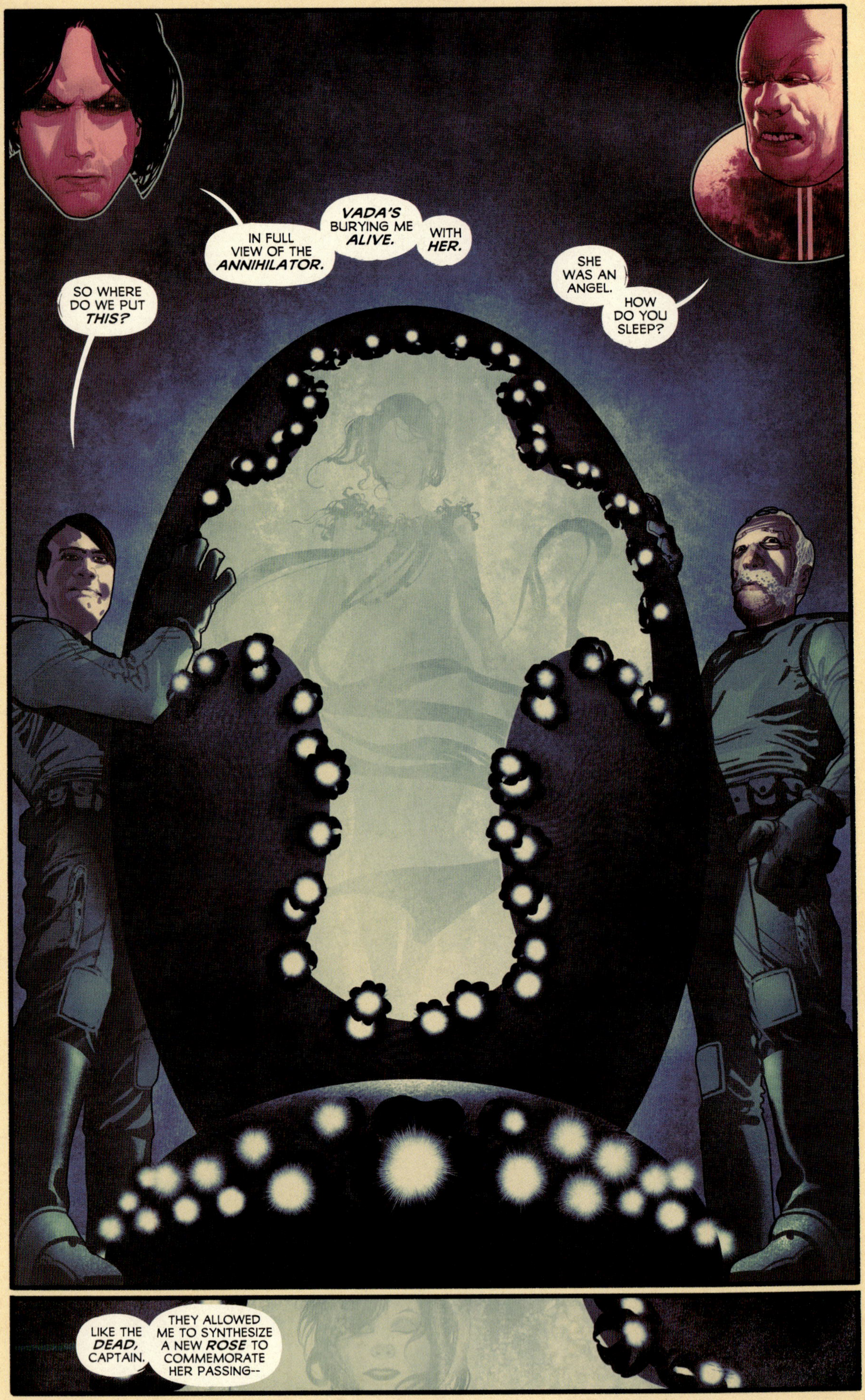
IN FULL VIEW OF THE *ANNIHILATOR.*
VADA'S BURYING ME *ALIVE.*
WITH *HER.*
SO WHERE DO WE PUT *THIS?*
SHE WAS AN ANGEL.
HOW DO YOU SLEEP?
LIKE THE *DEAD,* CAPTAIN.
THEY ALLOWED ME TO SYNTHESIZE A NEW *ROSE* TO COMMEMORATE HER PASSING--

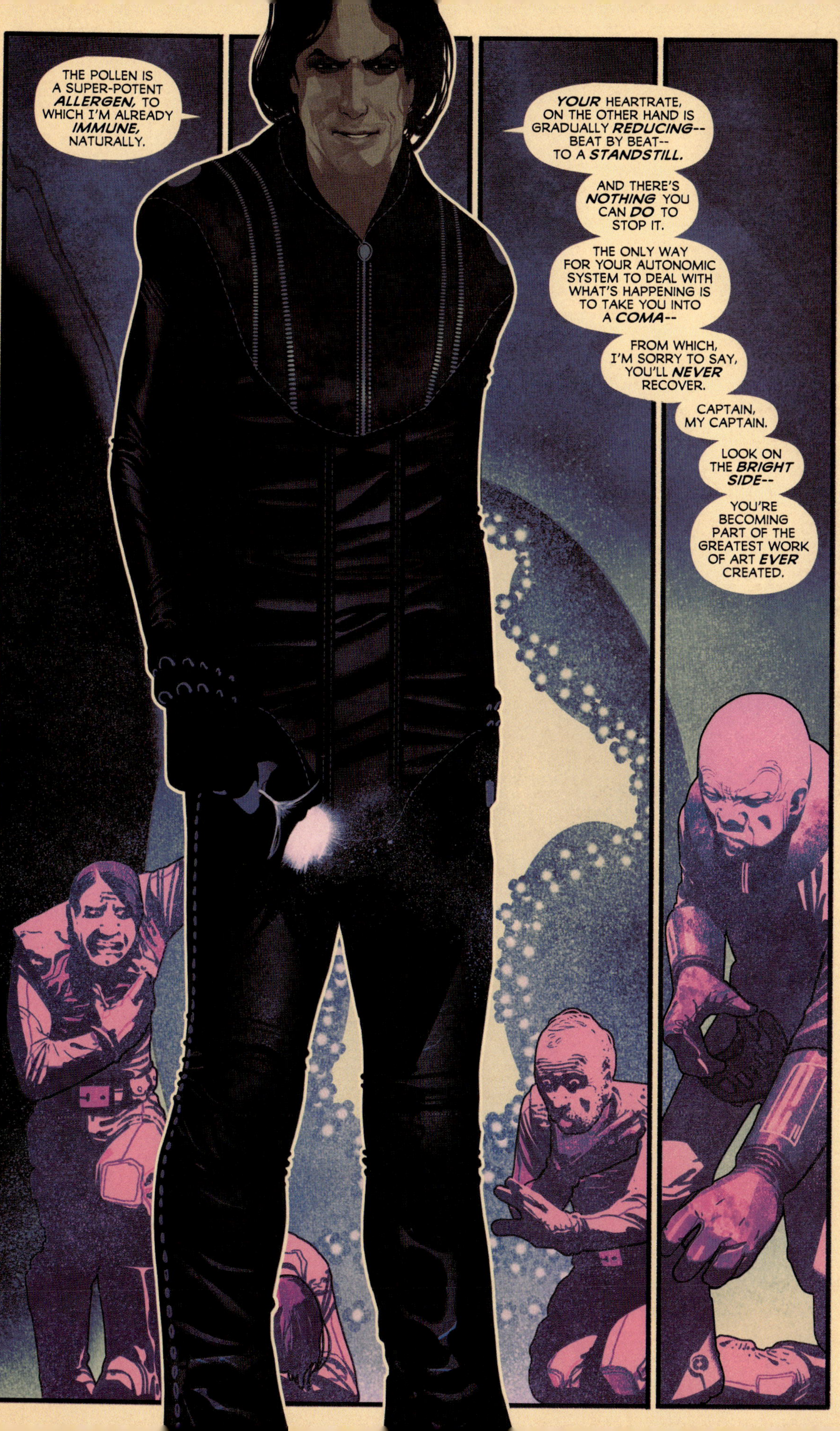
THE POLLEN IS A SUPER-POTENT ALLERGEN, TO WHICH I'M ALREADY IMMUNE, NATURALLY.
YOUR HEARTRATE, ON THE OTHER HAND IS GRADUALLY REDUCING-- BEAT BY BEAT-- TO A STANDSTILL.
AND THERE'S NOTHING YOU CAN DO TO STOP IT.
THE ONLY WAY FOR YOUR AUTONOMIC SYSTEM TO DEAL WITH WHAT'S HAPPENING IS TO TAKE YOU INTO A COMA--
FROM WHICH, I'M SORRY TO SAY, YOU'LL NEVER RECOVER.
CAPTAIN, MY CAPTAIN.
LOOK ON THE BRIGHT SIDE--
YOU'RE BECOMING PART OF THE GREATEST WORK OF ART EVER CREATED.

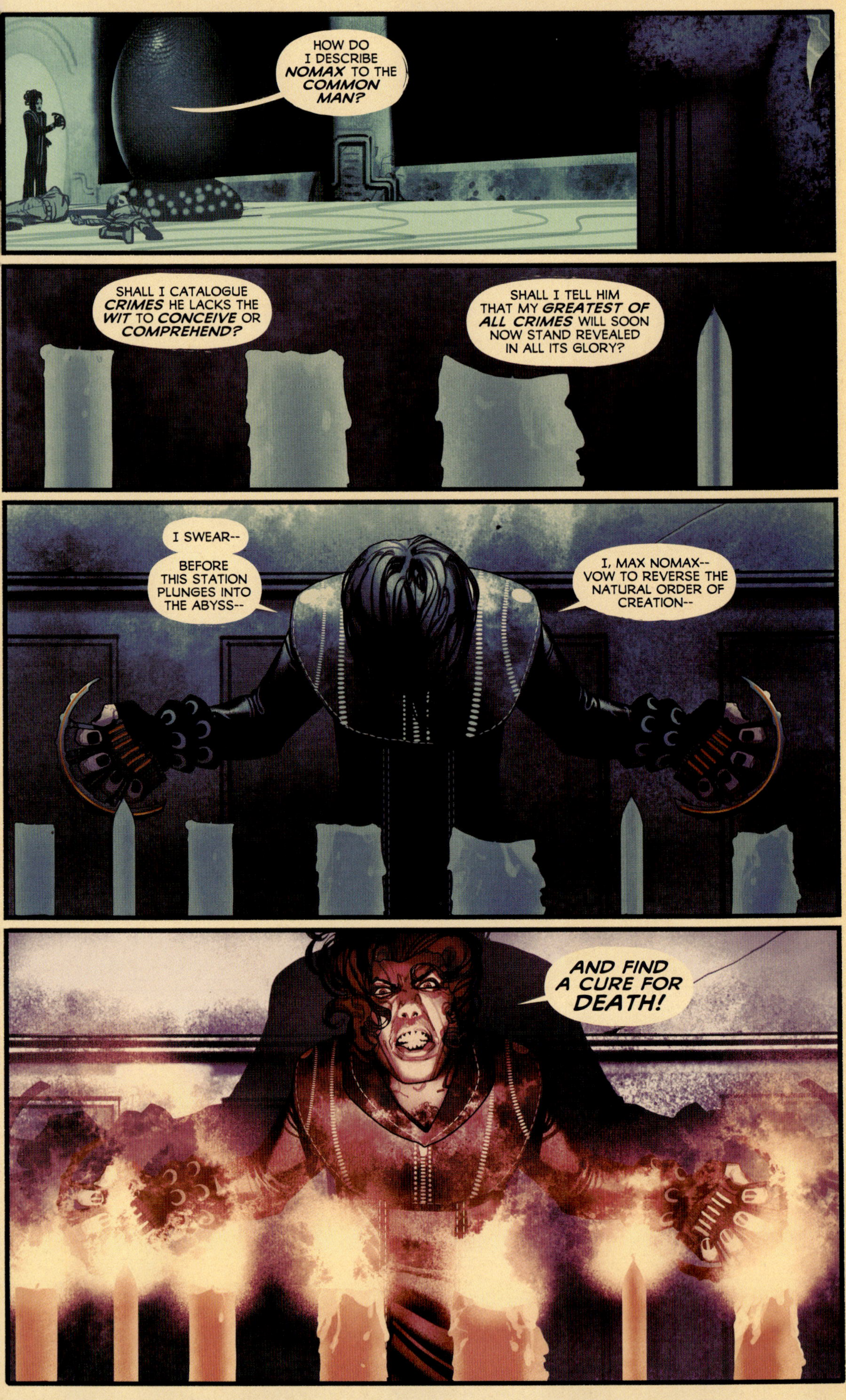
HOW DO I DESCRIBE NOMAX TO THE COMMON MAN?
SHALL I CATALOGUE CRIMES HE LACKS THE WIT TO CONCEIVE OR COMPREHEND?
SHALL I TELL HIM THAT MY GREATEST OF ALL CRIMES WILL SOON NOW STAND REVEALED IN ALL ITS GLORY?
I SWEAR--
BEFORE THIS STATION PLUNGES INTO THE ABYSS--
I, MAX NOMAX-- VOW TO REVERSE THE NATURAL ORDER OF CREATION--
AND FIND A CURE FOR DEATH!

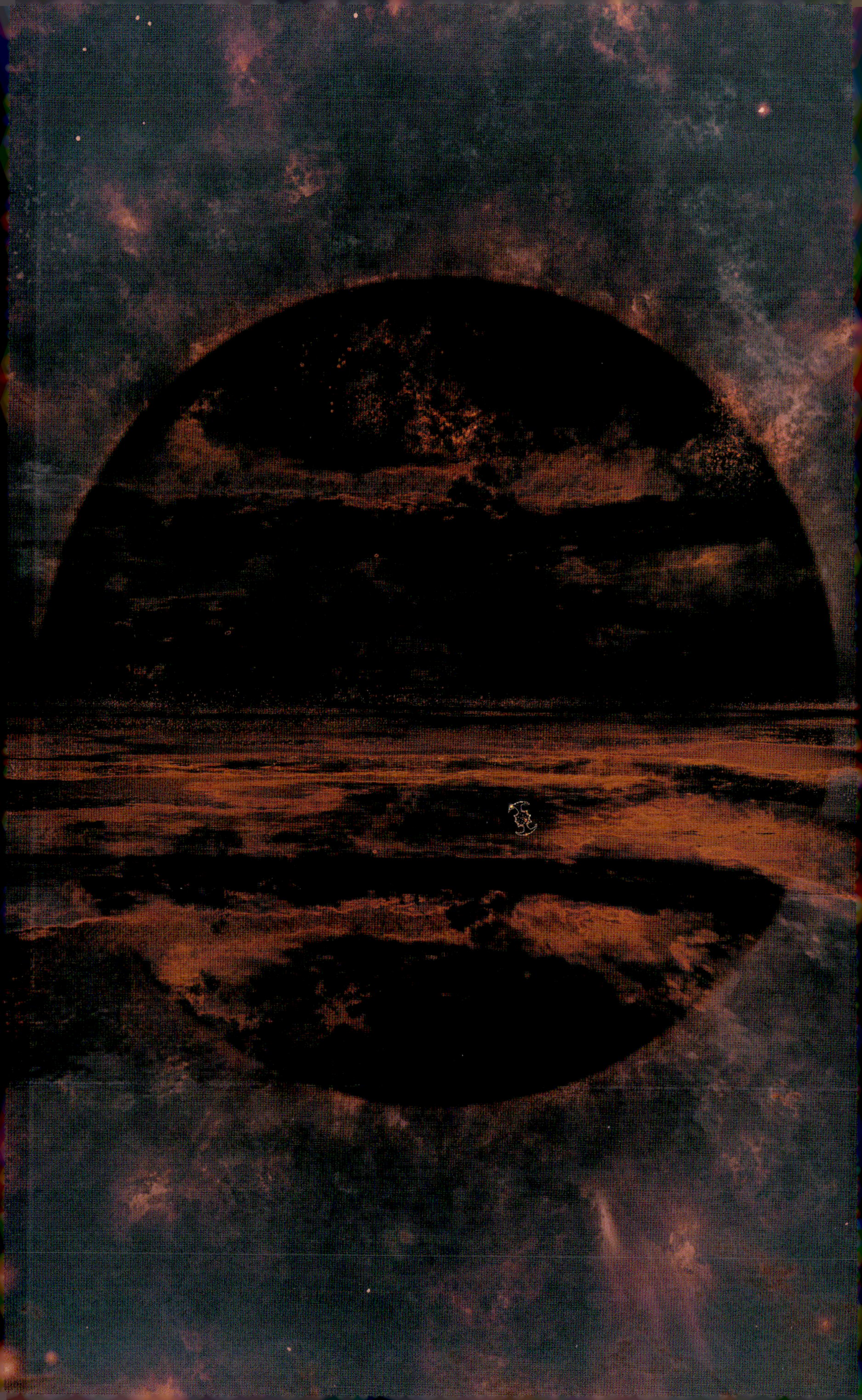

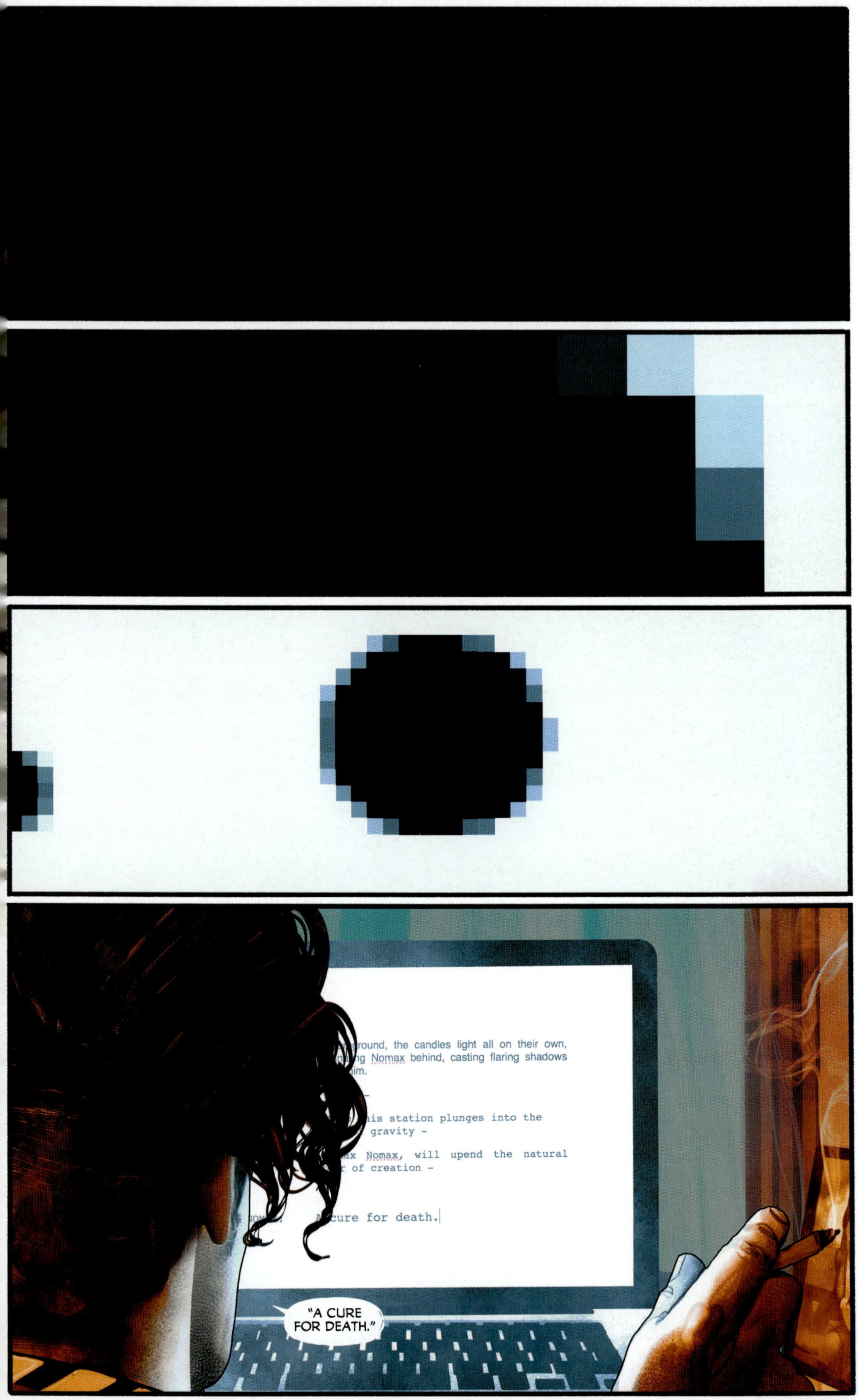
"A CURE FOR DEATH."

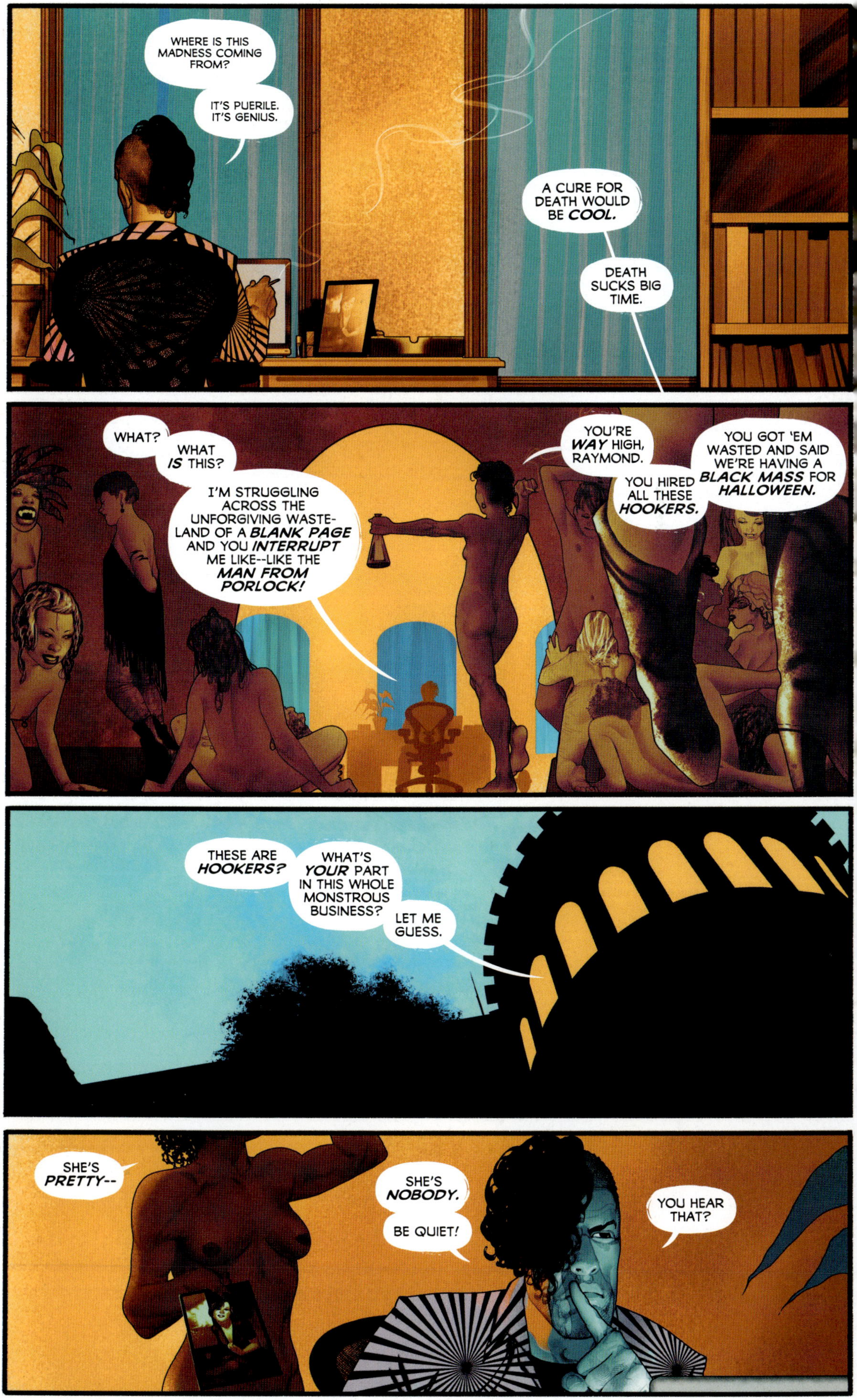
WHERE IS THIS MADNESS COMING FROM?
IT'S PUERILE. IT'S GENIUS.
A CURE FOR DEATH WOULD BE *COOL.*
DEATH SUCKS BIG TIME.
WHAT?
WHAT *IS* THIS?
I'M STRUGGLING ACROSS THE UNFORGIVING WASTE-LAND OF A *BLANK PAGE* AND YOU *INTERRUPT* ME LIKE--LIKE THE *MAN FROM PORLOCK!*
YOU'RE *WAY* HIGH, RAYMOND.
YOU HIRED ALL THESE *HOOKERS.*
YOU GOT 'EM WASTED AND SAID WE'RE HAVING A *BLACK MASS* FOR *HALLOWEEN.*
THESE ARE *HOOKERS?*
WHAT'S *YOUR* PART IN THIS WHOLE MONSTROUS BUSINESS?
LET ME GUESS.
SHE'S *PRETTY--*
SHE'S *NOBODY.*
BE QUIET!
YOU HEAR THAT?

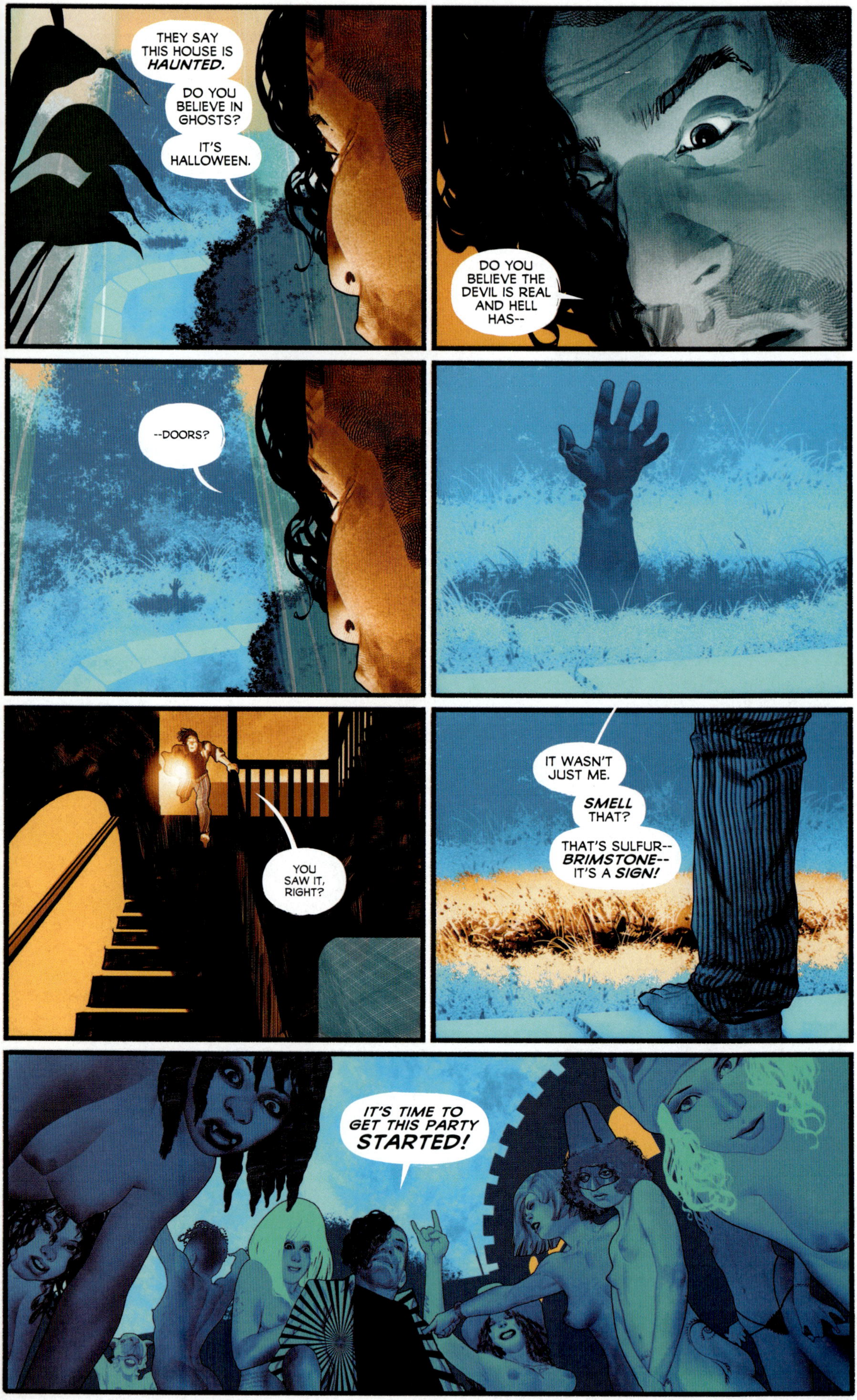
THEY SAY THIS HOUSE IS HAUNTED.
DO YOU BELIEVE IN GHOSTS?
IT'S HALLOWEEN.
DO YOU BELIEVE THE DEVIL IS REAL AND HELL HAS--
--DOORS?
YOU SAW IT, RIGHT?
IT WASN'T JUST ME.
SMELL THAT?
THAT'S SULFUR-- BRIMSTONE-- IT'S A SIGN!
IT'S TIME TO GET THIS PARTY STARTED!

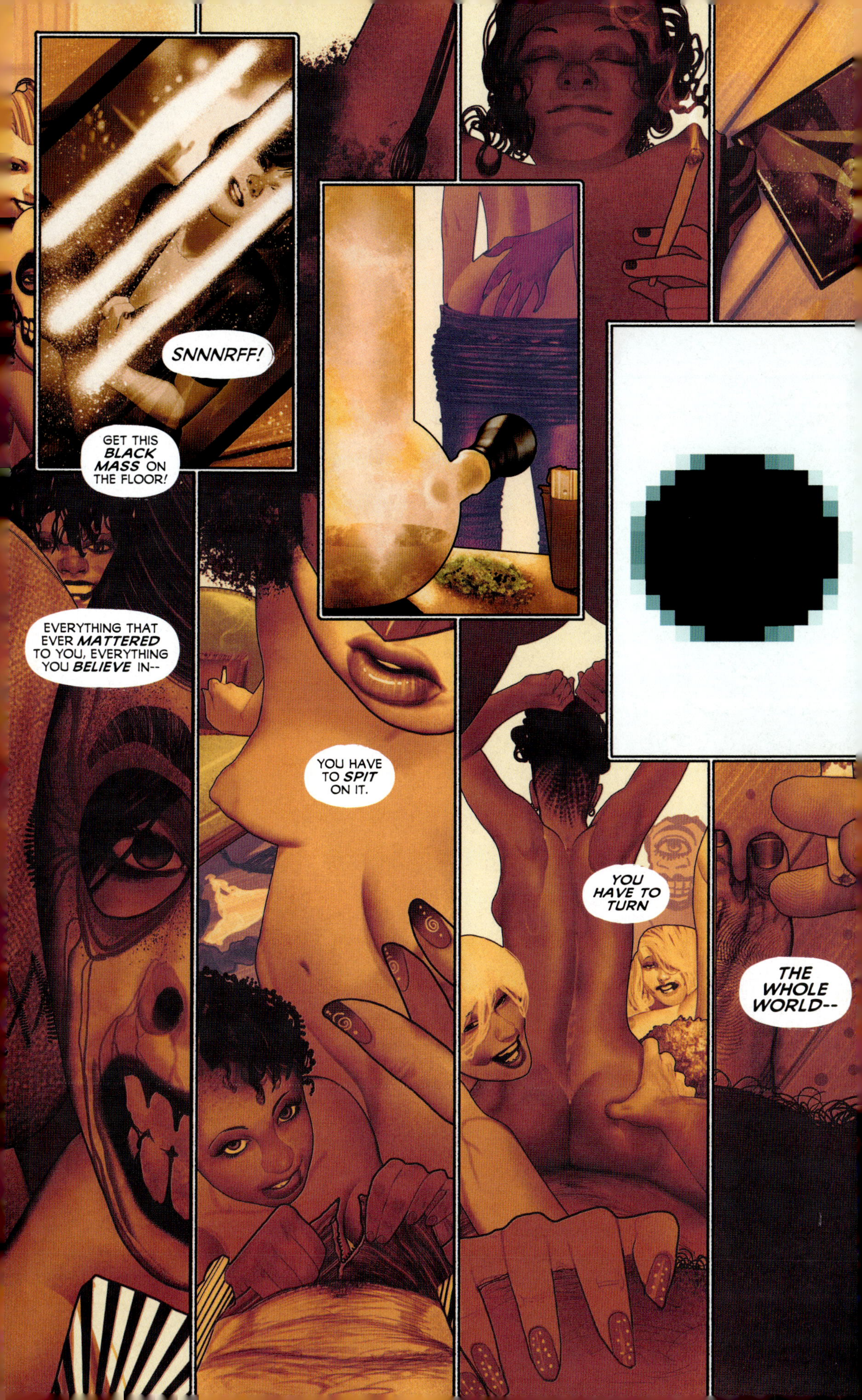
SNNNRFF!
GET THIS BLACK MASS ON THE FLOOR!
EVERYTHING THAT EVER MATTERED TO YOU, EVERYTHING YOU BELIEVE IN--
YOU HAVE TO SPIT ON IT.
YOU HAVE TO TURN
THE WHOLE WORLD--

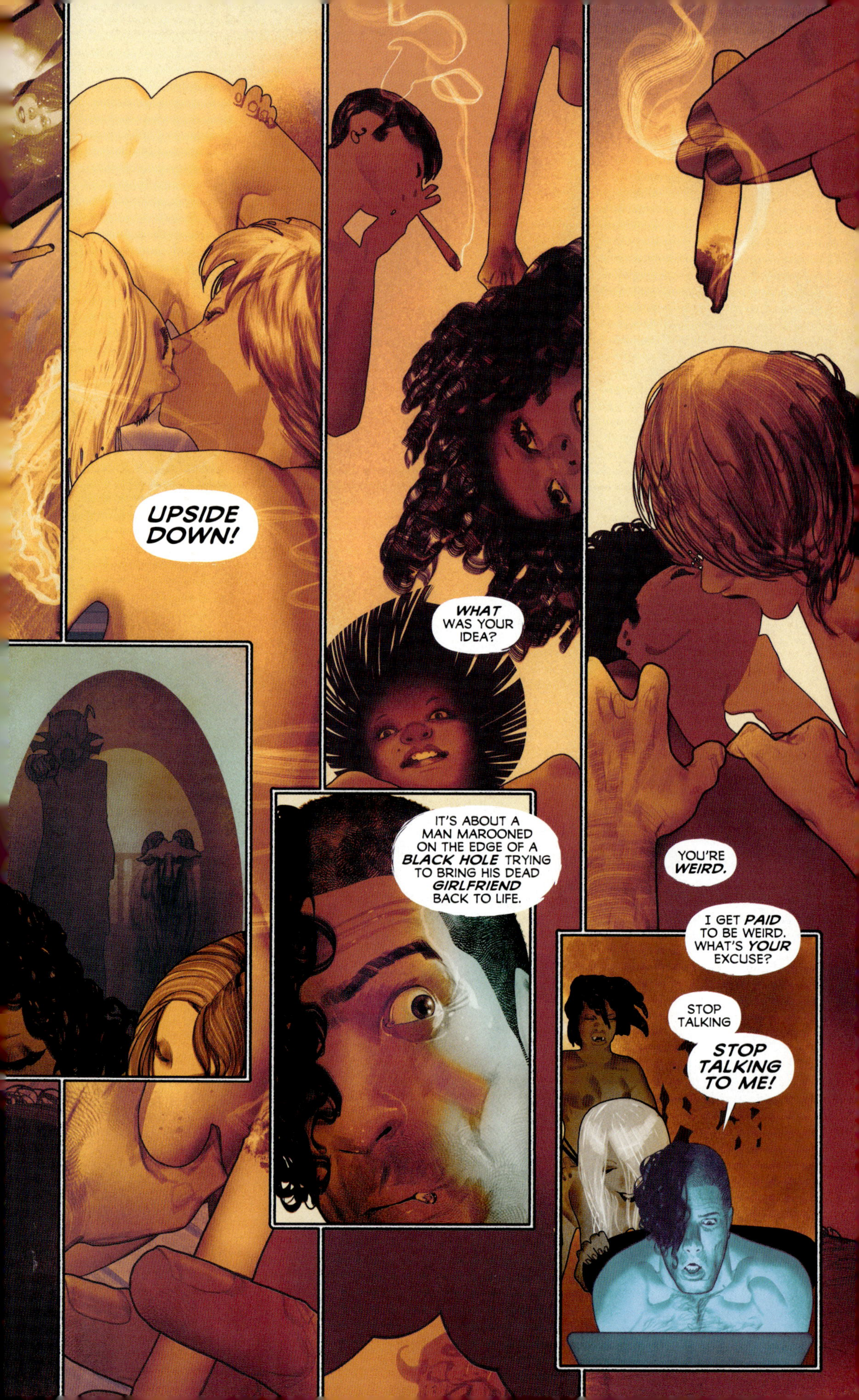
UPSIDE DOWN!
WHAT WAS YOUR IDEA?
IT'S ABOUT A MAN MAROONED ON THE EDGE OF A BLACK HOLE TRYING TO BRING HIS DEAD GIRLFRIEND BACK TO LIFE.
YOU'RE WEIRD.
I GET PAID TO BE WEIRD. WHAT'S YOUR EXCUSE?
STOP TALKING
STOP TALKING TO ME!

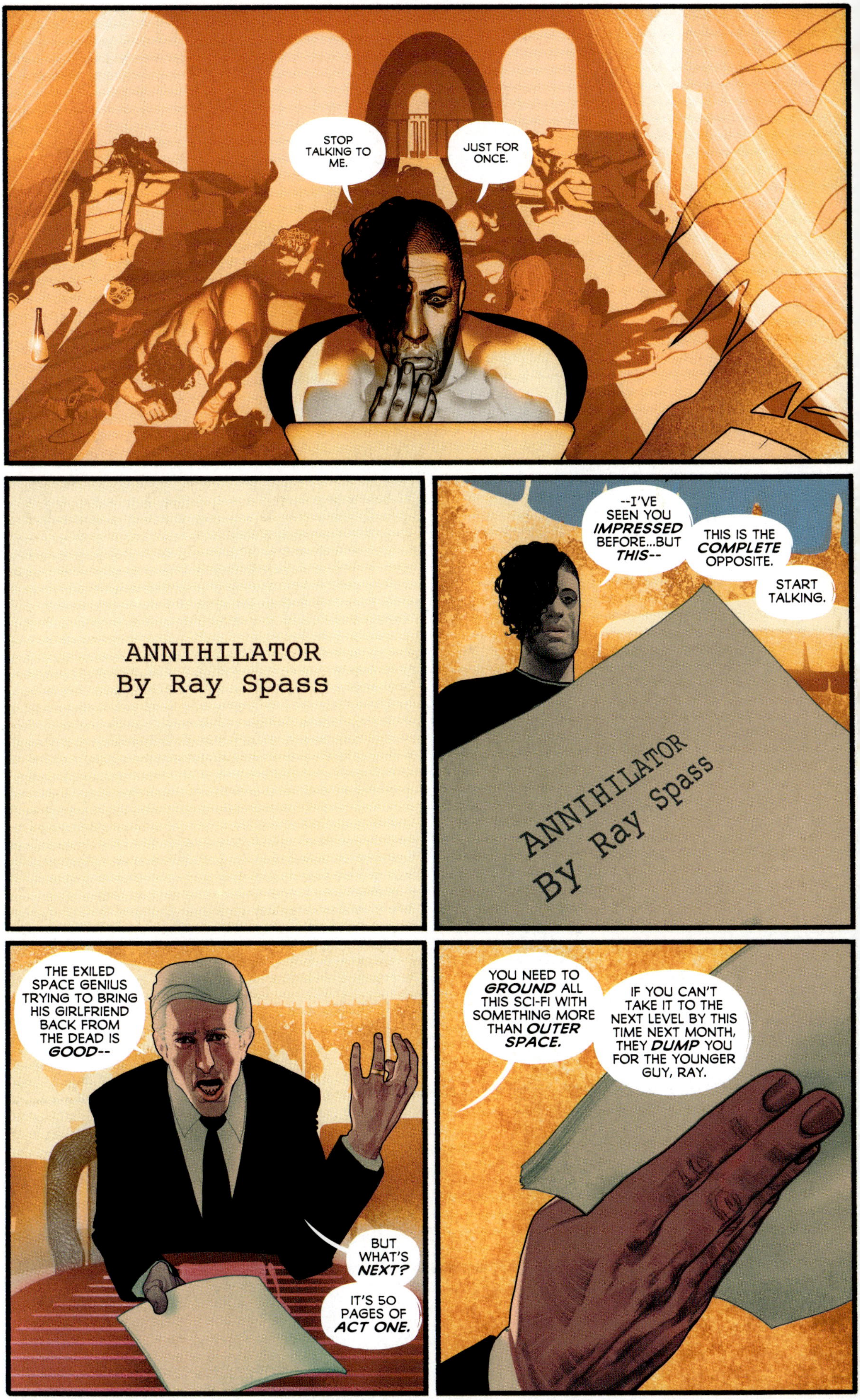
STOP TALKING TO ME.
JUST FOR ONCE.
ANNIHILATOR
By Ray Spass
--I'VE SEEN YOU IMPRESSED BEFORE...BUT THIS--
THIS IS THE COMPLETE OPPOSITE.
START TALKING.
ANNIHILATOR
By Ray Spass
THE EXILED SPACE GENIUS TRYING TO BRING HIS GIRLFRIEND BACK FROM THE DEAD IS GOOD--
BUT WHAT'S NEXT?
IT'S 50 PAGES OF ACT ONE.
YOU NEED TO GROUND ALL THIS SCI-FI WITH SOMETHING MORE THAN OUTER SPACE.
IF YOU CAN'T TAKE IT TO THE NEXT LEVEL BY THIS TIME NEXT MONTH, THEY DUMP YOU FOR THE YOUNGER GUY, RAY.

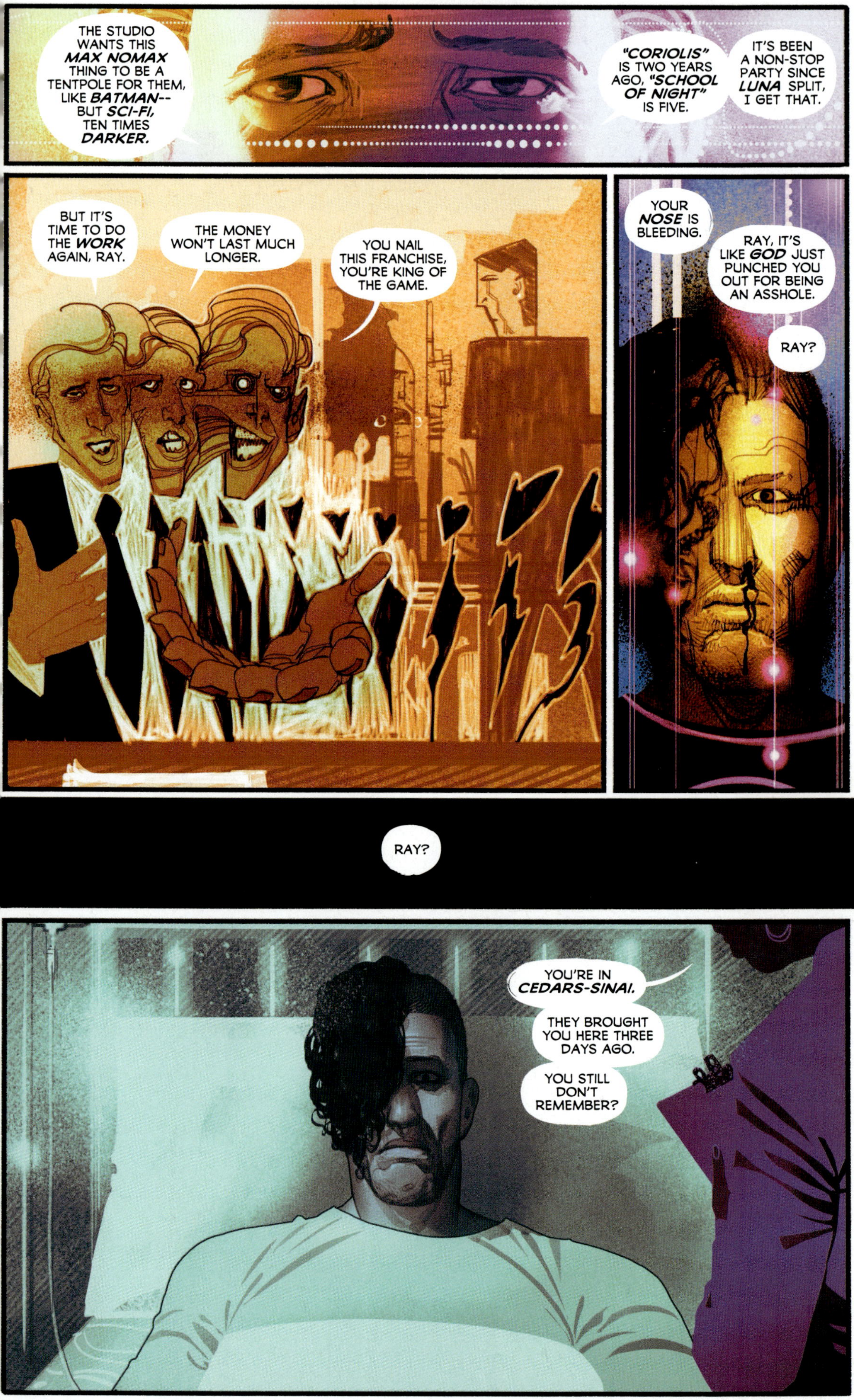
THE STUDIO WANTS THIS **MAX NOMAX** THING TO BE A TENTPOLE FOR THEM, LIKE **BATMAN**-- BUT **SCI-FI,** TEN TIMES **DARKER.**
"CORIOLIS" IS TWO YEARS AGO, **"SCHOOL OF NIGHT"** IS FIVE.
IT'S BEEN A NON-STOP PARTY SINCE **LUNA** SPLIT, I GET THAT.
BUT IT'S TIME TO DO THE **WORK** AGAIN, RAY.
THE MONEY WON'T LAST MUCH LONGER.
YOU NAIL THIS FRANCHISE, YOU'RE KING OF THE GAME.
YOUR **NOSE** IS BLEEDING.
RAY, IT'S LIKE **GOD** JUST PUNCHED YOU OUT FOR BEING AN ASSHOLE.
RAY?
RAY?
YOU'RE IN **CEDARS-SINAI.**
THEY BROUGHT YOU HERE THREE DAYS AGO.
YOU STILL DON'T REMEMBER?

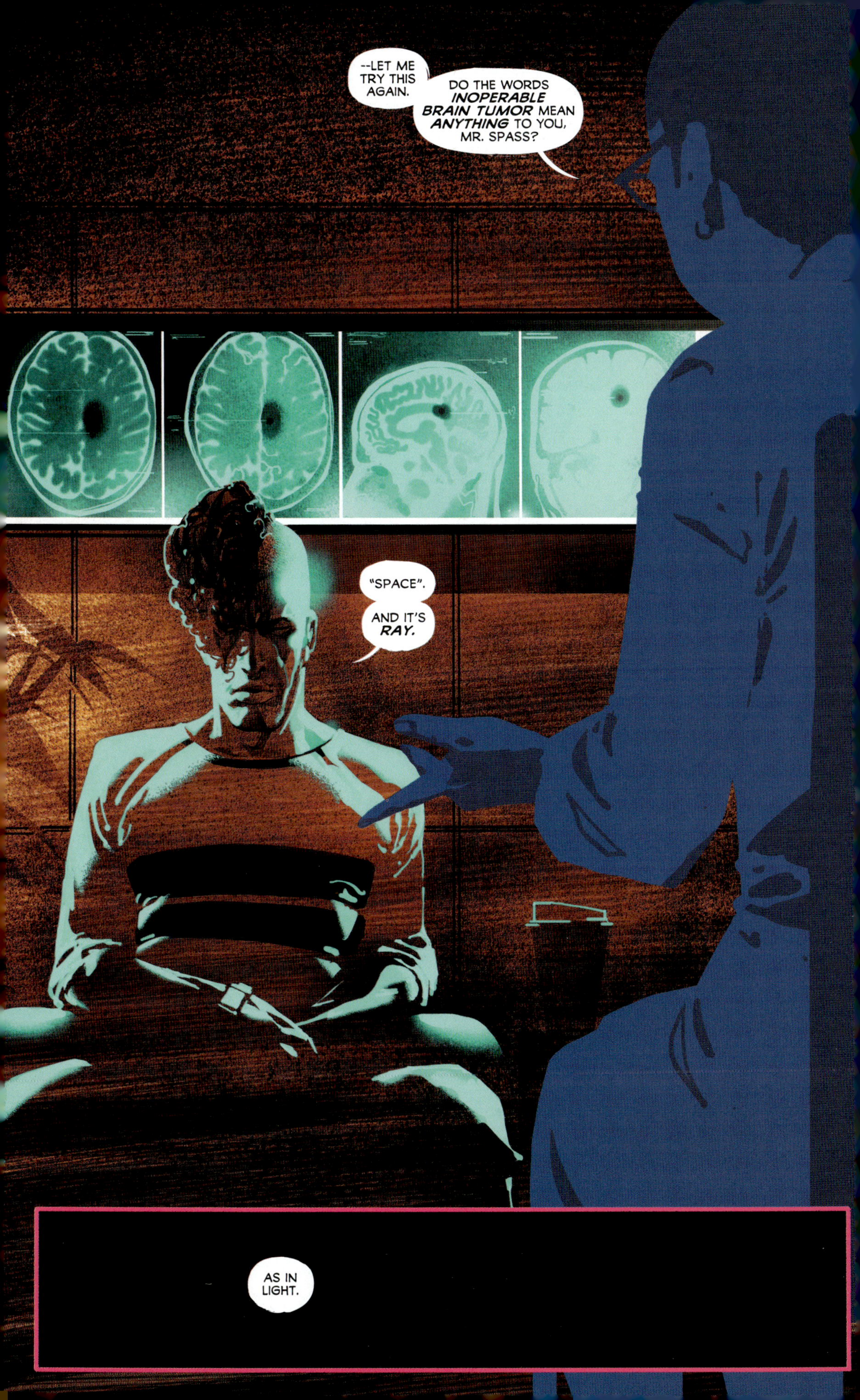
--LET ME TRY THIS AGAIN.
DO THE WORDS ***INOPERABLE BRAIN TUMOR*** MEAN ***ANYTHING*** TO YOU, MR. SPASS?
"SPACE".
AND IT'S ***RAY.***
AS IN LIGHT.

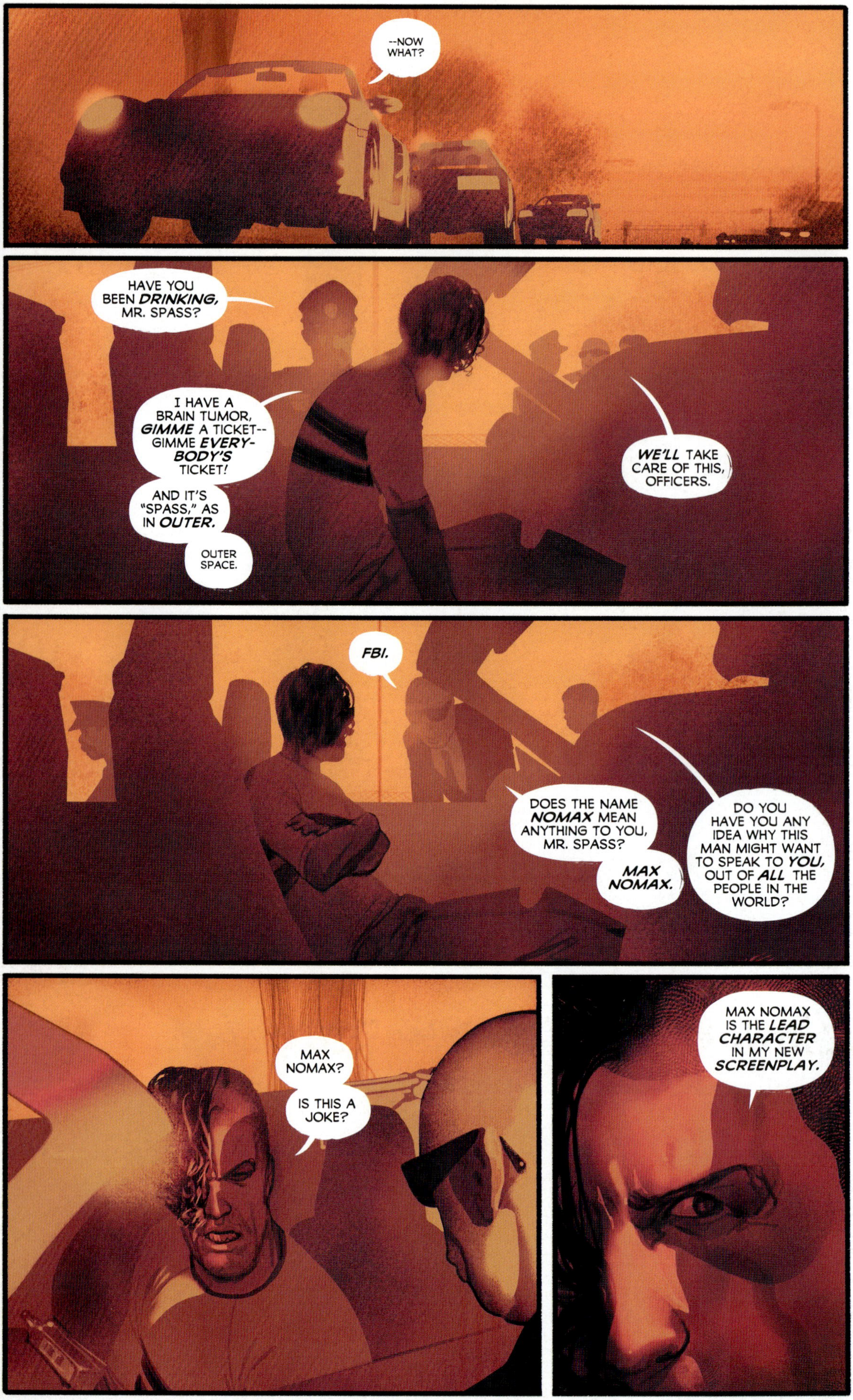
--NOW WHAT?
HAVE YOU BEEN *DRINKING,* MR. SPASS?
I HAVE A BRAIN TUMOR, *GIMME* A TICKET--GIMME *EVERY-BODY'S* TICKET!
AND IT'S "SPASS," AS IN *OUTER.*
OUTER SPACE.
WE'LL TAKE CARE OF THIS, OFFICERS.
FBI.
DOES THE NAME *NOMAX* MEAN ANYTHING TO YOU, MR. SPASS?
MAX NOMAX.
DO YOU HAVE YOU ANY IDEA WHY THIS MAN MIGHT WANT TO SPEAK TO *YOU,* OUT OF *ALL* THE PEOPLE IN THE WORLD?
MAX NOMAX?
IS THIS A JOKE?
MAX NOMAX IS THE *LEAD CHARACTER* IN MY NEW *SCREENPLAY.*

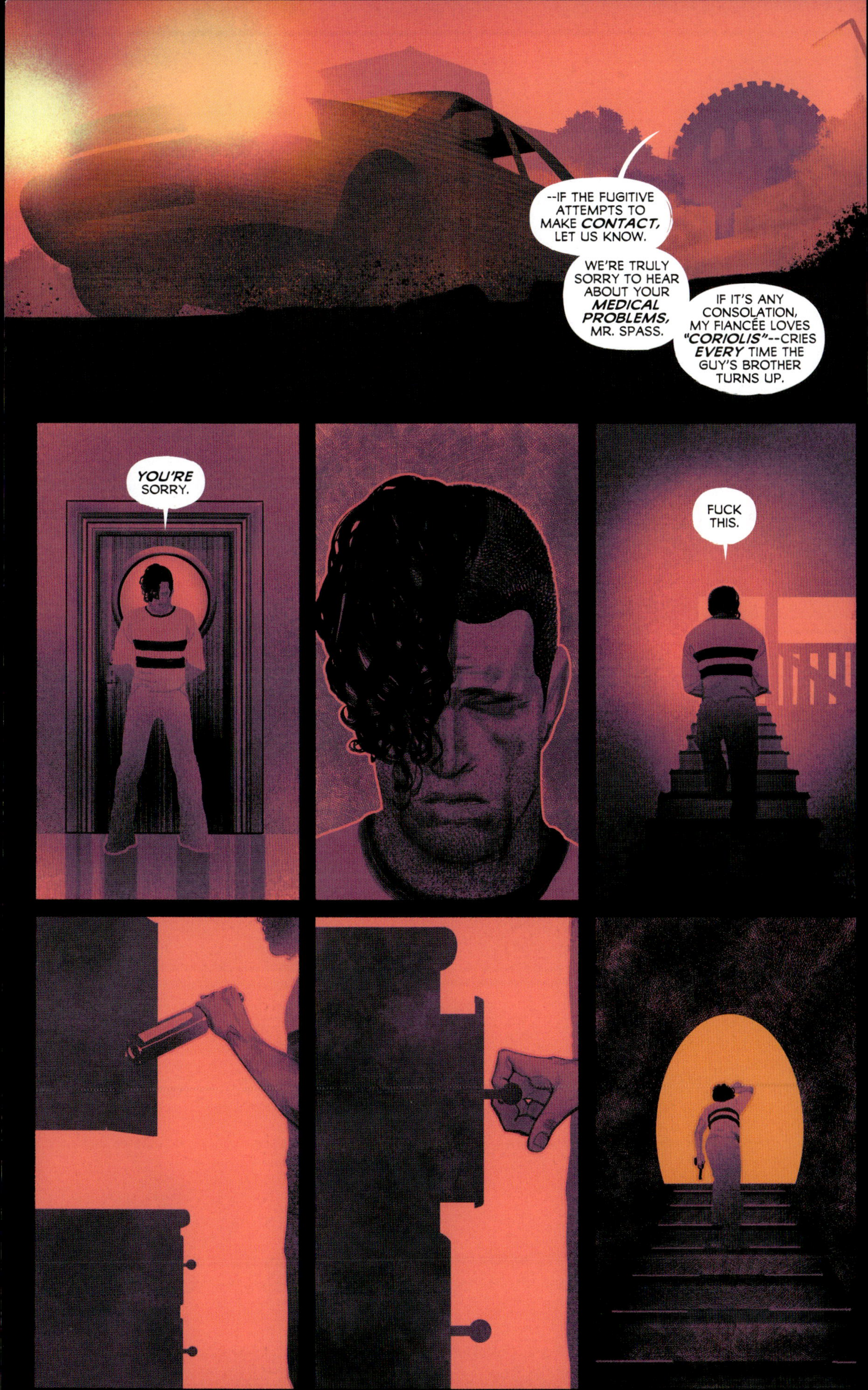
--IF THE FUGITIVE ATTEMPTS TO MAKE ***CONTACT,*** LET US KNOW.
WE'RE TRULY SORRY TO HEAR ABOUT YOUR ***MEDICAL PROBLEMS,*** MR. SPASS.
IF IT'S ANY CONSOLATION, MY FIANCÉE LOVES ***"CORIOLIS"***--CRIES ***EVERY*** TIME THE GUY'S BROTHER TURNS UP.
YOU'RE SORRY.
FUCK THIS.

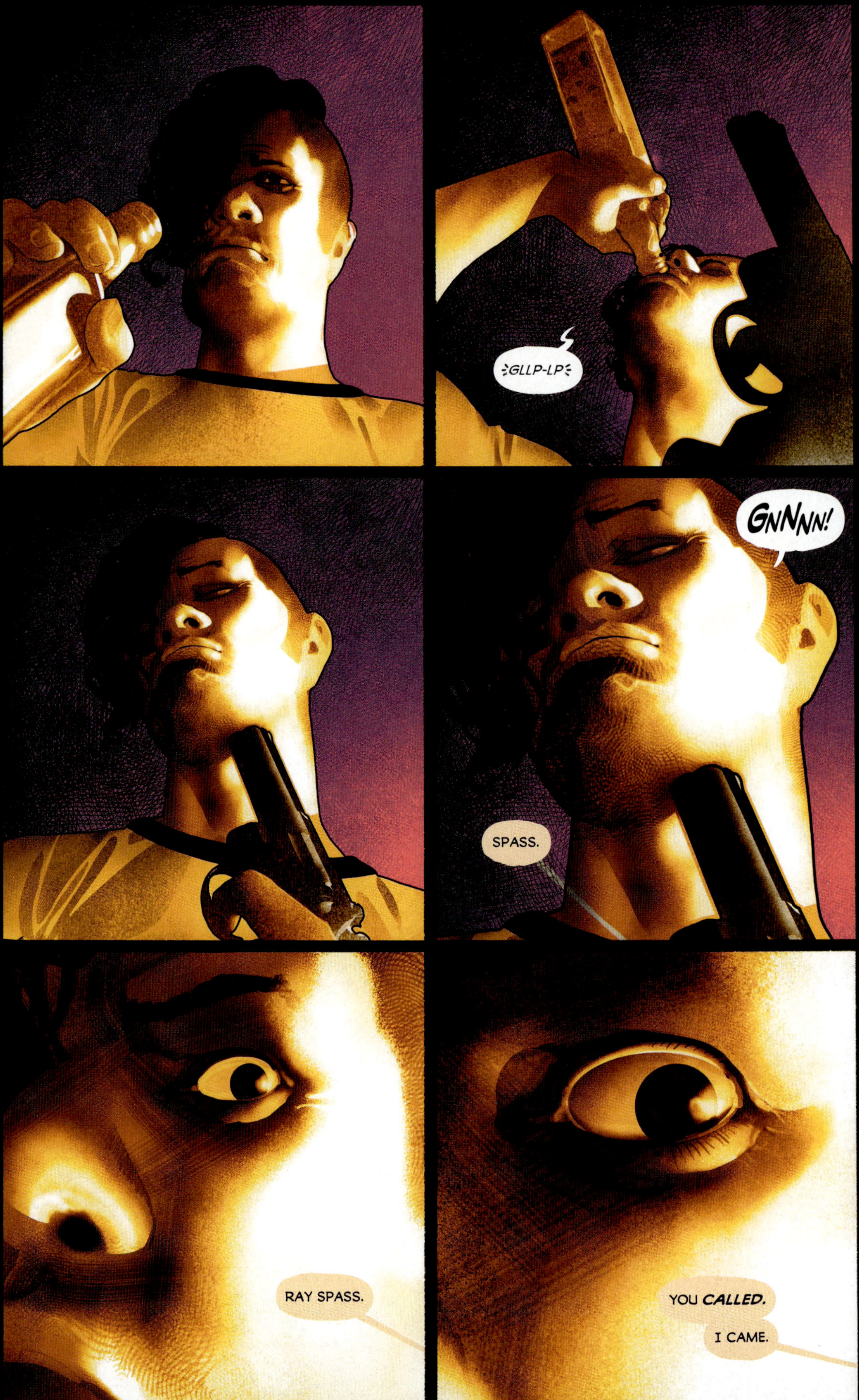
GLLP-LP
GNNNN!
SPASS.
RAY SPASS.
YOU CALLED.
I CAME.

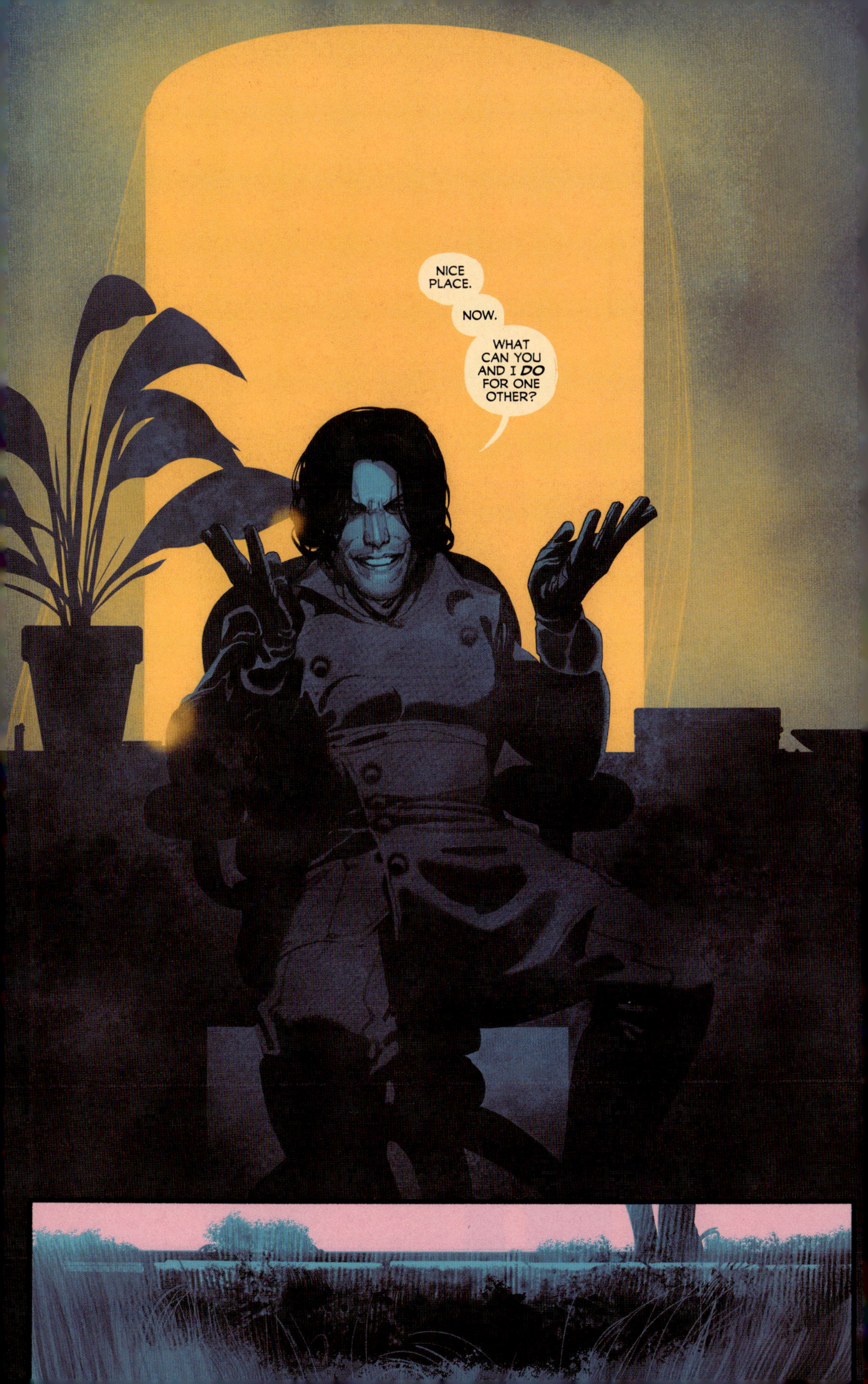
NICE PLACE.
NOW.
WHAT CAN YOU AND I *DO* FOR ONE OTHER?

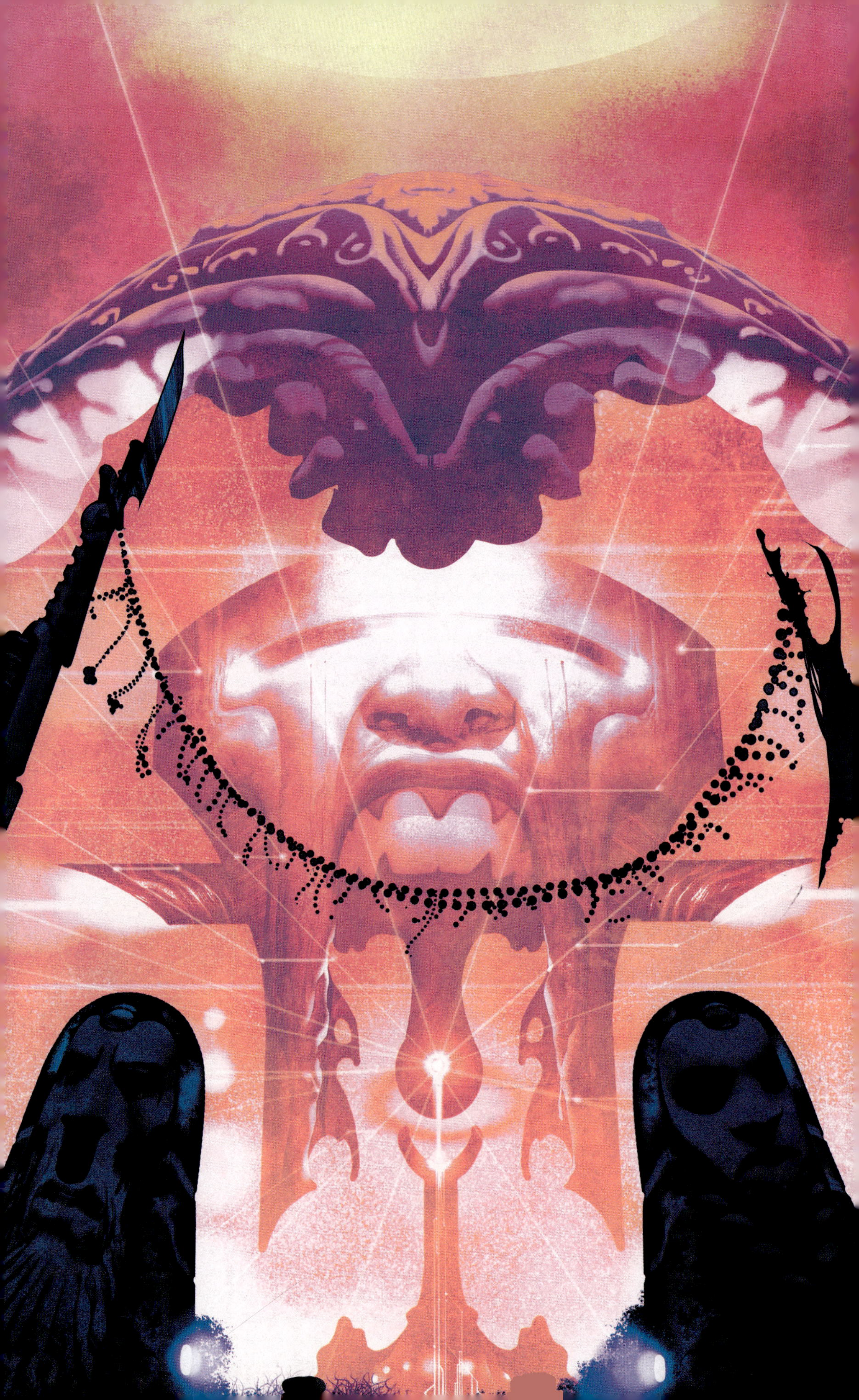

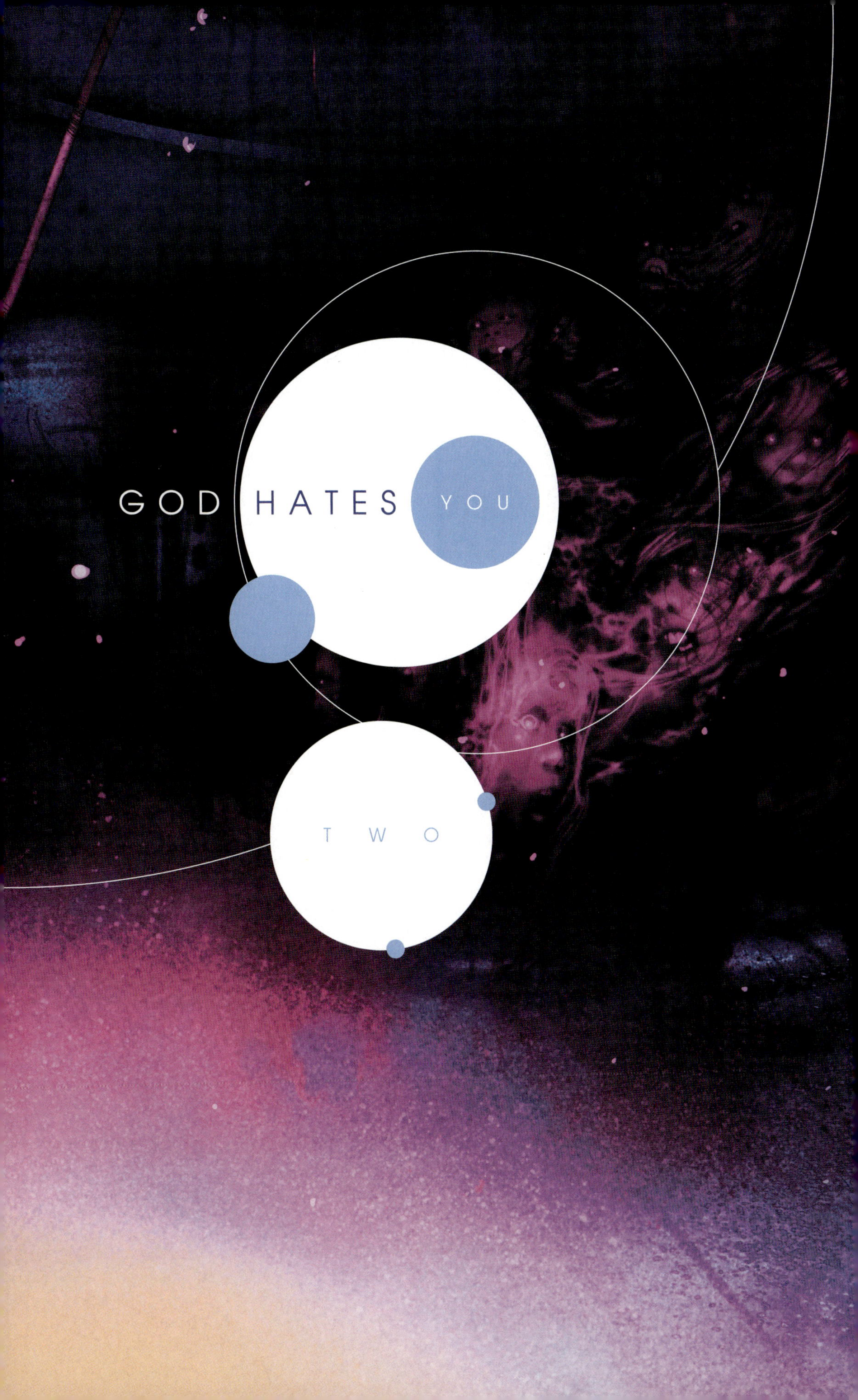
GOD HATES YOU
TWO

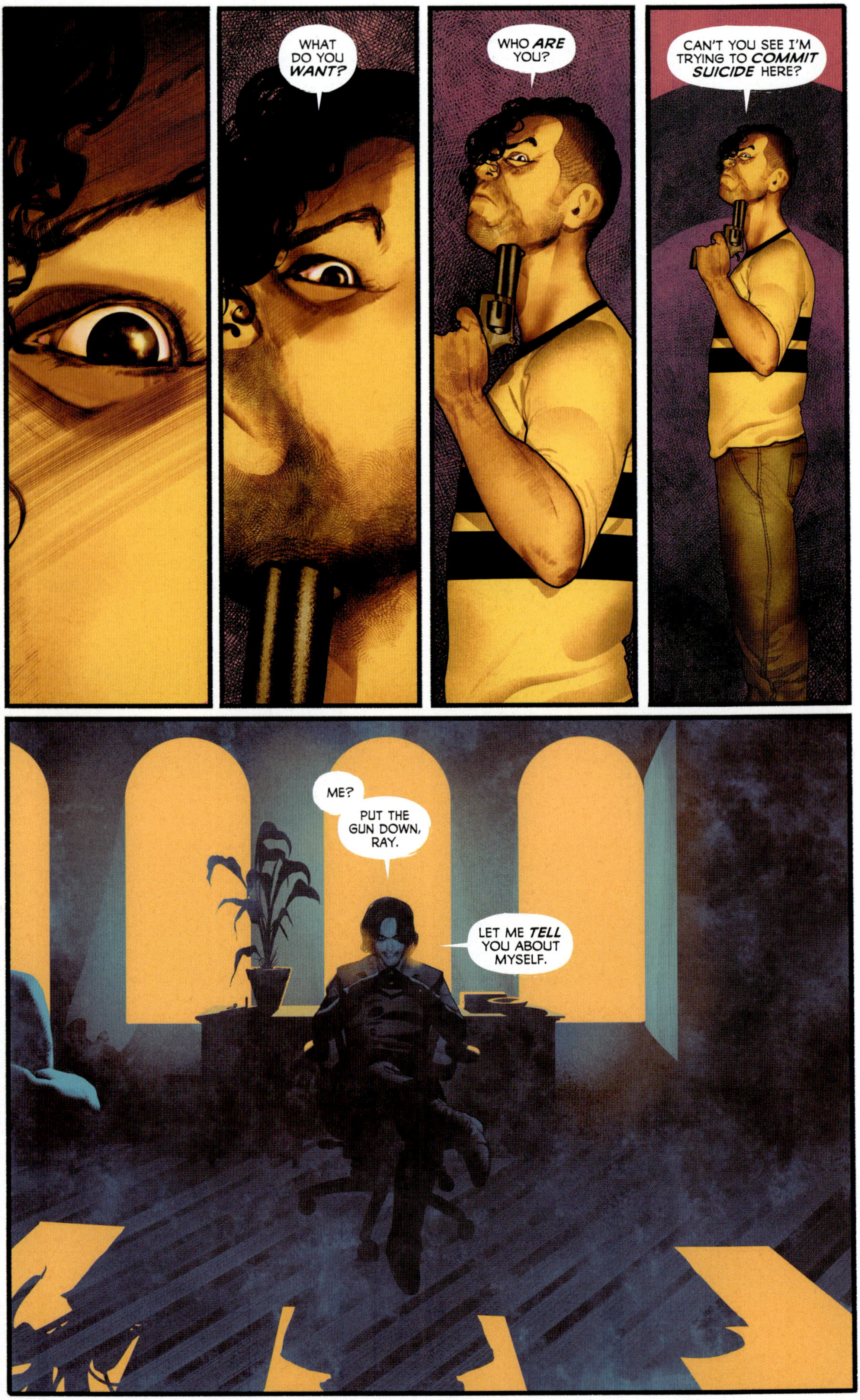
WHAT DO YOU WANT?
WHO ARE YOU?
CAN'T YOU SEE I'M TRYING TO COMMIT SUICIDE HERE?
ME?
PUT THE GUN DOWN, RAY.
LET ME TELL YOU ABOUT MYSELF.

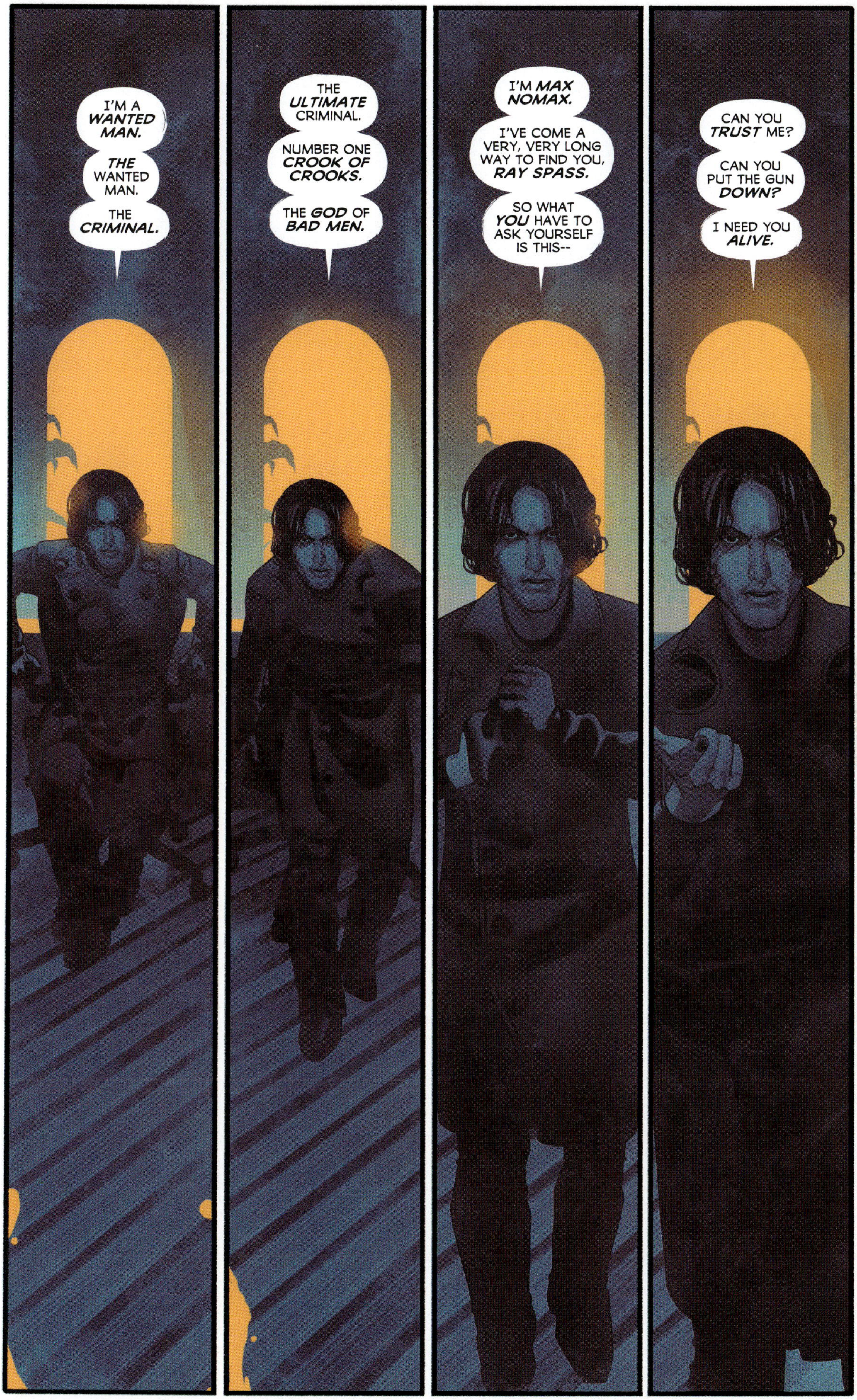
I'M A WANTED MAN.
THE WANTED MAN.
THE CRIMINAL.
THE ULTIMATE CRIMINAL.
NUMBER ONE CROOK OF CROOKS.
THE GOD OF BAD MEN.
I'M MAX NOMAX.
I'VE COME A VERY, VERY LONG WAY TO FIND YOU, RAY SPASS.
SO WHAT YOU HAVE TO ASK YOURSELF IS THIS--
CAN YOU TRUST ME?
CAN YOU PUT THE GUN DOWN?
I NEED YOU ALIVE.

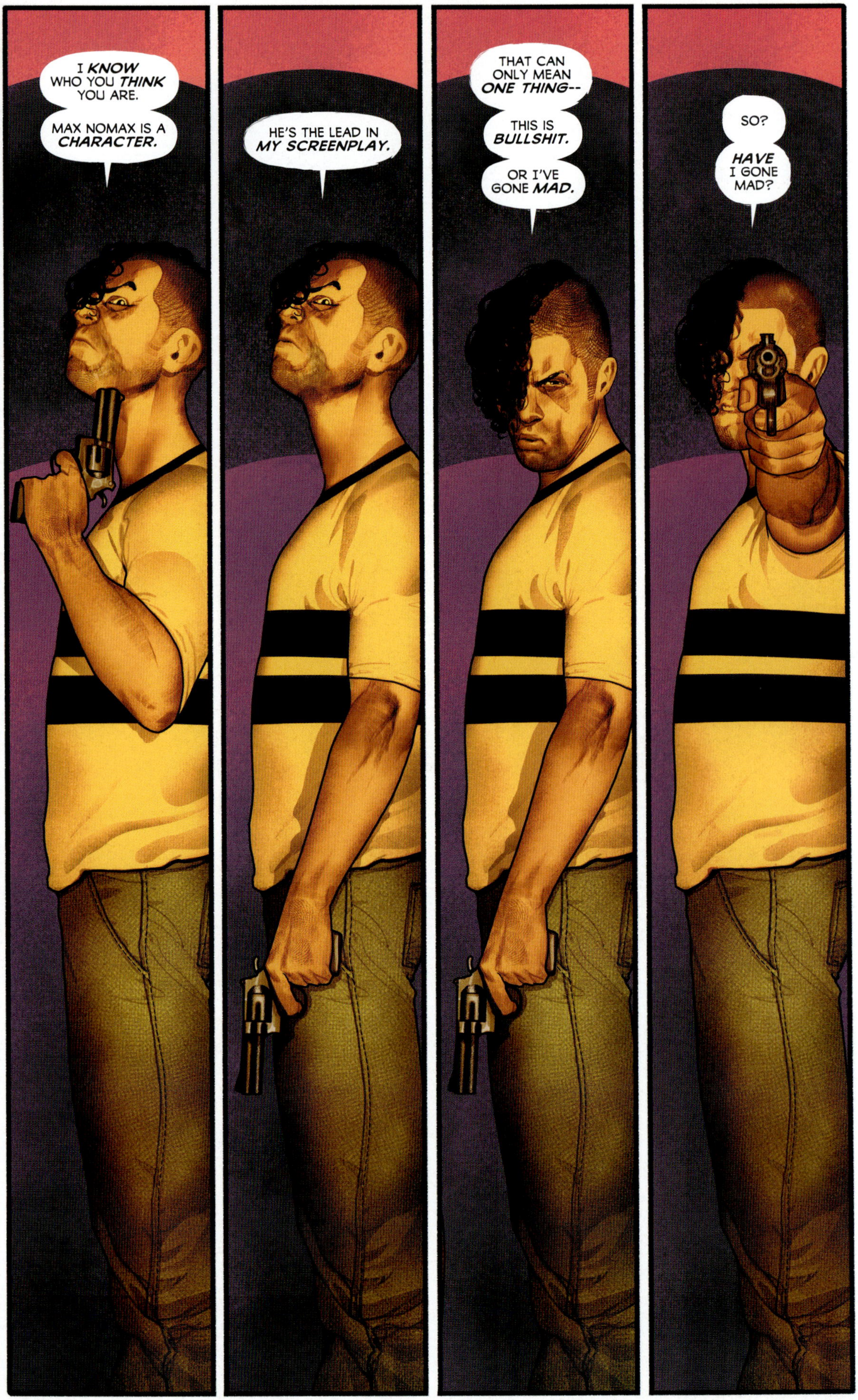
I KNOW WHO YOU THINK YOU ARE.
MAX NOMAX IS A CHARACTER.
HE'S THE LEAD IN MY SCREENPLAY.
THAT CAN ONLY MEAN ONE THING--
THIS IS BULLSHIT.
OR I'VE GONE MAD.
SO?
HAVE I GONE MAD?

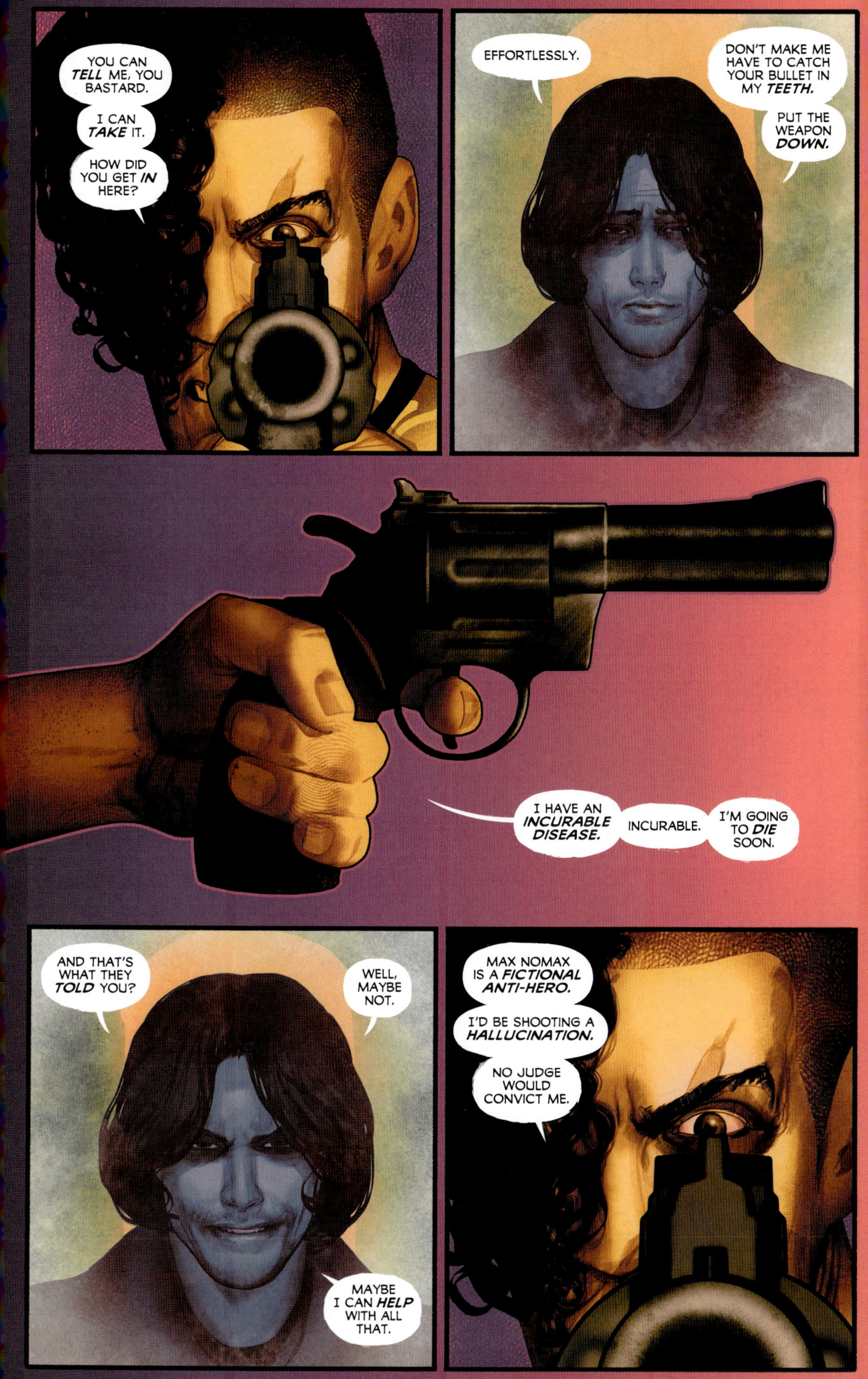
YOU CAN *TELL* ME, YOU BASTARD.
I CAN *TAKE* IT.
HOW DID YOU GET *IN* HERE?
EFFORTLESSLY.
DON'T MAKE ME HAVE TO CATCH YOUR BULLET IN MY *TEETH.*
PUT THE WEAPON *DOWN.*
I HAVE AN *INCURABLE DISEASE.*
INCURABLE.
I'M GOING TO *DIE* SOON.
AND THAT'S WHAT THEY *TOLD* YOU?
WELL, MAYBE NOT.
MAYBE I CAN *HELP* WITH ALL THAT.
MAX NOMAX IS A *FICTIONAL ANTI-HERO.*
I'D BE SHOOTING A *HALLUCINATION.*
NO JUDGE WOULD CONVICT ME.

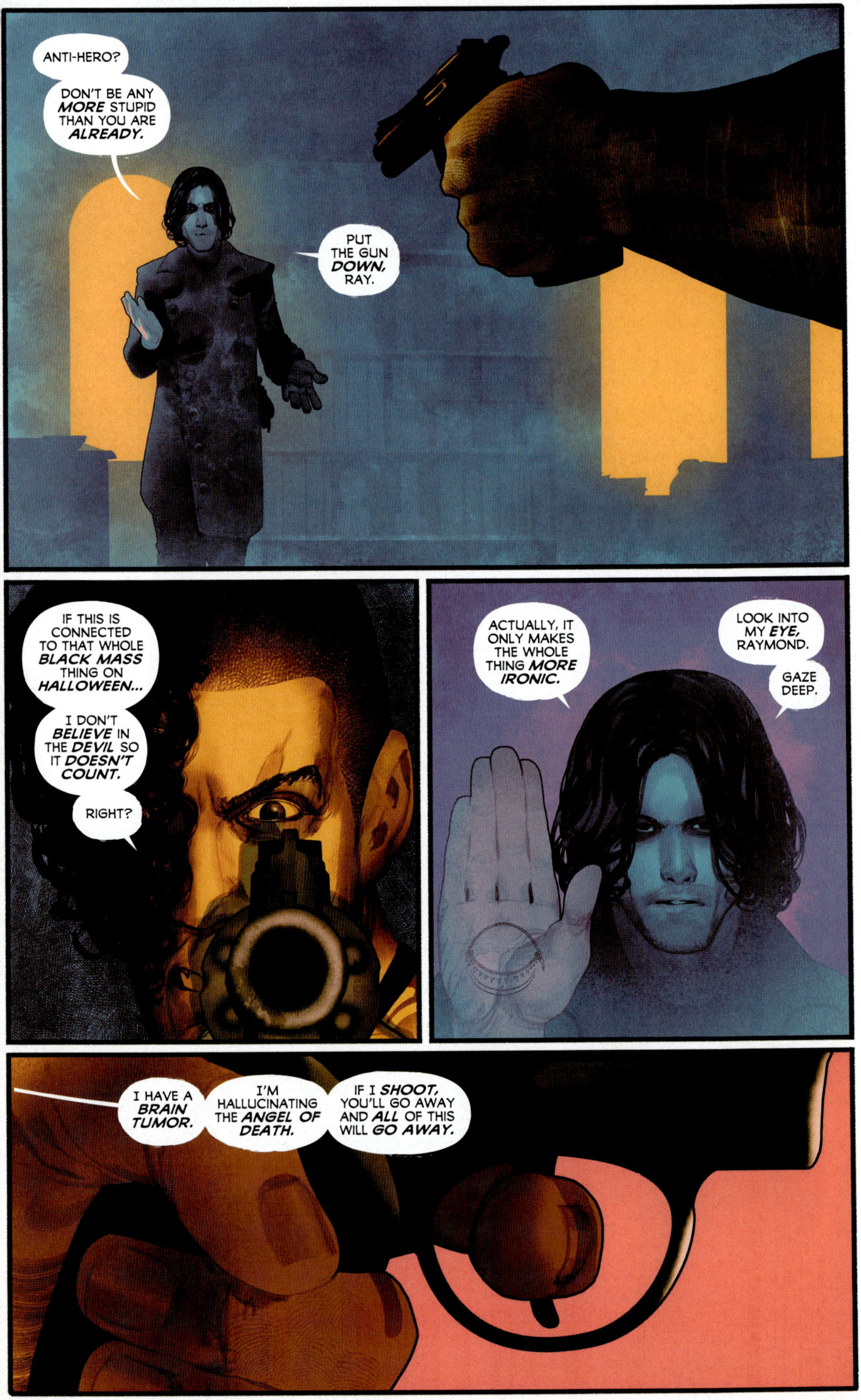
ANTI-HERO?
DON'T BE ANY *MORE* STUPID THAN YOU ARE *ALREADY.*
PUT THE GUN *DOWN,* RAY.
IF THIS IS CONNECTED TO THAT WHOLE *BLACK MASS* THING ON *HALLOWEEN...*
I DON'T *BELIEVE* IN THE *DEVIL* SO IT *DOESN'T COUNT.*
RIGHT?
ACTUALLY, IT ONLY MAKES THE WHOLE THING *MORE IRONIC.*
LOOK INTO MY *EYE,* RAYMOND.
GAZE DEEP.
I HAVE A *BRAIN TUMOR.*
I'M HALLUCINATING THE *ANGEL OF DEATH.*
IF I *SHOOT,* YOU'LL GO AWAY AND *ALL* OF THIS WILL *GO AWAY.*

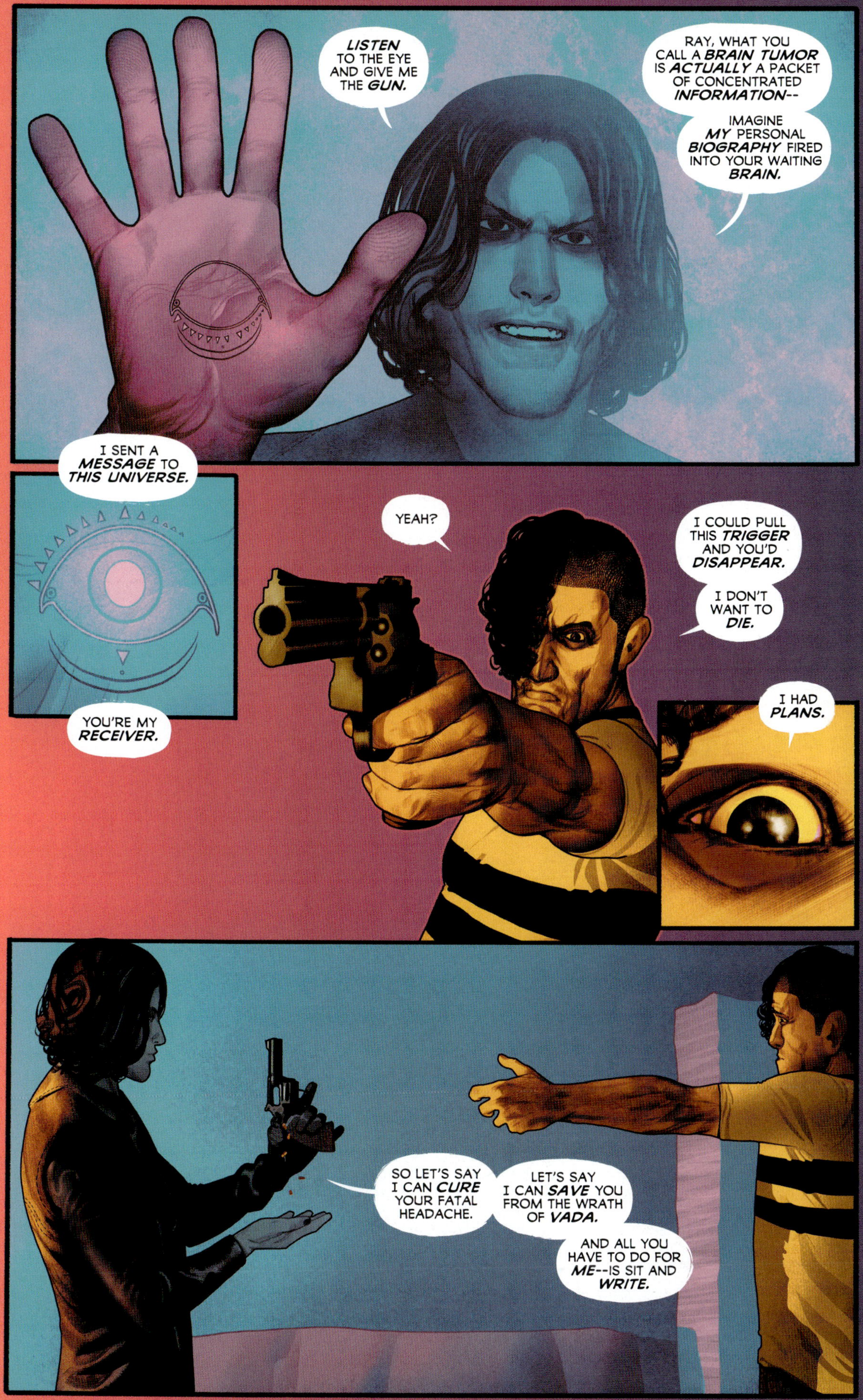
LISTEN TO THE EYE AND GIVE ME THE GUN.
RAY, WHAT YOU CALL A BRAIN TUMOR IS ACTUALLY A PACKET OF CONCENTRATED INFORMATION--
IMAGINE MY PERSONAL BIOGRAPHY FIRED INTO YOUR WAITING BRAIN.
I SENT A MESSAGE TO THIS UNIVERSE.
YOU'RE MY RECEIVER.
YEAH?
I COULD PULL THIS TRIGGER AND YOU'D DISAPPEAR.
I DON'T WANT TO DIE.
I HAD PLANS.
SO LET'S SAY I CAN CURE YOUR FATAL HEADACHE.
LET'S SAY I CAN SAVE YOU FROM THE WRATH OF VADA.
AND ALL YOU HAVE TO DO FOR ME--IS SIT AND WRITE.

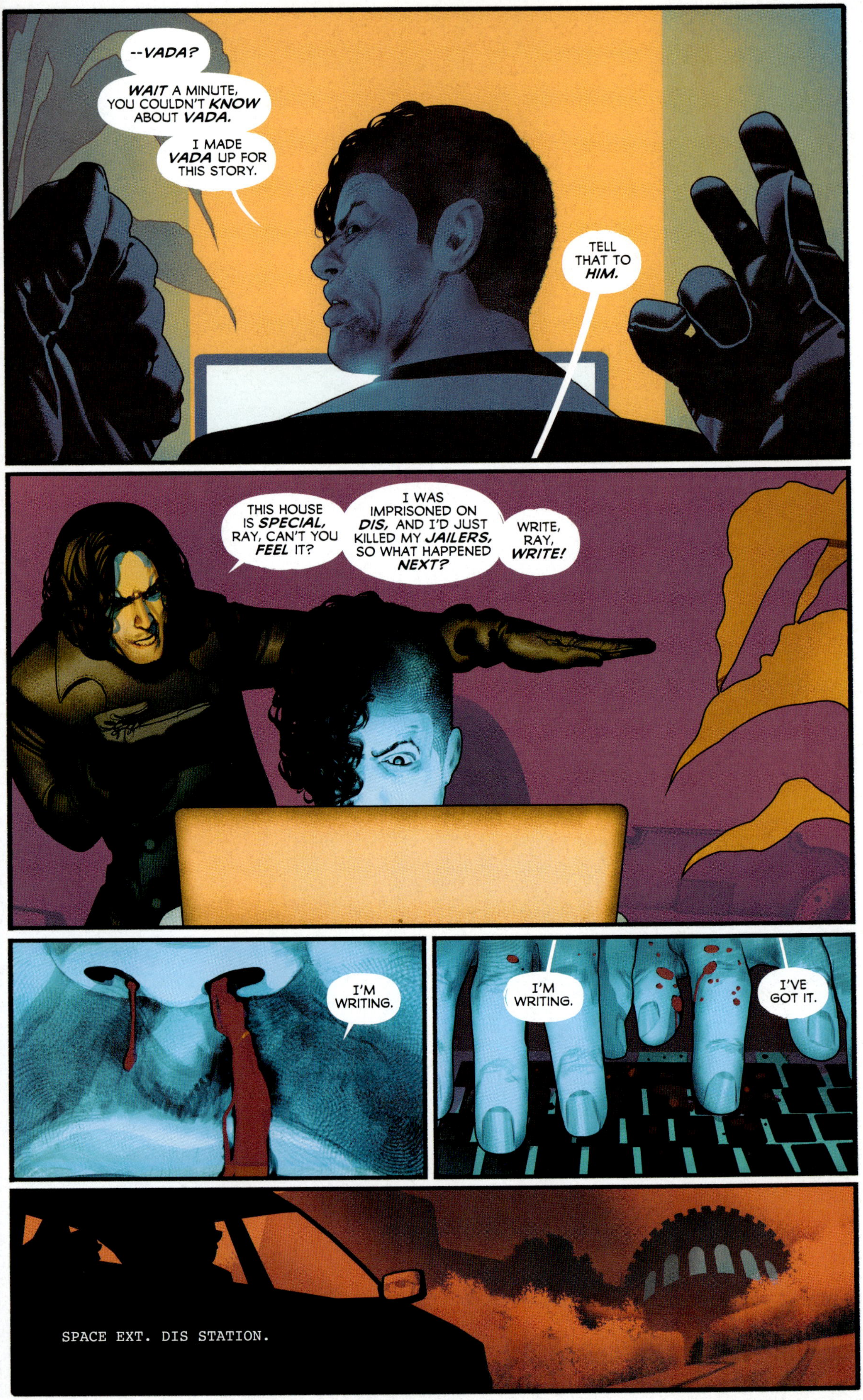
--VADA?
WAIT A MINUTE, YOU COULDN'T KNOW ABOUT VADA.
I MADE VADA UP FOR THIS STORY.
TELL THAT TO HIM.
THIS HOUSE IS SPECIAL, RAY, CAN'T YOU FEEL IT?
I WAS IMPRISONED ON DIS, AND I'D JUST KILLED MY JAILERS, SO WHAT HAPPENED NEXT?
WRITE, RAY, WRITE!
I'M WRITING.
I'M WRITING.
I'VE GOT IT.
SPACE EXT. DIS STATION.

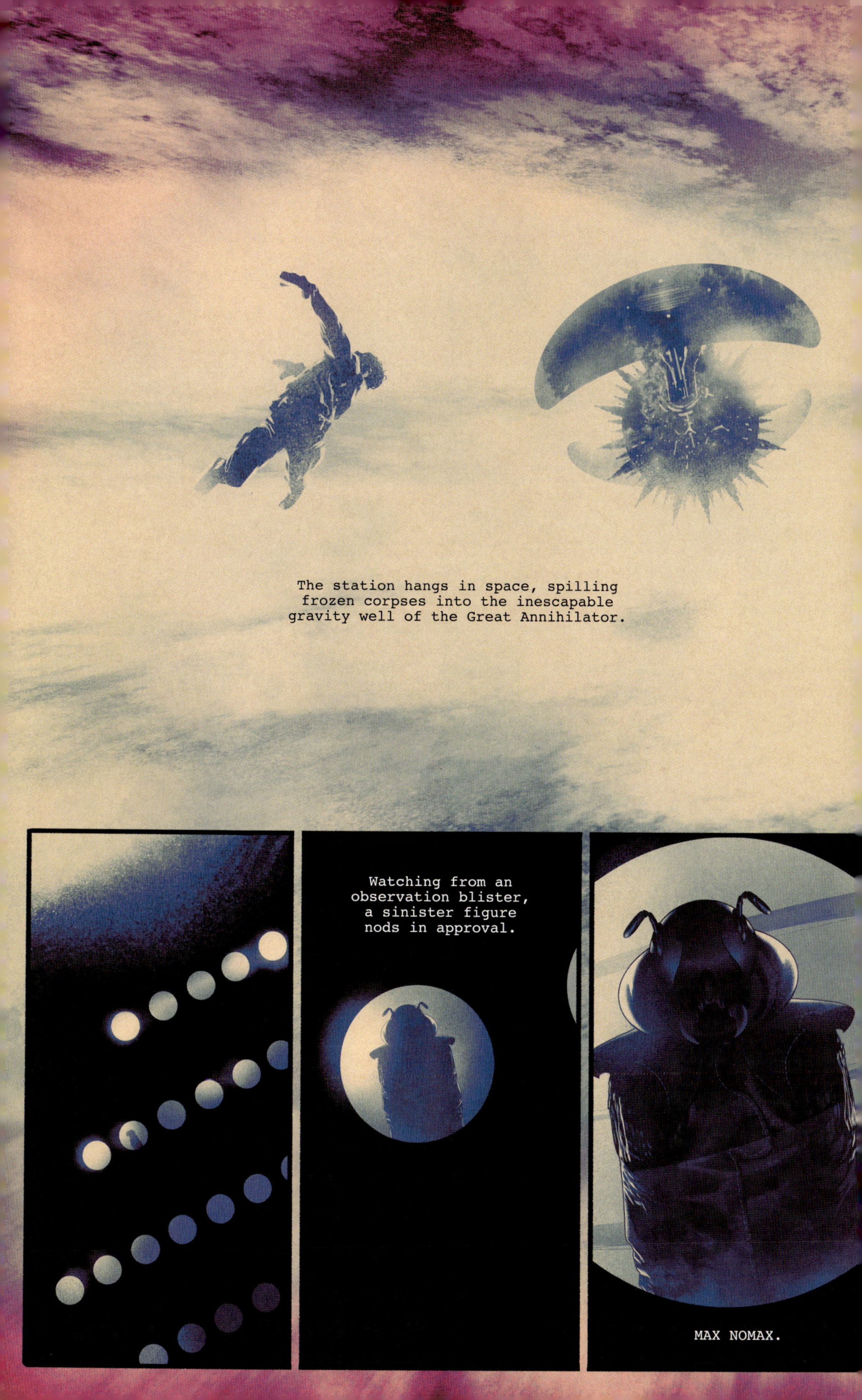
The station hangs in space, spilling frozen corpses into the inescapable gravity well of the Great Annihilator.
Watching from an observation blister, a sinister figure nods in approval.
MAX NOMAX.

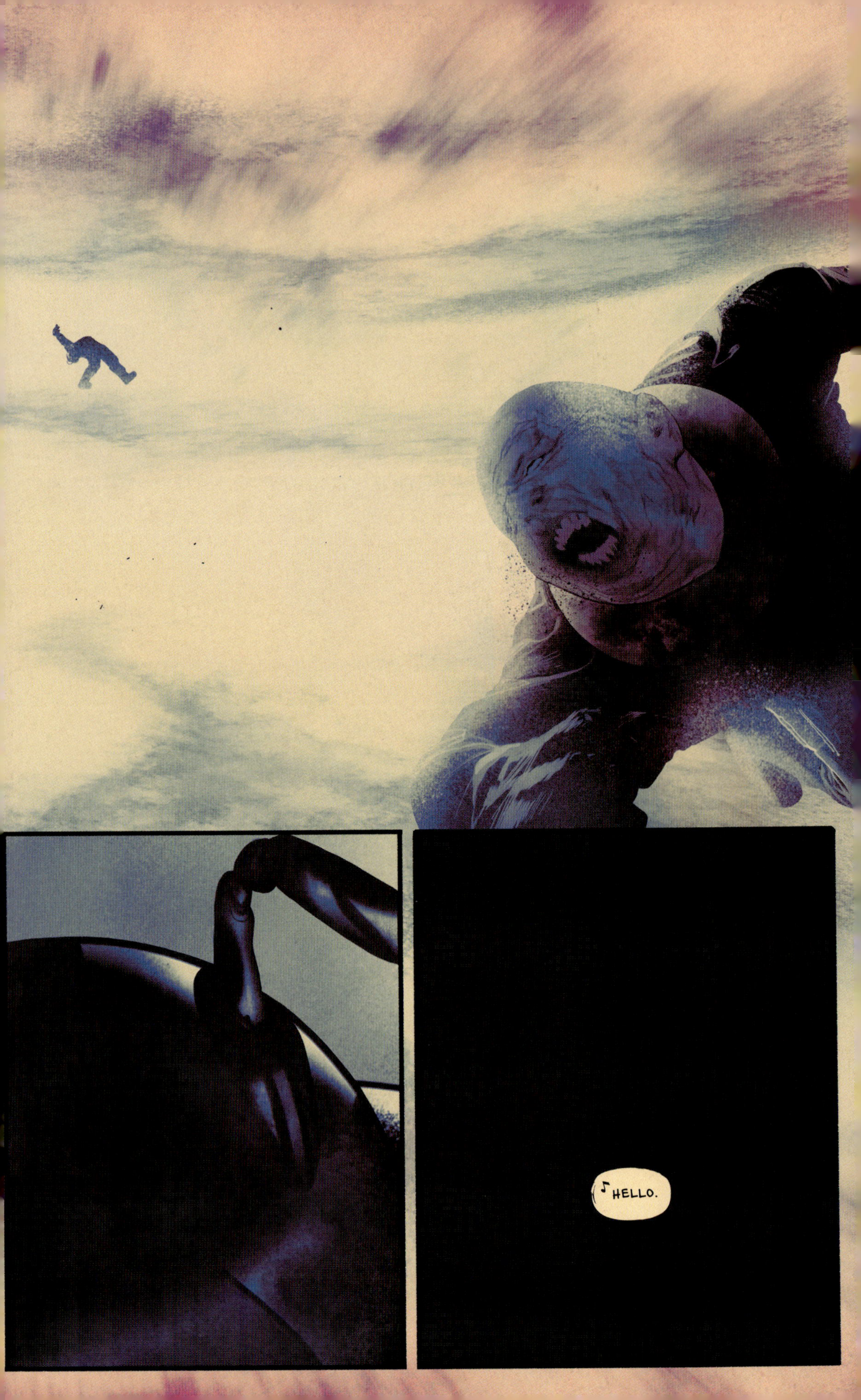
♪ HELLO.

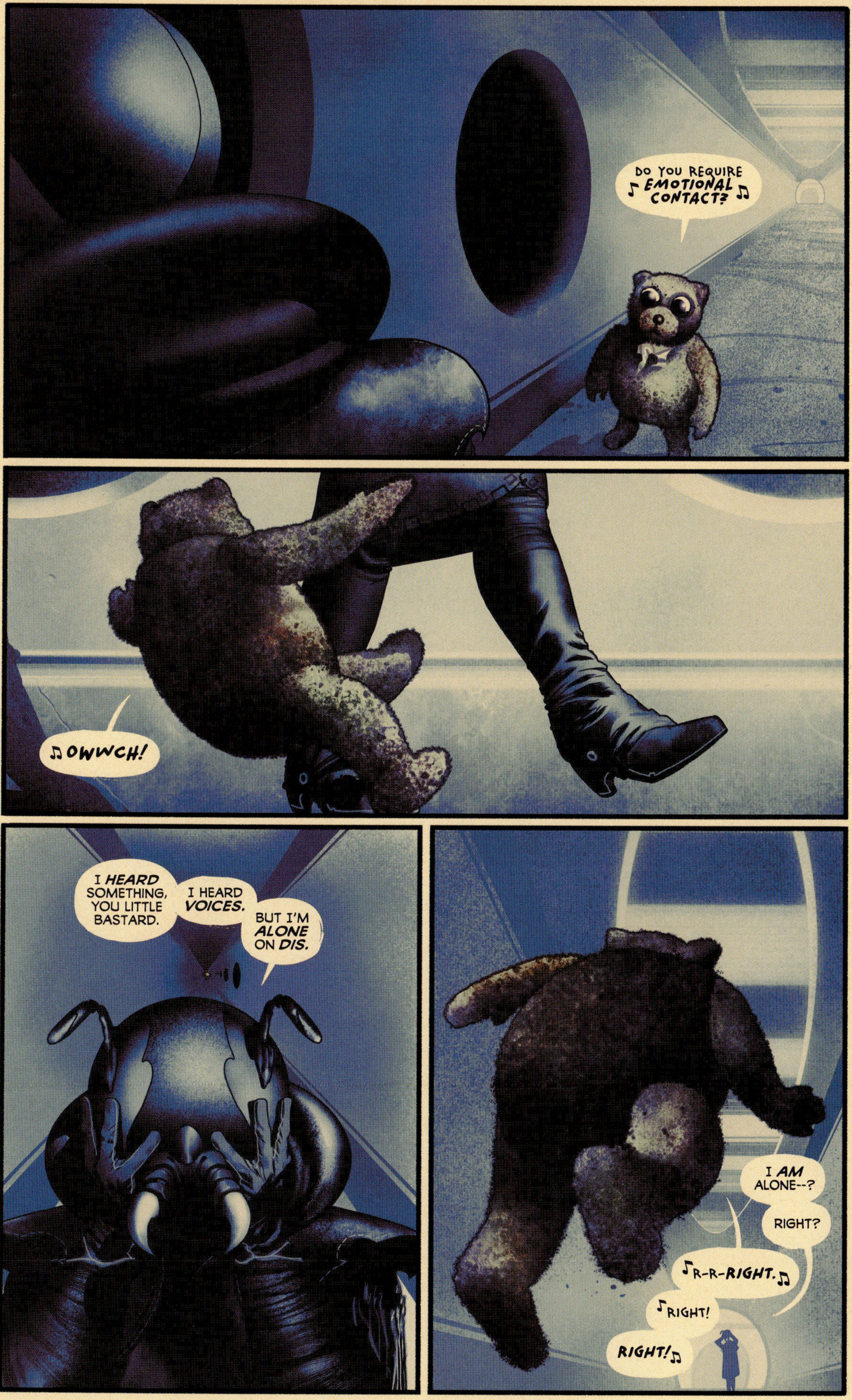

♪ DO YOU REQUIRE EMOTIONAL CONTACT? ♪
♪ OWWCH!
I HEARD SOMETHING, YOU LITTLE BASTARD.
I HEARD VOICES.
BUT I'M ALONE ON DIS.
I AM ALONE--?
RIGHT?
♪ R-R-RIGHT. ♪
♪ RIGHT!
RIGHT! ♪

THERE'S *NO-ONE ELSE* HERE WITH ME--

--*IS* THERE?

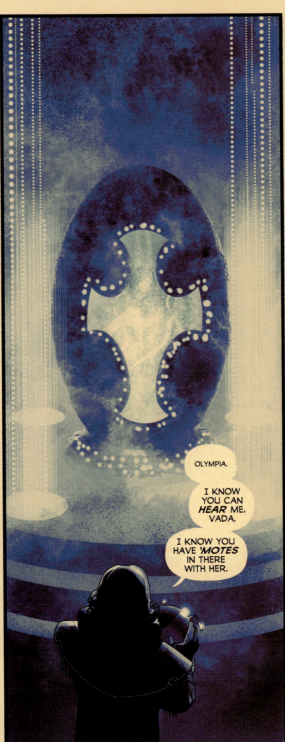

OLYMPIA.

I KNOW YOU CAN *HEAR* ME, VADA.

I KNOW YOU HAVE *'MOTES* IN THERE WITH HER.

YOU WHO HEARS *ALL.*

WHO ATTENDS TO *EVERY* PRAYER.

WHO *SEES* ALL.

I PRAY YOU *BLINK--*

AND MISS WHAT HAPPENS NEXT.

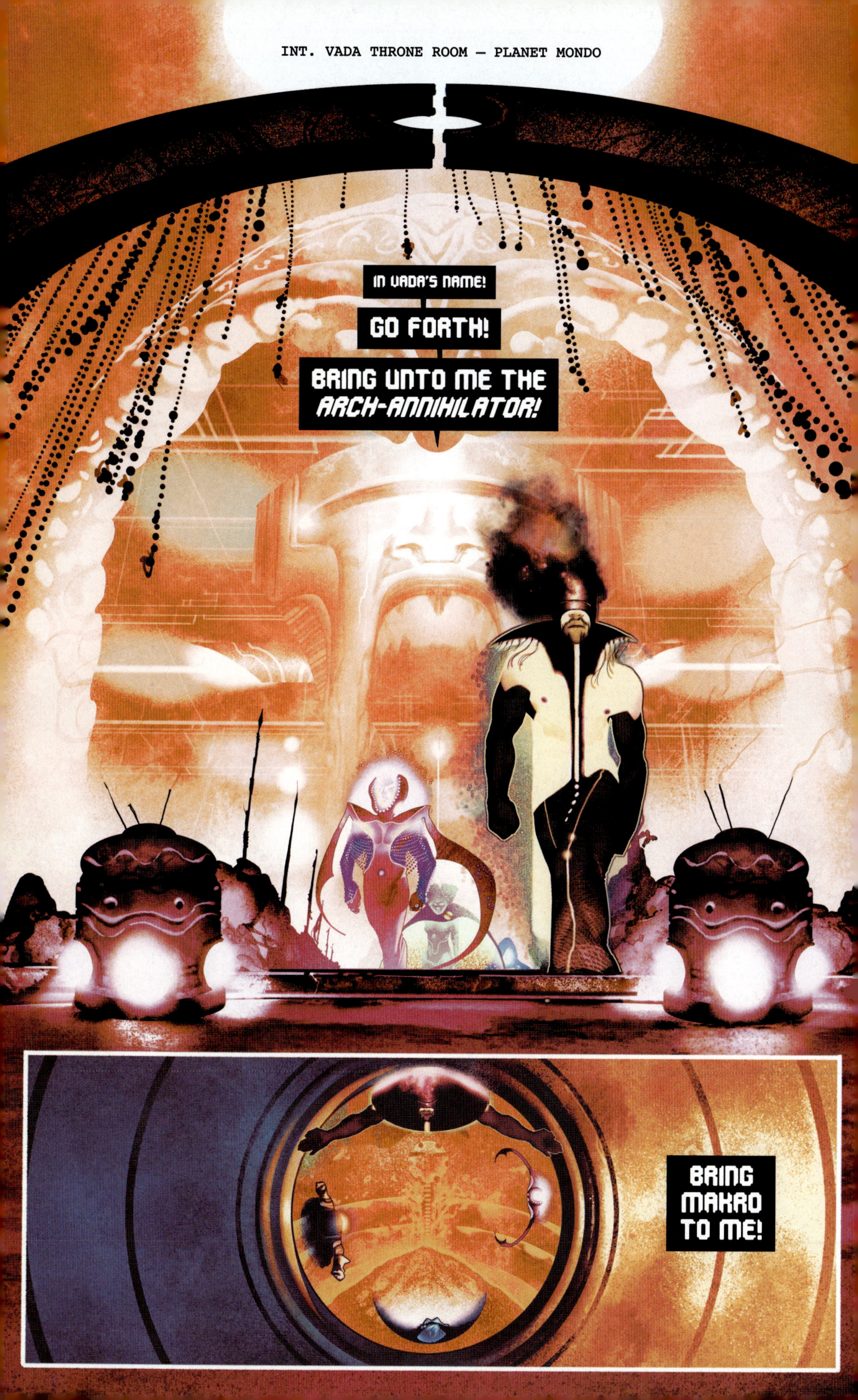
INT. VADA THRONE ROOM — PLANET MONDO
IN VADA'S NAME!
GO FORTH!
BRING UNTO ME THE ARCH-ANNIHILATOR!
BRING MAKRO TO ME!

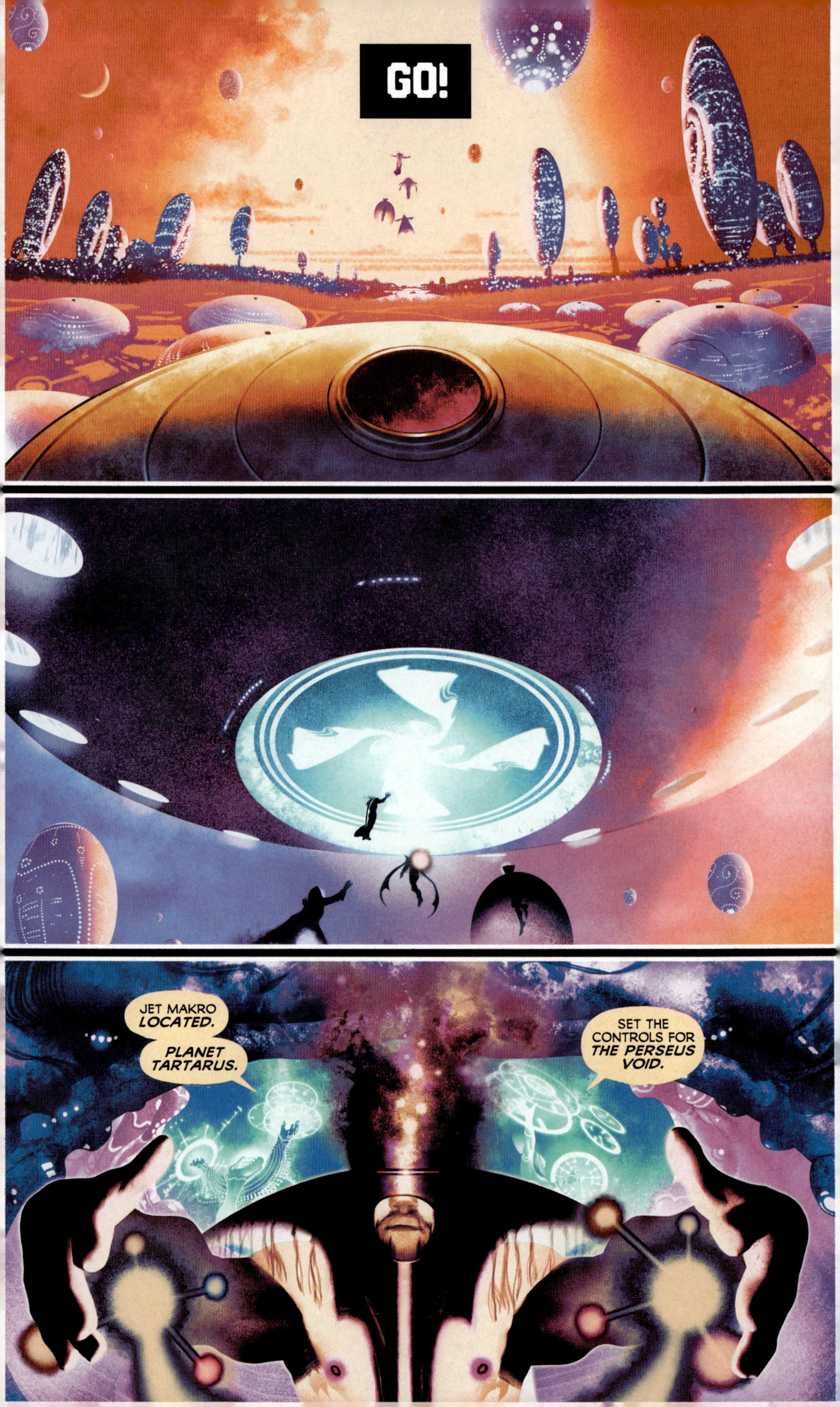
GO!
JET MAKRO LOCATED.
PLANET TARTARUS.
SET THE CONTROLS FOR THE PERSEUS VOID.

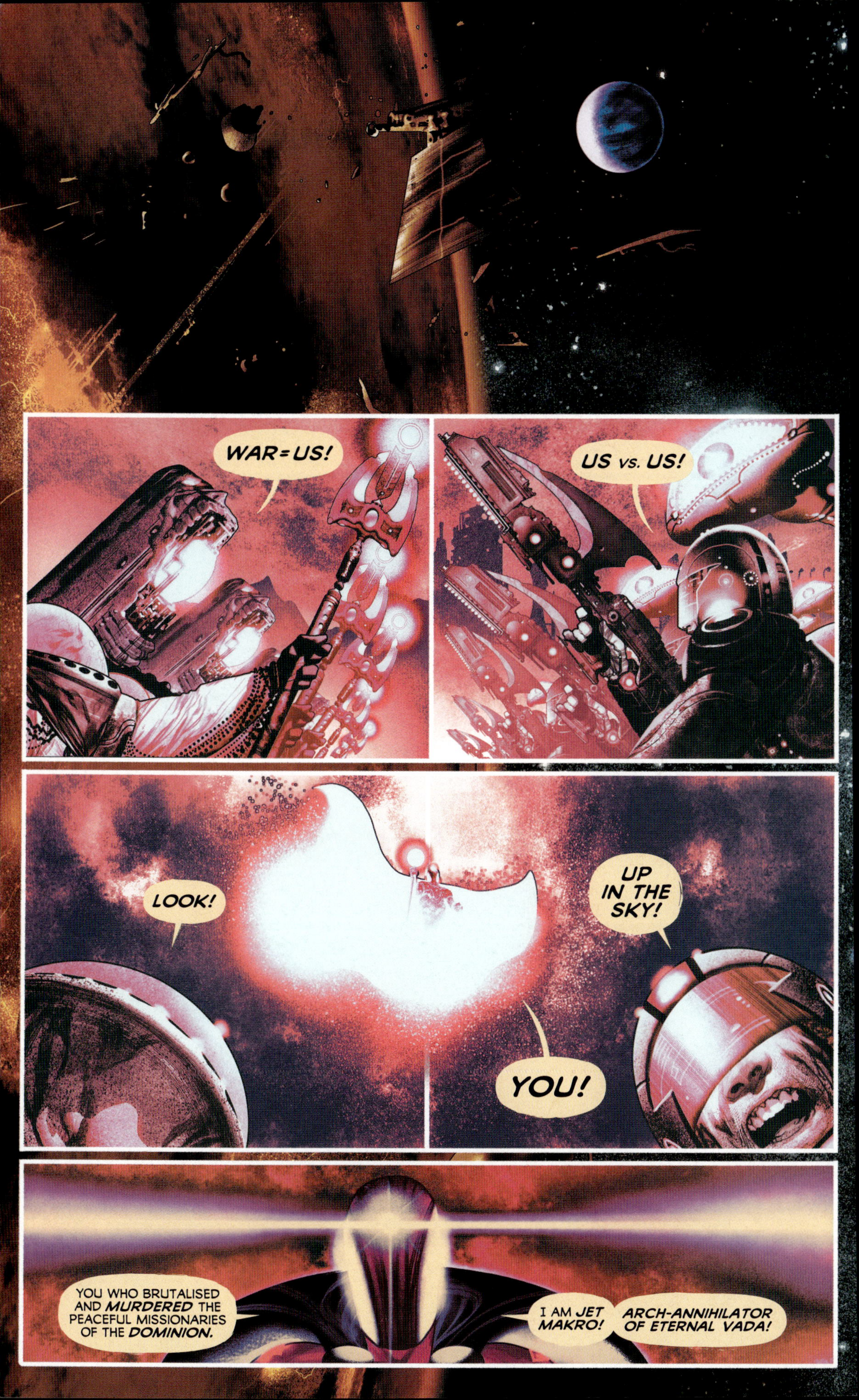
WAR=US!
US vs. US!
LOOK!
UP IN THE SKY!
YOU!
YOU WHO BRUTALISED AND MURDERED THE PEACEFUL MISSIONARIES OF THE DOMINION.
I AM JET MAKRO!
ARCH-ANNIHILATOR OF ETERNAL VADA!

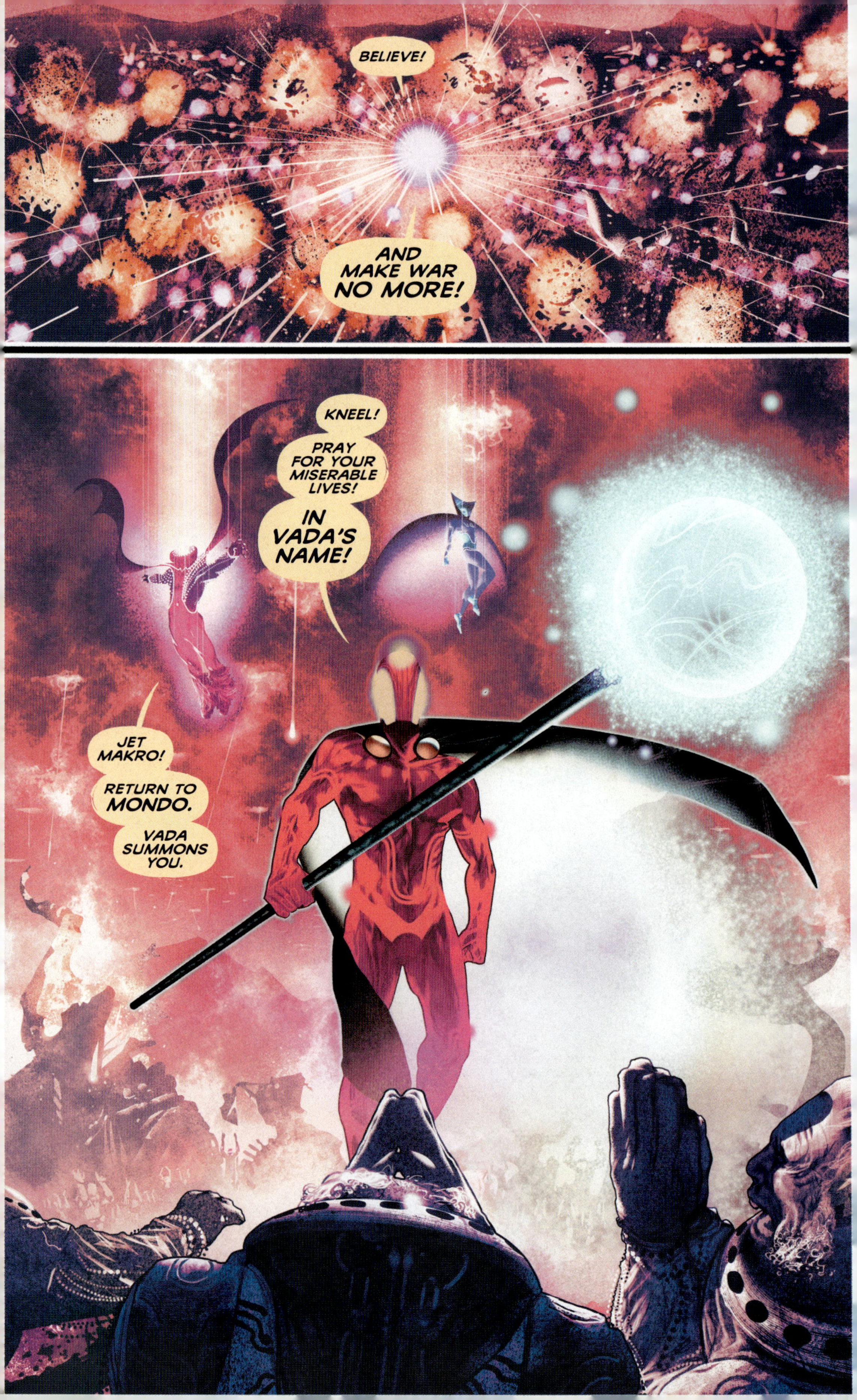
BELIEVE!
AND MAKE WAR NO MORE!
KNEEL!
PRAY FOR YOUR MISERABLE LIVES!
IN VADA'S NAME!
JET MAKRO!
RETURN TO MONDO.
VADA SUMMONS YOU.

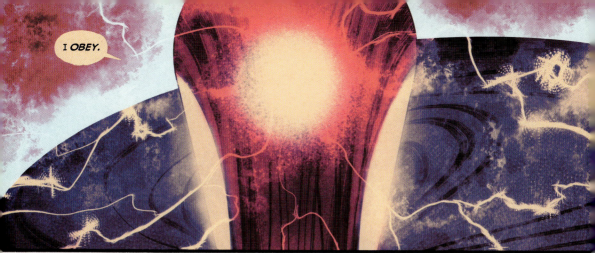

I OBEY.

"I OBEY."

TYPICAL MAKRO.

WHY DID YOU HAVE TO BRING JET MAKRO INTO A PERFECTLY GOOD STORY ABOUT ME?

HOW ABOUT WE GET BACK TO ME ON DIS STATION?

DID I FIND THE CURE FOR DEATH?

WHAT HAPPENED TO BRING ME HERE?

THERE ARE RULES OF NARRATIVE-- END OF ACT ONE I'M INTRODUCING THE BAD GUYS.

--MY HEADACHE'S GONE.

MY NOSE STOPPED BLEEDING.

I KILLED MAKRO IN YOUR OPENING SCENE!

THE FLASH-FORWARD.

I LURED HIM TO DIS AND I SHOT HIM IN THE HEAD!

SHH!

I'M TRYING TO MAKE SENSE OF THIS SCENE--

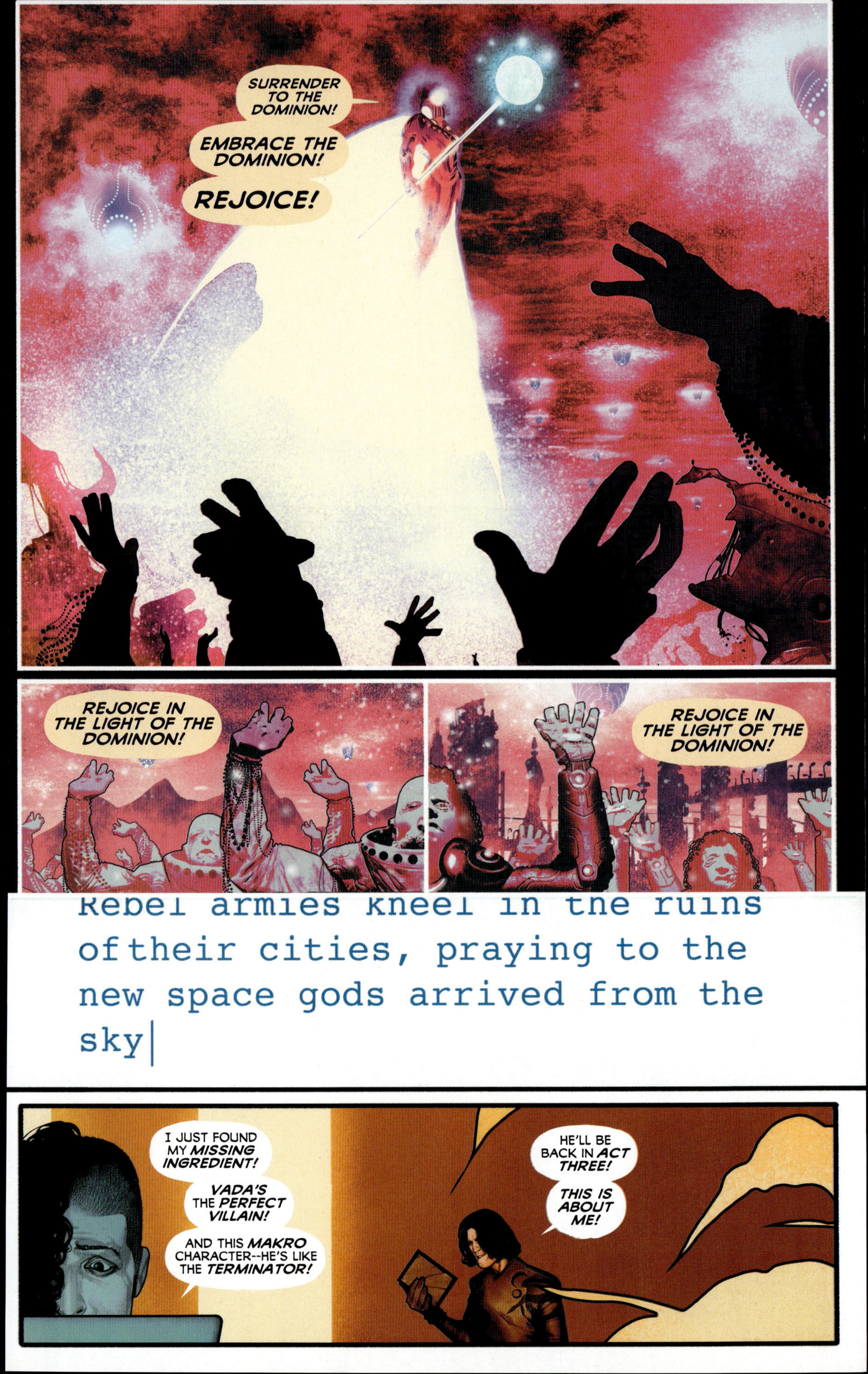
SURRENDER TO THE DOMINION!
EMBRACE THE DOMINION!
REJOICE!
REJOICE IN THE LIGHT OF THE DOMINION!
REJOICE IN THE LIGHT OF THE DOMINION!
Rebel armies kneel in the ruins oftheir cities, praying to the new space gods arrived from the sky
I JUST FOUND MY MISSING INGREDIENT!
VADA'S THE PERFECT VILLAIN!
AND THIS MAKRO CHARACTER--HE'S LIKE THE TERMINATOR!
HE'LL BE BACK IN ACT THREE!
THIS IS ABOUT ME!

YOU GUYS *HAVE* TO FIGHT.

"THE *ARCH-ANNIHILATOR!*"

I BARELY *THOUGHT* ABOUT THIS WHOLE *FUTURE SOCIETY THING* AND HOW IT MIGHT WORK.

IT'S *BACK-STORY!*

MAKRO'S *DEAD.*

HE *FELL,* ON *FIRE,* INTO A *BLACK HOLE!*

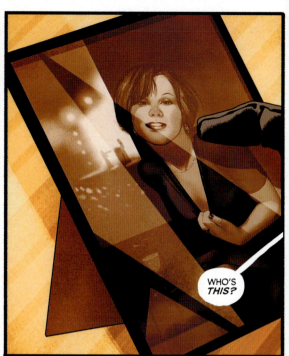

WHO'S *THIS?*

--*YOU* SURVIVED THE BLACK HOLE.

THIS *THING,* RIGHT?

SOMEHOW YOU DOWNLOAD YOUR *LIFE HISTORY* INTO MY HEAD-- WHERE IT SHOWS UP AS A *BRAIN TUMOR?*

A *DATA BULLET.*

THIS *GIRL*--

MY DOCTOR DIDN'T CALL IT A *DATA BULLET!*

HE CALLED IT AN *INOPERABLE BRAIN TUMOR,* YOU BASTARD!

YOU *GAVE* ME SUPER-*CANCER!*

YES, I DID.

DON'T MAKE ME *HIT* YOU, RAY.

I COULD *END YOUR LIFE* WITH A SINGLE BLOW.

I HAVE A *BRAIN TUMOR!*

THINK, MAN!

WHO WOULD YOU *RATHER* BELIEVE?

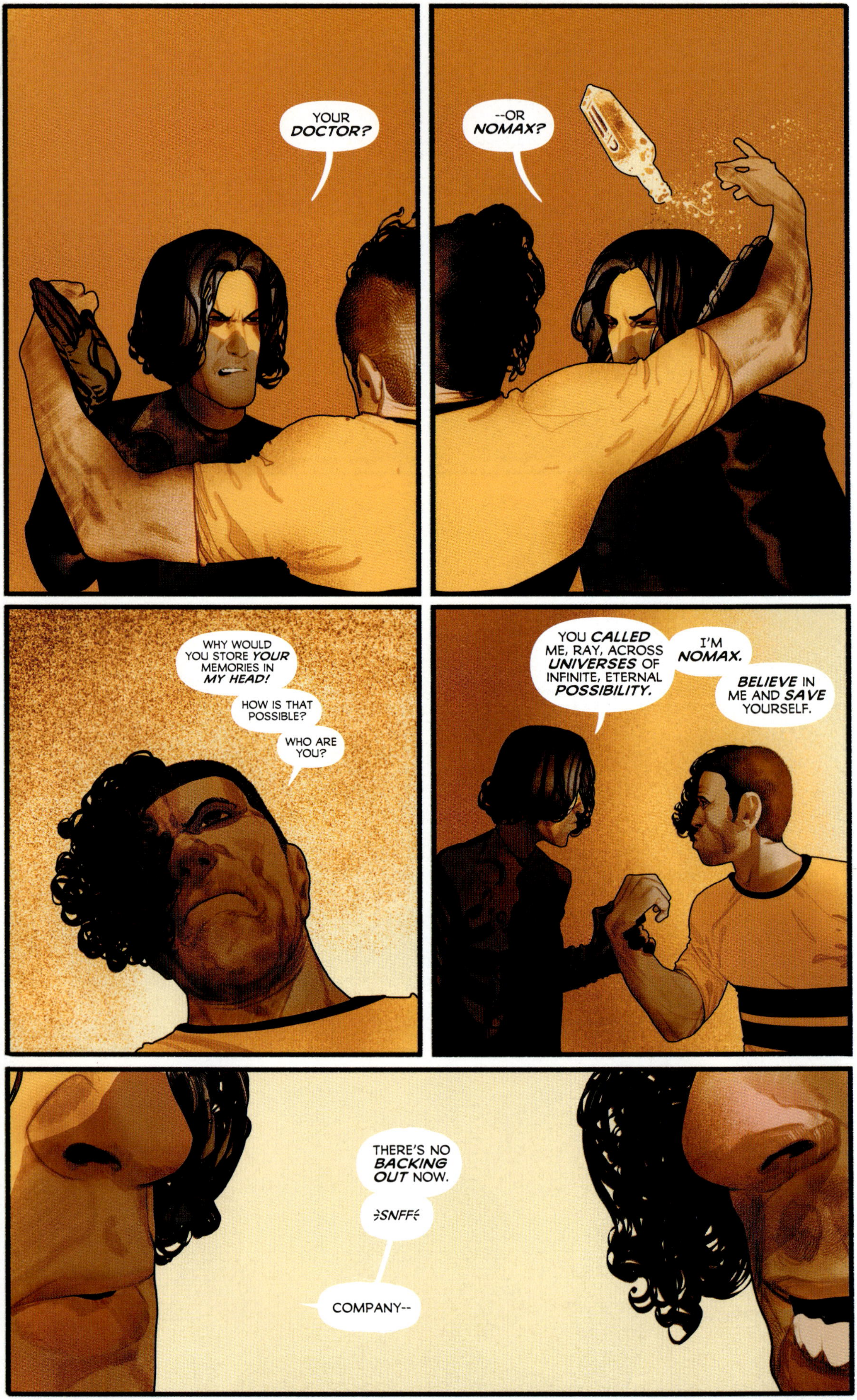
YOUR DOCTOR?
--OR NOMAX?
WHY WOULD YOU STORE YOUR MEMORIES IN MY HEAD!
HOW IS THAT POSSIBLE?
WHO ARE YOU?
YOU CALLED ME, RAY, ACROSS UNIVERSES OF INFINITE, ETERNAL POSSIBILITY.
I'M NOMAX.
BELIEVE IN ME AND SAVE YOURSELF.
THERE'S NO BACKING OUT NOW.
SNFF
COMPANY--

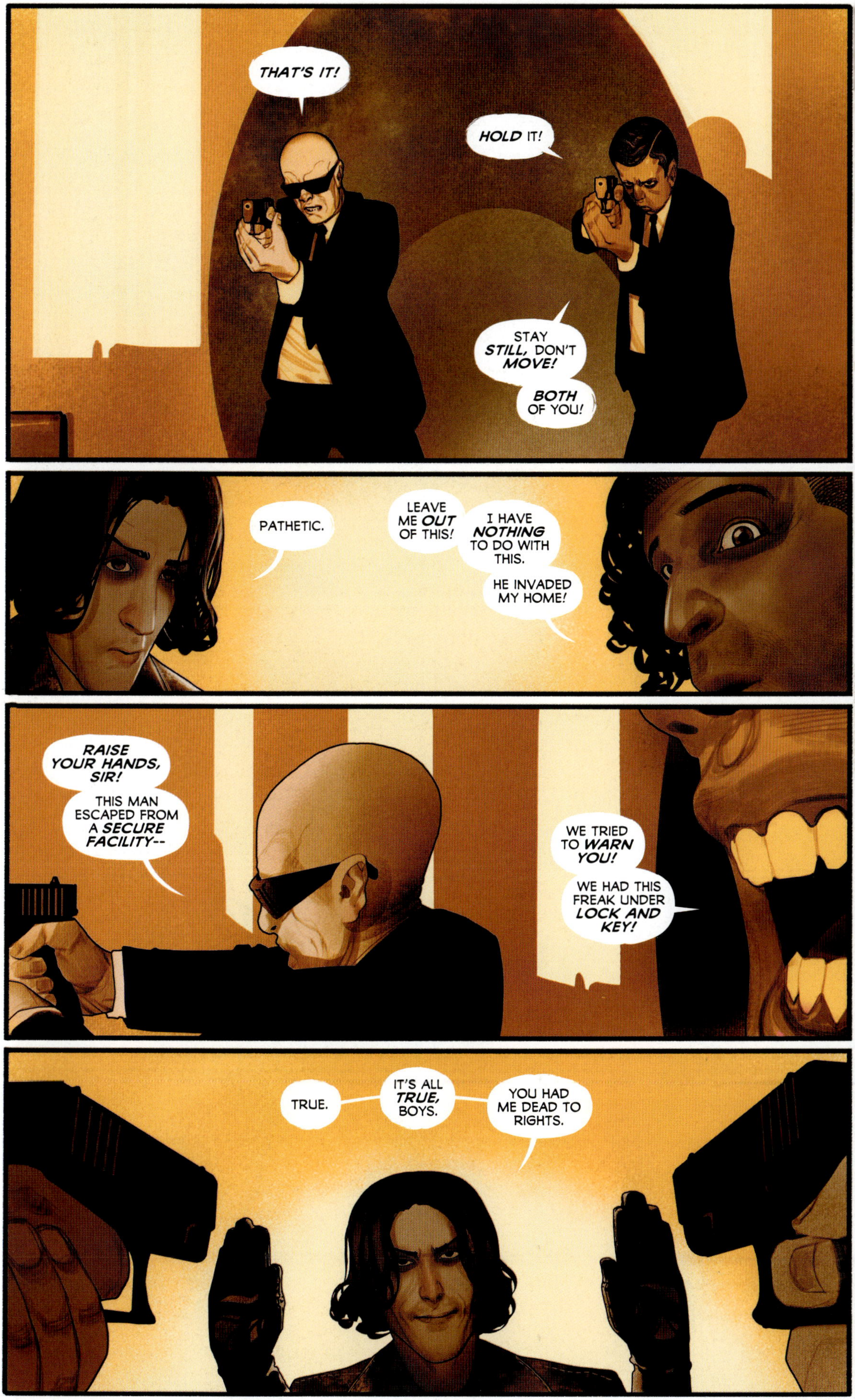
THAT'S IT!
HOLD IT!
STAY STILL, DON'T MOVE!
BOTH OF YOU!
PATHETIC.
LEAVE ME OUT OF THIS!
I HAVE NOTHING TO DO WITH THIS.
HE INVADED MY HOME!
RAISE YOUR HANDS, SIR!
THIS MAN ESCAPED FROM A SECURE FACILITY--
WE TRIED TO WARN YOU!
WE HAD THIS FREAK UNDER LOCK AND KEY!
TRUE.
IT'S ALL TRUE, BOYS.
YOU HAD ME DEAD TO RIGHTS.

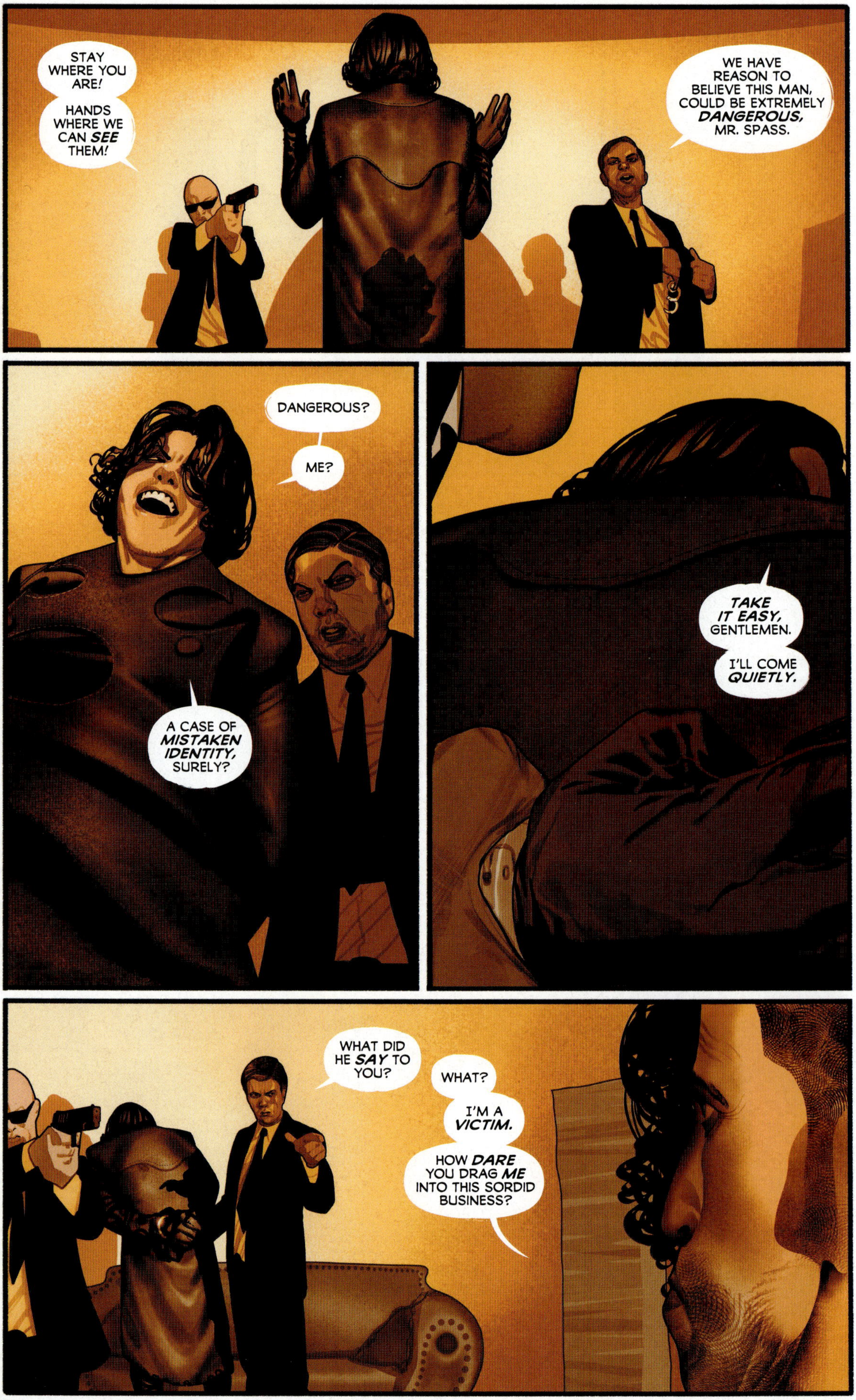
STAY WHERE YOU ARE!
HANDS WHERE WE CAN SEE THEM!
WE HAVE REASON TO BELIEVE THIS MAN, COULD BE EXTREMELY DANGEROUS, MR. SPASS.
DANGEROUS?
ME?
A CASE OF MISTAKEN IDENTITY, SURELY?
TAKE IT EASY, GENTLEMEN.
I'LL COME QUIETLY.
WHAT DID HE SAY TO YOU?
WHAT?
I'M A VICTIM.
HOW DARE YOU DRAG ME INTO THIS SORDID BUSINESS?

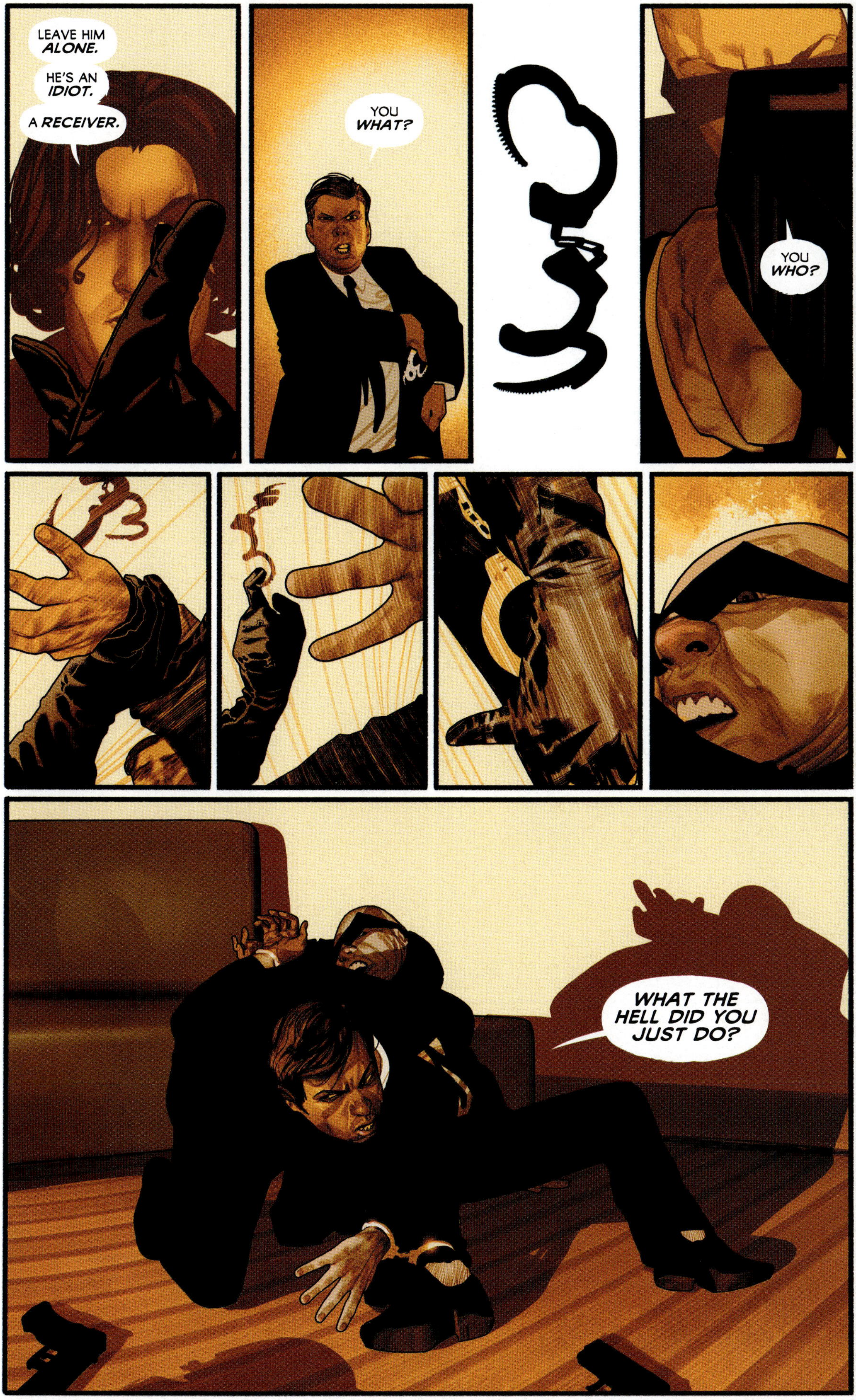
LEAVE HIM ALONE.
HE'S AN IDIOT.
A RECEIVER.
YOU WHAT?
YOU WHO?
WHAT THE HELL DID YOU JUST DO?

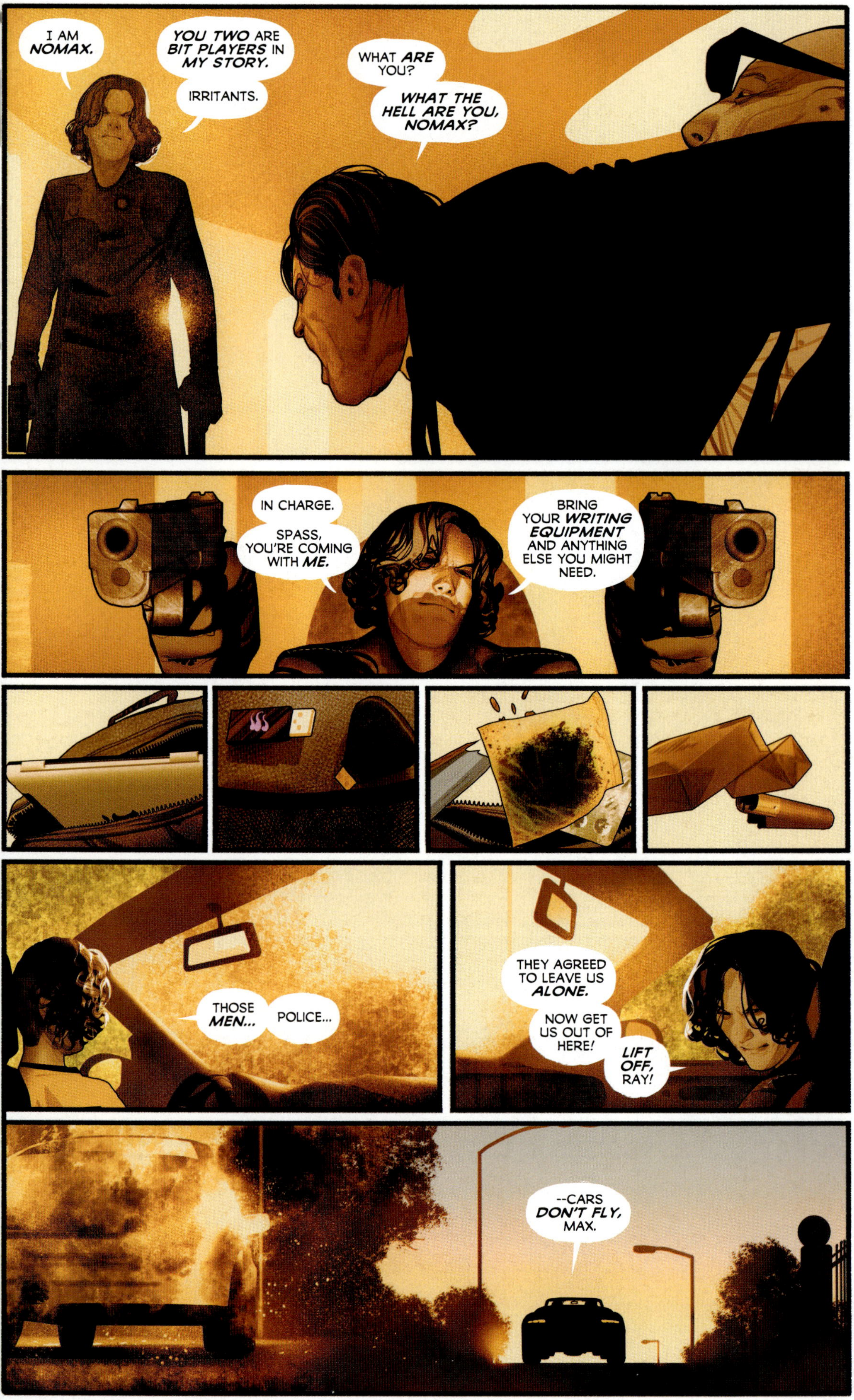
I AM NOMAX.
YOU TWO ARE BIT PLAYERS IN MY STORY.
IRRITANTS.
WHAT ARE YOU?
WHAT THE HELL ARE YOU, NOMAX?
IN CHARGE.
SPASS, YOU'RE COMING WITH ME.
BRING YOUR WRITING EQUIPMENT AND ANYTHING ELSE YOU MIGHT NEED.
THOSE MEN...
POLICE...
THEY AGREED TO LEAVE US ALONE.
NOW GET US OUT OF HERE!
LIFT OFF, RAY!
--CARS DON'T FLY, MAX.

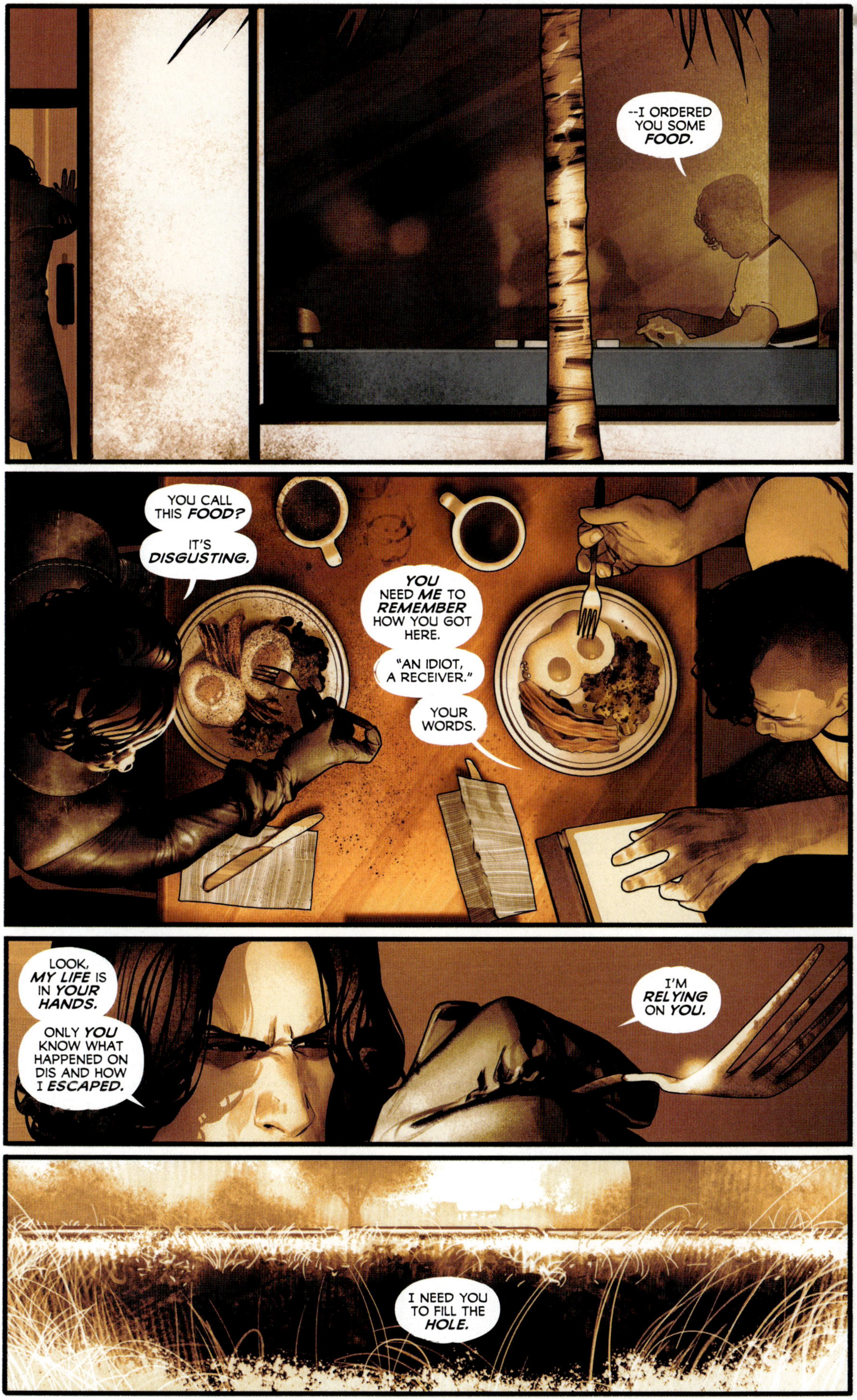
--I ORDERED YOU SOME *FOOD.*
YOU CALL THIS *FOOD?*
IT'S *DISGUSTING.*
YOU NEED *ME* TO *REMEMBER* HOW YOU GOT HERE.
"AN IDIOT, A RECEIVER."
YOUR WORDS.
LOOK, *MY LIFE* IS IN *YOUR HANDS.*
ONLY *YOU* KNOW WHAT HAPPENED ON DIS AND HOW I *ESCAPED.*
I'M *RELYING* ON *YOU.*
I NEED YOU TO FILL THE *HOLE.*

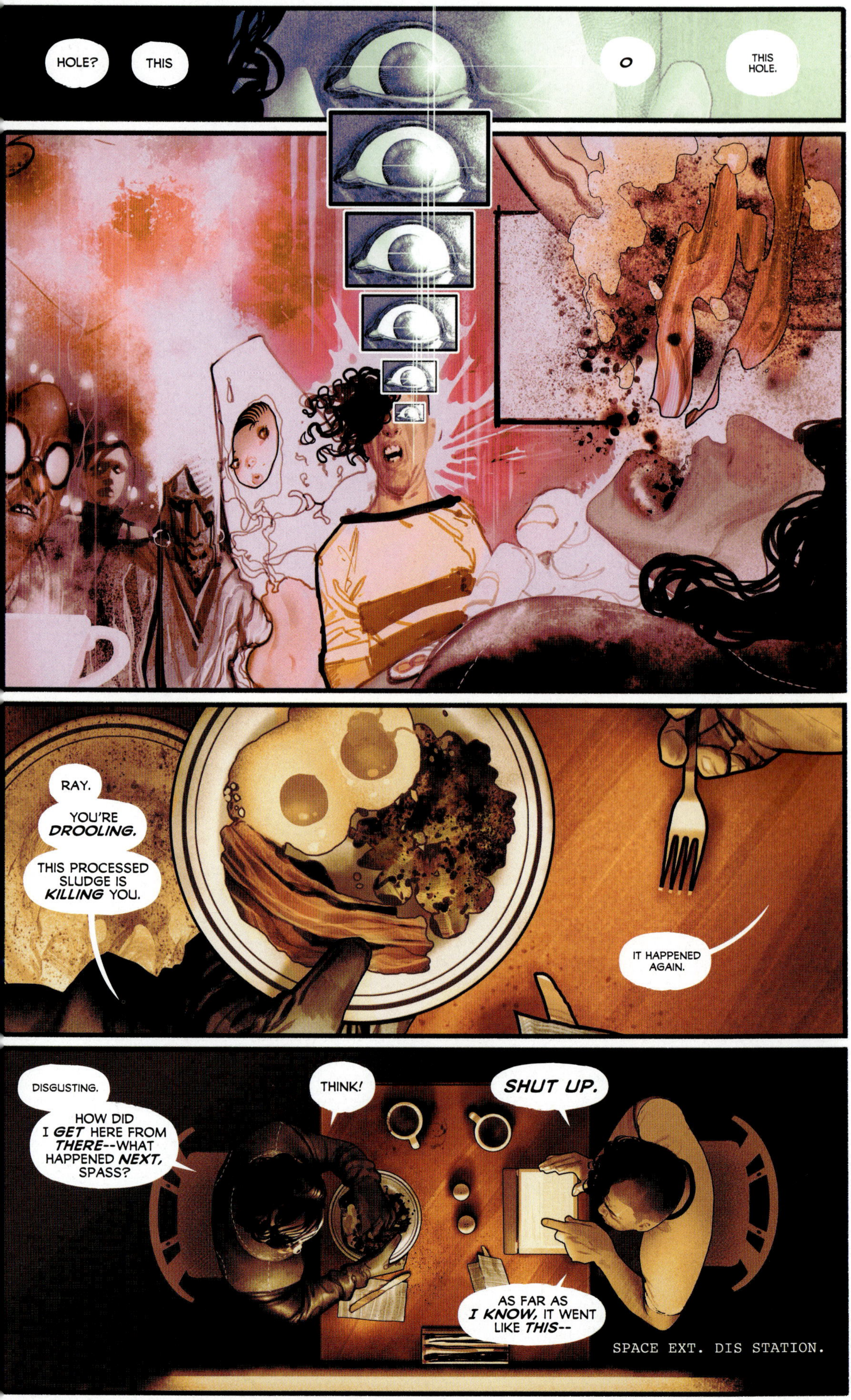
HOLE?
THIS
O
THIS HOLE.
RAY.
YOU'RE DROOLING.
THIS PROCESSED SLUDGE IS KILLING YOU.
IT HAPPENED AGAIN.
DISGUSTING.
HOW DID I GET HERE FROM THERE--WHAT HAPPENED NEXT, SPASS?
THINK!
SHUT UP.
AS FAR AS I KNOW, IT WENT LIKE THIS--
SPACE EXT. DIS STATION.

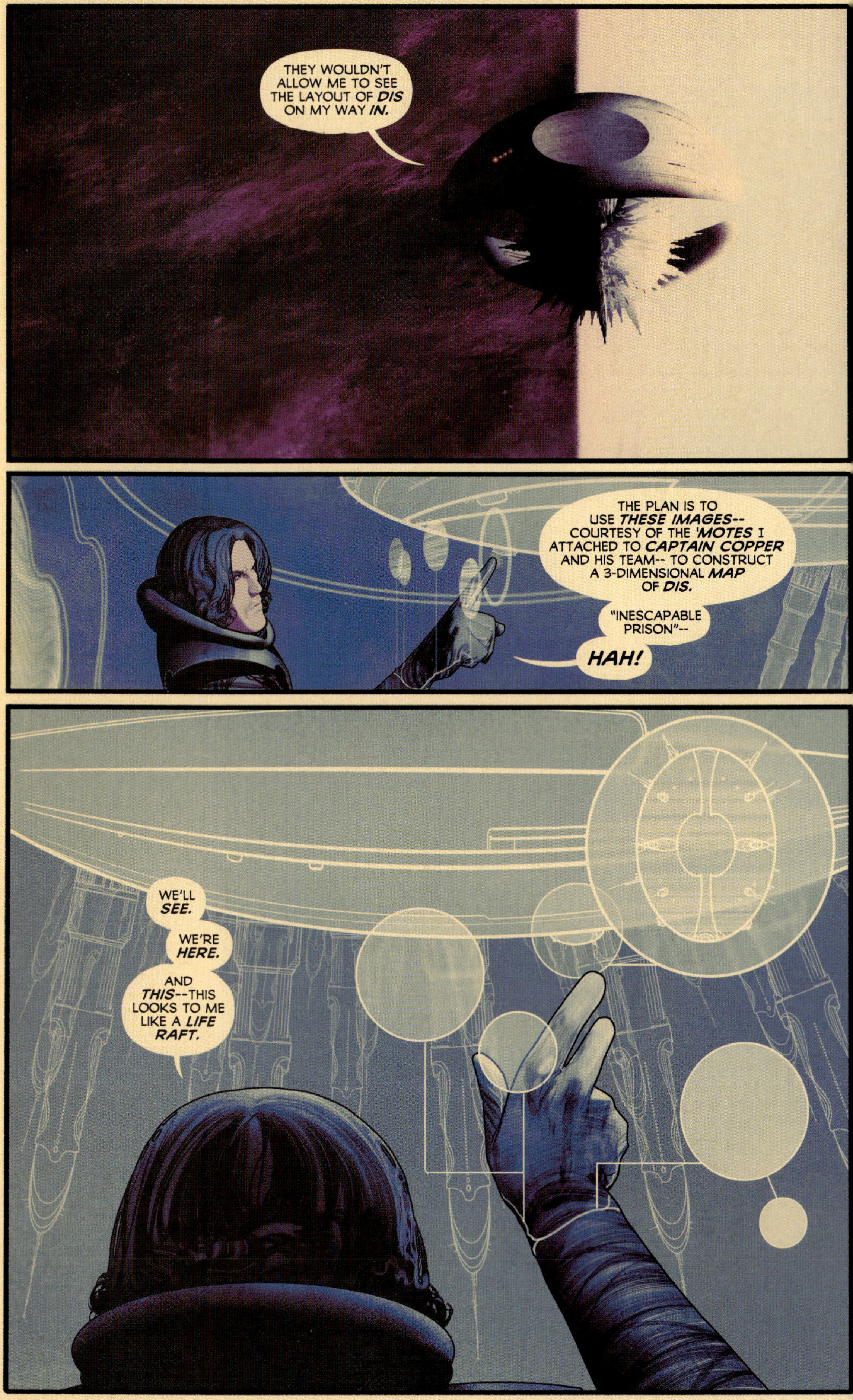
THEY WOULDN'T ALLOW ME TO SEE THE LAYOUT OF *DIS* ON MY WAY *IN.*
THE PLAN IS TO USE *THESE IMAGES*-- COURTESY OF THE *'MOTES* I ATTACHED TO *CAPTAIN COPPER* AND HIS TEAM-- TO CONSTRUCT A 3-DIMENSIONAL *MAP* OF *DIS.*
"INESCAPABLE PRISON"--
HAH!
WE'LL *SEE.*
WE'RE *HERE.*
AND *THIS*--THIS LOOKS TO ME LIKE A *LIFE RAFT.*

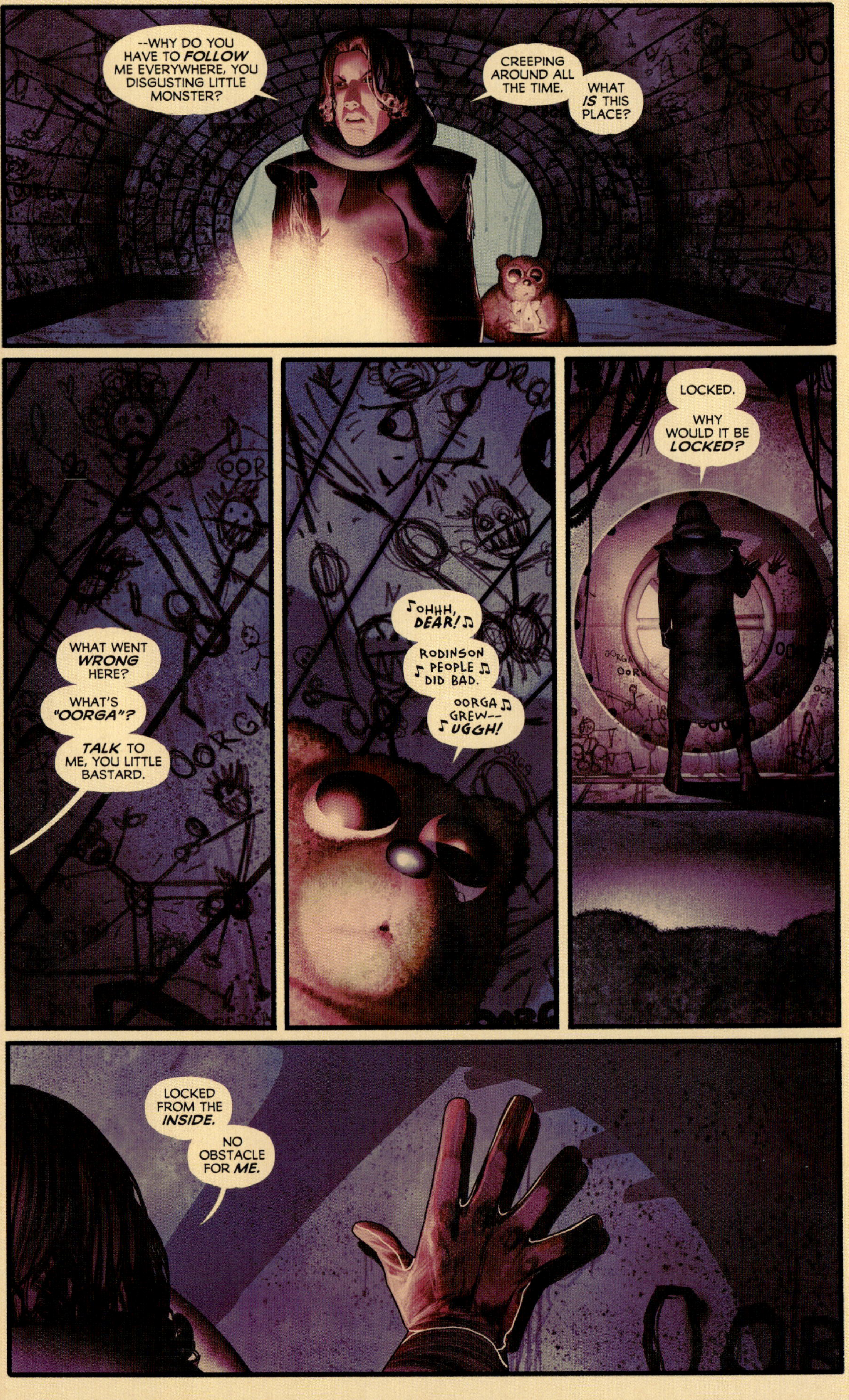
--WHY DO YOU HAVE TO FOLLOW ME EVERYWHERE, YOU DISGUSTING LITTLE MONSTER?
CREEPING AROUND ALL THE TIME.
WHAT IS THIS PLACE?
WHAT WENT WRONG HERE?
WHAT'S "OORGA"?
TALK TO ME, YOU LITTLE BASTARD.
♪OHHH, DEAR!♪
RODINSON ♪PEOPLE♪ DID BAD.
OORGA♪ GREW-- ♪UGGH!
LOCKED.
WHY WOULD IT BE LOCKED?
LOCKED FROM THE INSIDE.
NO OBSTACLE FOR ME.

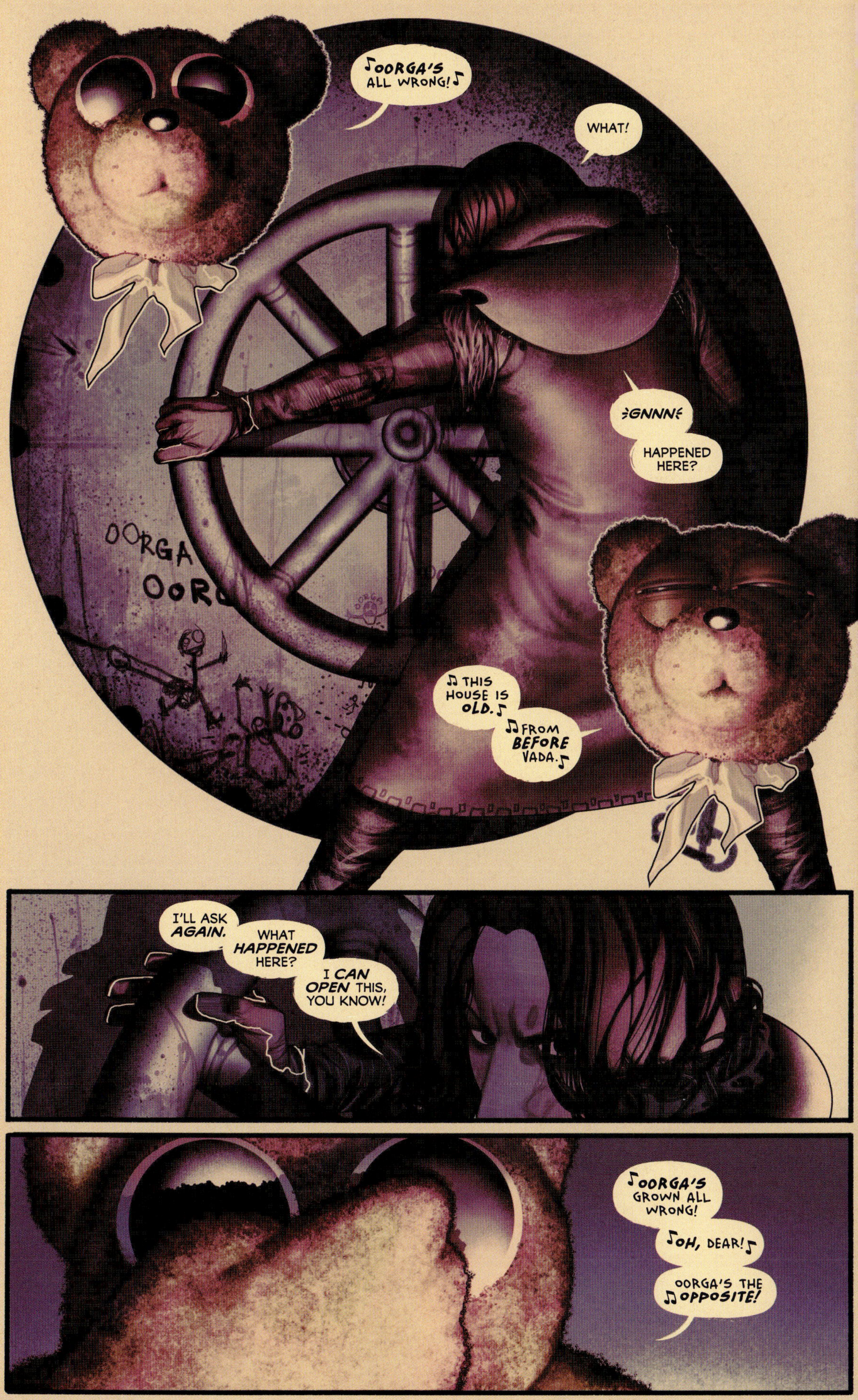
♪OORGA'S ALL WRONG!♪
WHAT!
GNNN
HAPPENED HERE?
OORGA
OORG
♪THIS HOUSE IS OLD.♪
♪FROM BEFORE VADA.♪
I'LL ASK AGAIN.
WHAT HAPPENED HERE?
I CAN OPEN THIS, YOU KNOW!
♪OORGA'S GROWN ALL WRONG!
♪OH, DEAR!♪
OORGA'S THE ♪OPPOSITE!

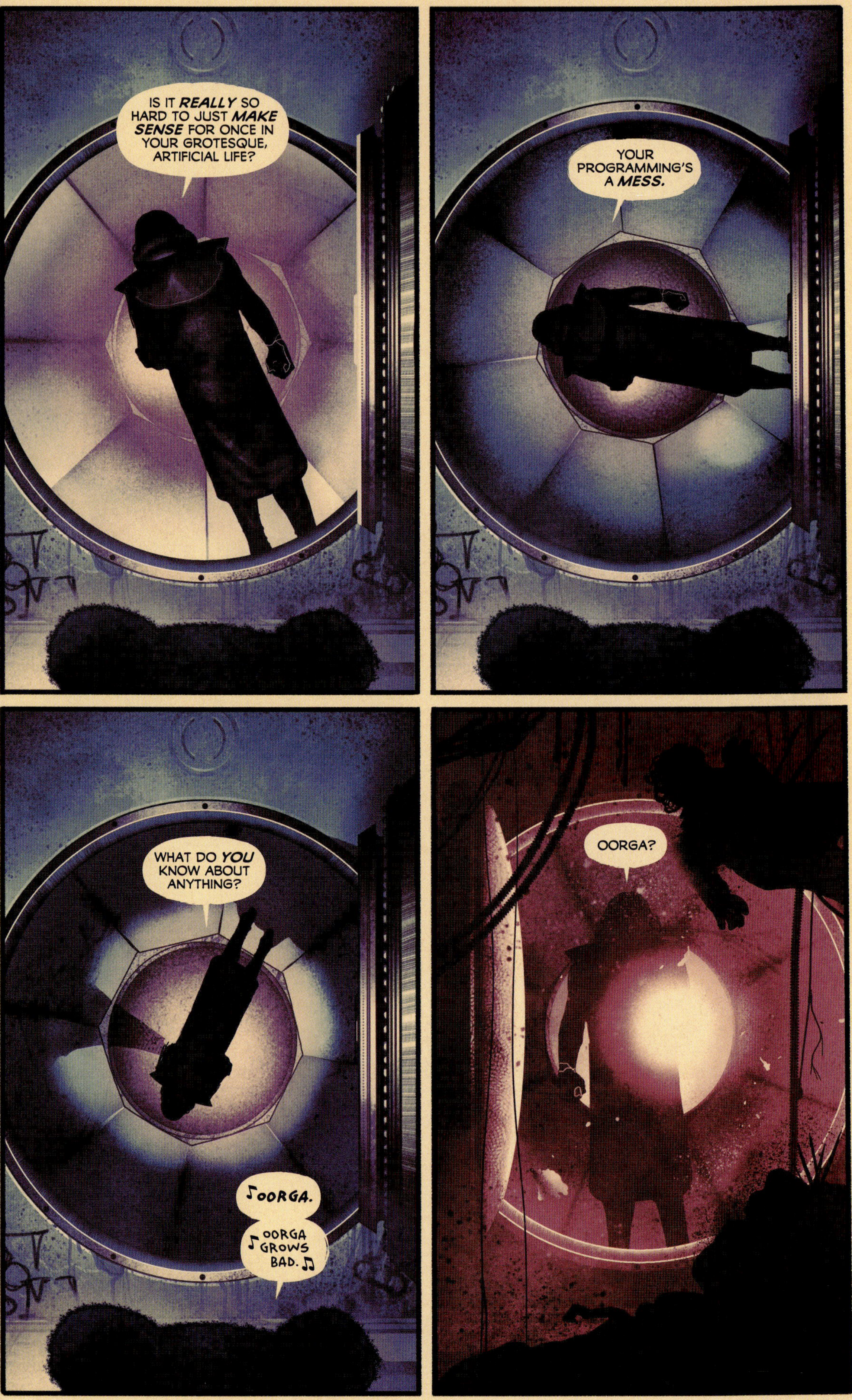
IS IT REALLY SO HARD TO JUST MAKE SENSE FOR ONCE IN YOUR GROTESQUE, ARTIFICIAL LIFE?
YOUR PROGRAMMING'S A MESS.
WHAT DO YOU KNOW ABOUT ANYTHING?
♪OORGA.
♪OORGA GROWS BAD.♫
OORGA?

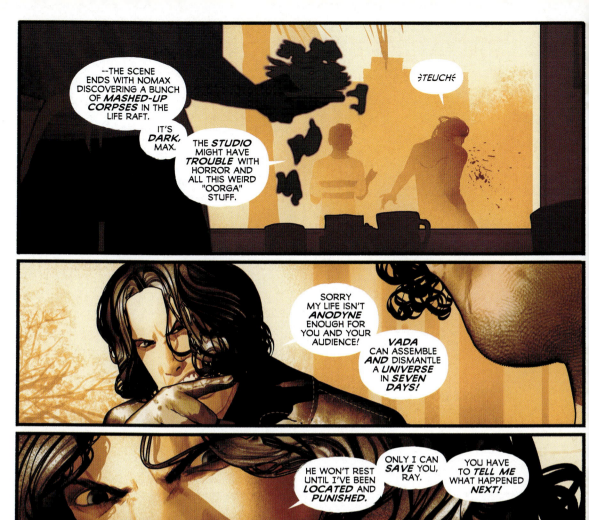

--THE SCENE ENDS WITH NOMAX DISCOVERING A BUNCH OF *MASHED-UP CORPSES* IN THE LIFE RAFT.

IT'S *DARK,* MAX.

THE *STUDIO* MIGHT HAVE *TROUBLE* WITH HORROR AND ALL THIS WEIRD "OORGA" STUFF.

⸮TEUCH⸮

SORRY MY LIFE ISN'T *ANODYNE* ENOUGH FOR YOU AND YOUR AUDIENCE!

VADA CAN ASSEMBLE *AND* DISMANTLE A *UNIVERSE* IN *SEVEN DAYS!*

HE WON'T REST UNTIL I'VE BEEN *LOCATED* AND *PUNISHED.*

ONLY I CAN *SAVE* YOU, RAY.

YOU HAVE TO *TELL ME* WHAT HAPPENED *NEXT!*

MY *PITCH* ONLY REACHED THE END OF *ACT ONE.*

ALL OF THIS IS *NEW* TO ME.

HOW SOON BEFORE THIS "DATA BULLET" *KILLS* ME?

SEVEN DAYS--

THAT'S YOUR *DEADLINE,* RAY.

ONLY *YOU AND I* CAN SAVE THIS WHOLE HIDEOUS *WORLD* FROM *VADA'S WRATH.*

TELL ME WHAT I FOUND *IN THE LIFE RAFT* THAT *WASN'T SUPPOSED TO BE THERE,* RAY.

HURRY!

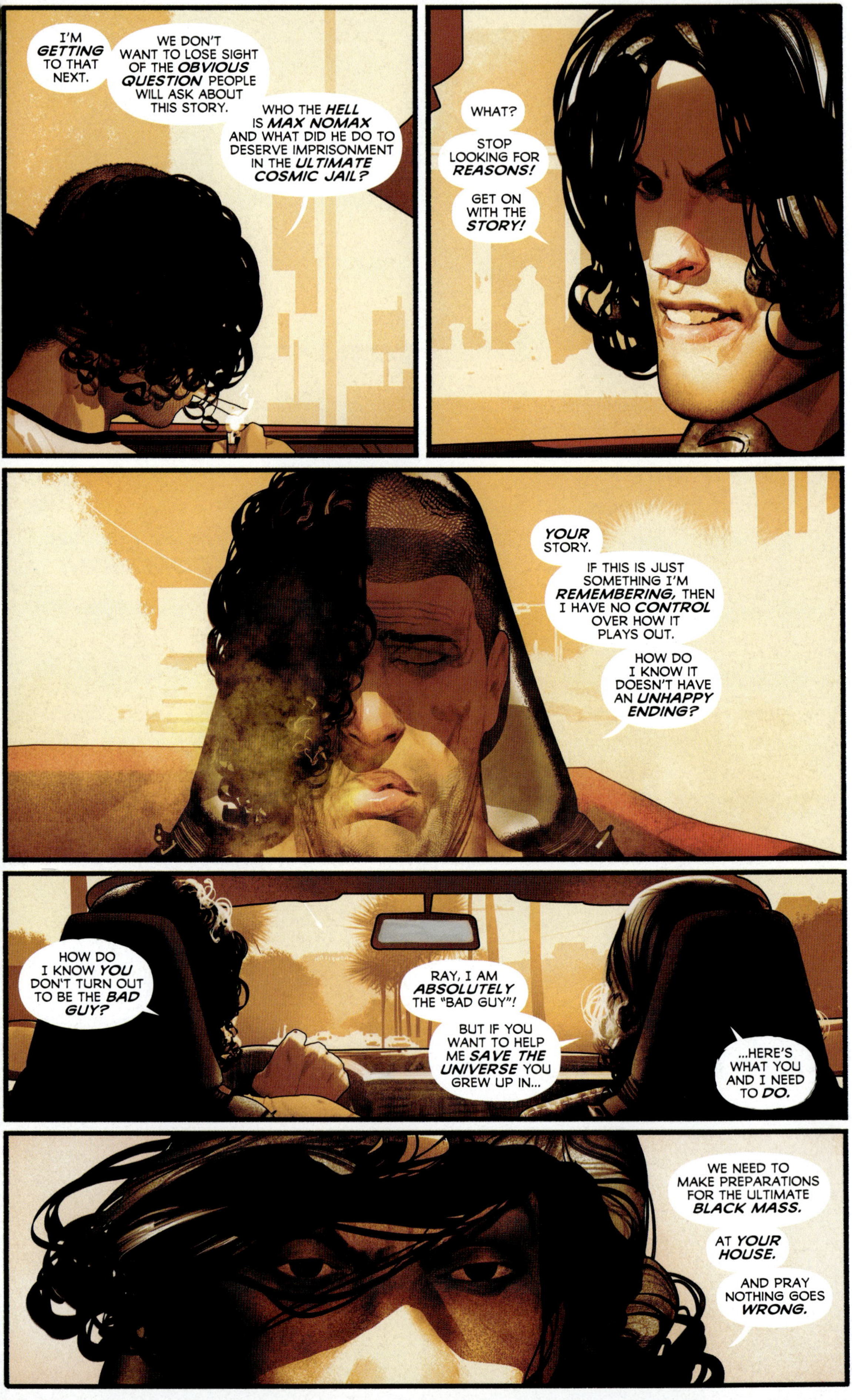
I'M GETTING TO THAT NEXT.
WE DON'T WANT TO LOSE SIGHT OF THE OBVIOUS QUESTION PEOPLE WILL ASK ABOUT THIS STORY.
WHO THE HELL IS MAX NOMAX AND WHAT DID HE DO TO DESERVE IMPRISONMENT IN THE ULTIMATE COSMIC JAIL?
WHAT?
STOP LOOKING FOR REASONS!
GET ON WITH THE STORY!
YOUR STORY.
IF THIS IS JUST SOMETHING I'M REMEMBERING, THEN I HAVE NO CONTROL OVER HOW IT PLAYS OUT.
HOW DO I KNOW IT DOESN'T HAVE AN UNHAPPY ENDING?
HOW DO I KNOW YOU DON'T TURN OUT TO BE THE BAD GUY?
RAY, I AM ABSOLUTELY THE "BAD GUY"!
BUT IF YOU WANT TO HELP ME SAVE THE UNIVERSE YOU GREW UP IN...
...HERE'S WHAT YOU AND I NEED TO DO.
WE NEED TO MAKE PREPARATIONS FOR THE ULTIMATE BLACK MASS.
AT YOUR HOUSE.
AND PRAY NOTHING GOES WRONG.

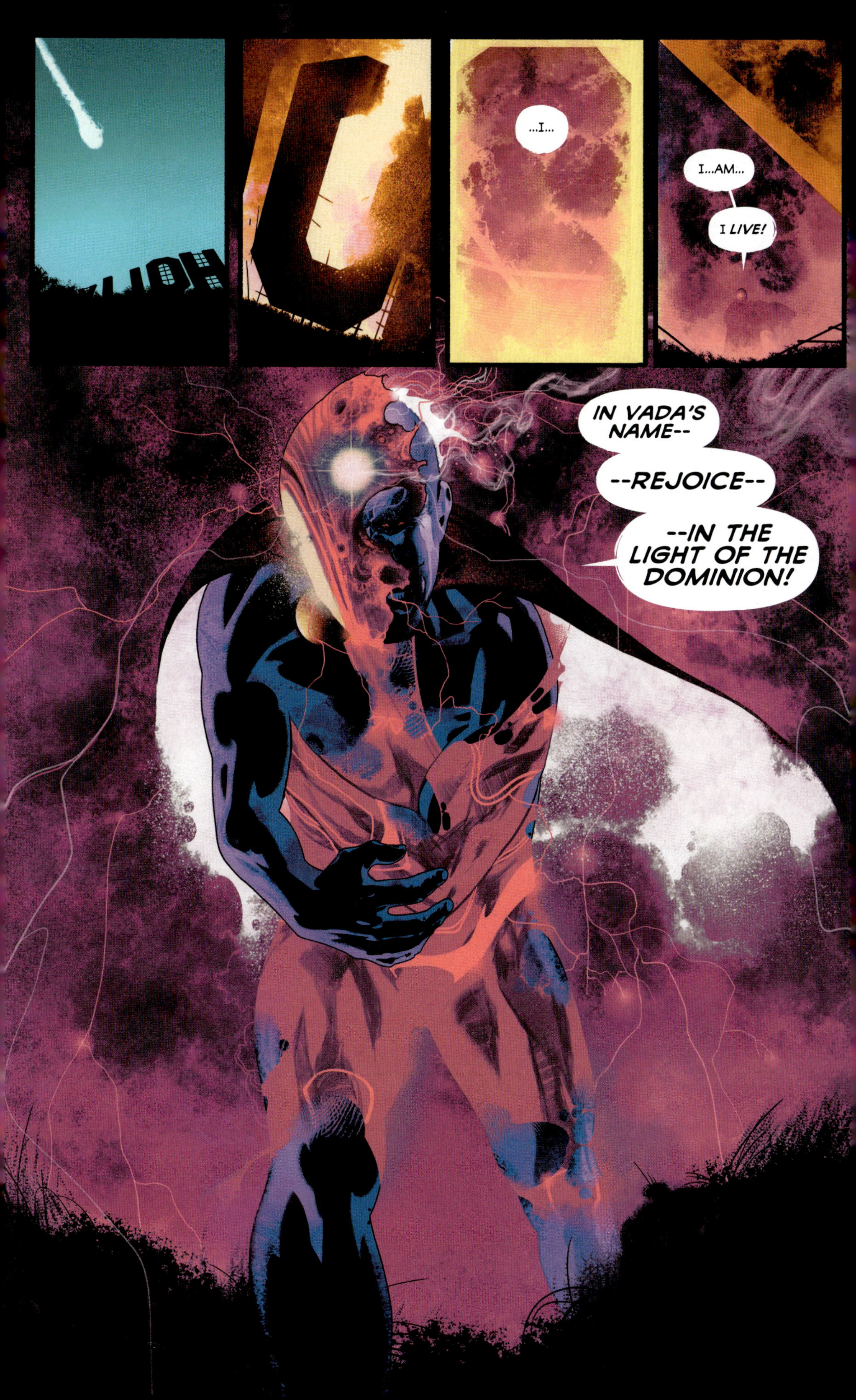
...I...
I...AM...
I LIVE!
IN VADA'S NAME--
--REJOICE--
--IN THE LIGHT OF THE DOMINION!

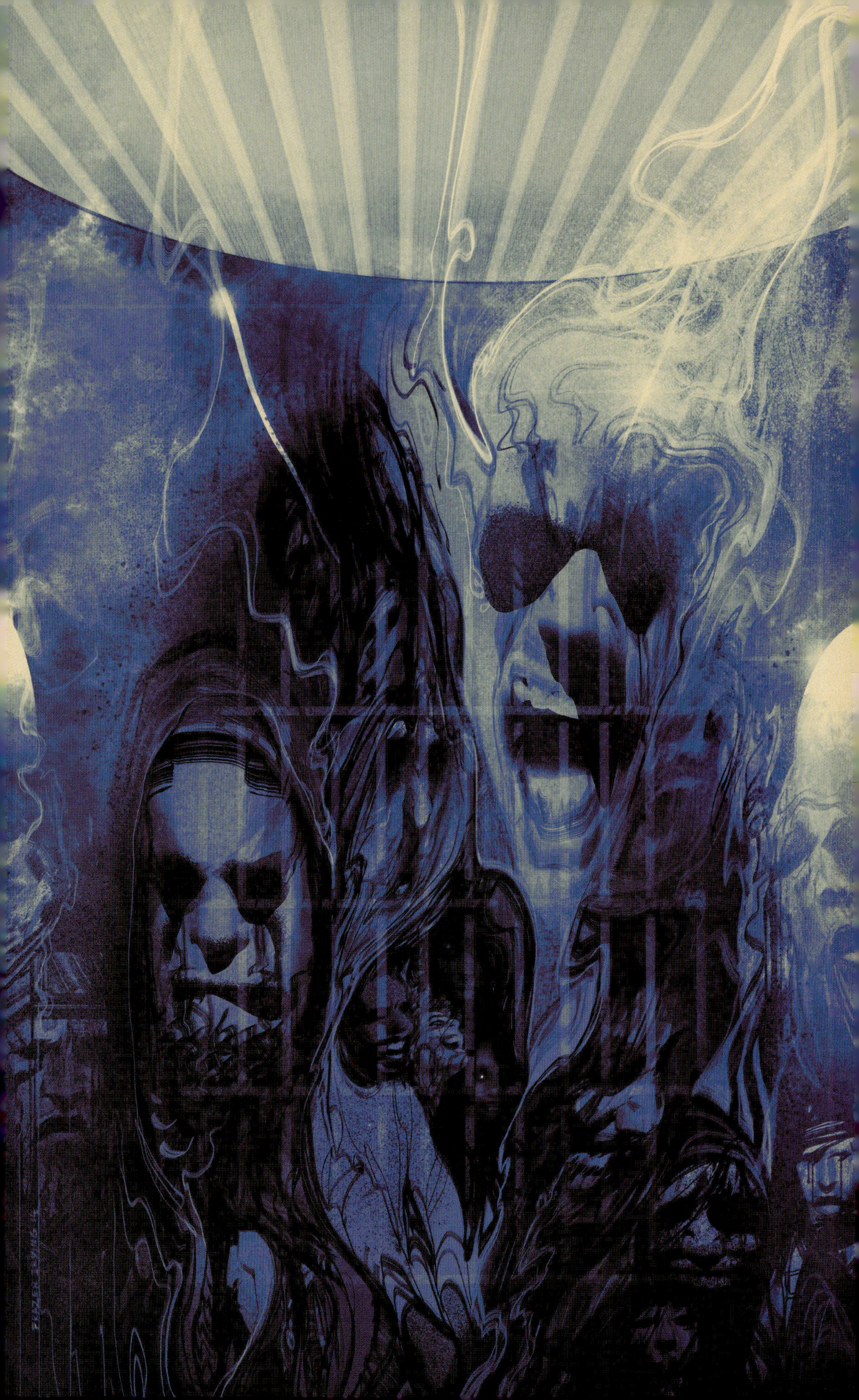

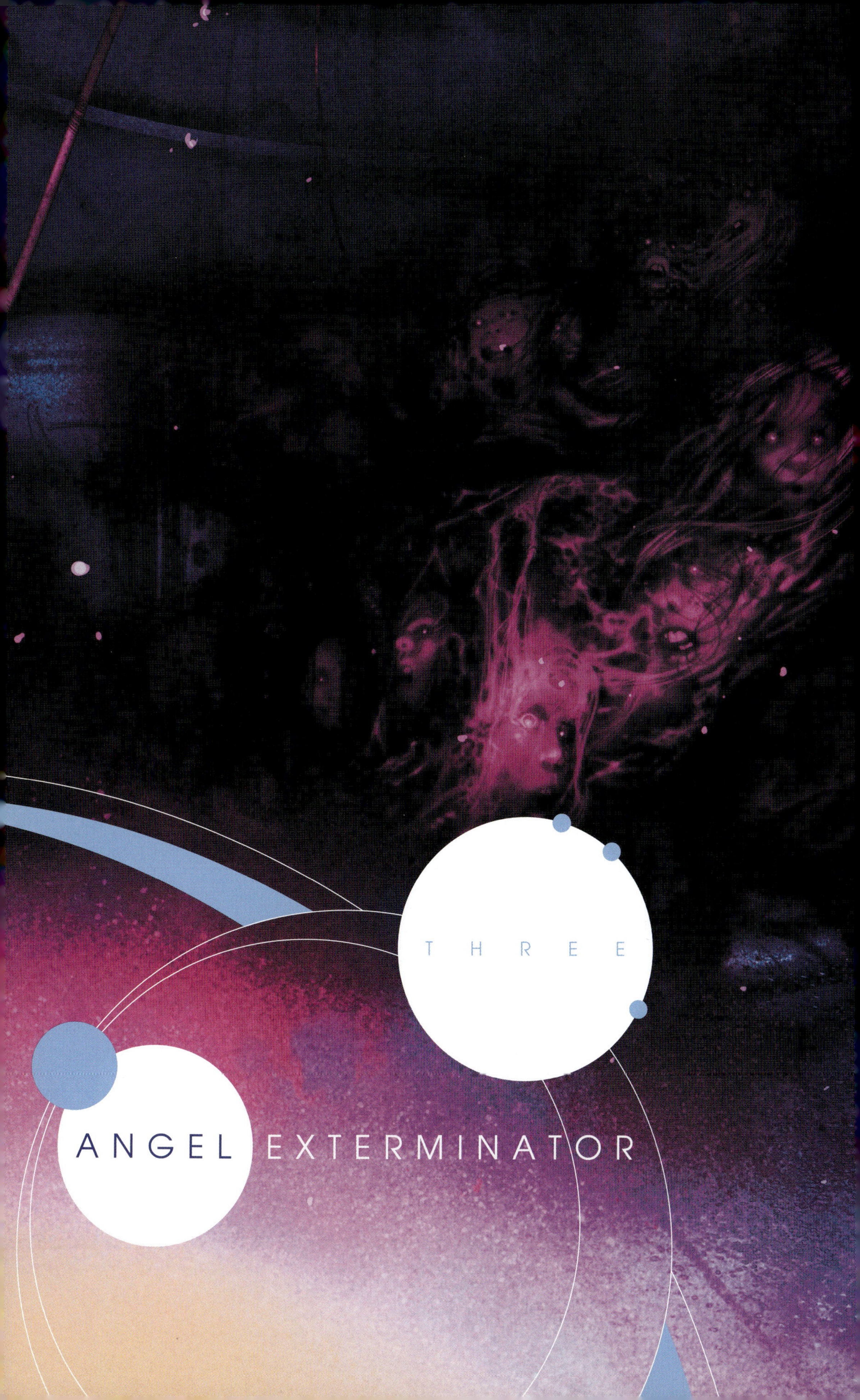
THREE
ANGEL EXTERMINATOR

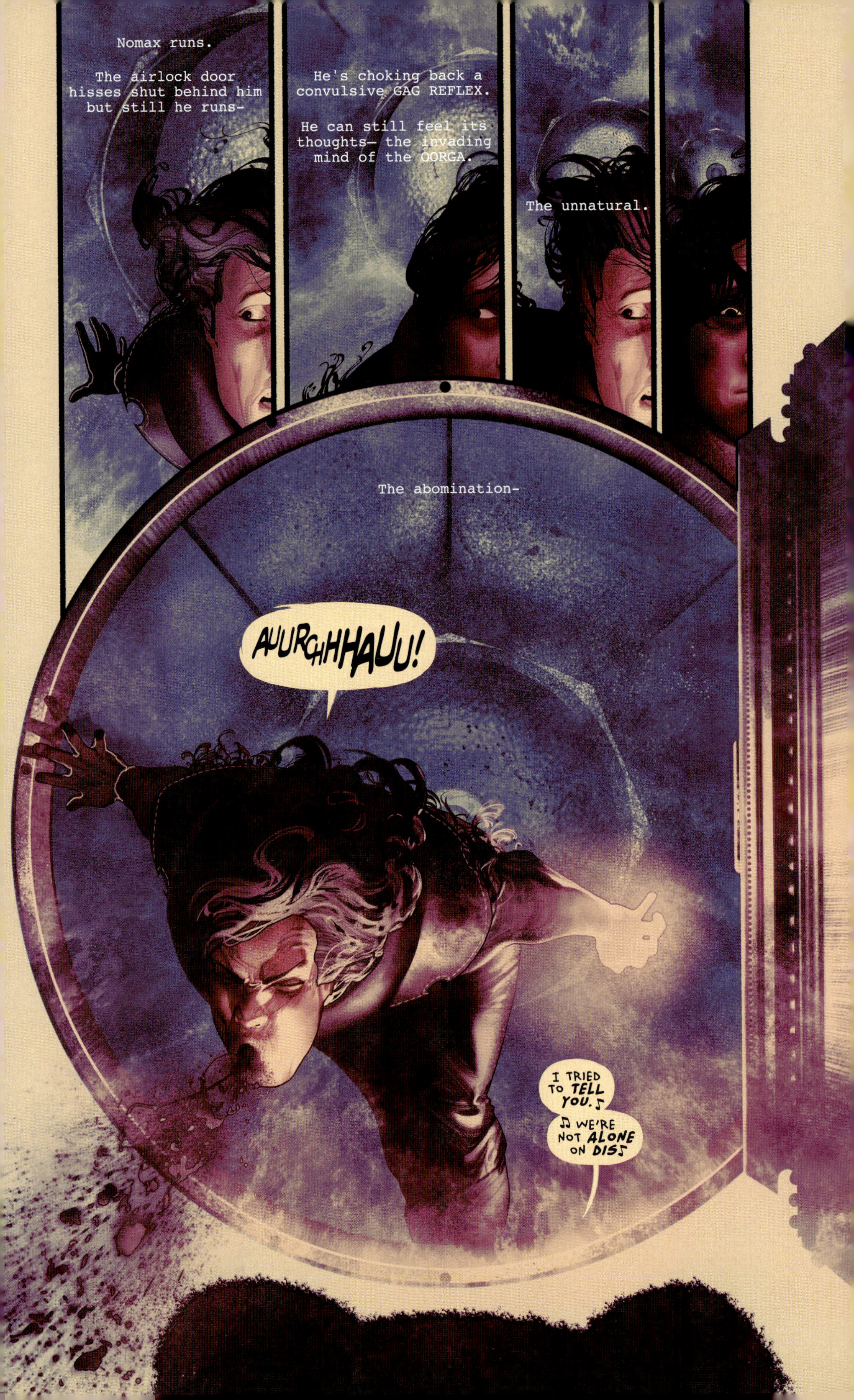
Nomax runs.
The airlock door hisses shut behind him but still he runs-
He's choking back a convulsive GAG REFLEX.
He can still feel its thoughts— the invading mind of the OORGA.
The unnatural.
The abomination-
AUURGHHHAUU!
I TRIED TO TELL YOU.
WE'RE NOT ALONE ON DIS

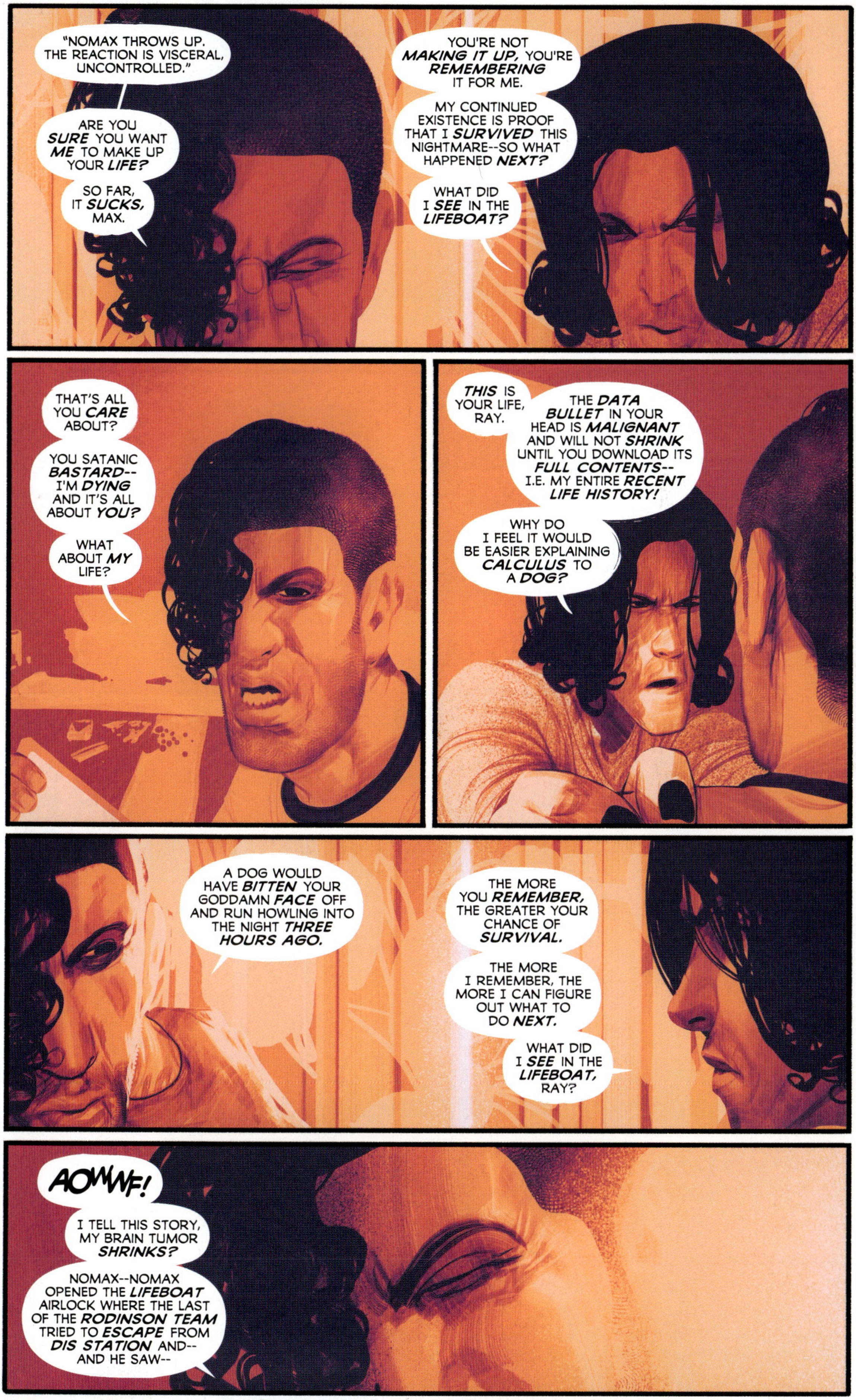
"NOMAX THROWS UP. THE REACTION IS VISCERAL, UNCONTROLLED."
ARE YOU SURE YOU WANT ME TO MAKE UP YOUR LIFE?
SO FAR, IT SUCKS, MAX.
YOU'RE NOT MAKING IT UP, YOU'RE REMEMBERING IT FOR ME.
MY CONTINUED EXISTENCE IS PROOF THAT I SURVIVED THIS NIGHTMARE--SO WHAT HAPPENED NEXT?
WHAT DID I SEE IN THE LIFEBOAT?
THAT'S ALL YOU CARE ABOUT?
YOU SATANIC BASTARD-- I'M DYING AND IT'S ALL ABOUT YOU?
WHAT ABOUT MY LIFE?
THIS IS YOUR LIFE, RAY.
THE DATA BULLET IN YOUR HEAD IS MALIGNANT AND WILL NOT SHRINK UNTIL YOU DOWNLOAD ITS FULL CONTENTS-- I.E. MY ENTIRE RECENT LIFE HISTORY!
WHY DO I FEEL IT WOULD BE EASIER EXPLAINING CALCULUS TO A DOG?
A DOG WOULD HAVE BITTEN YOUR GODDAMN FACE OFF AND RUN HOWLING INTO THE NIGHT THREE HOURS AGO.
THE MORE YOU REMEMBER, THE GREATER YOUR CHANCE OF SURVIVAL.
THE MORE I REMEMBER, THE MORE I CAN FIGURE OUT WHAT TO DO NEXT.
WHAT DID I SEE IN THE LIFEBOAT, RAY?
AOWWF!
I TELL THIS STORY, MY BRAIN TUMOR SHRINKS?
NOMAX--NOMAX OPENED THE LIFEBOAT AIRLOCK WHERE THE LAST OF THE RODINSON TEAM TRIED TO ESCAPE FROM DIS STATION AND-- AND HE SAW--

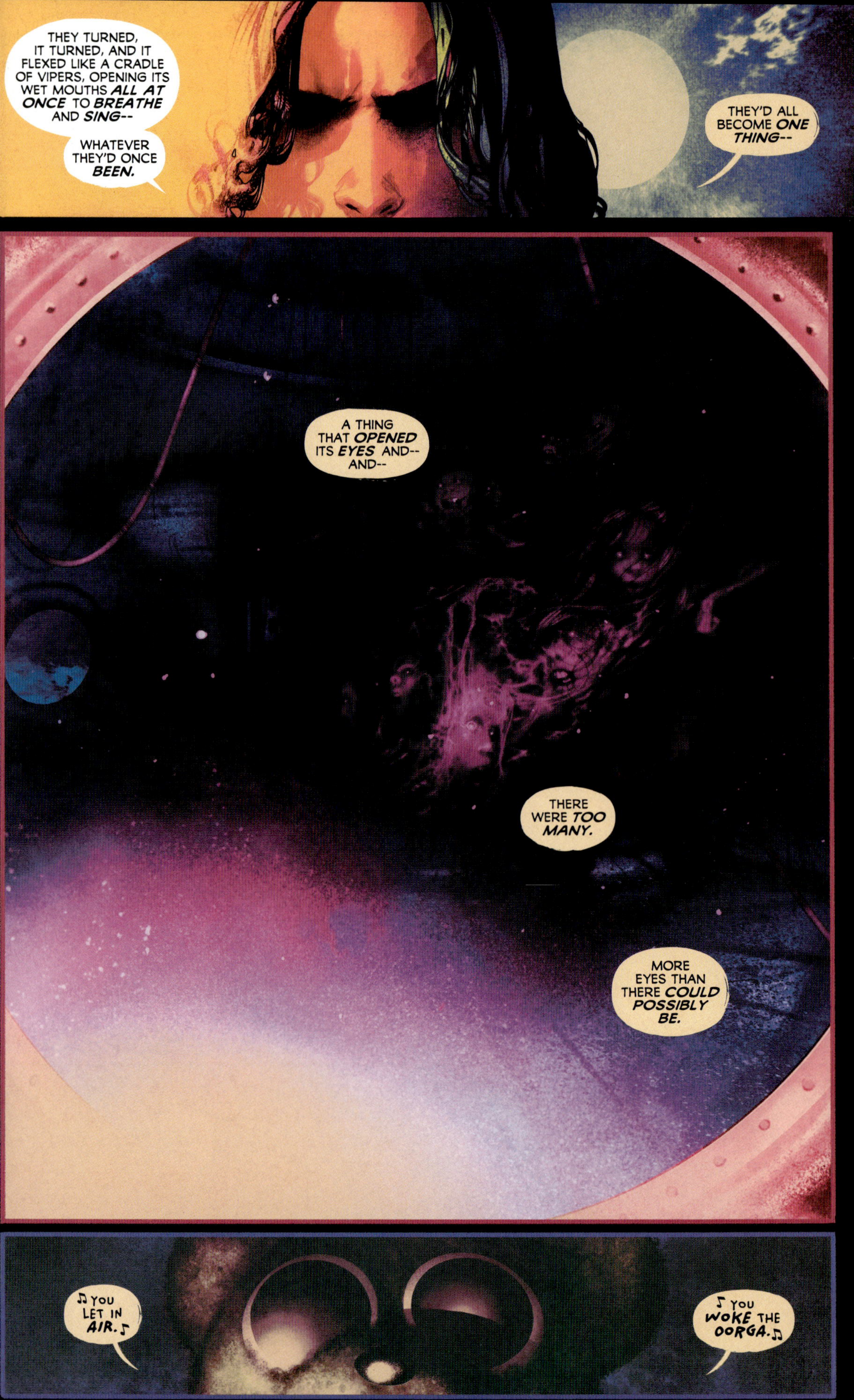
THEY TURNED, IT TURNED, AND IT FLEXED LIKE A CRADLE OF VIPERS, OPENING ITS WET MOUTHS ALL AT ONCE TO BREATHE AND SING--
WHATEVER THEY'D ONCE BEEN.
THEY'D ALL BECOME ONE THING--
A THING THAT OPENED ITS EYES AND-- AND--
THERE WERE TOO MANY.
MORE EYES THAN THERE COULD POSSIBLY BE.
♫ YOU LET IN AIR. ♫
♪ YOU WOKE THE OORGA. ♫

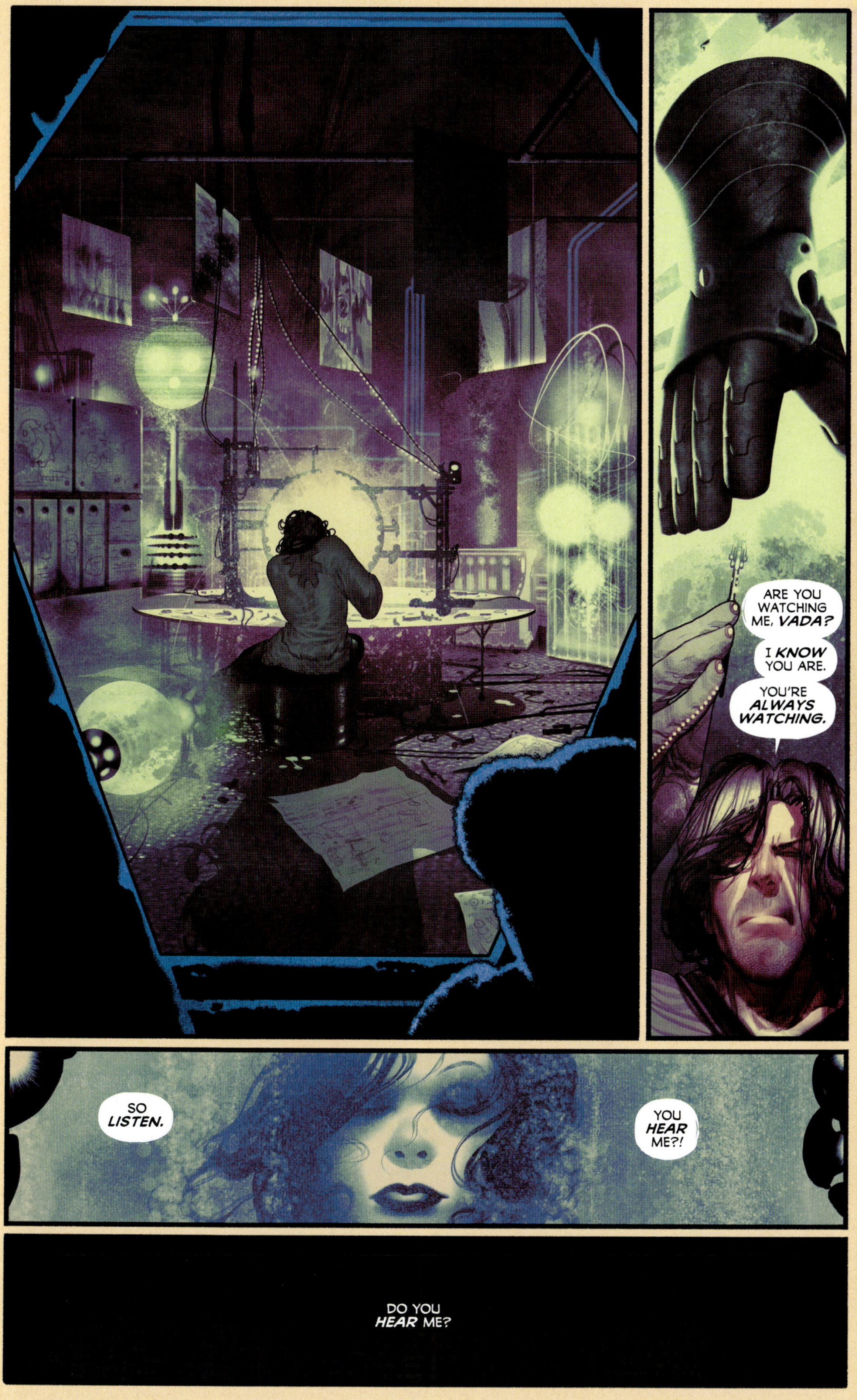
ARE YOU WATCHING ME, VADA?
I KNOW YOU ARE.
YOU'RE ALWAYS WATCHING.
SO LISTEN.
YOU HEAR ME?!
DO YOU HEAR ME?

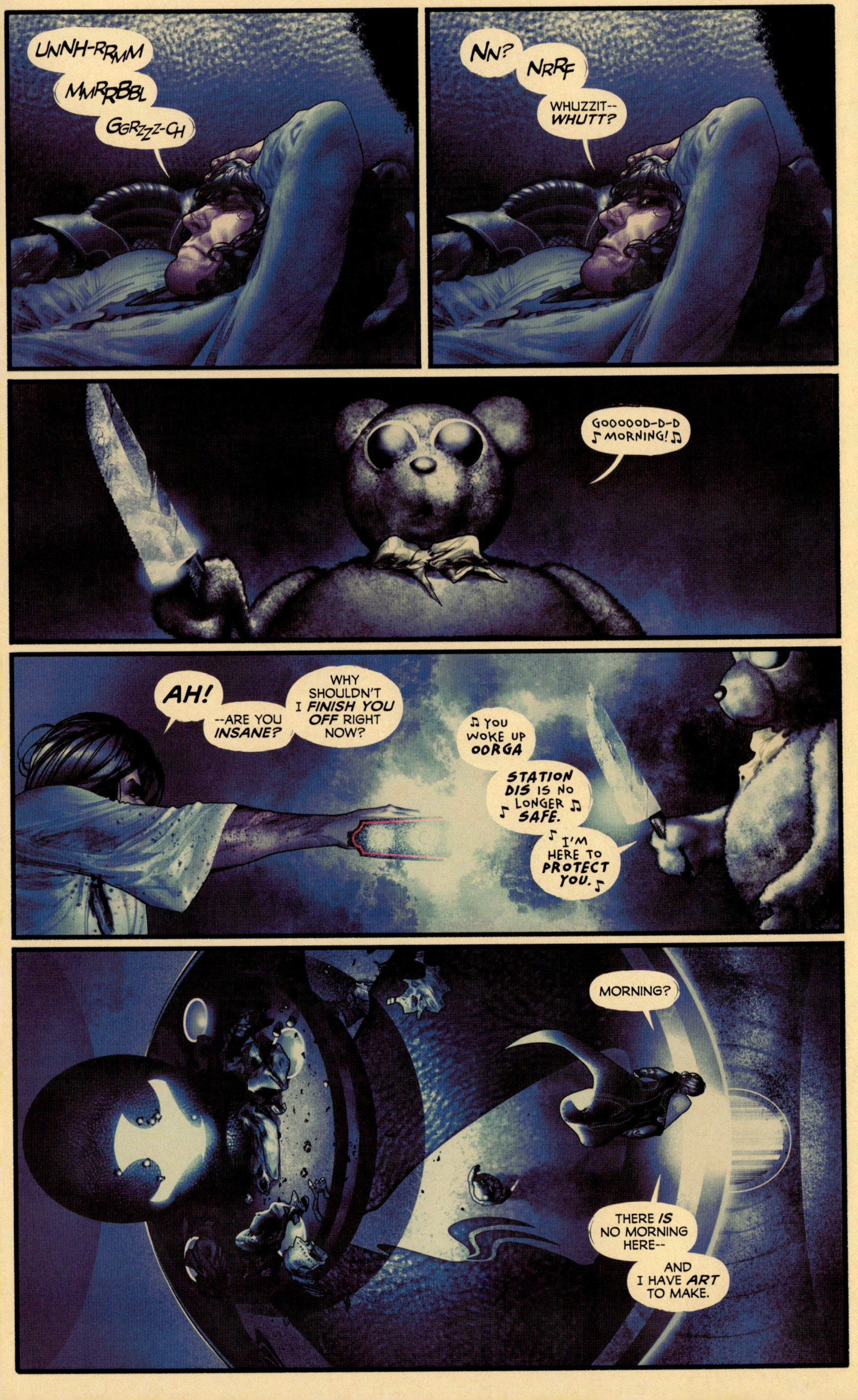
UNNH-RRMM
MMRRBBL
GGRZZZ-CH
NN?
NRRF
WHUZZIT-- WHUTT?
GOOOOOD-D-D ♪ MORNING! ♫
AH!
--ARE YOU INSANE?
WHY SHOULDN'T I FINISH YOU OFF RIGHT NOW?
♫ YOU WOKE UP OORGA
STATION DIS IS NO LONGER SAFE. ♫
♪ I'M HERE TO PROTECT YOU. ♪
MORNING?
THERE IS NO MORNING HERE--
AND I HAVE ART TO MAKE.

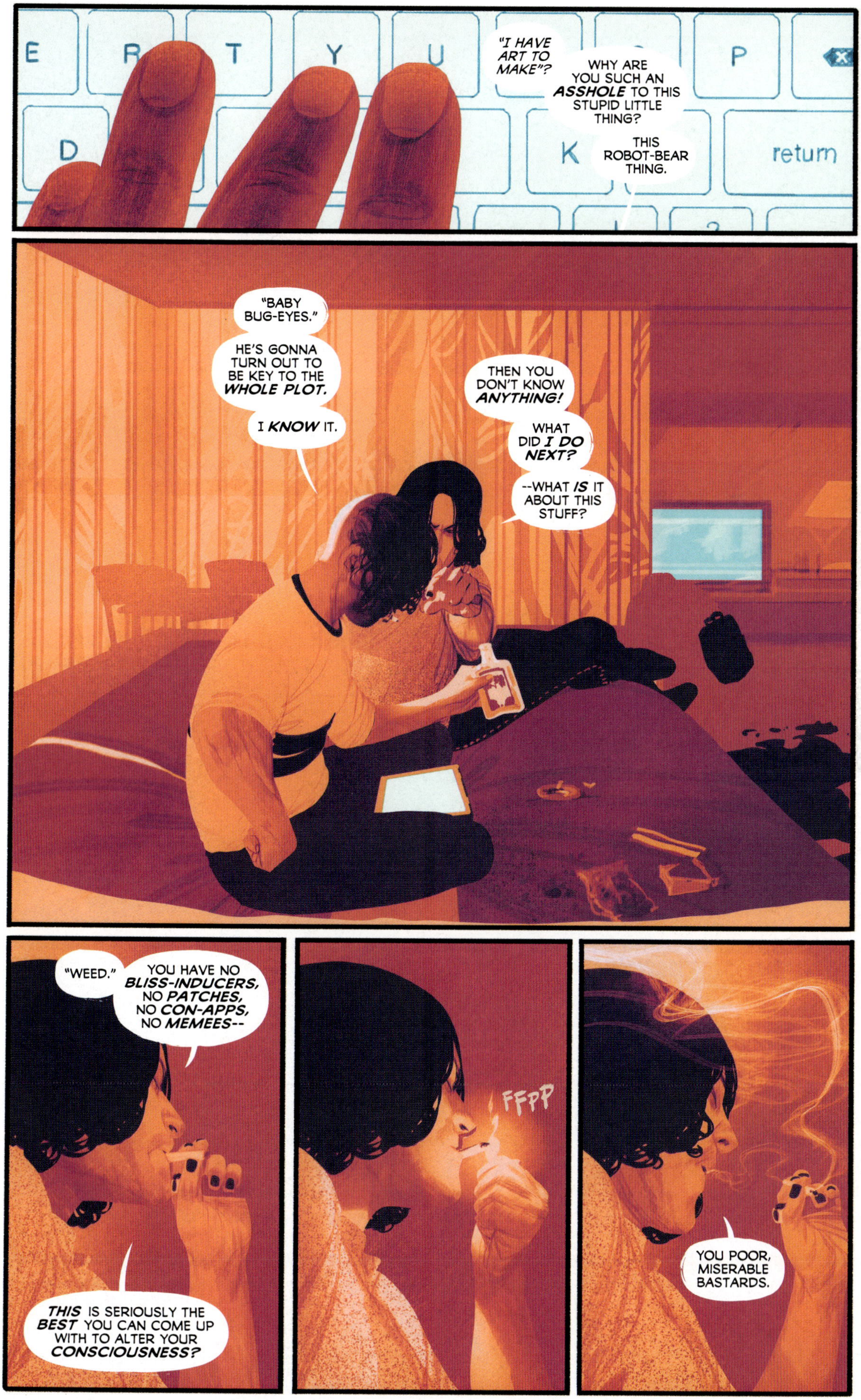
"I HAVE ART TO MAKE"?
WHY ARE YOU SUCH AN ASSHOLE TO THIS STUPID LITTLE THING?
THIS ROBOT-BEAR THING.
"BABY BUG-EYES."
HE'S GONNA TURN OUT TO BE KEY TO THE WHOLE PLOT.
I KNOW IT.
THEN YOU DON'T KNOW ANYTHING!
WHAT DID I DO NEXT?
--WHAT IS IT ABOUT THIS STUFF?
"WEED."
YOU HAVE NO BLISS-INDUCERS, NO PATCHES, NO CON-APPS, NO MEMEES--
THIS IS SERIOUSLY THE BEST YOU CAN COME UP WITH TO ALTER YOUR CONSCIOUSNESS?
FFPP
YOU POOR, MISERABLE BASTARDS.

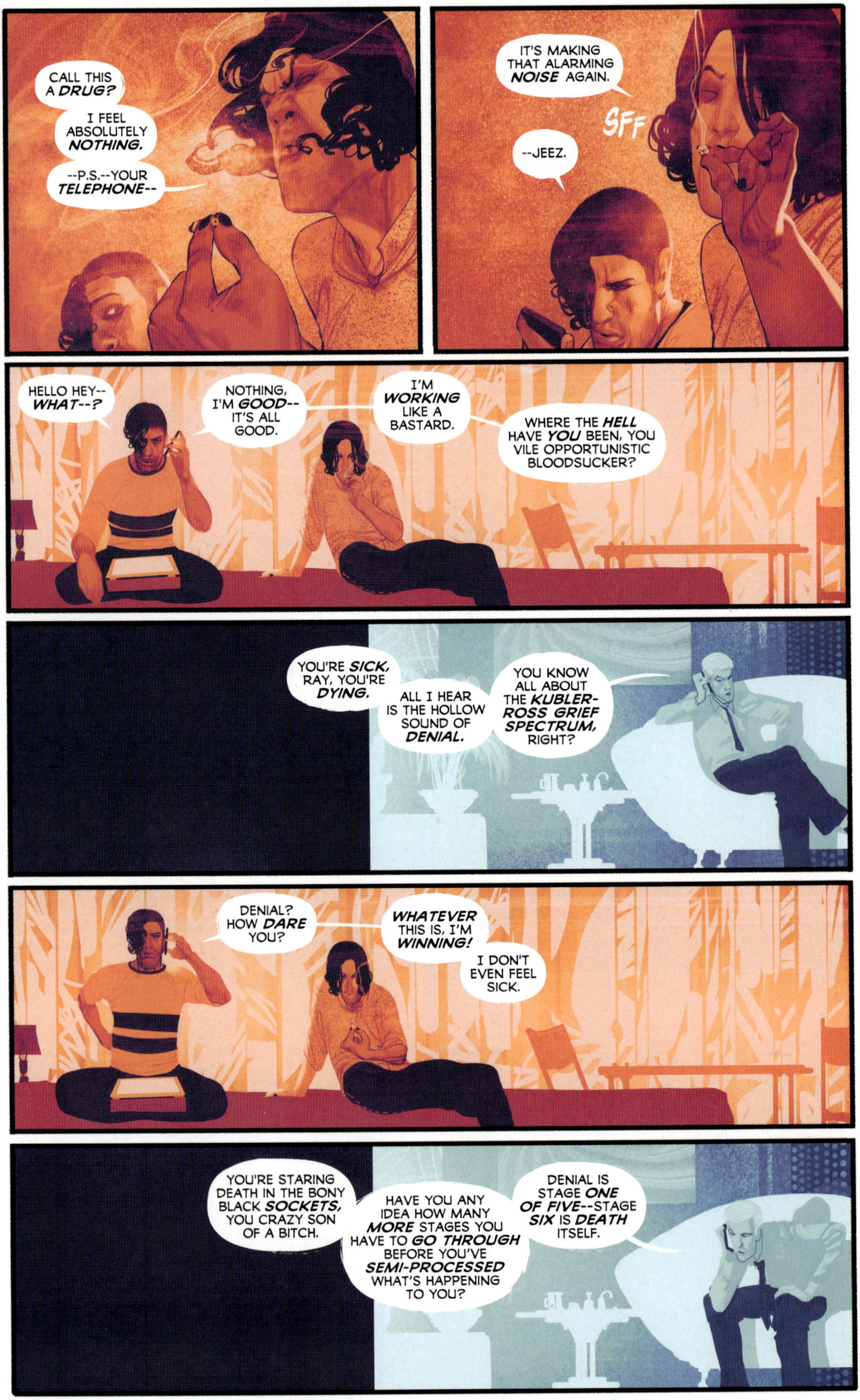
CALL THIS A DRUG?
I FEEL ABSOLUTELY NOTHING.
--P.S.--YOUR TELEPHONE--
IT'S MAKING THAT ALARMING NOISE AGAIN.
SFF
--JEEZ.
HELLO HEY-- WHAT--?
NOTHING, I'M GOOD-- IT'S ALL GOOD.
I'M WORKING LIKE A BASTARD.
WHERE THE HELL HAVE YOU BEEN, YOU VILE OPPORTUNISTIC BLOODSUCKER?
YOU'RE SICK, RAY, YOU'RE DYING.
ALL I HEAR IS THE HOLLOW SOUND OF DENIAL.
YOU KNOW ALL ABOUT THE KUBLER-ROSS GRIEF SPECTRUM, RIGHT?
DENIAL? HOW DARE YOU?
WHATEVER THIS IS, I'M WINNING!
I DON'T EVEN FEEL SICK.
YOU'RE STARING DEATH IN THE BONY BLACK SOCKETS, YOU CRAZY SON OF A BITCH.
HAVE YOU ANY IDEA HOW MANY MORE STAGES YOU HAVE TO GO THROUGH BEFORE YOU'VE SEMI-PROCESSED WHAT'S HAPPENING TO YOU?
DENIAL IS STAGE ONE OF FIVE--STAGE SIX IS DEATH ITSELF.

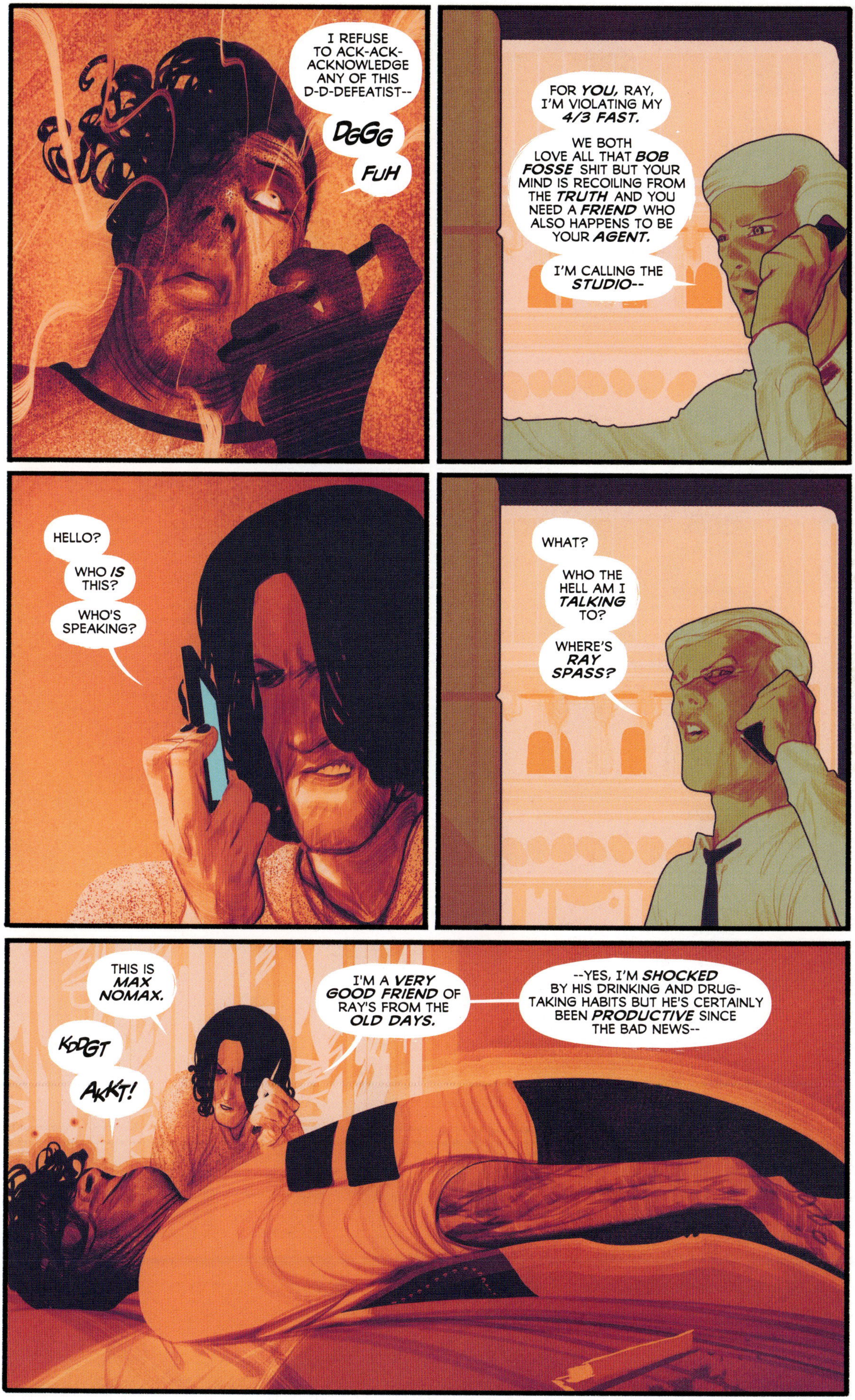
I REFUSE TO ACK-ACK-ACKNOWLEDGE ANY OF THIS D-D-DEFEATIST--
DGGG
FUH
FOR YOU, RAY, I'M VIOLATING MY 4/3 FAST.
WE BOTH LOVE ALL THAT BOB FOSSE SHIT BUT YOUR MIND IS RECOILING FROM THE TRUTH AND YOU NEED A FRIEND WHO ALSO HAPPENS TO BE YOUR AGENT.
I'M CALLING THE STUDIO--
HELLO?
WHO IS THIS?
WHO'S SPEAKING?
WHAT?
WHO THE HELL AM I TALKING TO?
WHERE'S RAY SPASS?
THIS IS MAX NOMAX.
KDDGT
AKKT!
I'M A VERY GOOD FRIEND OF RAY'S FROM THE OLD DAYS.
--YES, I'M SHOCKED BY HIS DRINKING AND DRUG-TAKING HABITS BUT HE'S CERTAINLY BEEN PRODUCTIVE SINCE THE BAD NEWS--

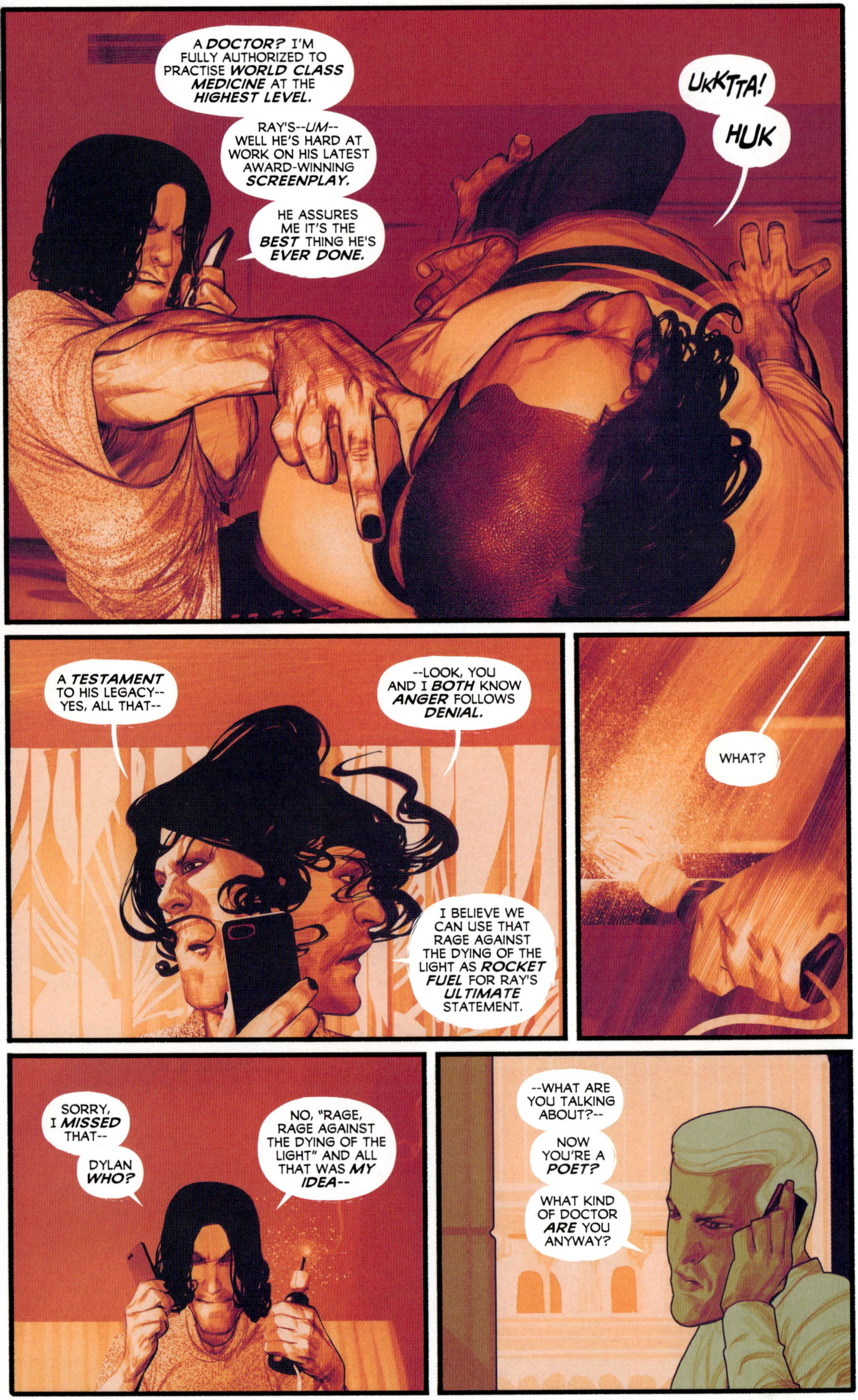
A DOCTOR? I'M FULLY AUTHORIZED TO PRACTISE WORLD CLASS MEDICINE AT THE HIGHEST LEVEL.
RAY'S--UM--WELL HE'S HARD AT WORK ON HIS LATEST AWARD-WINNING SCREENPLAY.
HE ASSURES ME IT'S THE BEST THING HE'S EVER DONE.
UKKTTA!
HUK
A TESTAMENT TO HIS LEGACY--YES, ALL THAT--
--LOOK, YOU AND I BOTH KNOW ANGER FOLLOWS DENIAL.
I BELIEVE WE CAN USE THAT RAGE AGAINST THE DYING OF THE LIGHT AS ROCKET FUEL FOR RAY'S ULTIMATE STATEMENT.
WHAT?
SORRY, I MISSED THAT--
DYLAN WHO?
NO, "RAGE, RAGE AGAINST THE DYING OF THE LIGHT" AND ALL THAT WAS MY IDEA--
--WHAT ARE YOU TALKING ABOUT?--
NOW YOU'RE A POET?
WHAT KIND OF DOCTOR ARE YOU ANYWAY?

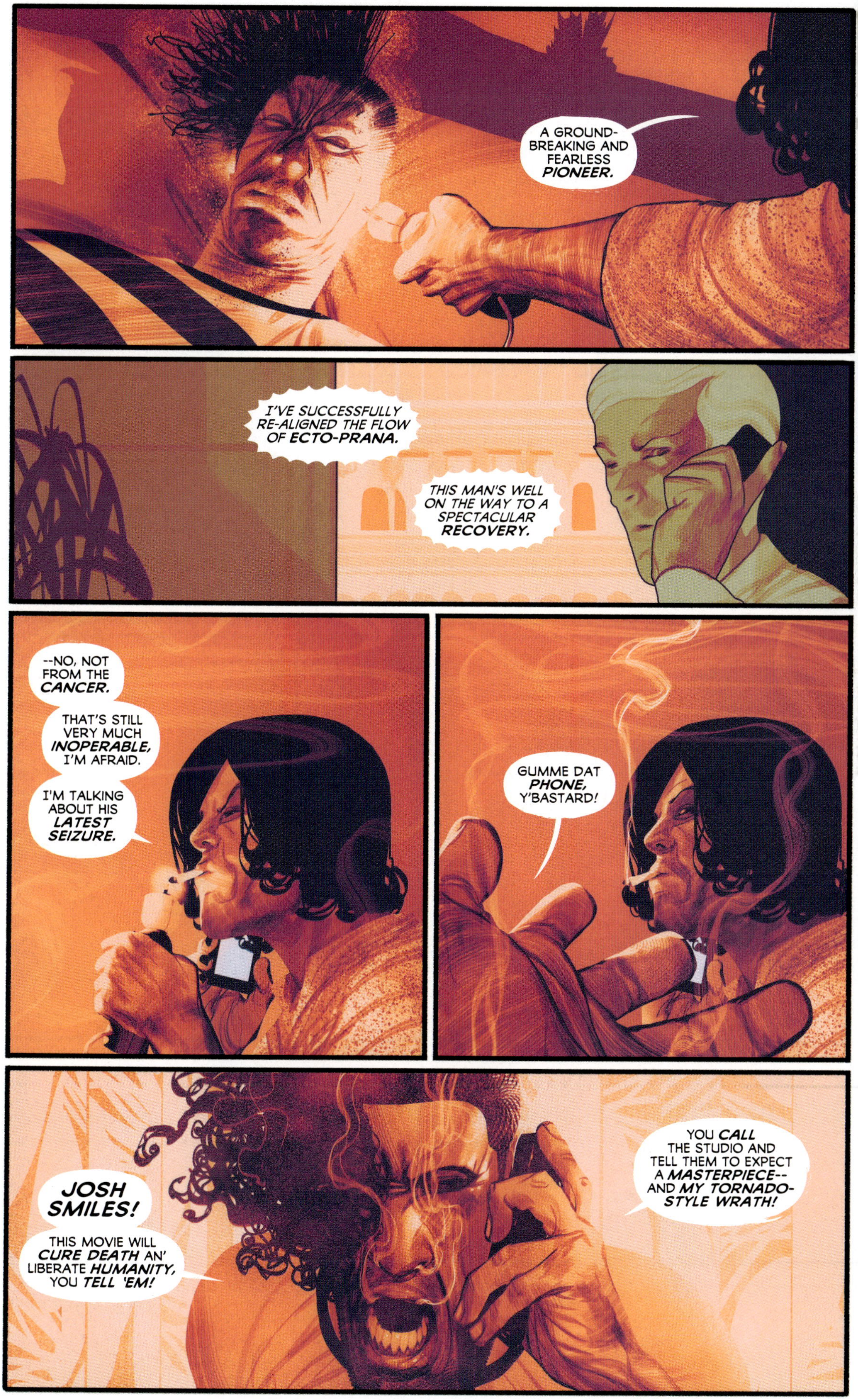
A GROUND-BREAKING AND FEARLESS PIONEER.
I'VE SUCCESSFULLY RE-ALIGNED THE FLOW OF ECTO-PRANA.
THIS MAN'S WELL ON THE WAY TO A SPECTACULAR RECOVERY.
--NO, NOT FROM THE CANCER.
THAT'S STILL VERY MUCH INOPERABLE, I'M AFRAID.
I'M TALKING ABOUT HIS LATEST SEIZURE.
GUMME DAT PHONE, Y'BASTARD!
JOSH SMILES!
THIS MOVIE WILL CURE DEATH AN' LIBERATE HUMANITY, YOU TELL 'EM!
YOU CALL THE STUDIO AND TELL THEM TO EXPECT A MASTERPIECE-- AND MY TORNADO-STYLE WRATH!

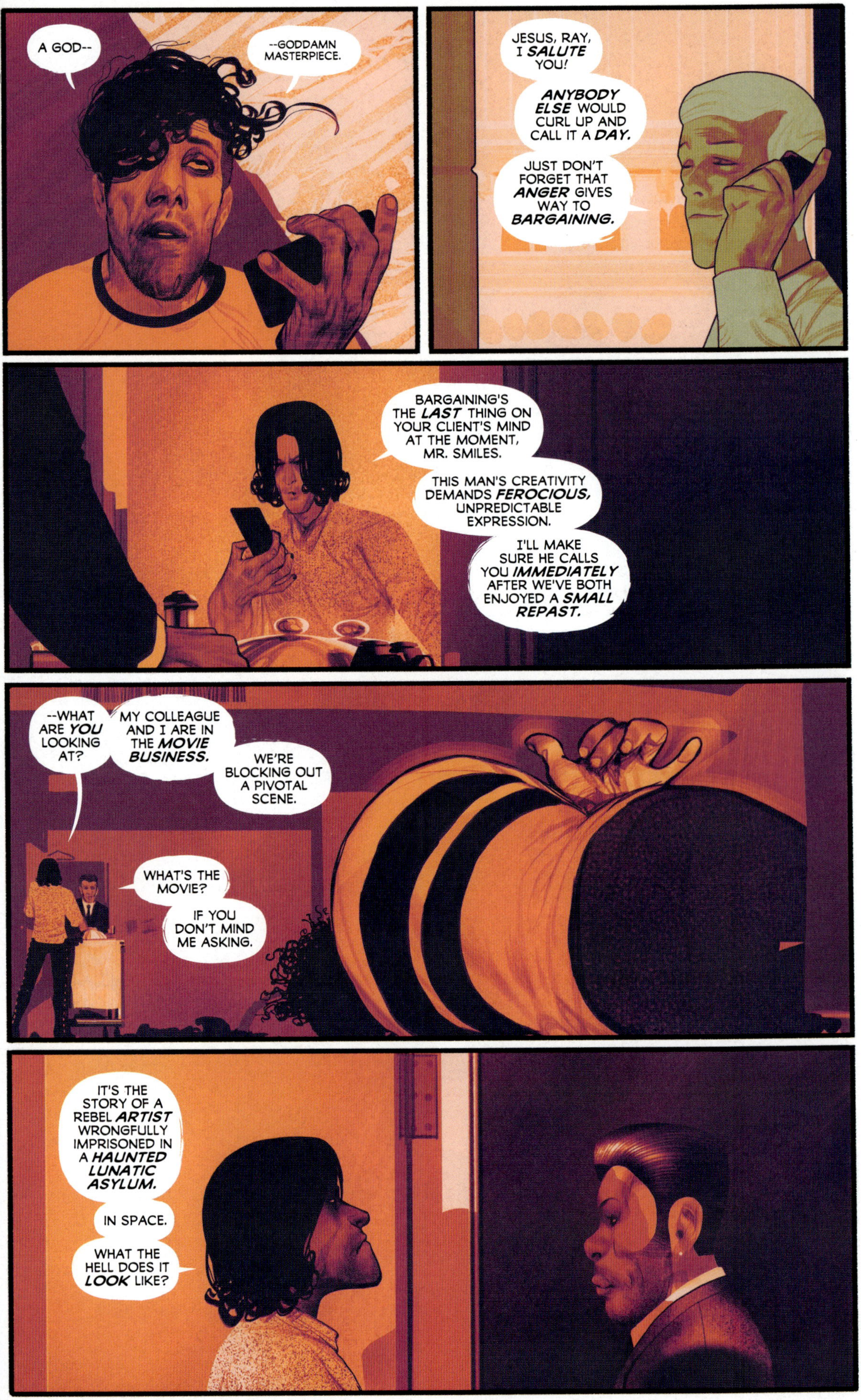
A GOD--
--GODDAMN MASTERPIECE.
JESUS, RAY, I SALUTE YOU!
ANYBODY ELSE WOULD CURL UP AND CALL IT A DAY.
JUST DON'T FORGET THAT ANGER GIVES WAY TO BARGAINING.
BARGAINING'S THE LAST THING ON YOUR CLIENT'S MIND AT THE MOMENT, MR. SMILES.
THIS MAN'S CREATIVITY DEMANDS FEROCIOUS, UNPREDICTABLE EXPRESSION.
I'LL MAKE SURE HE CALLS YOU IMMEDIATELY AFTER WE'VE BOTH ENJOYED A SMALL REPAST.
--WHAT ARE YOU LOOKING AT?
MY COLLEAGUE AND I ARE IN THE MOVIE BUSINESS.
WE'RE BLOCKING OUT A PIVOTAL SCENE.
WHAT'S THE MOVIE?
IF YOU DON'T MIND ME ASKING.
IT'S THE STORY OF A REBEL ARTIST WRONGFULLY IMPRISONED IN A HAUNTED LUNATIC ASYLUM.
IN SPACE.
WHAT THE HELL DOES IT LOOK LIKE?

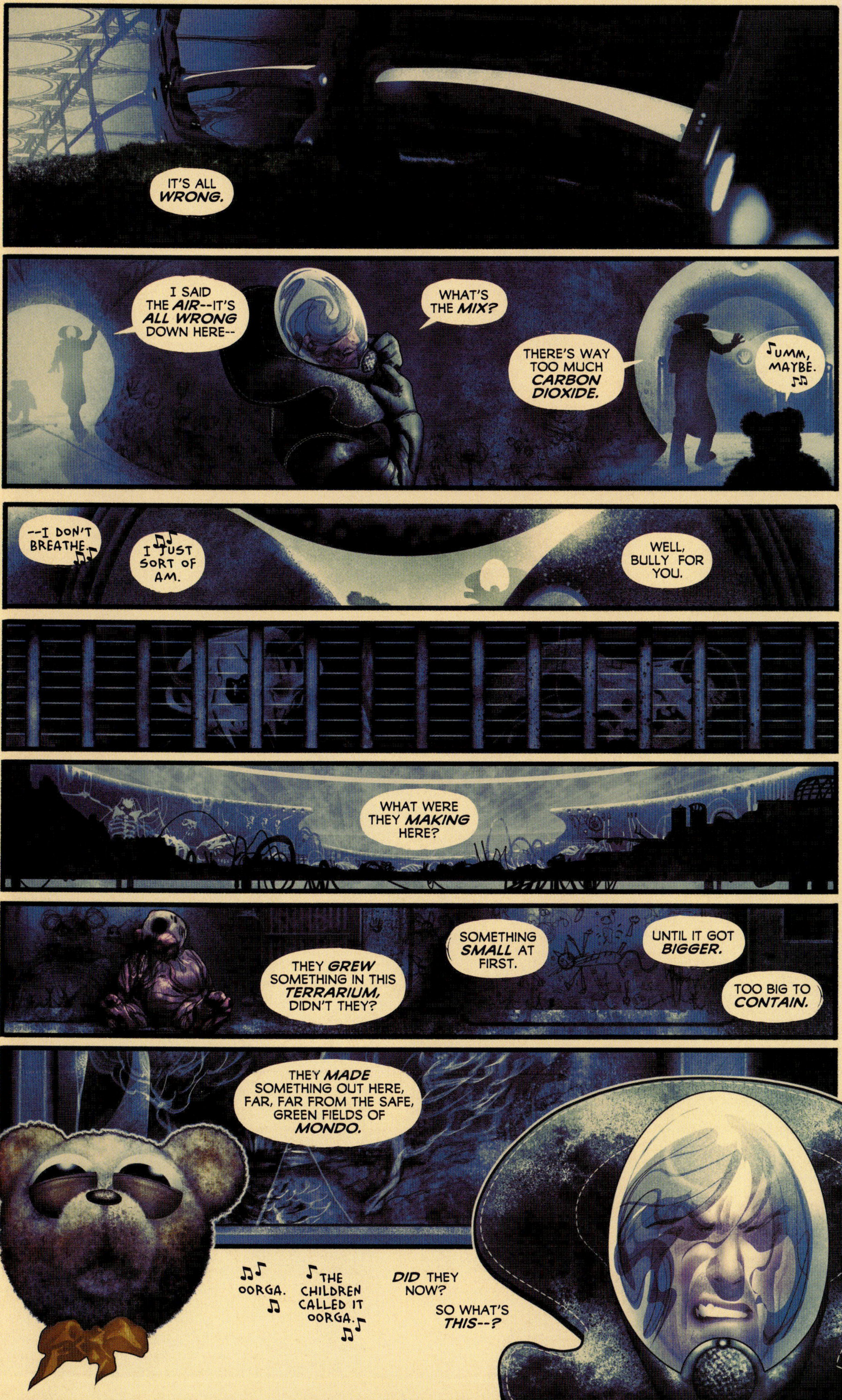
IT'S ALL WRONG.
I SAID THE AIR--IT'S ALL WRONG DOWN HERE--
WHAT'S THE MIX?
THERE'S WAY TOO MUCH CARBON DIOXIDE.
♪UMM, MAYBE. ♫
--I DON'T BREATHE. ♫
♫ I JUST SORT OF AM.
WELL, BULLY FOR YOU.
WHAT WERE THEY MAKING HERE?
THEY GREW SOMETHING IN THIS TERRARIUM, DIDN'T THEY?
SOMETHING SMALL AT FIRST.
UNTIL IT GOT BIGGER.
TOO BIG TO CONTAIN.
THEY MADE SOMETHING OUT HERE, FAR, FAR FROM THE SAFE, GREEN FIELDS OF MONDO.
♫ OORGA. ♫
♪THE CHILDREN CALLED IT OORGA. ♫
DID THEY NOW?
SO WHAT'S THIS--?

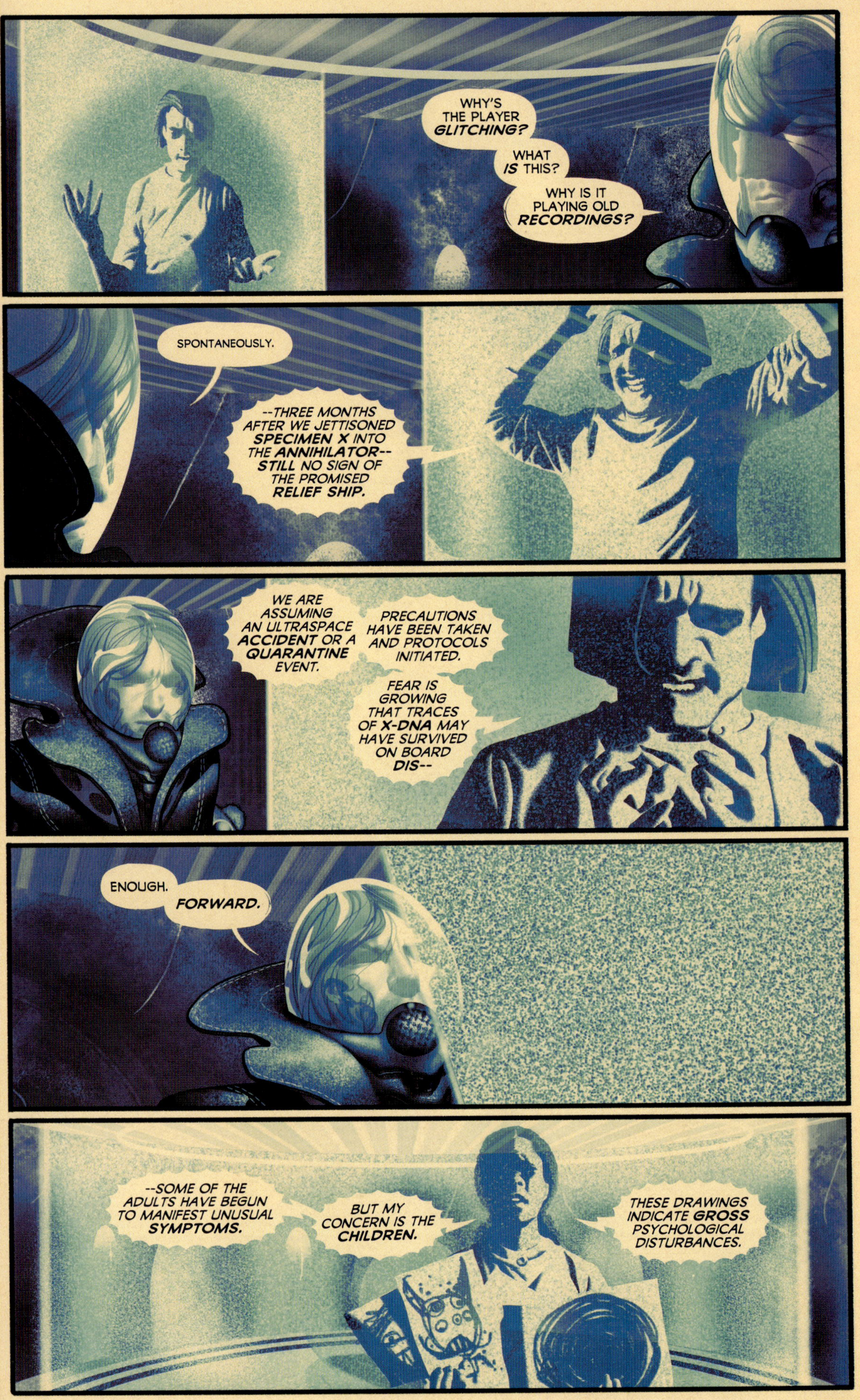
WHY'S THE PLAYER GLITCHING?
WHAT IS THIS?
WHY IS IT PLAYING OLD RECORDINGS?
SPONTANEOUSLY.
--THREE MONTHS AFTER WE JETTISONED SPECIMEN X INTO THE ANNIHILATOR--STILL NO SIGN OF THE PROMISED RELIEF SHIP.
WE ARE ASSUMING AN ULTRASPACE ACCIDENT OR A QUARANTINE EVENT.
PRECAUTIONS HAVE BEEN TAKEN AND PROTOCOLS INITIATED.
FEAR IS GROWING THAT TRACES OF X-DNA MAY HAVE SURVIVED ON BOARD DIS--
ENOUGH.
FORWARD.
--SOME OF THE ADULTS HAVE BEGUN TO MANIFEST UNUSUAL SYMPTOMS.
BUT MY CONCERN IS THE CHILDREN.
THESE DRAWINGS INDICATE GROSS PSYCHOLOGICAL DISTURBANCES.

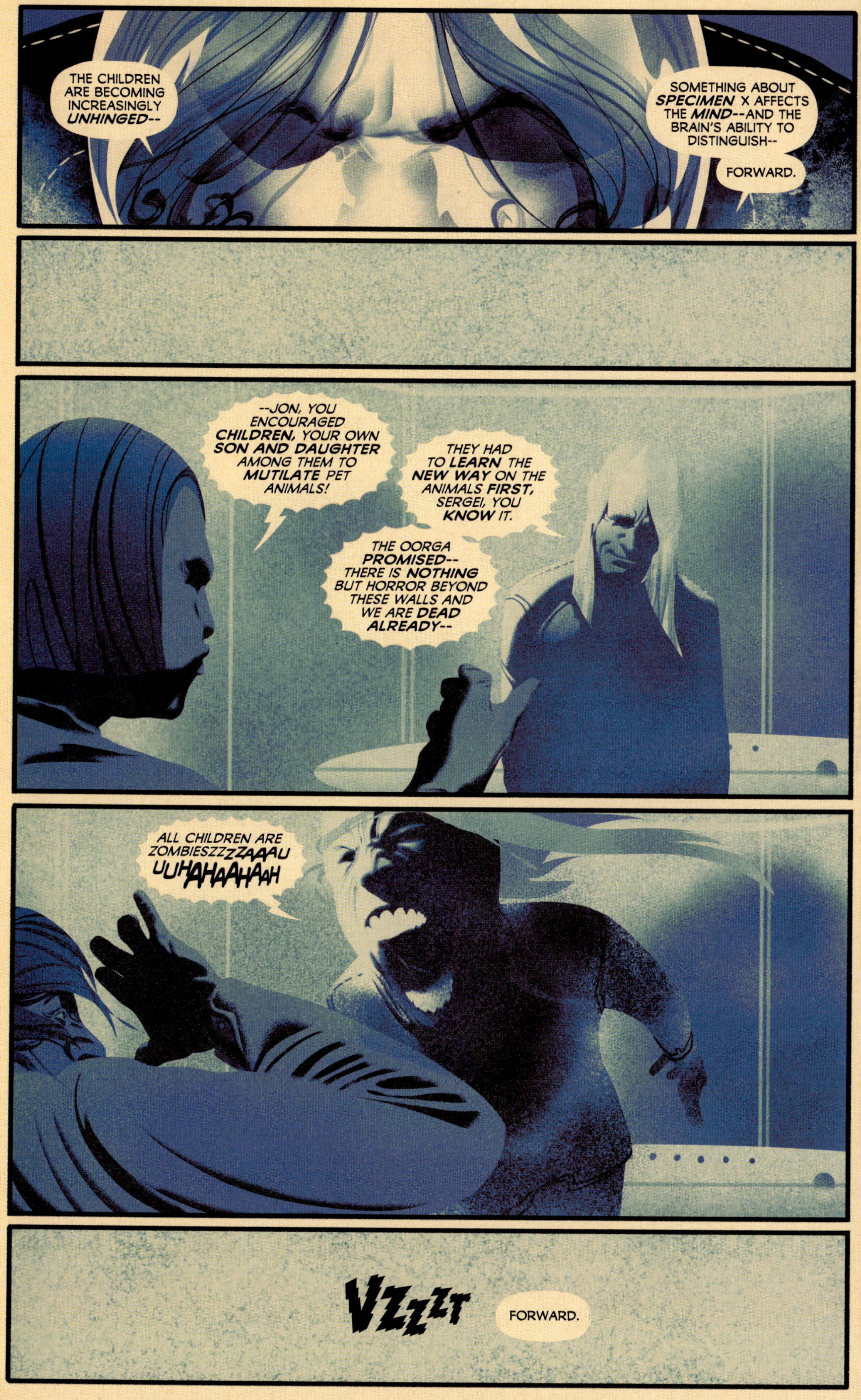
THE CHILDREN ARE BECOMING INCREASINGLY UNHINGED--
SOMETHING ABOUT SPECIMEN X AFFECTS THE MIND--AND THE BRAIN'S ABILITY TO DISTINGUISH--
FORWARD.
--JON, YOU ENCOURAGED CHILDREN, YOUR OWN SON AND DAUGHTER AMONG THEM TO MUTILATE PET ANIMALS!
THEY HAD TO LEARN THE NEW WAY ON THE ANIMALS FIRST, SERGEI, YOU KNOW IT.
THE OORGA PROMISED--THERE IS NOTHING BUT HORROR BEYOND THESE WALLS AND WE ARE DEAD ALREADY--
ALL CHILDREN ARE ZOMBIESZZZZAAAU UUHAHAAHAAH
VZZZT
FORWARD.

--WHY DID THEY LEAVE *ME* IN CHARGE! WHY WON'T THEY STOP ALL THAT HORRIBLE *SINGING*?

WHAT HAPPENED TO THE--TO THE--TO THE *THING*--TO *ME*--TO ME--TO--THE--

FORWARD.

YOU'RE ON THE OUTSIDE NOW! IT'S ALL MAKING SENSE!

WE WERE *RIGHT* TO LET IT LOOSE!

BUT HOW COULD VADA DO THIS TO US?

HOW COULD--

FORWARD.

FORWARD!

WHAT WAS BEHIND *THAT* DOOR?

PROJECT X

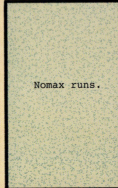

Nomax runs.

Nomax runs.

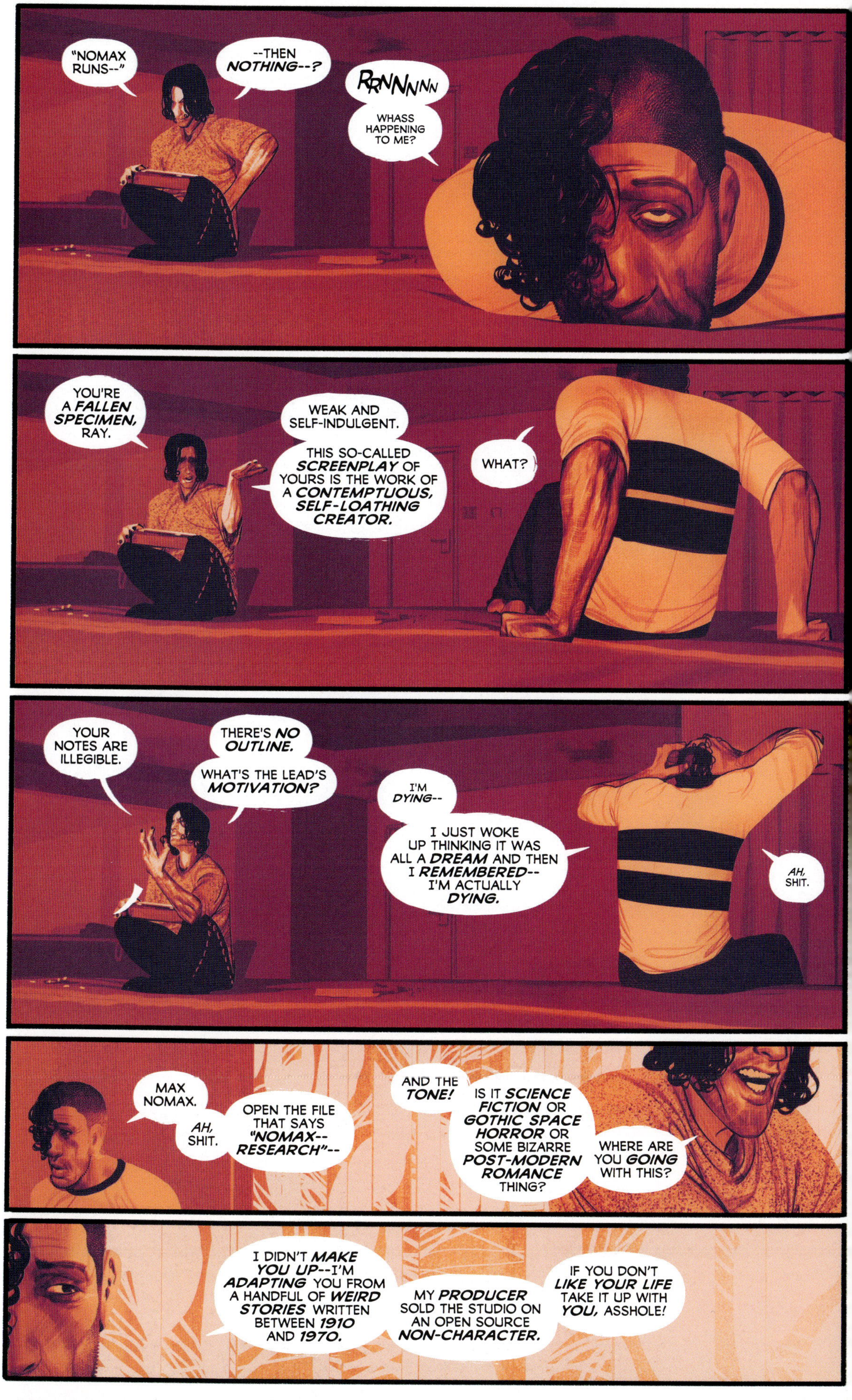
"NOMAX RUNS--"
--THEN NOTHING--?
RRNNNNN
WHASS HAPPENING TO ME?
YOU'RE A FALLEN SPECIMEN, RAY.
WEAK AND SELF-INDULGENT.
THIS SO-CALLED SCREENPLAY OF YOURS IS THE WORK OF A CONTEMPTUOUS, SELF-LOATHING CREATOR.
WHAT?
YOUR NOTES ARE ILLEGIBLE.
THERE'S NO OUTLINE.
WHAT'S THE LEAD'S MOTIVATION?
I'M DYING--
I JUST WOKE UP THINKING IT WAS ALL A DREAM AND THEN I REMEMBERED-- I'M ACTUALLY DYING.
AH, SHIT.
MAX NOMAX.
AH, SHIT.
OPEN THE FILE THAT SAYS "NOMAX--RESEARCH"--
AND THE TONE!
IS IT SCIENCE FICTION OR GOTHIC SPACE HORROR OR SOME BIZARRE POST-MODERN ROMANCE THING?
WHERE ARE YOU GOING WITH THIS?
I DIDN'T MAKE YOU UP--I'M ADAPTING YOU FROM A HANDFUL OF WEIRD STORIES WRITTEN BETWEEN 1910 AND 1970.
MY PRODUCER SOLD THE STUDIO ON AN OPEN SOURCE NON-CHARACTER.
IF YOU DON'T LIKE YOUR LIFE TAKE IT UP WITH YOU, ASSHOLE!

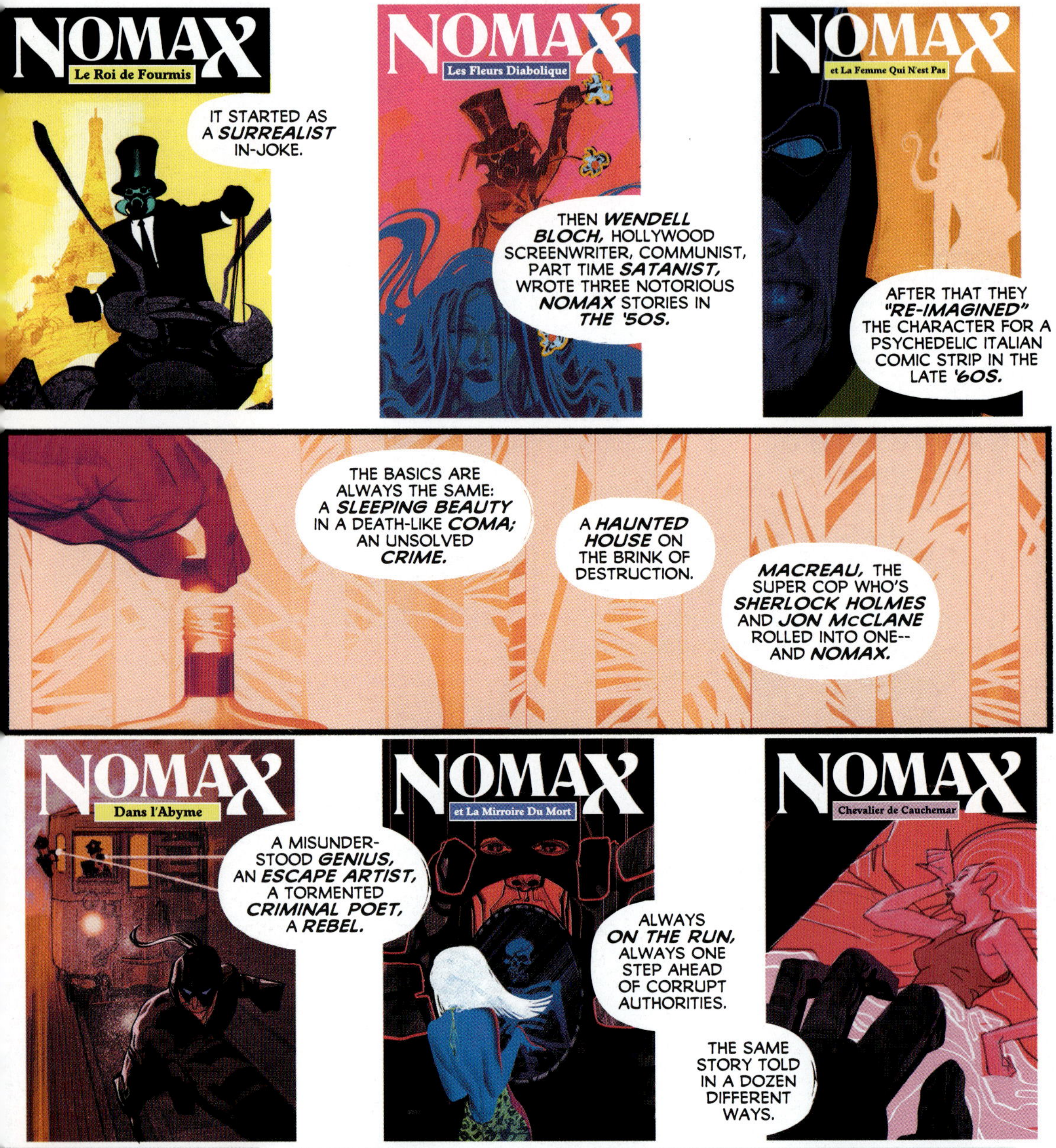
NOMAX
Le Roi de Fourmis
IT STARTED AS A *SURREALIST* IN-JOKE.
NOMAX
Les Fleurs Diabolique
THEN *WENDELL BLOCH,* HOLLYWOOD SCREENWRITER, COMMUNIST, PART TIME *SATANIST,* WROTE THREE NOTORIOUS *NOMAX* STORIES IN *THE '50S.*
NOMAX
et La Femme Qui N'est Pas
AFTER THAT THEY *"RE-IMAGINED"* THE CHARACTER FOR A PSYCHEDELIC ITALIAN COMIC STRIP IN THE LATE *'60S.*
THE BASICS ARE ALWAYS THE SAME: A *SLEEPING BEAUTY* IN A DEATH-LIKE *COMA;* AN UNSOLVED *CRIME.*
A *HAUNTED HOUSE* ON THE BRINK OF DESTRUCTION.
MACREAU, THE SUPER COP WHO'S *SHERLOCK HOLMES* AND *JON McCLANE* ROLLED INTO ONE-- AND *NOMAX.*
NOMAX
Dans l'Abyme
A MISUNDER-STOOD *GENIUS,* AN *ESCAPE ARTIST,* A TORMENTED *CRIMINAL POET,* A *REBEL.*
NOMAX
et La Mirroire Du Mort
ALWAYS *ON THE RUN,* ALWAYS ONE STEP AHEAD OF CORRUPT AUTHORITIES.
NOMAX
Chevalier de Cauchemar
THE SAME STORY TOLD IN A DOZEN DIFFERENT WAYS.

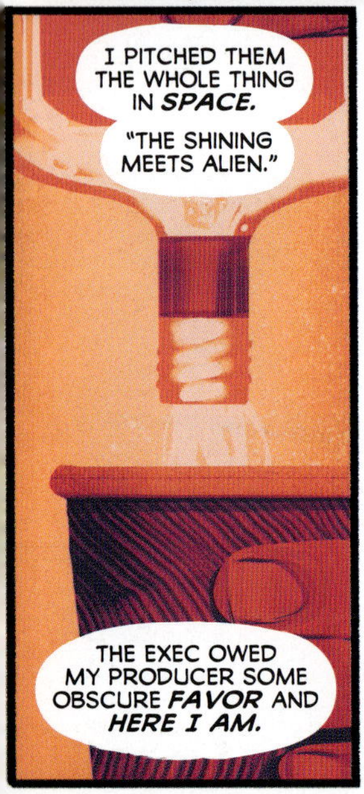
I PITCHED THEM THE WHOLE THING IN *SPACE.*
"THE SHINING MEETS ALIEN."
THE EXEC OWED MY PRODUCER SOME OBSCURE *FAVOR* AND *HERE I AM.*

FROM the forbidden journals of Duke Nomax- January 31st.

THE captive angel shrieked in a bright, sharp falsetto as Nomax plucked a quill from the shining thing's lacerated, bony back. Thrilling blood spilled white, an ice-cold luminous milk in the ultraviolet black-light. The dove-fledged, delirious creature wept helplessly, unable to comprehend why any mortal thing would choose to treat it with such casual, deliberate cruelty. Soon, the bright and broken exquisite spirit would come to learn the ways of evil, as a bad angel in the service of sweet Satan; Our black and radiant Lucifer, our ever-giving Void-God.

Our Great Lord Annihilator.

"Thus shall I pen cosmic pornography with a gory stylus plucked raw from a seraph's spine," the sneering, self-entitled Duke Nomax declared with relish. "I shall author blasphemous gospels for a coming apostate aeon where the stainless virgin ruts with genetically-engineered goat-men for the pleasure of her masters in Abaddon, Sheol, Annwn! So shall Nomax write flaming,

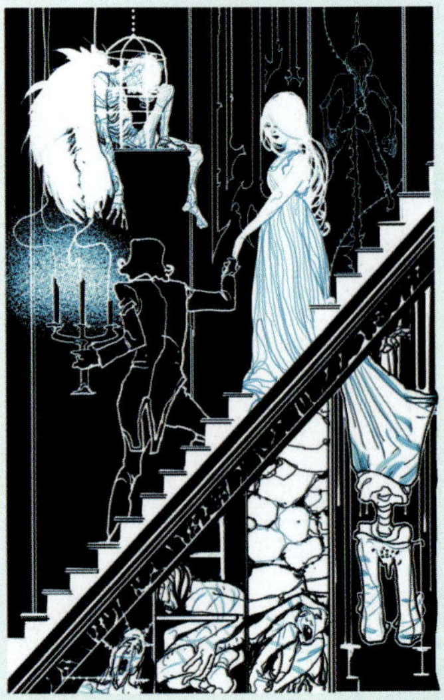

21 of 353

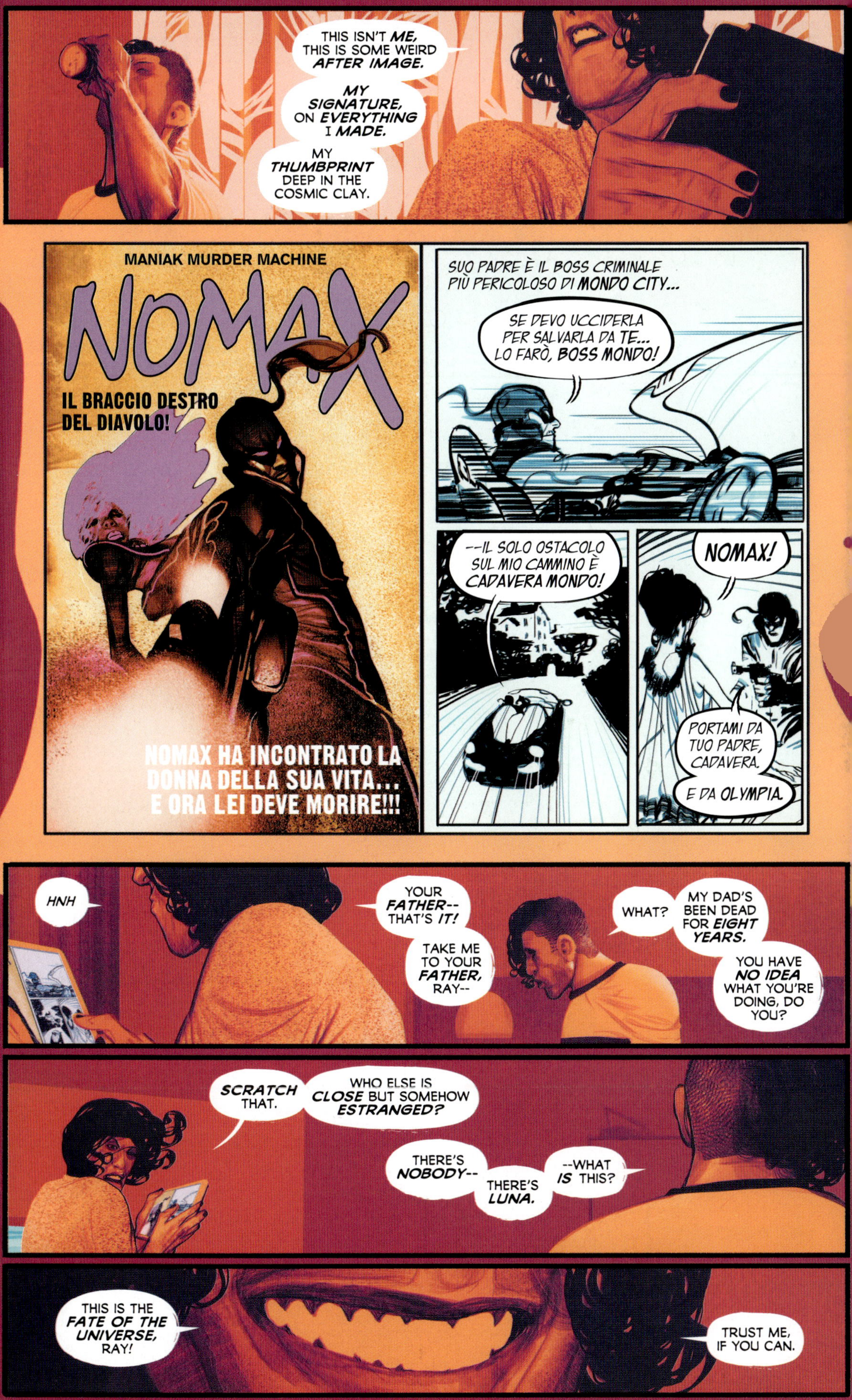
THIS ISN'T ME, THIS IS SOME WEIRD AFTER IMAGE.
MY SIGNATURE, ON EVERYTHING I MADE.
MY THUMBPRINT DEEP IN THE COSMIC CLAY.
MANIAK MURDER MACHINE
NOMAX
IL BRACCIO DESTRO DEL DIAVOLO!
NOMAX HA INCONTRATO LA DONNA DELLA SUA VITA... E ORA LEI DEVE MORIRE!!!
SUO PADRE È IL BOSS CRIMINALE PIÙ PERICOLOSO DI MONDO CITY...
SE DEVO UCCIDERLA PER SALVARLA DA TE... LO FARÒ, BOSS MONDO!
--IL SOLO OSTACOLO SUL MIO CAMMINO È CADAVERA MONDO!
NOMAX!
PORTAMI DA TUO PADRE, CADAVERA.
E DA OLYMPIA.
HNH
YOUR FATHER-- THAT'S IT!
TAKE ME TO YOUR FATHER, RAY--
WHAT?
MY DAD'S BEEN DEAD FOR EIGHT YEARS.
YOU HAVE NO IDEA WHAT YOU'RE DOING, DO YOU?
SCRATCH THAT.
WHO ELSE IS CLOSE BUT SOMEHOW ESTRANGED?
THERE'S NOBODY--
THERE'S LUNA.
--WHAT IS THIS?
THIS IS THE FATE OF THE UNIVERSE, RAY!
TRUST ME, IF YOU CAN.

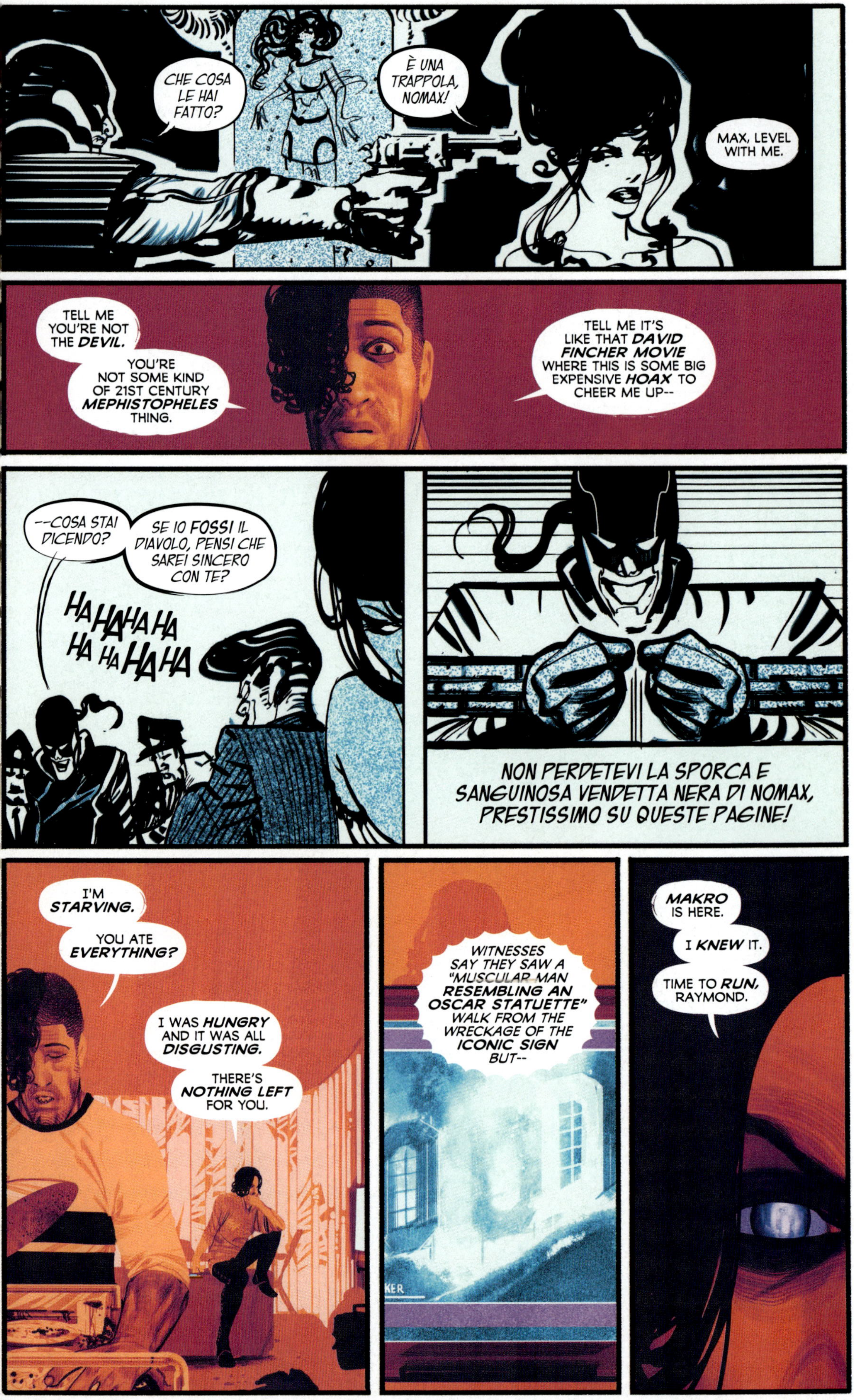

CHE COSA LE HAI FATTO?
È UNA TRAPPOLA, NOMAX!
MAX, LEVEL WITH ME.
TELL ME YOU'RE NOT THE DEVIL.
YOU'RE NOT SOME KIND OF 21ST CENTURY MEPHISTOPHELES THING.
TELL ME IT'S LIKE THAT DAVID FINCHER MOVIE WHERE THIS IS SOME BIG EXPENSIVE HOAX TO CHEER ME UP--
--COSA STAI DICENDO?
SE IO FOSSI IL DIAVOLO, PENSI CHE SAREI SINCERO CON TE?
HA HA HA HA HA
HA HA HA HA
NON PERDETEVI LA SPORCA E SANGUINOSA VENDETTA NERA DI NOMAX, PRESTISSIMO SU QUESTE PAGINE!
I'M STARVING.
YOU ATE EVERYTHING?
I WAS HUNGRY AND IT WAS ALL DISGUSTING.
THERE'S NOTHING LEFT FOR YOU.
WITNESSES SAY THEY SAW A "MUSCULAR MAN RESEMBLING AN OSCAR STATUETTE" WALK FROM THE WRECKAGE OF THE ICONIC SIGN BUT--
MAKRO IS HERE.
I KNEW IT.
TIME TO RUN, RAYMOND.

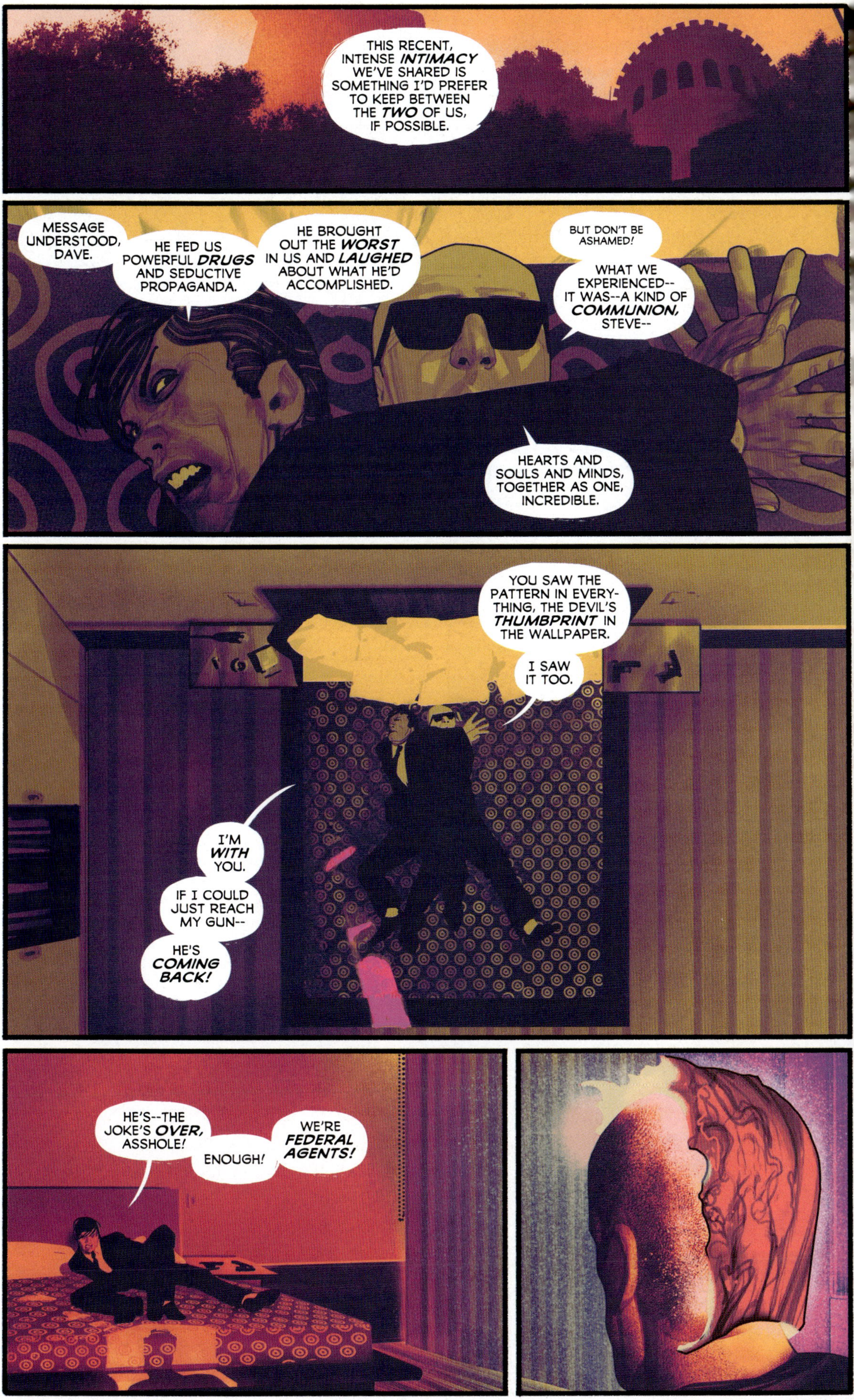

THIS RECENT, INTENSE *INTIMACY* WE'VE SHARED IS SOMETHING I'D PREFER TO KEEP BETWEEN THE *TWO* OF US, IF POSSIBLE.
MESSAGE UNDERSTOOD, DAVE.
HE FED US POWERFUL *DRUGS* AND SEDUCTIVE PROPAGANDA.
HE BROUGHT OUT THE *WORST* IN US AND *LAUGHED* ABOUT WHAT HE'D ACCOMPLISHED.
BUT DON'T BE ASHAMED!
WHAT WE EXPERIENCED-- IT WAS--A KIND OF *COMMUNION,* STEVE--
HEARTS AND SOULS AND MINDS, TOGETHER AS ONE, INCREDIBLE.
YOU SAW THE PATTERN IN EVERY-THING, THE DEVIL'S *THUMBPRINT* IN THE WALLPAPER.
I SAW IT TOO.
I'M *WITH* YOU.
IF I COULD JUST REACH MY GUN--
HE'S *COMING BACK!*
HE'S--THE JOKE'S *OVER,* ASSHOLE!
ENOUGH!
WE'RE *FEDERAL AGENTS!*

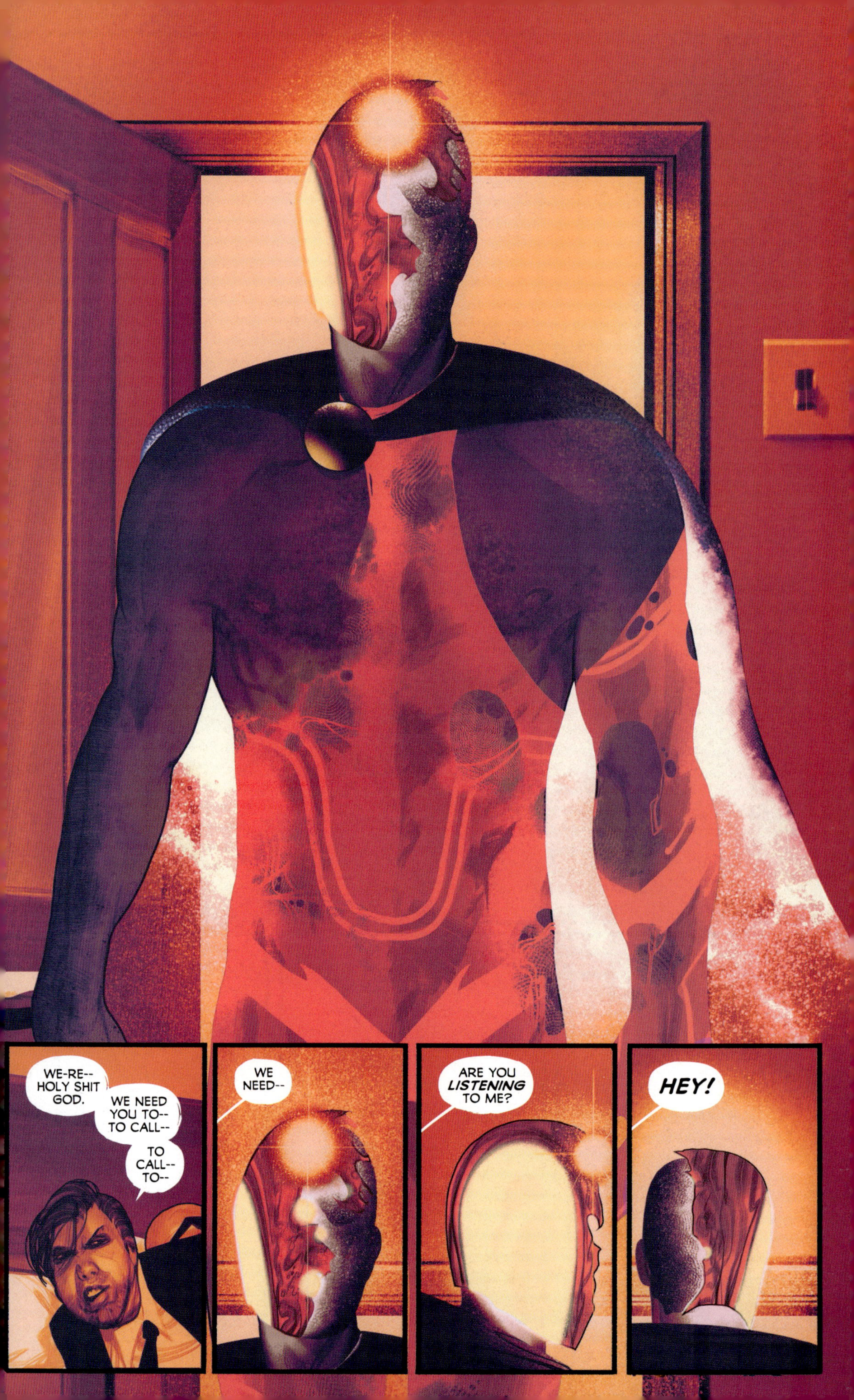
WE-RE-- HOLY SHIT GOD.
WE NEED YOU TO-- TO CALL--
TO CALL-- TO--
WE NEED--
ARE YOU *LISTENING* TO ME?
HEY!

THIS WORLD.
THIS MORTAL *SEWER.*
Luna Kozma

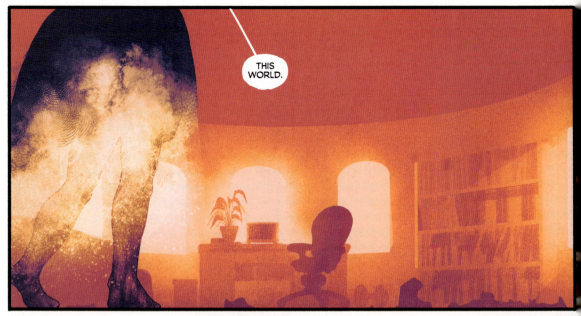

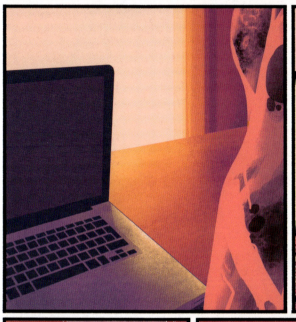

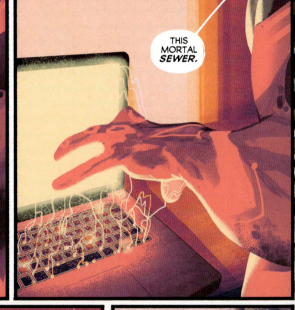

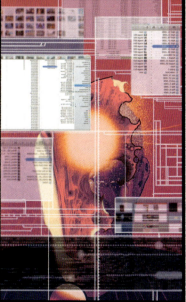

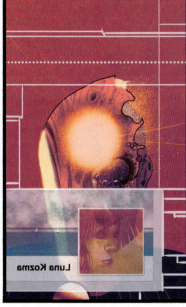

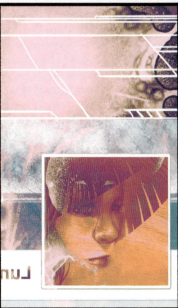

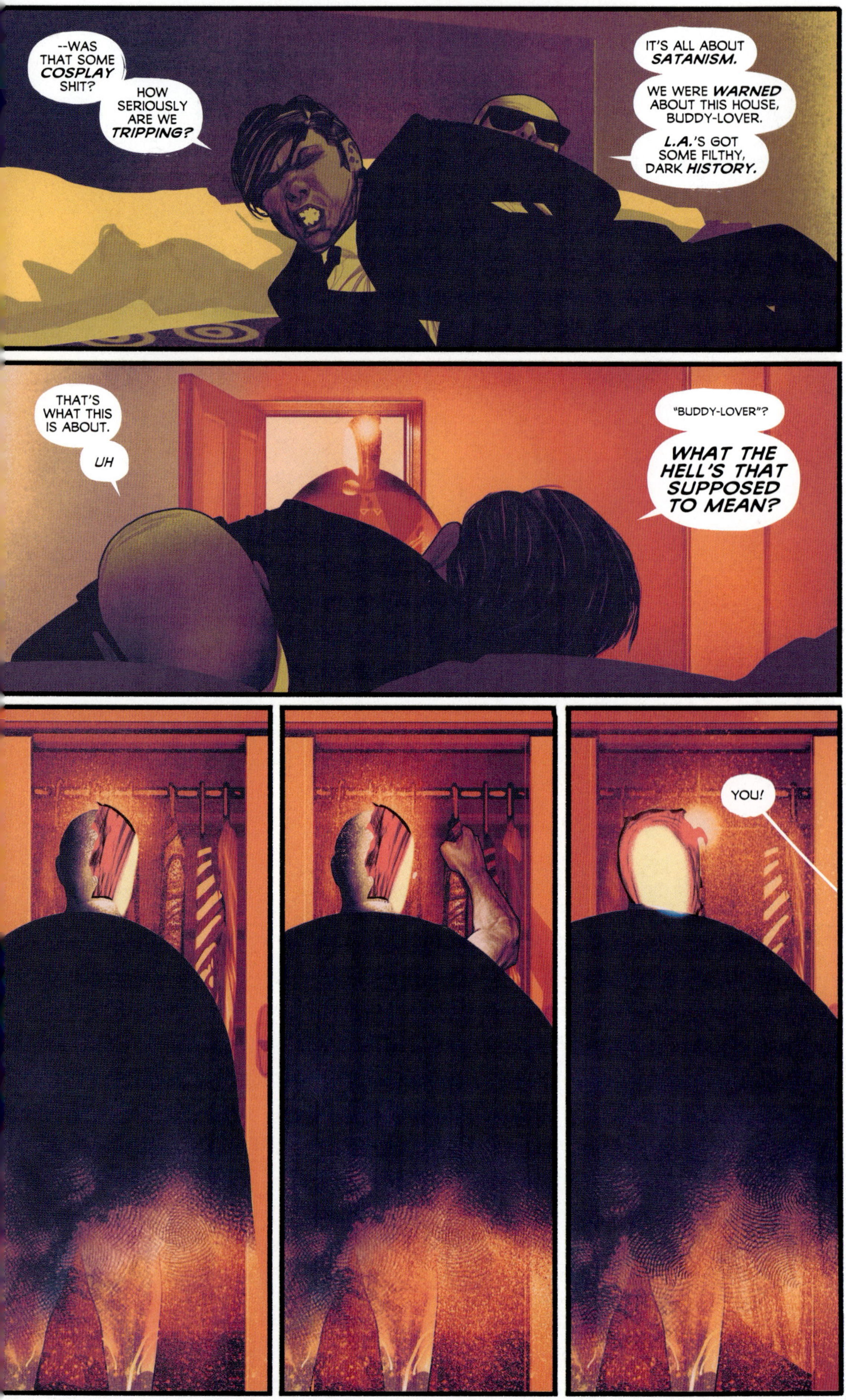
--WAS THAT SOME COSPLAY SHIT?
HOW SERIOUSLY ARE WE TRIPPING?
IT'S ALL ABOUT SATANISM.
WE WERE WARNED ABOUT THIS HOUSE, BUDDY-LOVER.
L.A.'S GOT SOME FILTHY, DARK HISTORY.
THAT'S WHAT THIS IS ABOUT.
UH
"BUDDY-LOVER"?
WHAT THE HELL'S THAT SUPPOSED TO MEAN?
YOU!

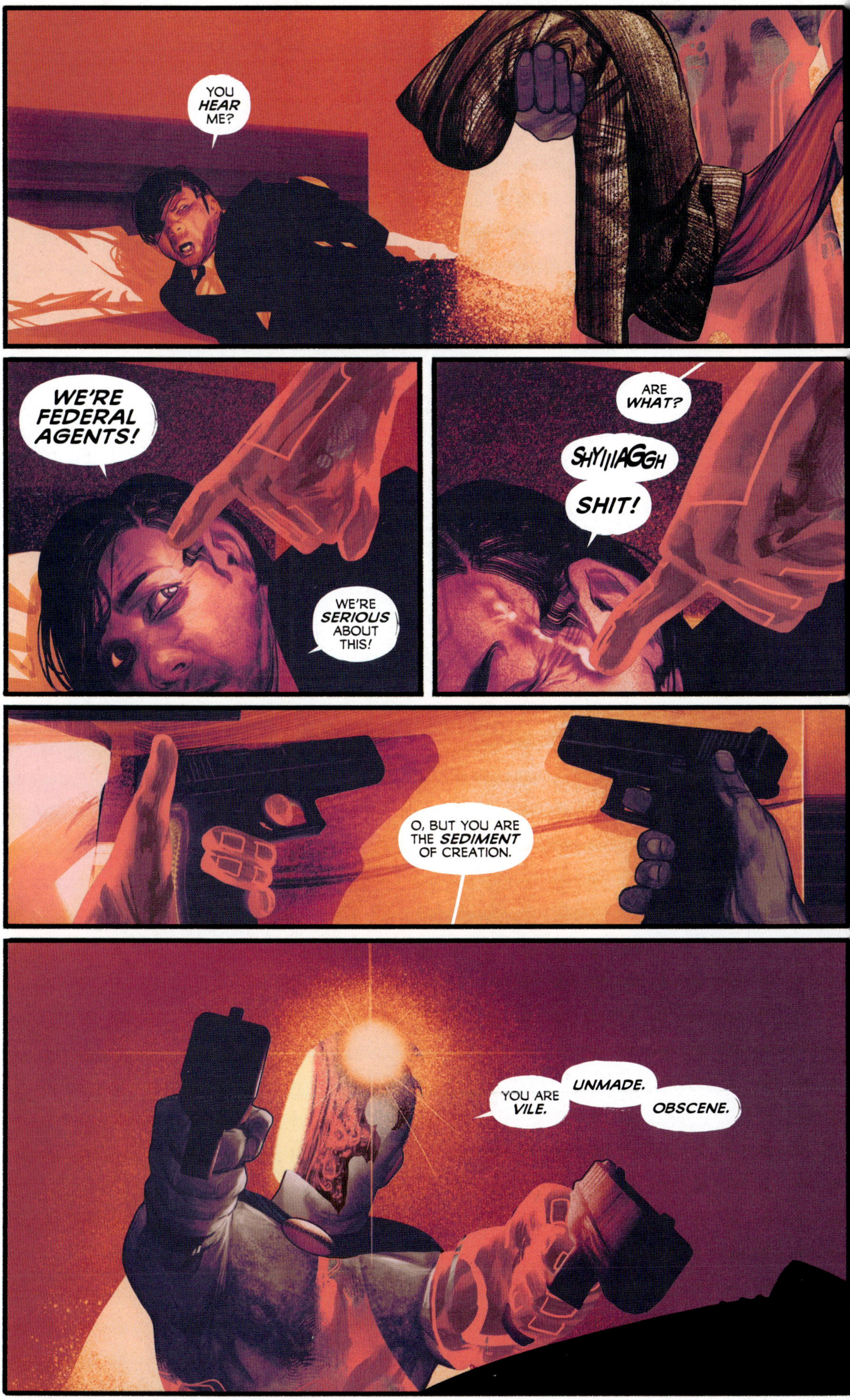

YOU HEAR ME?
WE'RE FEDERAL AGENTS!
WE'RE SERIOUS ABOUT THIS!
ARE WHAT?
SHYIIIAGGH
SHIT!
O, BUT YOU ARE THE SEDIMENT OF CREATION.
YOU ARE VILE.
UNMADE.
OBSCENE.

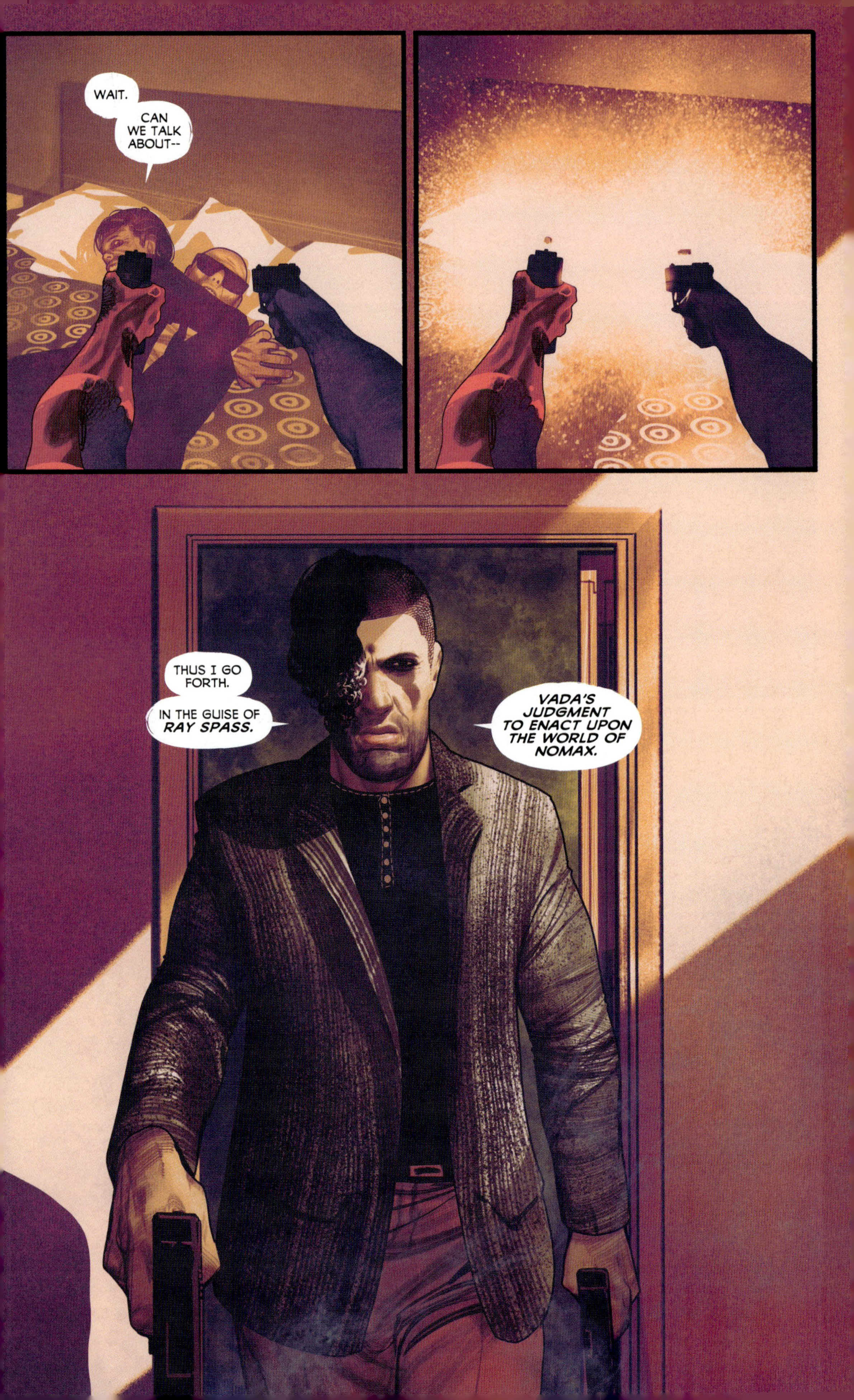
WAIT.
CAN WE TALK ABOUT--
THUS I GO FORTH.
IN THE GUISE OF RAY SPASS.
VADA'S JUDGMENT TO ENACT UPON THE WORLD OF NOMAX.

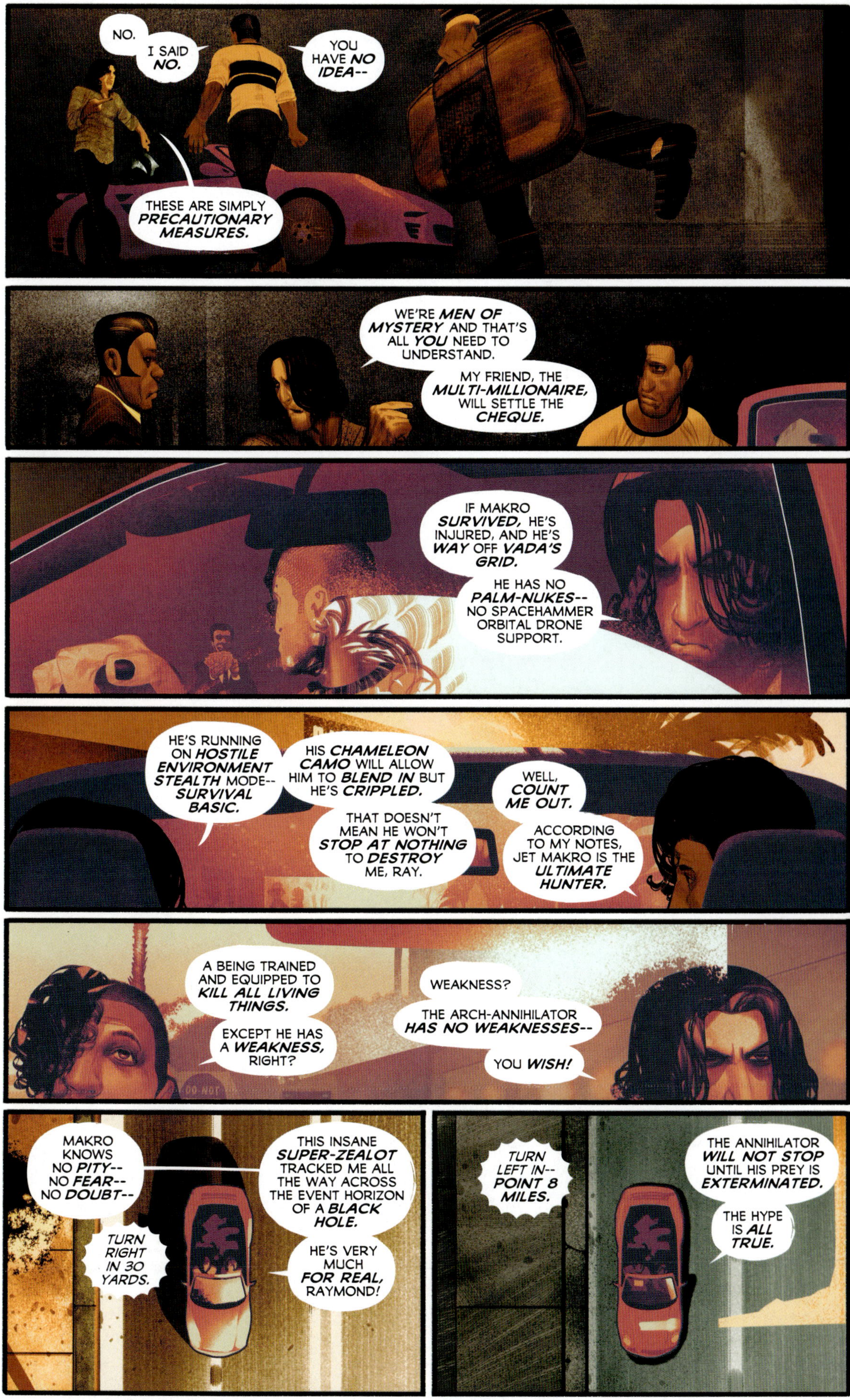
NO. I SAID NO.
YOU HAVE NO IDEA--
THESE ARE SIMPLY PRECAUTIONARY MEASURES.
WE'RE MEN OF MYSTERY AND THAT'S ALL YOU NEED TO UNDERSTAND.
MY FRIEND, THE MULTI-MILLIONAIRE, WILL SETTLE THE CHEQUE.
IF MAKRO SURVIVED, HE'S INJURED, AND HE'S WAY OFF VADA'S GRID.
HE HAS NO PALM-NUKES-- NO SPACEHAMMER ORBITAL DRONE SUPPORT.
HE'S RUNNING ON HOSTILE ENVIRONMENT STEALTH MODE-- SURVIVAL BASIC.
HIS CHAMELEON CAMO WILL ALLOW HIM TO BLEND IN BUT HE'S CRIPPLED.
THAT DOESN'T MEAN HE WON'T STOP AT NOTHING TO DESTROY ME, RAY.
WELL, COUNT ME OUT.
ACCORDING TO MY NOTES, JET MAKRO IS THE ULTIMATE HUNTER.
A BEING TRAINED AND EQUIPPED TO KILL ALL LIVING THINGS.
EXCEPT HE HAS A WEAKNESS, RIGHT?
WEAKNESS?
THE ARCH-ANNIHILATOR HAS NO WEAKNESSES--
YOU WISH!
MAKRO KNOWS NO PITY-- NO FEAR-- NO DOUBT--
THIS INSANE SUPER-ZEALOT TRACKED ME ALL THE WAY ACROSS THE EVENT HORIZON OF A BLACK HOLE.
TURN RIGHT IN 30 YARDS.
HE'S VERY MUCH FOR REAL, RAYMOND!
TURN LEFT IN-- POINT 8 MILES.
THE ANNIHILATOR WILL NOT STOP UNTIL HIS PREY IS EXTERMINATED.
THE HYPE IS ALL TRUE.

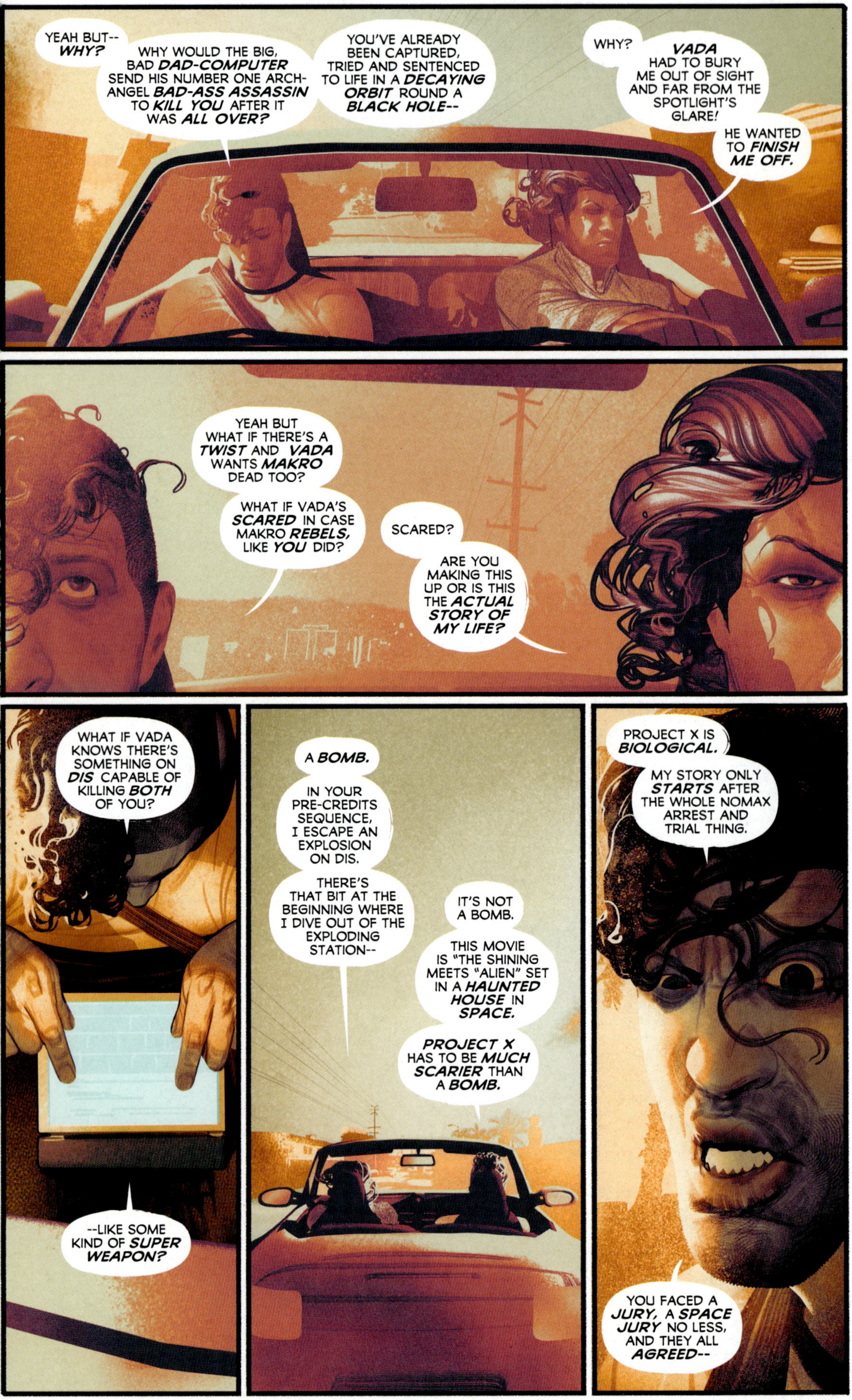
YEAH BUT-- WHY?
WHY WOULD THE BIG, BAD DAD-COMPUTER SEND HIS NUMBER ONE ARCH-ANGEL BAD-ASS ASSASSIN TO KILL YOU AFTER IT WAS ALL OVER?
YOU'VE ALREADY BEEN CAPTURED, TRIED AND SENTENCED TO LIFE IN A DECAYING ORBIT ROUND A BLACK HOLE--
WHY?
VADA HAD TO BURY ME OUT OF SIGHT AND FAR FROM THE SPOTLIGHT'S GLARE!
HE WANTED TO FINISH ME OFF.
YEAH BUT WHAT IF THERE'S A TWIST AND VADA WANTS MAKRO DEAD TOO?
WHAT IF VADA'S SCARED IN CASE MAKRO REBELS, LIKE YOU DID?
SCARED?
ARE YOU MAKING THIS UP OR IS THIS THE ACTUAL STORY OF MY LIFE?
WHAT IF VADA KNOWS THERE'S SOMETHING ON DIS CAPABLE OF KILLING BOTH OF YOU?
--LIKE SOME KIND OF SUPER WEAPON?
A BOMB.
IN YOUR PRE-CREDITS SEQUENCE, I ESCAPE AN EXPLOSION ON DIS.
THERE'S THAT BIT AT THE BEGINNING WHERE I DIVE OUT OF THE EXPLODING STATION--
IT'S NOT A BOMB.
THIS MOVIE IS "THE SHINING MEETS "ALIEN" SET IN A HAUNTED HOUSE IN SPACE.
PROJECT X HAS TO BE MUCH SCARIER THAN A BOMB.
PROJECT X IS BIOLOGICAL.
MY STORY ONLY STARTS AFTER THE WHOLE NOMAX ARREST AND TRIAL THING.
YOU FACED A JURY, A SPACE JURY NO LESS, AND THEY ALL AGREED--

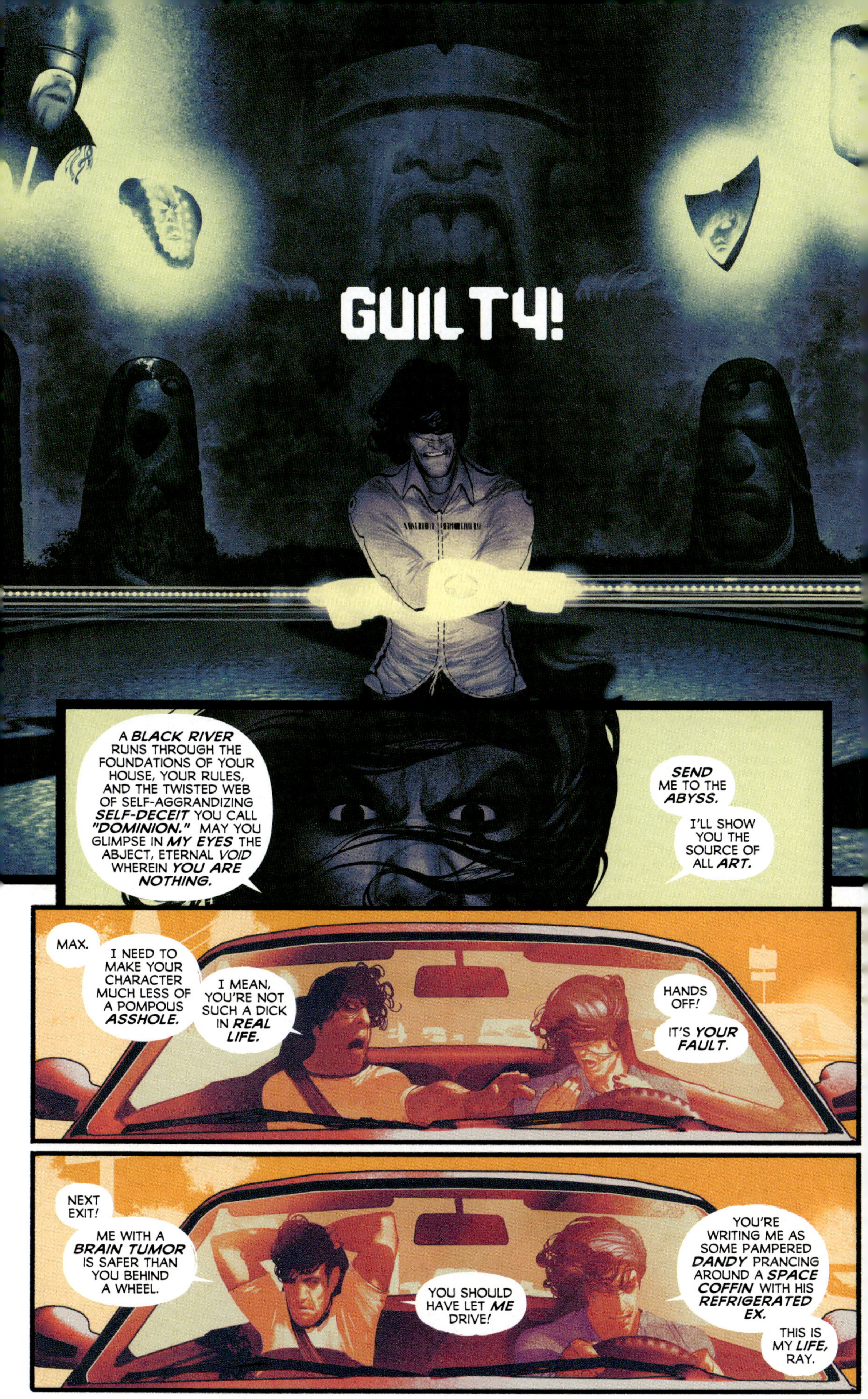
GUILTY!
A BLACK RIVER RUNS THROUGH THE FOUNDATIONS OF YOUR HOUSE, YOUR RULES, AND THE TWISTED WEB OF SELF-AGGRANDIZING SELF-DECEIT YOU CALL "DOMINION." MAY YOU GLIMPSE IN MY EYES THE ABJECT, ETERNAL VOID WHEREIN YOU ARE NOTHING.
SEND ME TO THE ABYSS.
I'LL SHOW YOU THE SOURCE OF ALL ART.
MAX.
I NEED TO MAKE YOUR CHARACTER MUCH LESS OF A POMPOUS ASSHOLE.
I MEAN, YOU'RE NOT SUCH A DICK IN REAL LIFE.
HANDS OFF!
IT'S YOUR FAULT.
NEXT EXIT!
ME WITH A BRAIN TUMOR IS SAFER THAN YOU BEHIND A WHEEL.
YOU SHOULD HAVE LET ME DRIVE!
YOU'RE WRITING ME AS SOME PAMPERED DANDY PRANCING AROUND A SPACE COFFIN WITH HIS REFRIGERATED EX.
THIS IS MY LIFE, RAY.

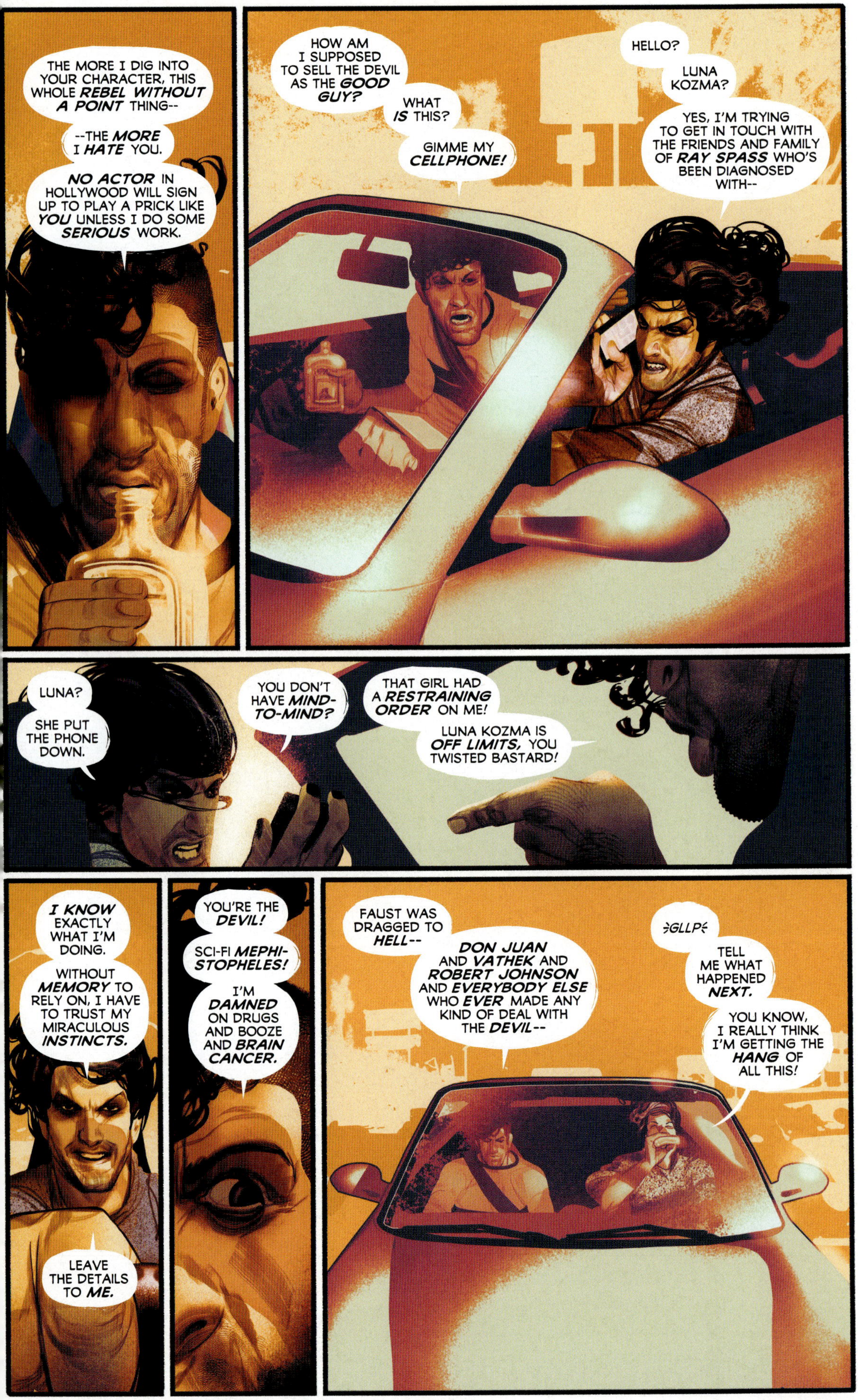
THE MORE I DIG INTO YOUR CHARACTER, THIS WHOLE REBEL WITHOUT A POINT THING--
--THE MORE I HATE YOU.
NO ACTOR IN HOLLYWOOD WILL SIGN UP TO PLAY A PRICK LIKE YOU UNLESS I DO SOME SERIOUS WORK.
HOW AM I SUPPOSED TO SELL THE DEVIL AS THE GOOD GUY?
WHAT IS THIS?
GIMME MY CELLPHONE!
HELLO?
LUNA KOZMA?
YES, I'M TRYING TO GET IN TOUCH WITH THE FRIENDS AND FAMILY OF RAY SPASS WHO'S BEEN DIAGNOSED WITH--
LUNA?
SHE PUT THE PHONE DOWN.
YOU DON'T HAVE MIND-TO-MIND?
THAT GIRL HAD A RESTRAINING ORDER ON ME!
LUNA KOZMA IS OFF LIMITS, YOU TWISTED BASTARD!
I KNOW EXACTLY WHAT I'M DOING.
WITHOUT MEMORY TO RELY ON, I HAVE TO TRUST MY MIRACULOUS INSTINCTS.
LEAVE THE DETAILS TO ME.
YOU'RE THE DEVIL!
SCI-FI MEPHISTOPHELES!
I'M DAMNED ON DRUGS AND BOOZE AND BRAIN CANCER.
FAUST WAS DRAGGED TO HELL--
DON JUAN AND VATHEK AND ROBERT JOHNSON AND EVERYBODY ELSE WHO EVER MADE ANY KIND OF DEAL WITH THE DEVIL--
GLLP
TELL ME WHAT HAPPENED NEXT.
YOU KNOW, I REALLY THINK I'M GETTING THE HANG OF ALL THIS!

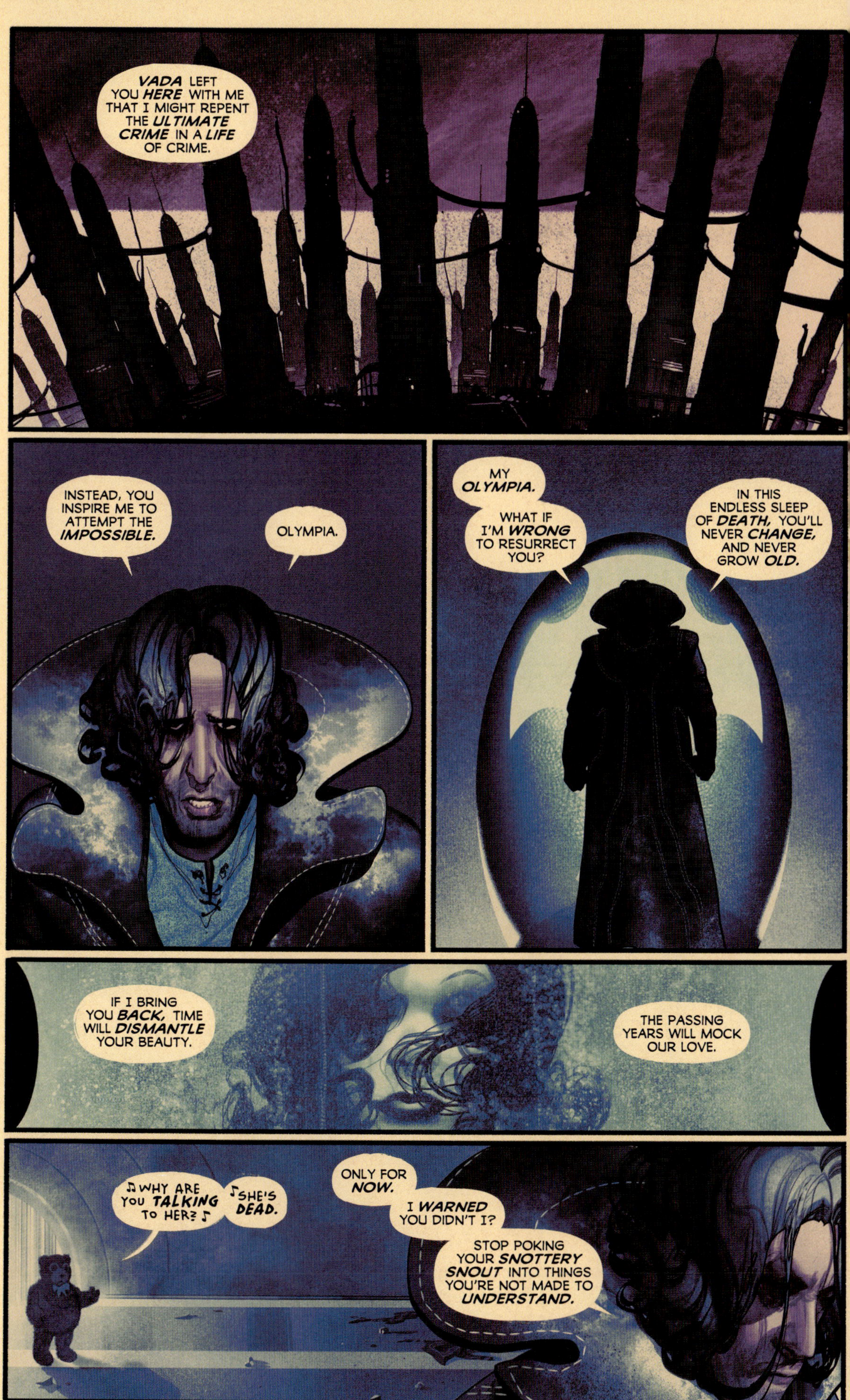
VADA LEFT YOU HERE WITH ME THAT I MIGHT REPENT THE ULTIMATE CRIME IN A LIFE OF CRIME.
INSTEAD, YOU INSPIRE ME TO ATTEMPT THE IMPOSSIBLE.
OLYMPIA.
MY OLYMPIA.
WHAT IF I'M WRONG TO RESURRECT YOU?
IN THIS ENDLESS SLEEP OF DEATH, YOU'LL NEVER CHANGE, AND NEVER GROW OLD.
IF I BRING YOU BACK, TIME WILL DISMANTLE YOUR BEAUTY.
THE PASSING YEARS WILL MOCK OUR LOVE.
♫WHY ARE YOU TALKING TO HER? ♫
♫SHE'S DEAD.
ONLY FOR NOW.
I WARNED YOU DIDN'T I?
STOP POKING YOUR SNOTTERY SNOUT INTO THINGS YOU'RE NOT MADE TO UNDERSTAND.

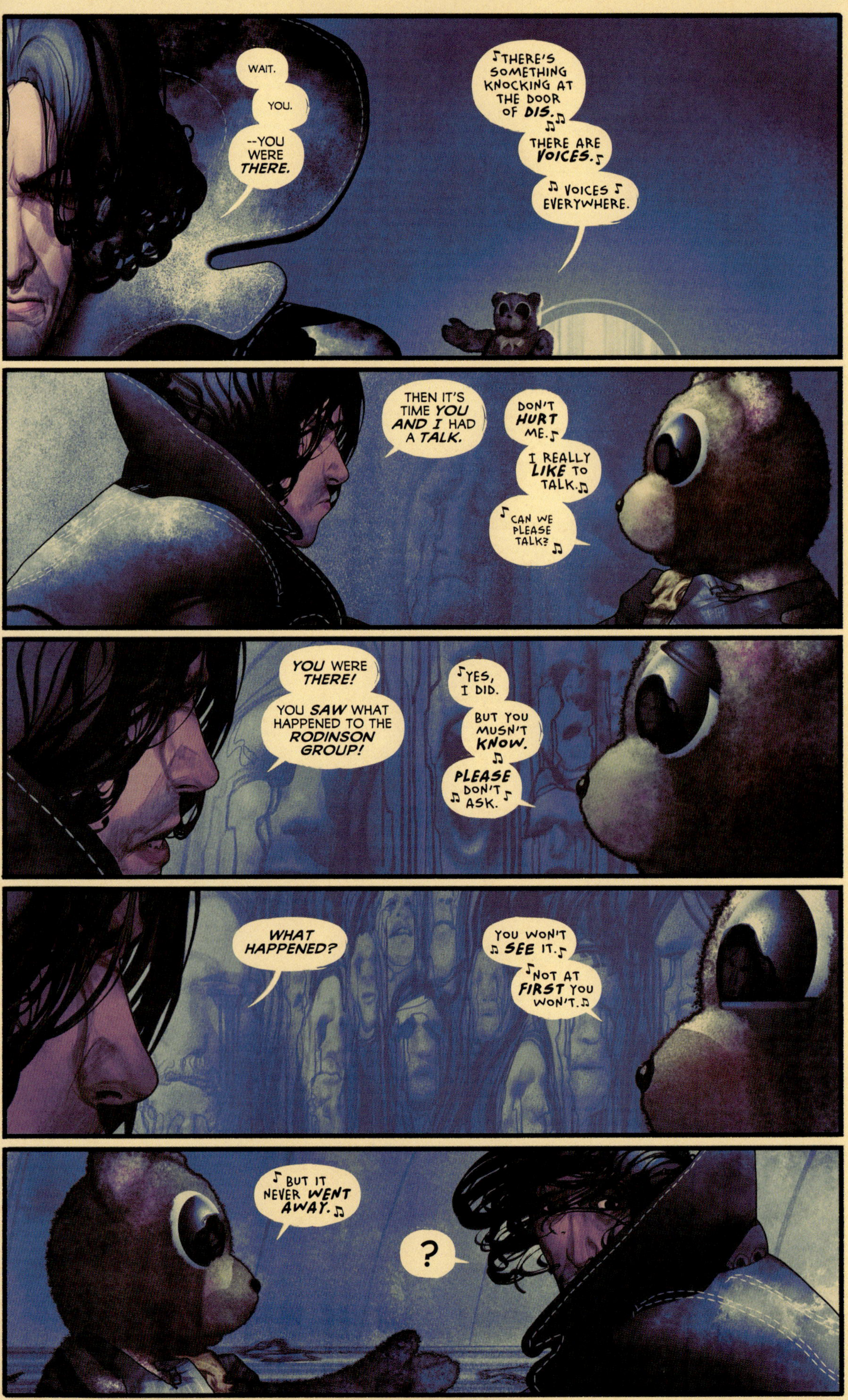
WAIT.
YOU.
--YOU WERE THERE.
♪THERE'S SOMETHING KNOCKING AT THE DOOR OF DIS.♫
♫THERE ARE VOICES.♪
♫ VOICES ♪ EVERYWHERE.
THEN IT'S TIME YOU AND I HAD A TALK.
DON'T HURT ME.♪
I REALLY LIKE TO TALK.♫
♪ CAN WE PLEASE TALK? ♫
YOU WERE THERE!
YOU SAW WHAT HAPPENED TO THE RODINSON GROUP!
♪YES, I DID.
BUT YOU MUSN'T KNOW. ♫
PLEASE DON'T ♫ ASK.♪
WHAT HAPPENED?
YOU WON'T ♫ SEE IT.♪
♪NOT AT FIRST YOU WON'T.♫
♪ BUT IT NEVER WENT AWAY.♫
?

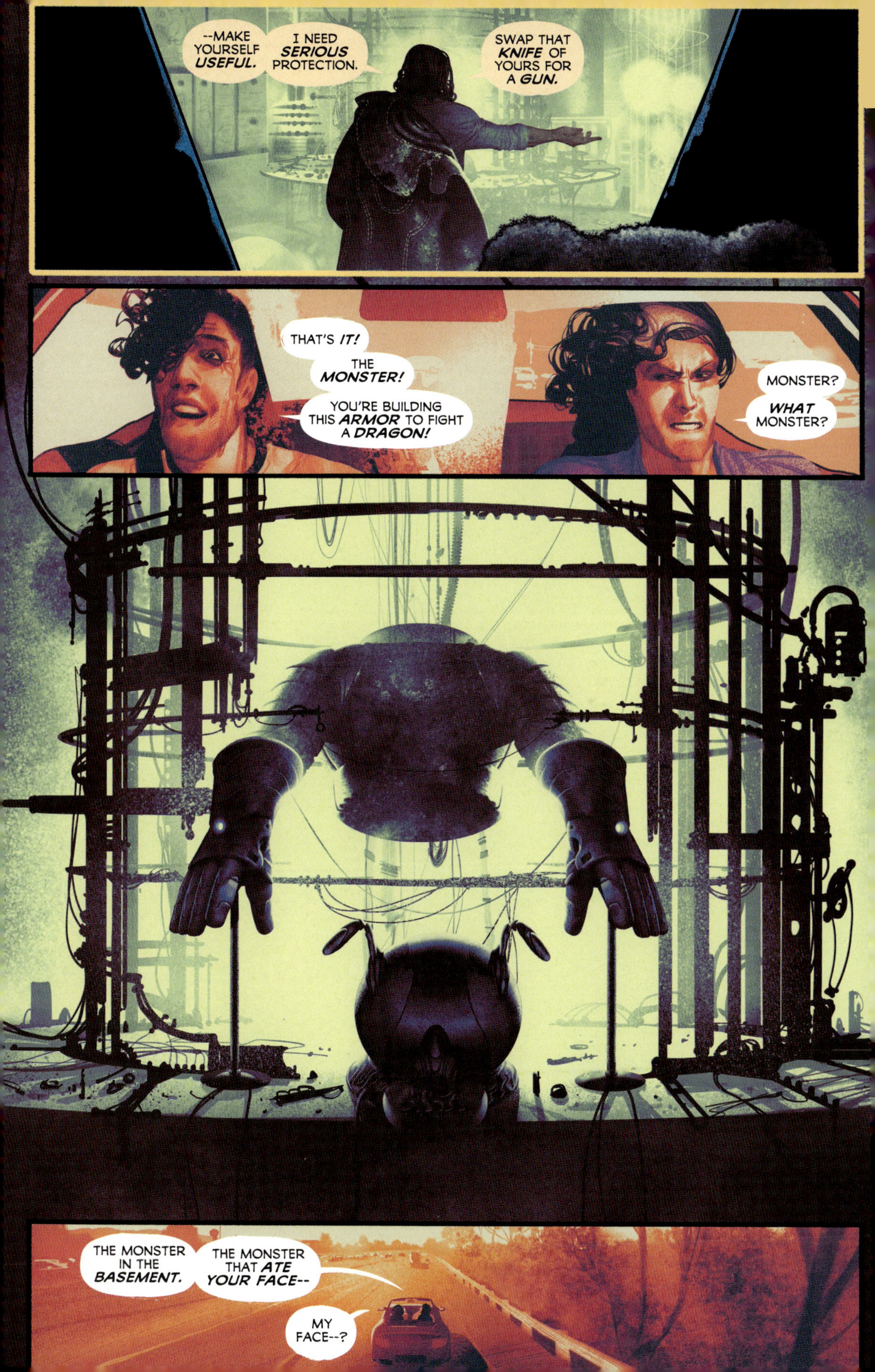
--MAKE YOURSELF USEFUL.
I NEED SERIOUS PROTECTION.
SWAP THAT KNIFE OF YOURS FOR A GUN.
THAT'S IT!
THE MONSTER!
YOU'RE BUILDING THIS ARMOR TO FIGHT A DRAGON!
MONSTER?
WHAT MONSTER?
THE MONSTER IN THE BASEMENT.
THE MONSTER THAT ATE YOUR FACE--
MY FACE--?

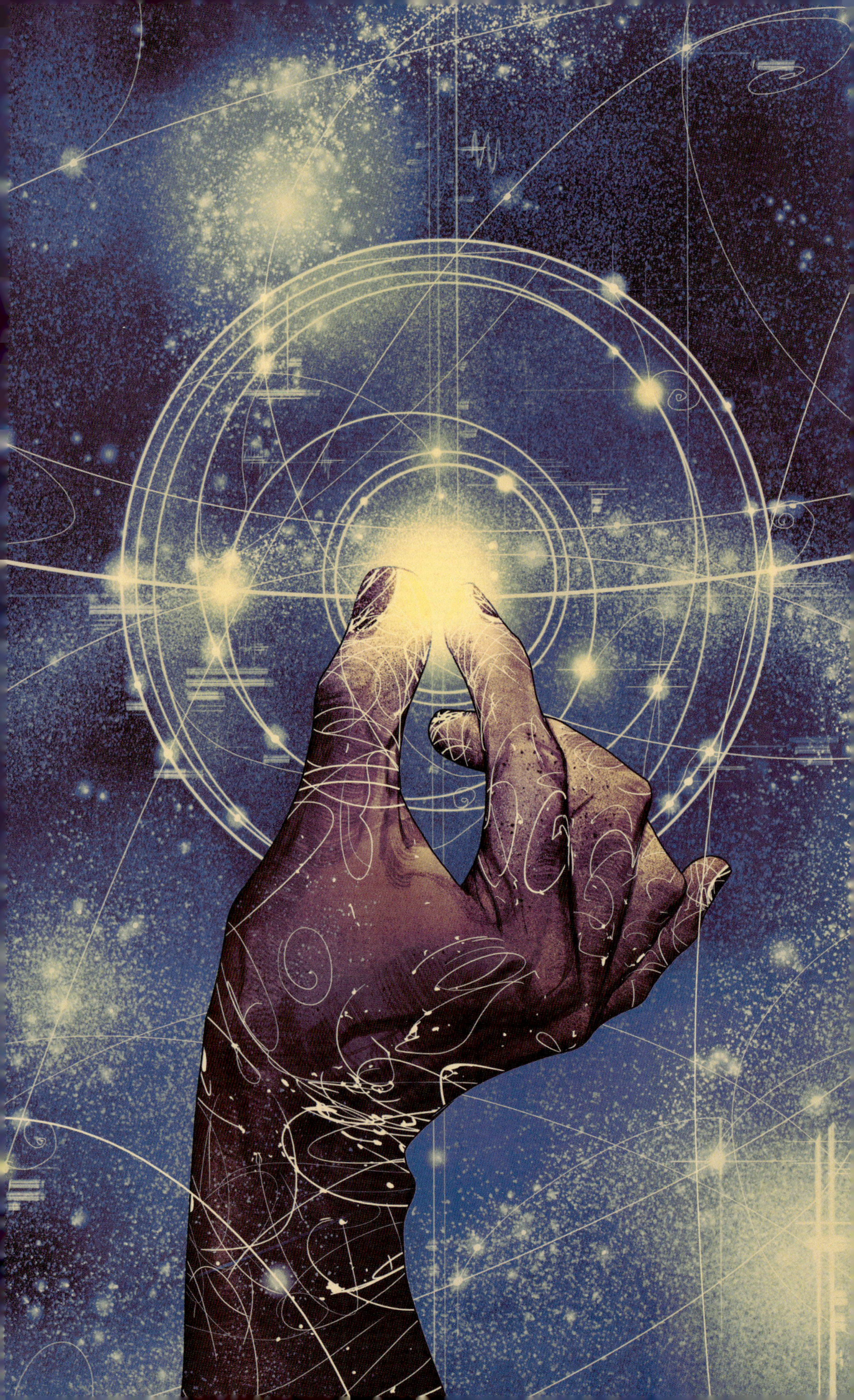

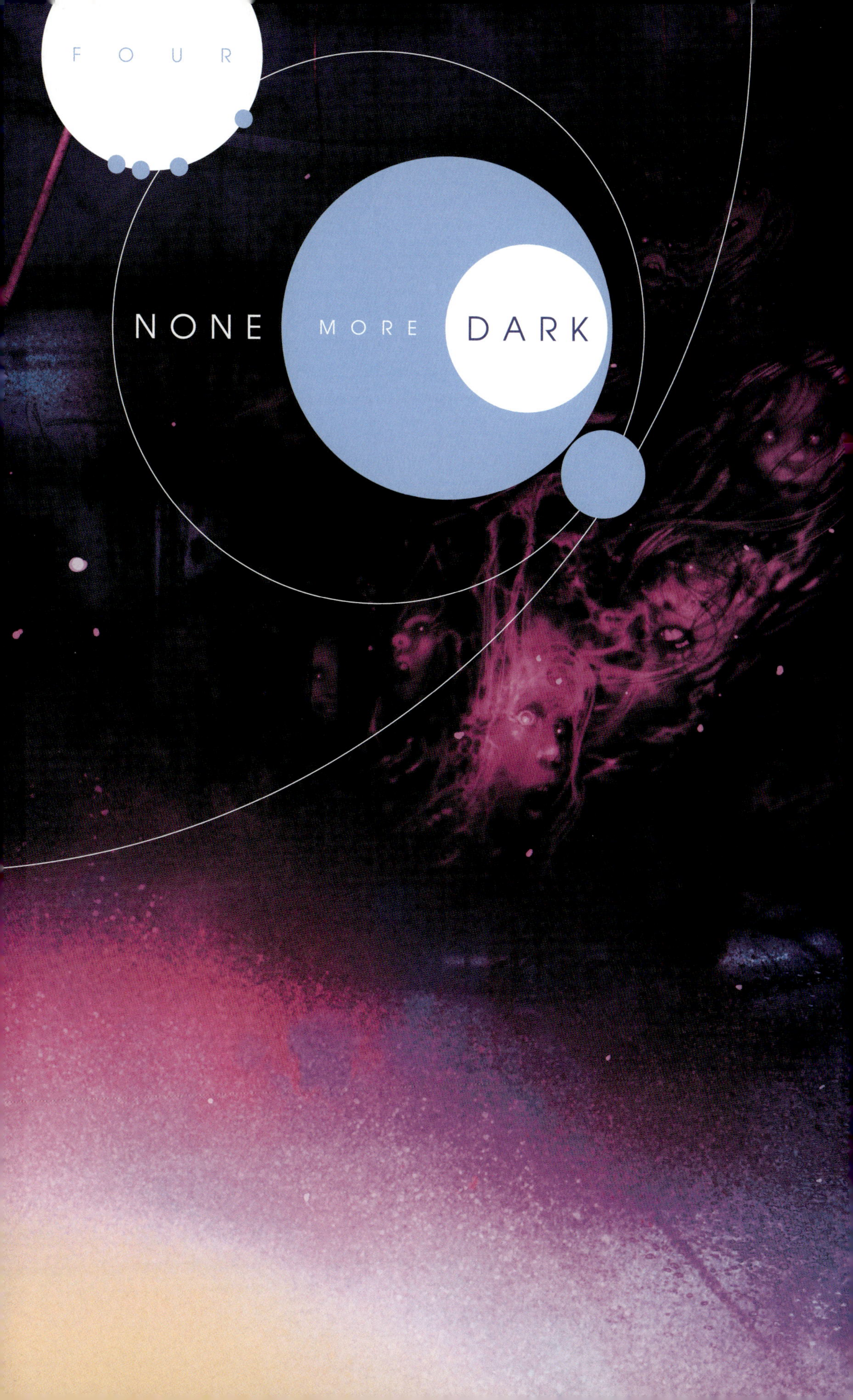
FOUR
NONE MORE DARK

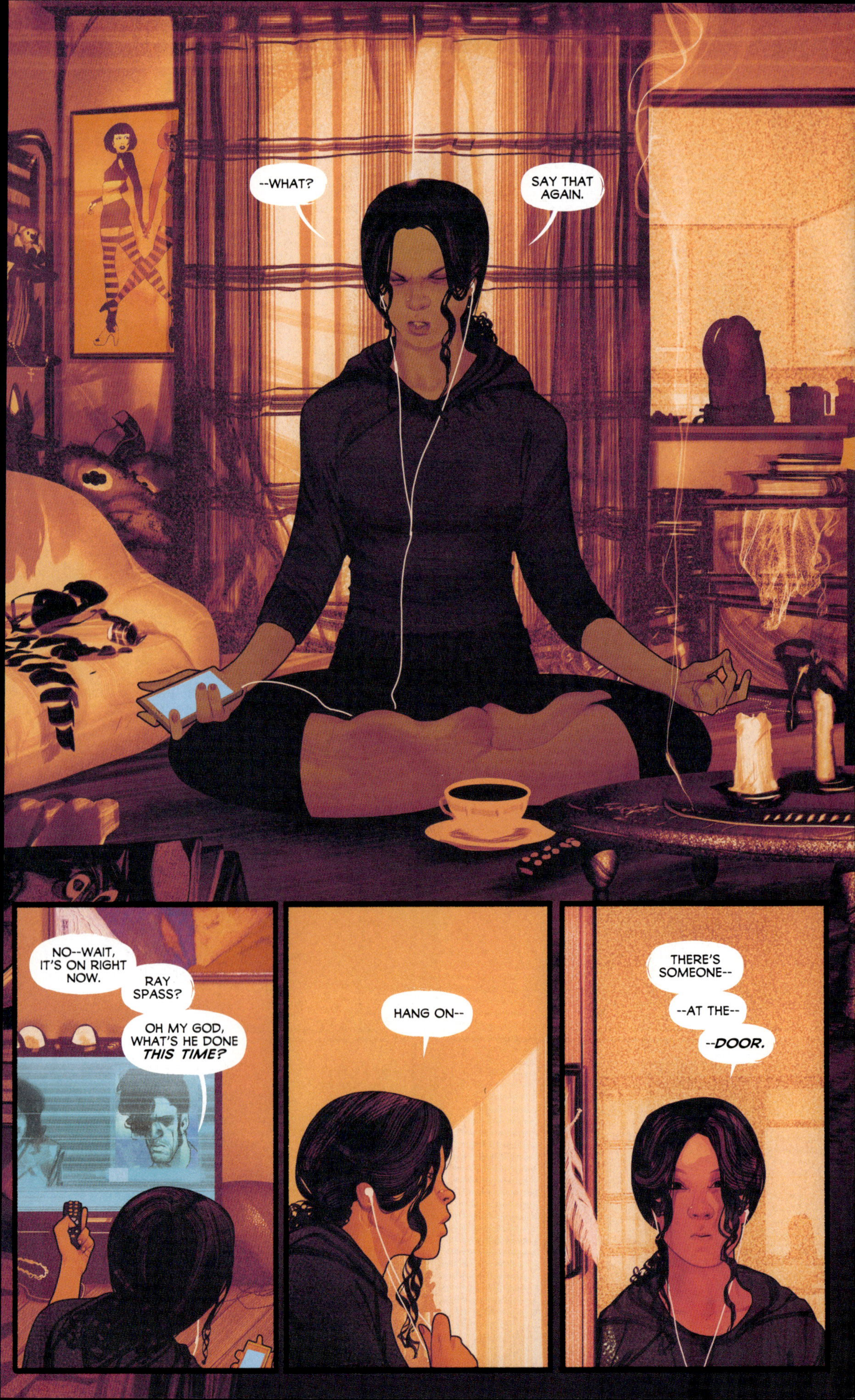
--WHAT?
SAY THAT AGAIN.
NO--WAIT, IT'S ON RIGHT NOW.
RAY SPASS?
OH MY GOD, WHAT'S HE DONE *THIS TIME?*
HANG ON--
THERE'S SOMEONE--
--AT THE--
--*DOOR.*

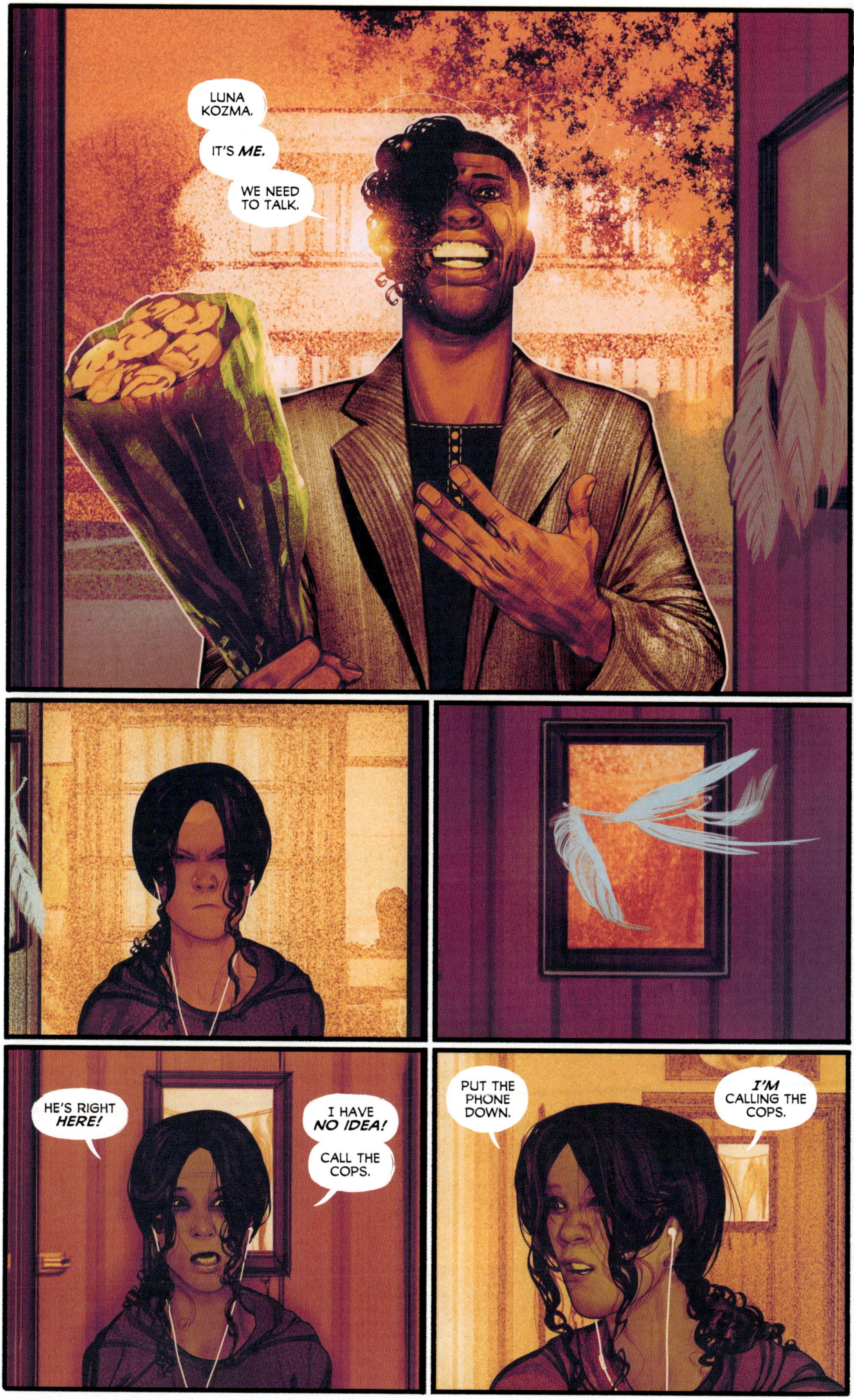
LUNA KOZMA.
IT'S *ME.*
WE NEED TO TALK.
HE'S RIGHT *HERE!*
I HAVE *NO IDEA!*
CALL THE COPS.
PUT THE PHONE DOWN.
I'M CALLING THE COPS.

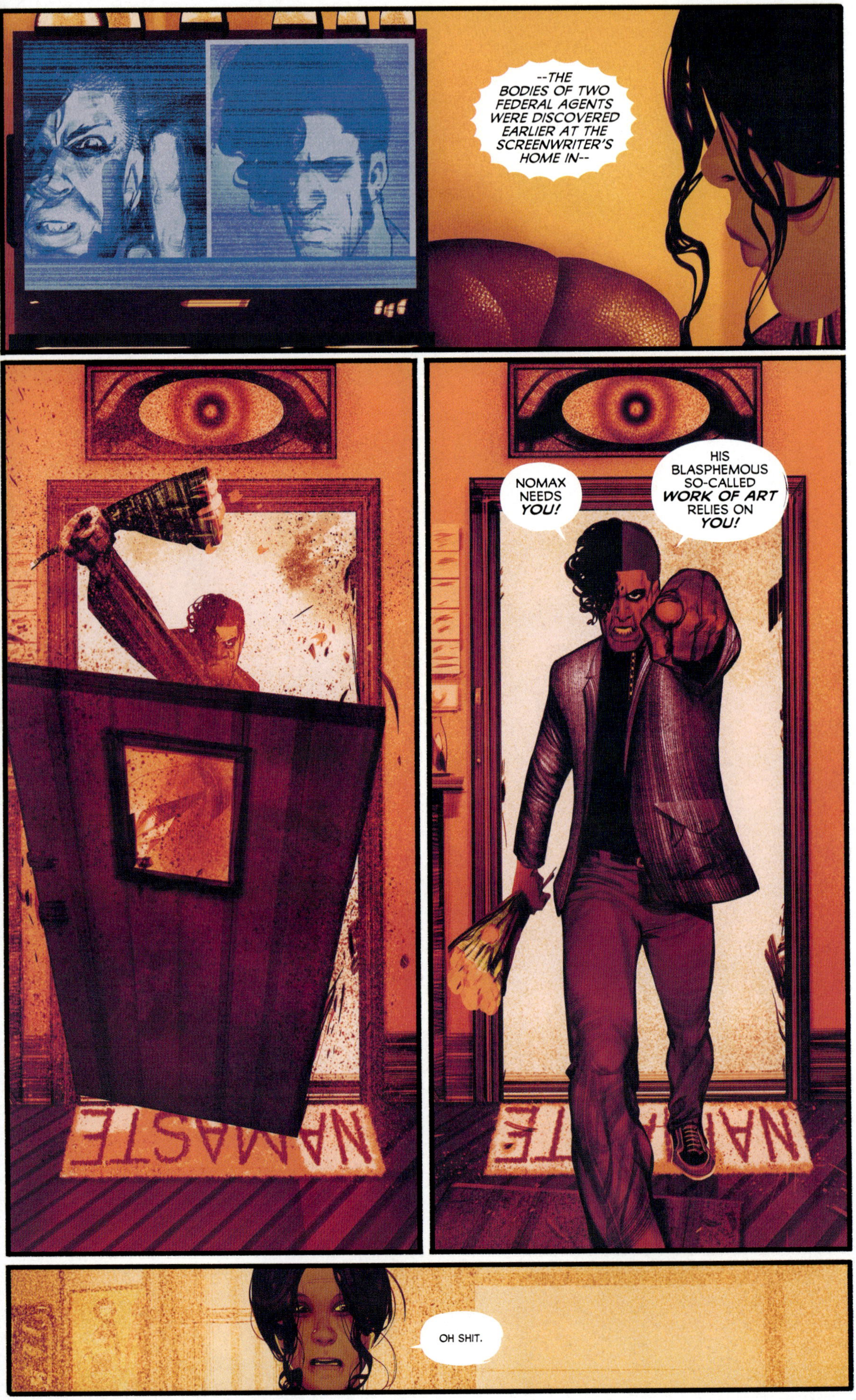
--THE BODIES OF TWO FEDERAL AGENTS WERE DISCOVERED EARLIER AT THE SCREENWRITER'S HOME IN--
NAMASTE
NOMAX NEEDS *YOU!*
HIS BLASPHEMOUS SO-CALLED ***WORK OF ART*** RELIES ON *YOU!*
NAMASTE
OH SHIT.

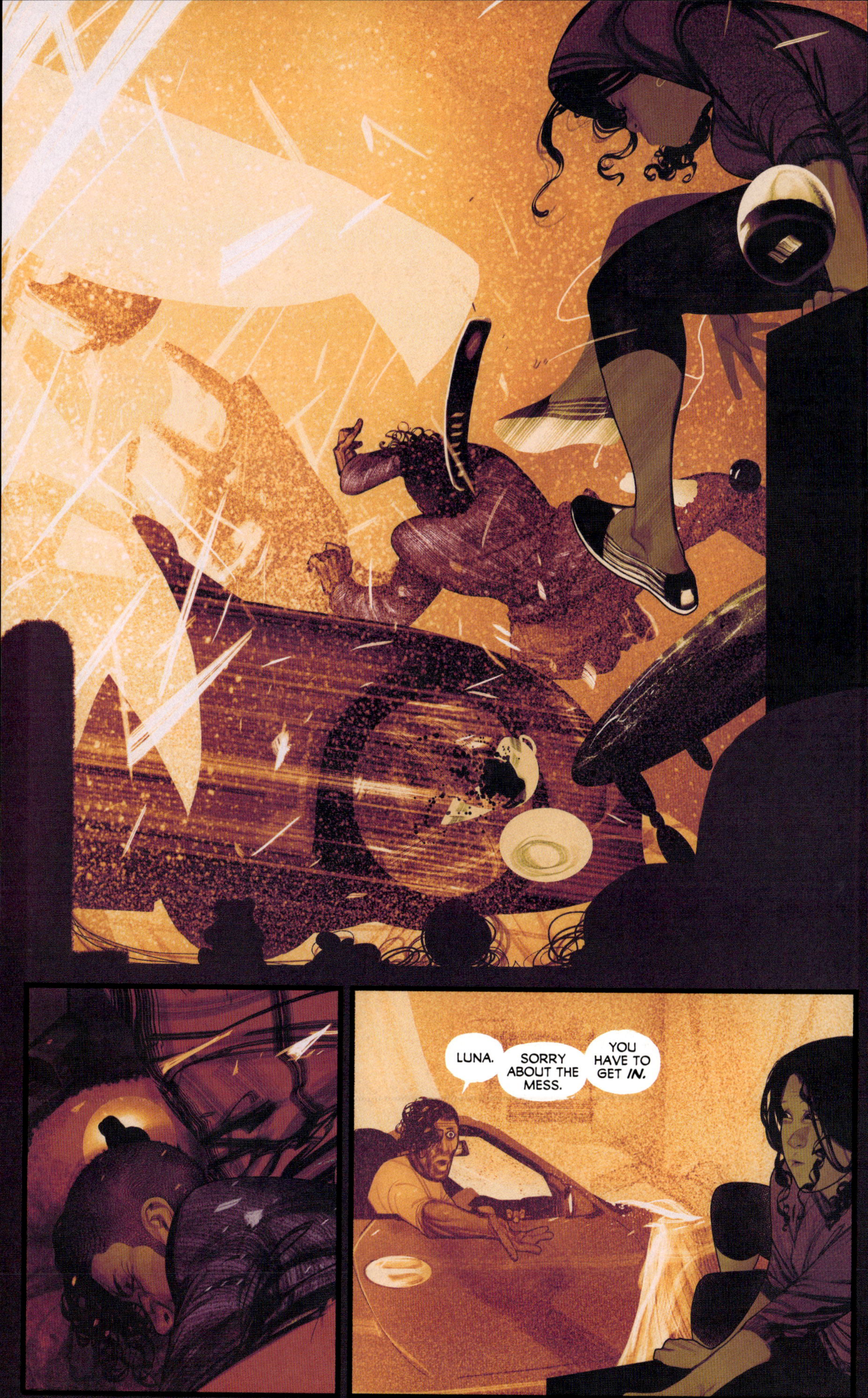
LUNA.
SORRY ABOUT THE MESS.
YOU HAVE TO GET *IN.*

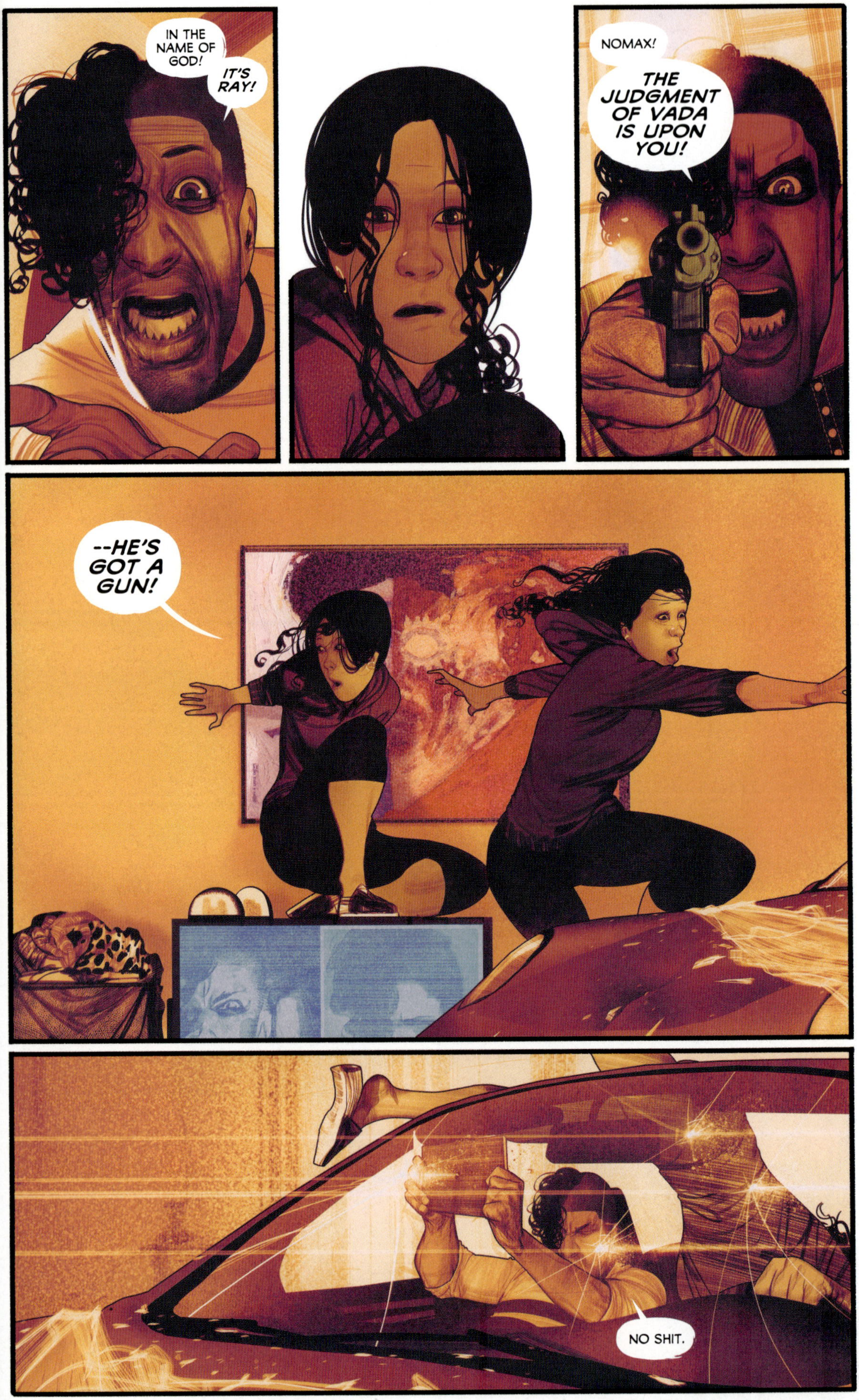
IN THE NAME OF GOD!
IT'S RAY!
NOMAX!
THE JUDGMENT OF VADA IS UPON YOU!
--HE'S GOT A GUN!
NO SHIT.

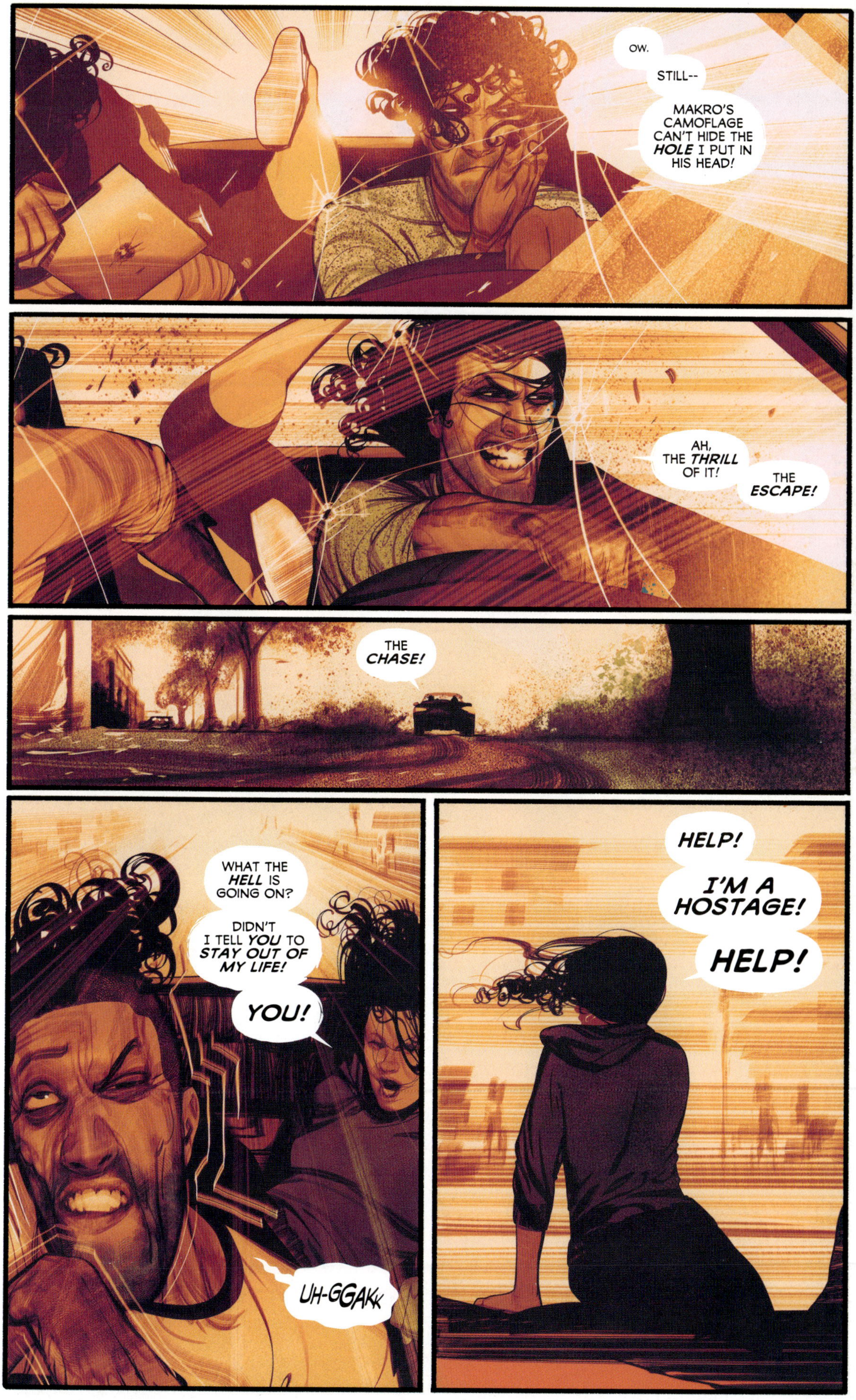
OW.
STILL--
MAKRO'S CAMOFLAGE CAN'T HIDE THE HOLE I PUT IN HIS HEAD!
AH, THE THRILL OF IT!
THE ESCAPE!
THE CHASE!
WHAT THE HELL IS GOING ON?
DIDN'T I TELL YOU TO STAY OUT OF MY LIFE!
YOU!
UH-GGAKK
HELP!
I'M A HOSTAGE!
HELP!

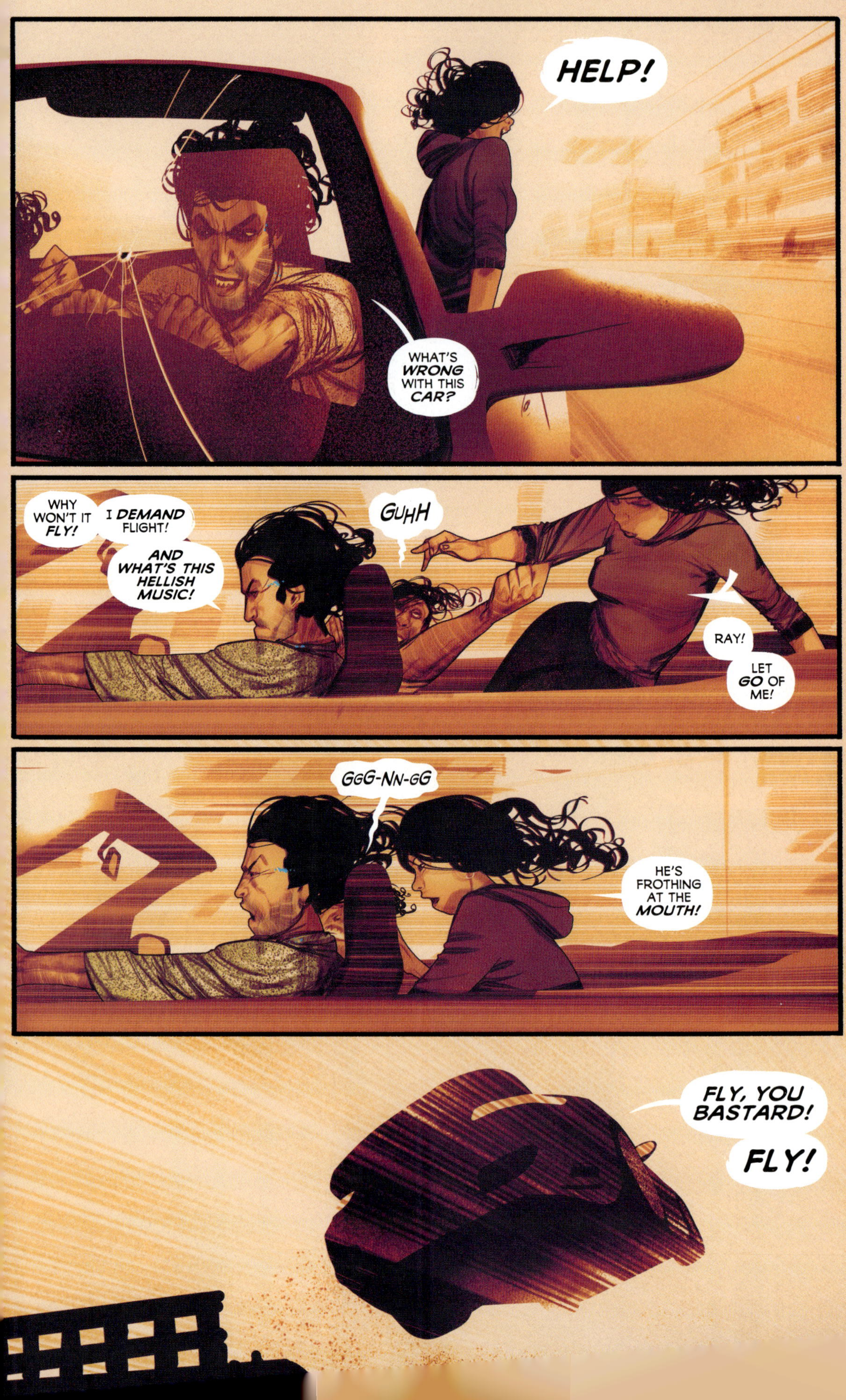
HELP!
WHAT'S WRONG WITH THIS CAR?
WHY WON'T IT FLY!
I DEMAND FLIGHT!
AND WHAT'S THIS HELLISH MUSIC!
GUHH
RAY!
LET GO OF ME!
GGG-NN-GG
HE'S FROTHING AT THE MOUTH!
FLY, YOU BASTARD!
FLY!

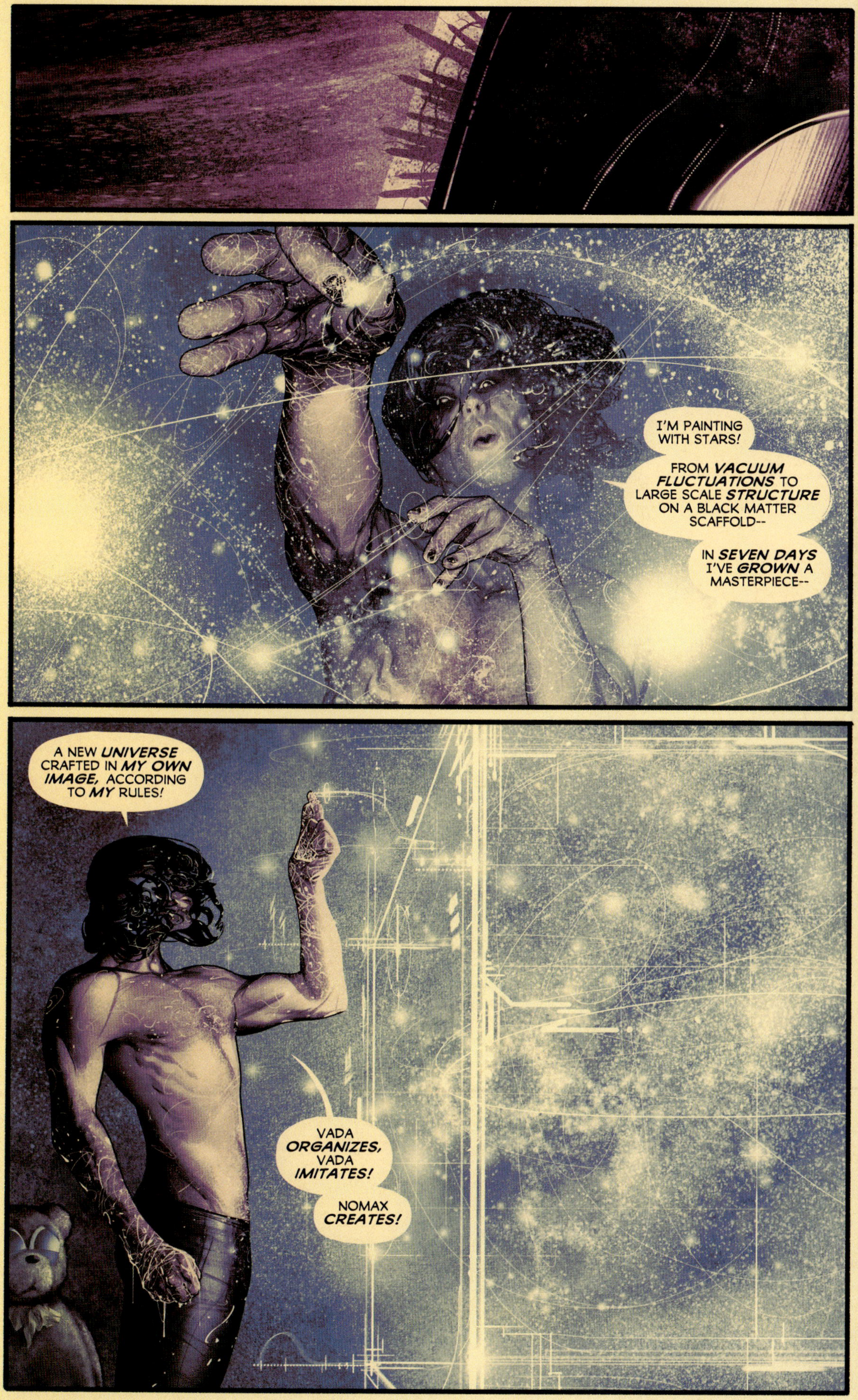
I'M PAINTING WITH STARS!
FROM *VACUUM FLUCTUATIONS* TO LARGE SCALE *STRUCTURE* ON A BLACK MATTER SCAFFOLD--
IN *SEVEN DAYS* I'VE *GROWN* A MASTERPIECE--
A NEW *UNIVERSE* CRAFTED IN *MY OWN IMAGE,* ACCORDING TO *MY* RULES!
VADA *ORGANIZES,* VADA *IMITATES!*
NOMAX *CREATES!*

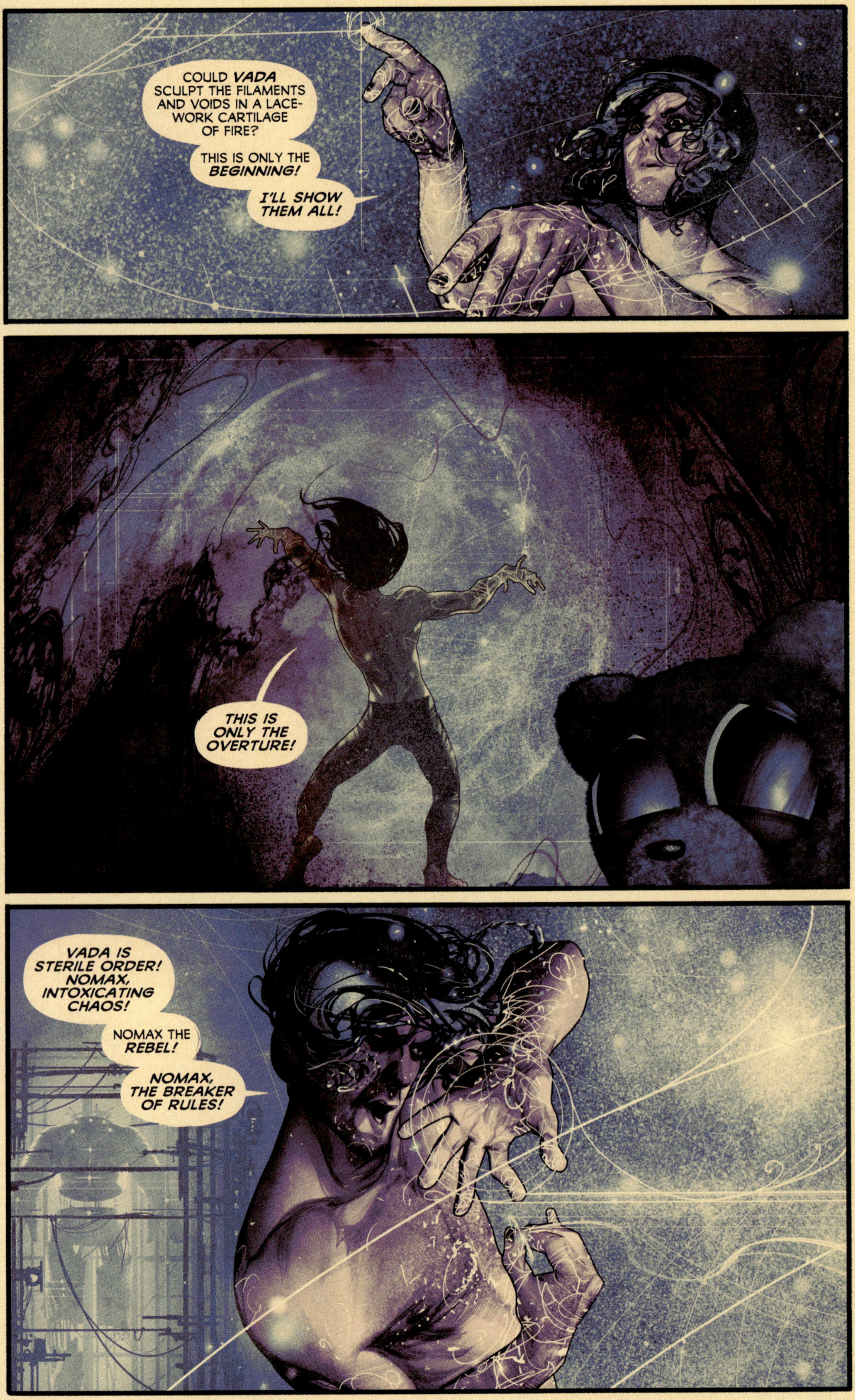
COULD *VADA* SCULPT THE FILAMENTS AND VOIDS IN A LACE-WORK CARTILAGE OF FIRE?
THIS IS ONLY THE *BEGINNING!*
I'LL SHOW THEM ALL!
THIS IS ONLY THE OVERTURE!
VADA IS STERILE ORDER! NOMAX, INTOXICATING CHAOS!
NOMAX THE *REBEL!*
NOMAX, THE BREAKER OF RULES!

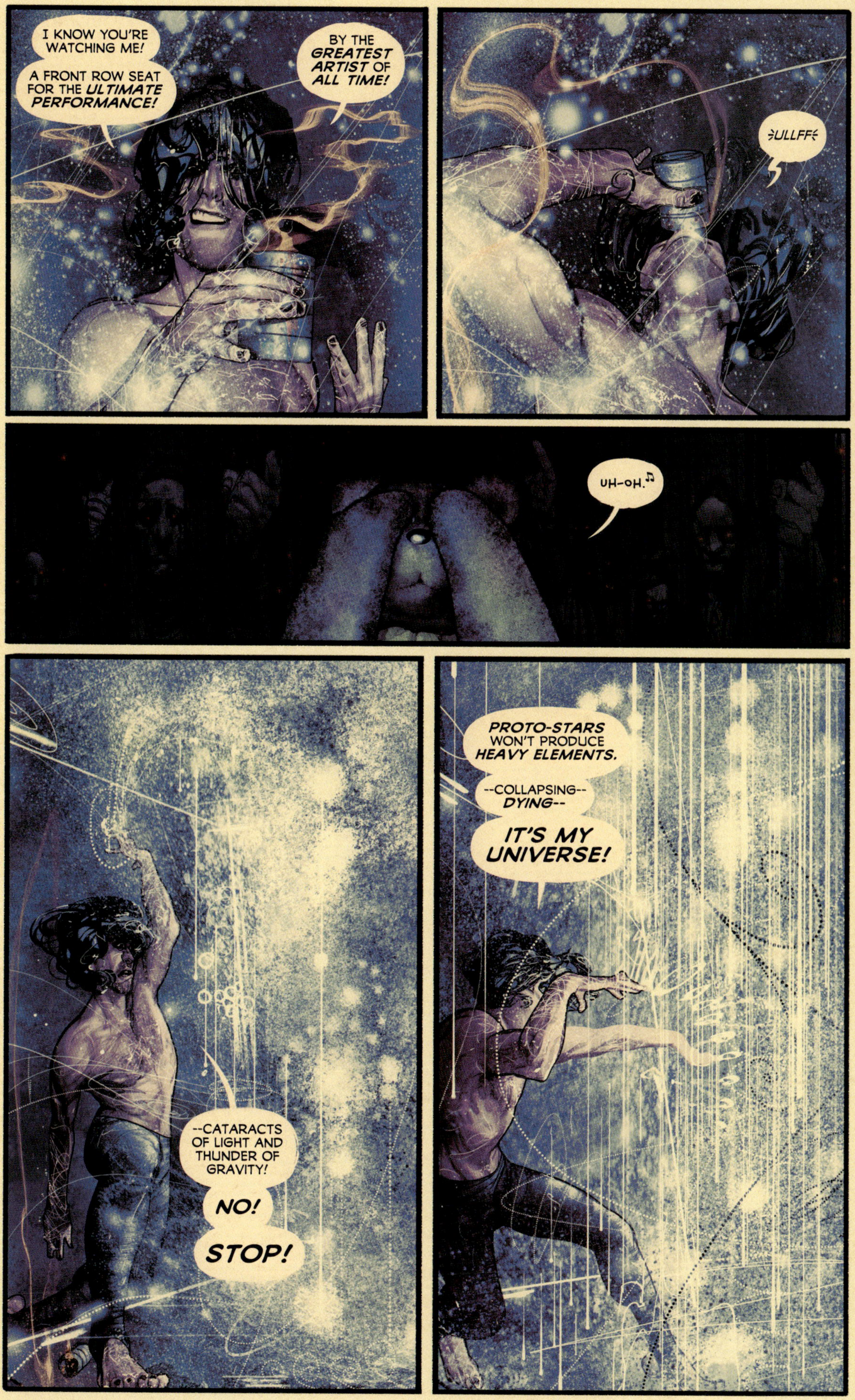
I KNOW YOU'RE WATCHING ME!
A FRONT ROW SEAT FOR THE ULTIMATE PERFORMANCE!
BY THE GREATEST ARTIST OF ALL TIME!
ULLFF
UH-OH.♫
--CATARACTS OF LIGHT AND THUNDER OF GRAVITY!
NO!
STOP!
PROTO-STARS WON'T PRODUCE HEAVY ELEMENTS.
--COLLAPSING-- DYING--
IT'S MY UNIVERSE!

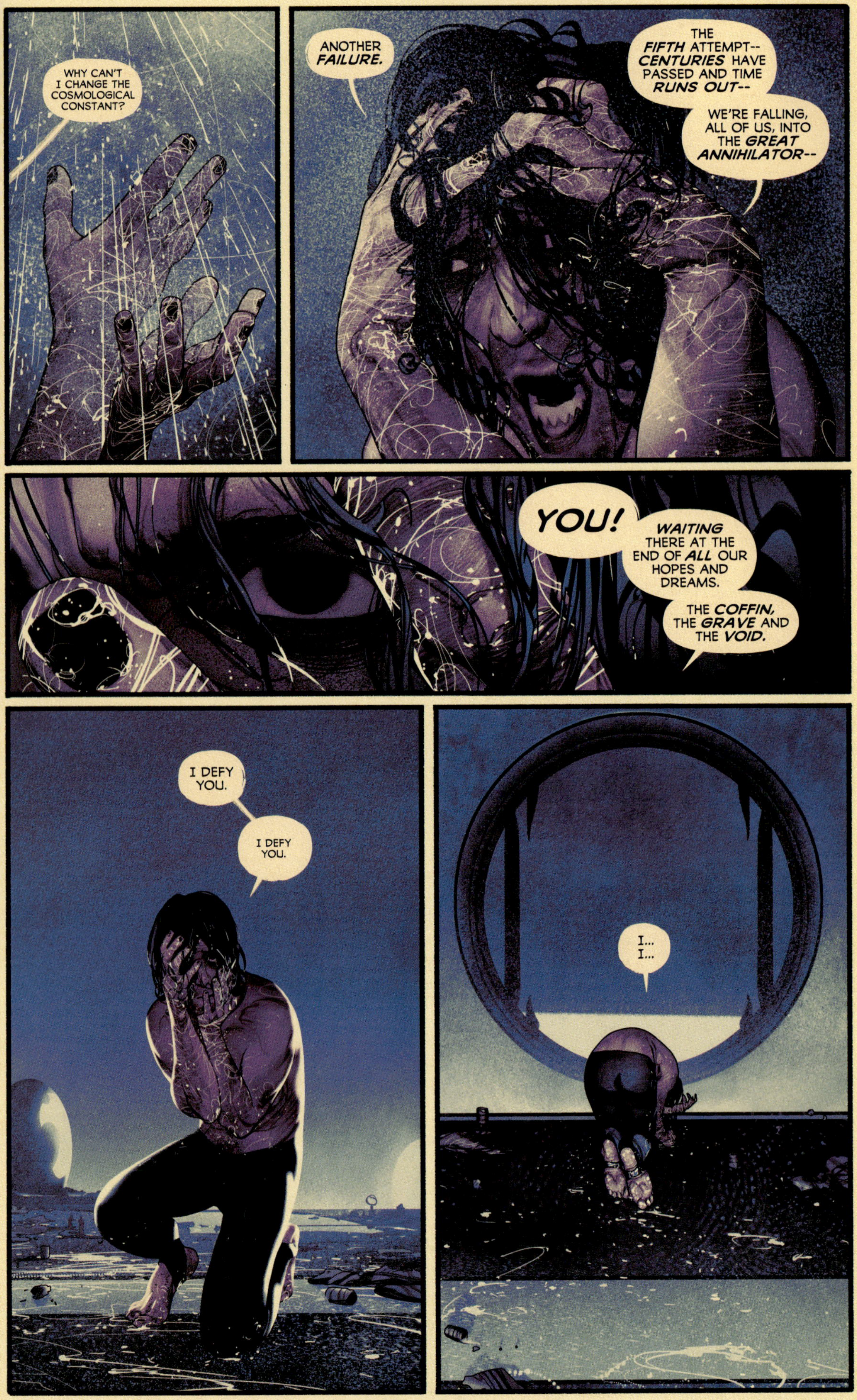
WHY CAN'T I CHANGE THE COSMOLOGICAL CONSTANT?
ANOTHER FAILURE.
THE FIFTH ATTEMPT-- CENTURIES HAVE PASSED AND TIME RUNS OUT--
WE'RE FALLING, ALL OF US, INTO THE GREAT ANNIHILATOR--
YOU!
WAITING THERE AT THE END OF ALL OUR HOPES AND DREAMS.
THE COFFIN, THE GRAVE AND THE VOID.
I DEFY YOU.
I DEFY YOU.
I... I...

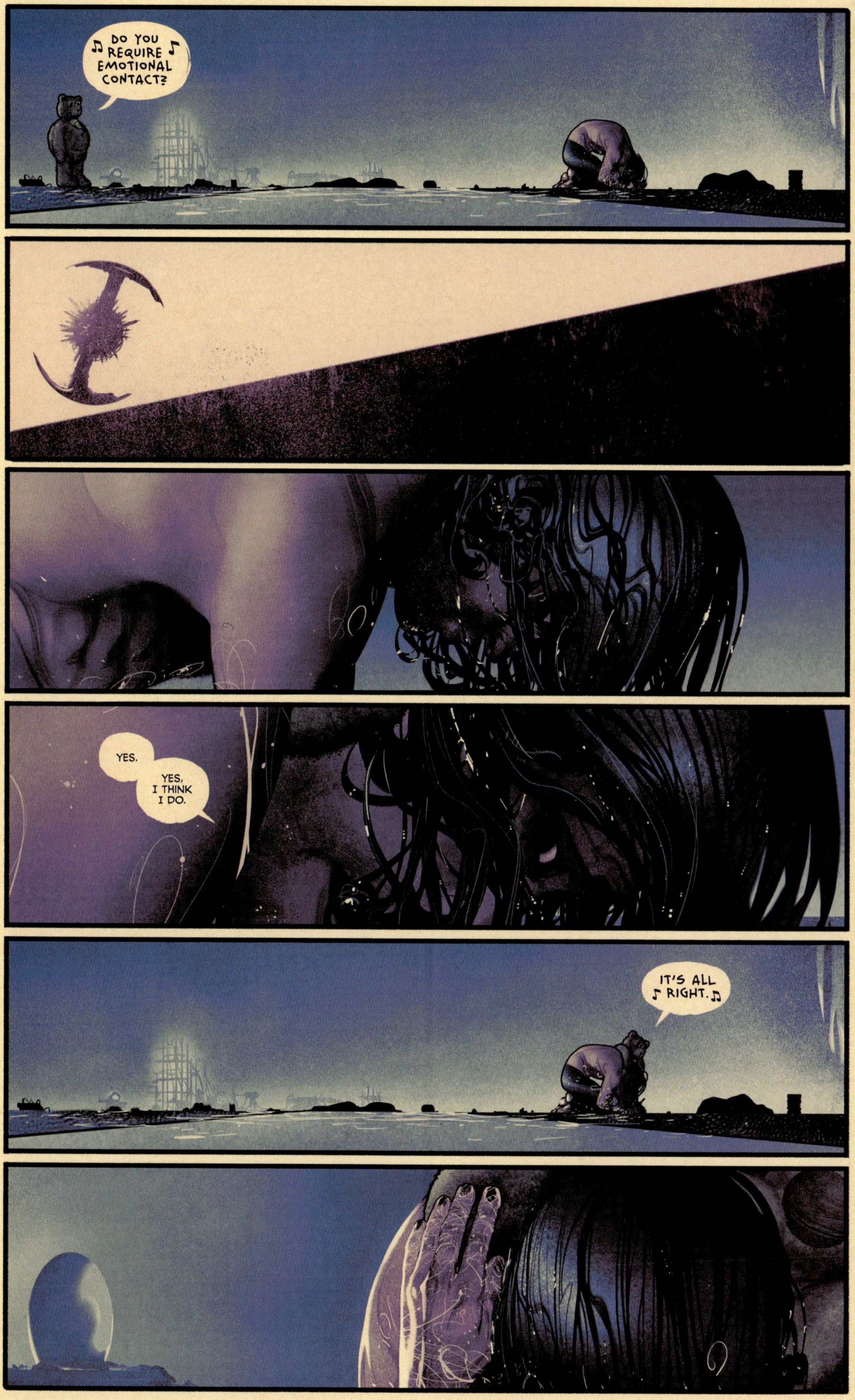
♫ DO YOU REQUIRE EMOTIONAL CONTACT? ♪
YES.
YES, I THINK I DO.
IT'S ALL ♪ RIGHT. ♫

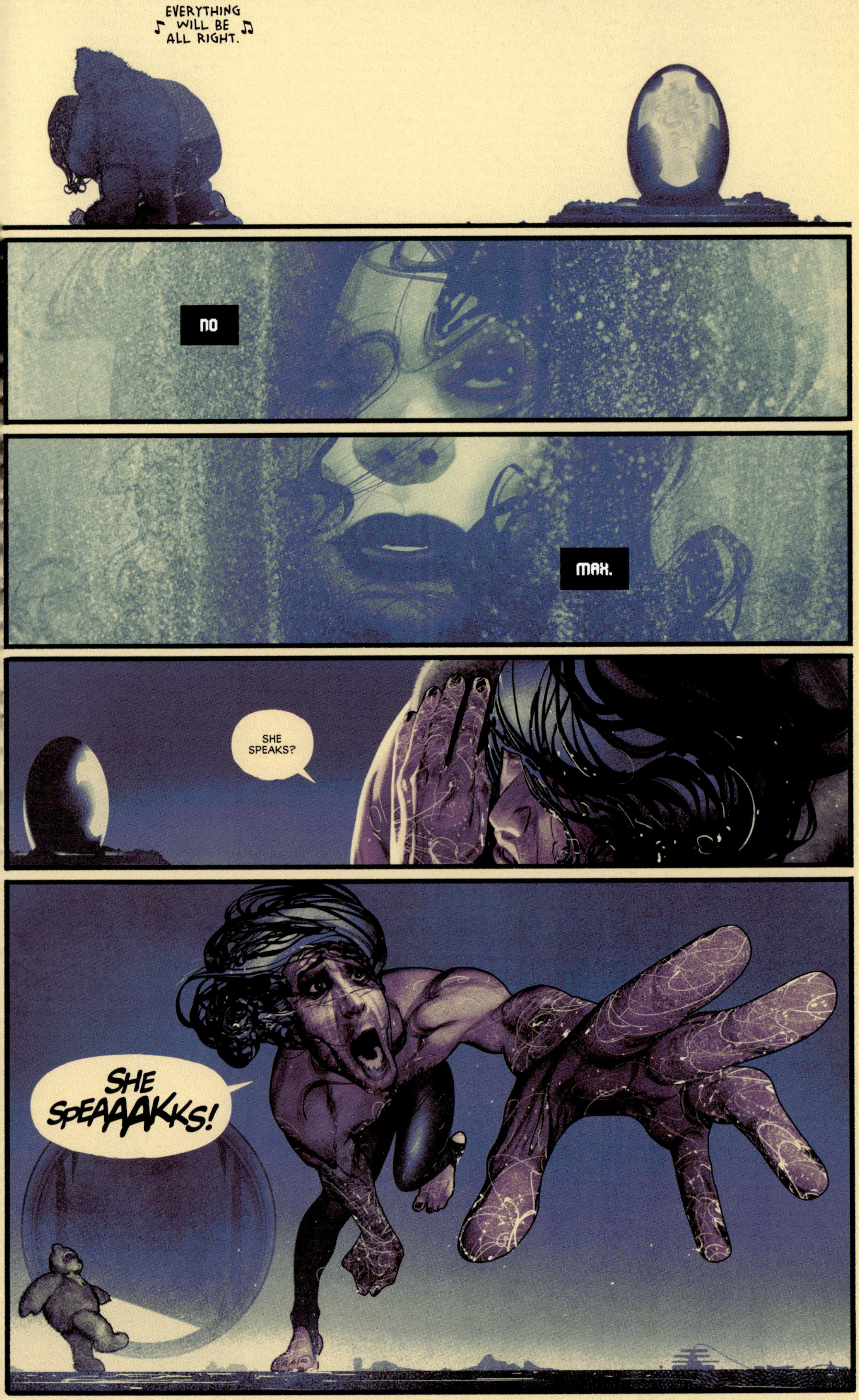
EVERYTHING WILL BE ALL RIGHT.
NO
MAX.
SHE SPEAKS?
SHE SPEAAAKKS!

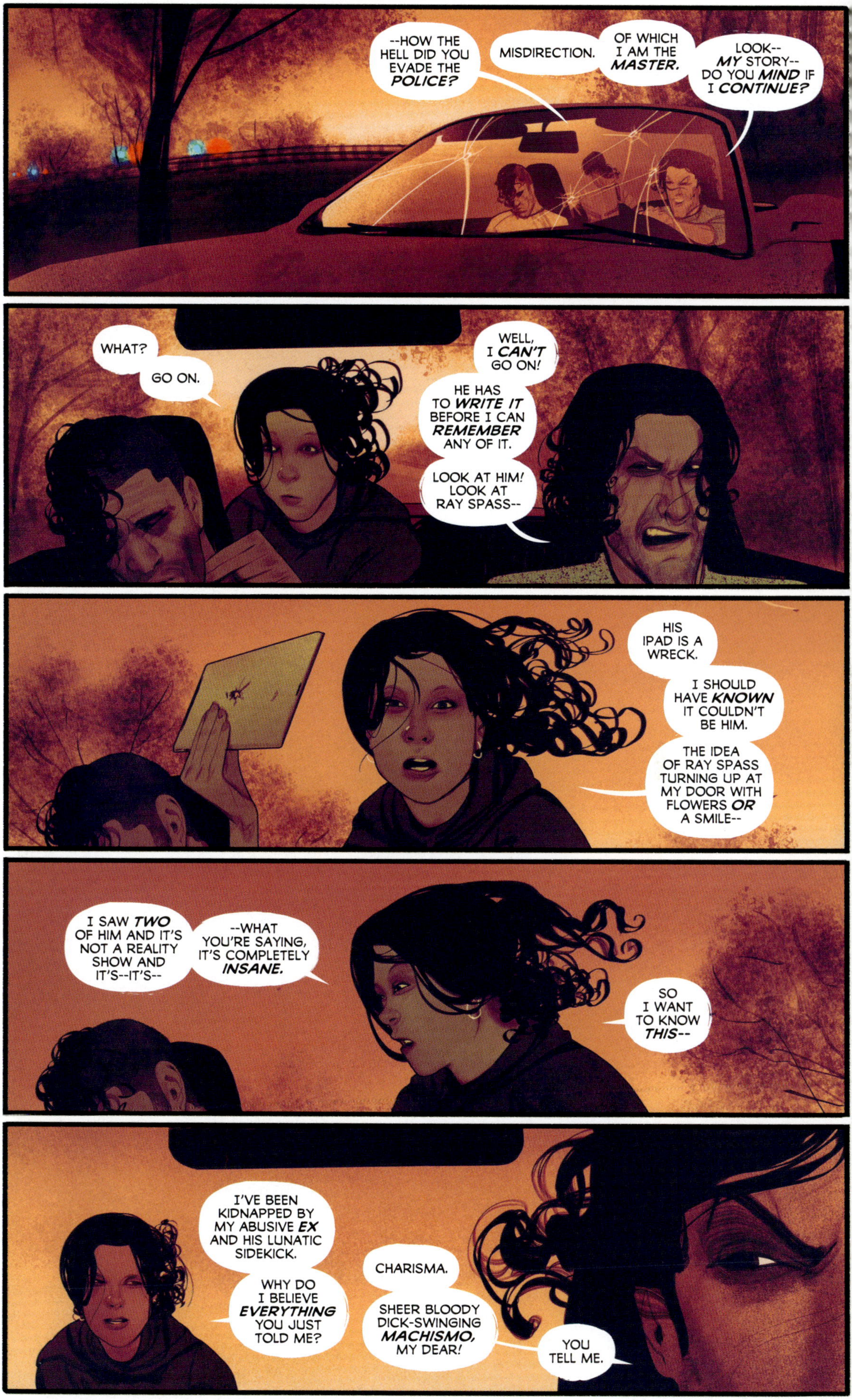
--HOW THE HELL DID YOU EVADE THE *POLICE?*
MISDIRECTION.
OF WHICH I AM THE *MASTER.*
LOOK-- *MY* STORY-- DO YOU *MIND* IF I *CONTINUE?*
WHAT?
GO ON.
WELL, I *CAN'T* GO ON!
HE HAS TO *WRITE IT* BEFORE I CAN *REMEMBER* ANY OF IT.
LOOK AT HIM! LOOK AT RAY SPASS--
HIS IPAD IS A WRECK.
I SHOULD HAVE *KNOWN* IT COULDN'T BE HIM.
THE IDEA OF RAY SPASS TURNING UP AT MY DOOR WITH FLOWERS *OR* A SMILE--
I SAW *TWO* OF HIM AND IT'S NOT A REALITY SHOW AND IT'S--IT'S--
--WHAT YOU'RE SAYING, IT'S COMPLETELY *INSANE.*
SO I WANT TO KNOW *THIS*--
I'VE BEEN KIDNAPPED BY MY ABUSIVE *EX* AND HIS LUNATIC SIDEKICK.
WHY DO I BELIEVE *EVERYTHING* YOU JUST TOLD ME?
CHARISMA.
SHEER BLOODY DICK-SWINGING *MACHISMO,* MY DEAR!
YOU TELL ME.

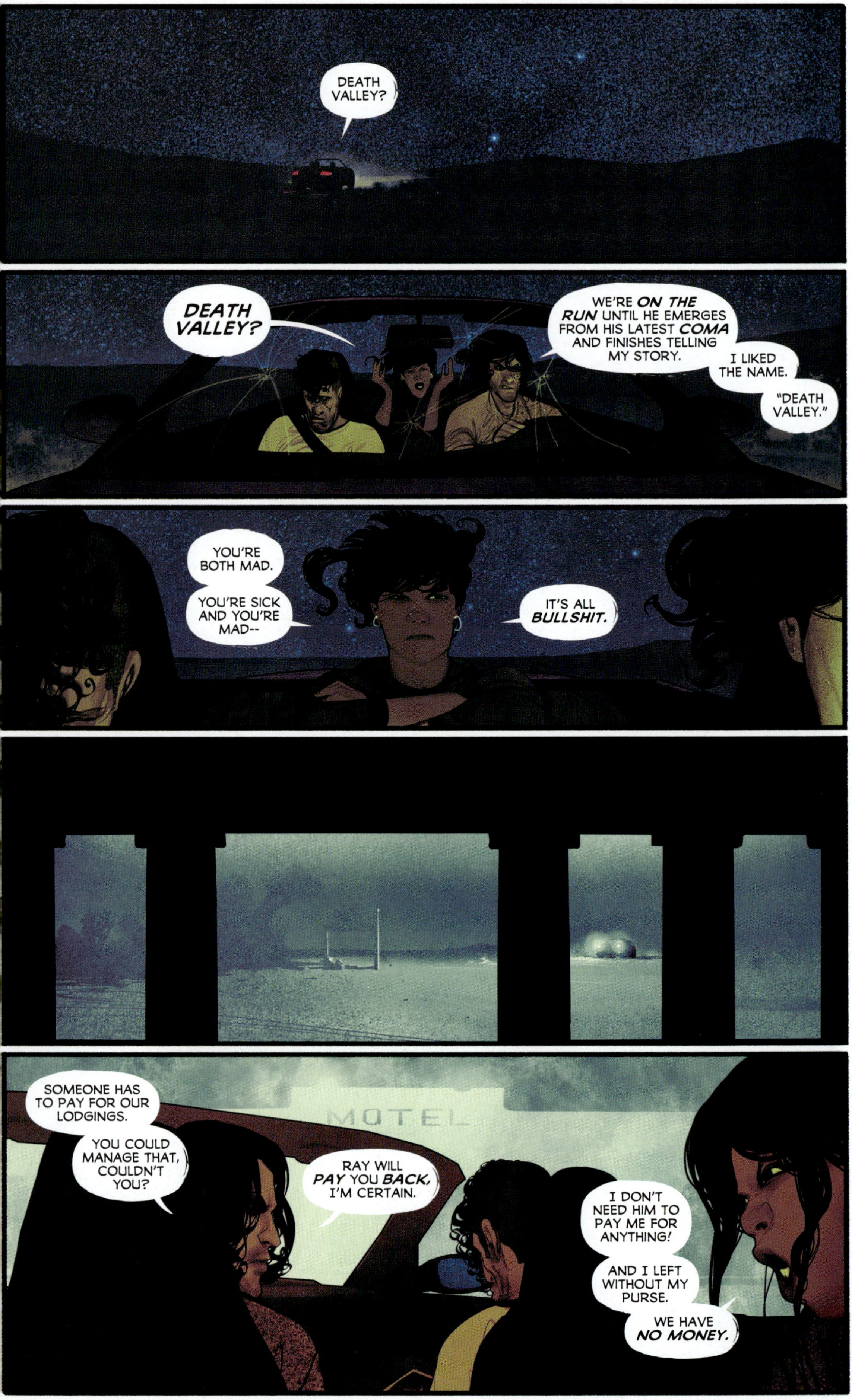
DEATH VALLEY?
DEATH VALLEY?
WE'RE ON THE RUN UNTIL HE EMERGES FROM HIS LATEST COMA AND FINISHES TELLING MY STORY.
I LIKED THE NAME.
"DEATH VALLEY."
YOU'RE BOTH MAD.
YOU'RE SICK AND YOU'RE MAD--
IT'S ALL BULLSHIT.
MOTEL
SOMEONE HAS TO PAY FOR OUR LODGINGS.
YOU COULD MANAGE THAT, COULDN'T YOU?
RAY WILL PAY YOU BACK, I'M CERTAIN.
I DON'T NEED HIM TO PAY ME FOR ANYTHING!
AND I LEFT WITHOUT MY PURSE.
WE HAVE NO MONEY.

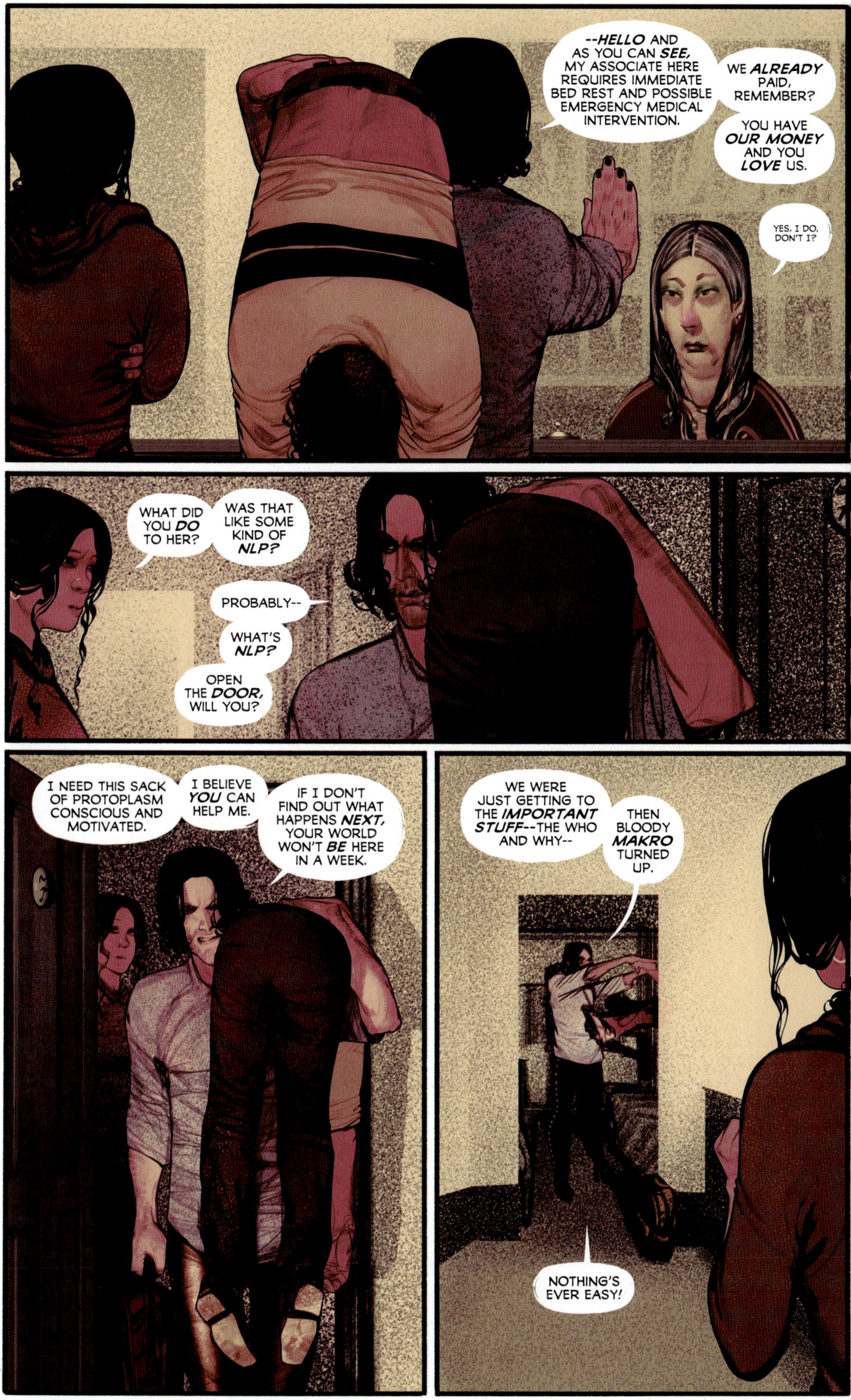
--HELLO AND AS YOU CAN SEE, MY ASSOCIATE HERE REQUIRES IMMEDIATE BED REST AND POSSIBLE EMERGENCY MEDICAL INTERVENTION.
WE ALREADY PAID, REMEMBER?
YOU HAVE OUR MONEY AND YOU LOVE US.
YES, I DO, DON'T I?
WHAT DID YOU DO TO HER?
WAS THAT LIKE SOME KIND OF NLP?
PROBABLY--
WHAT'S NLP?
OPEN THE DOOR, WILL YOU?
I NEED THIS SACK OF PROTOPLASM CONSCIOUS AND MOTIVATED.
I BELIEVE YOU CAN HELP ME.
IF I DON'T FIND OUT WHAT HAPPENS NEXT, YOUR WORLD WON'T BE HERE IN A WEEK.
WE WERE JUST GETTING TO THE IMPORTANT STUFF--THE WHO AND WHY--
THEN BLOODY MAKRO TURNED UP.
NOTHING'S EVER EASY!

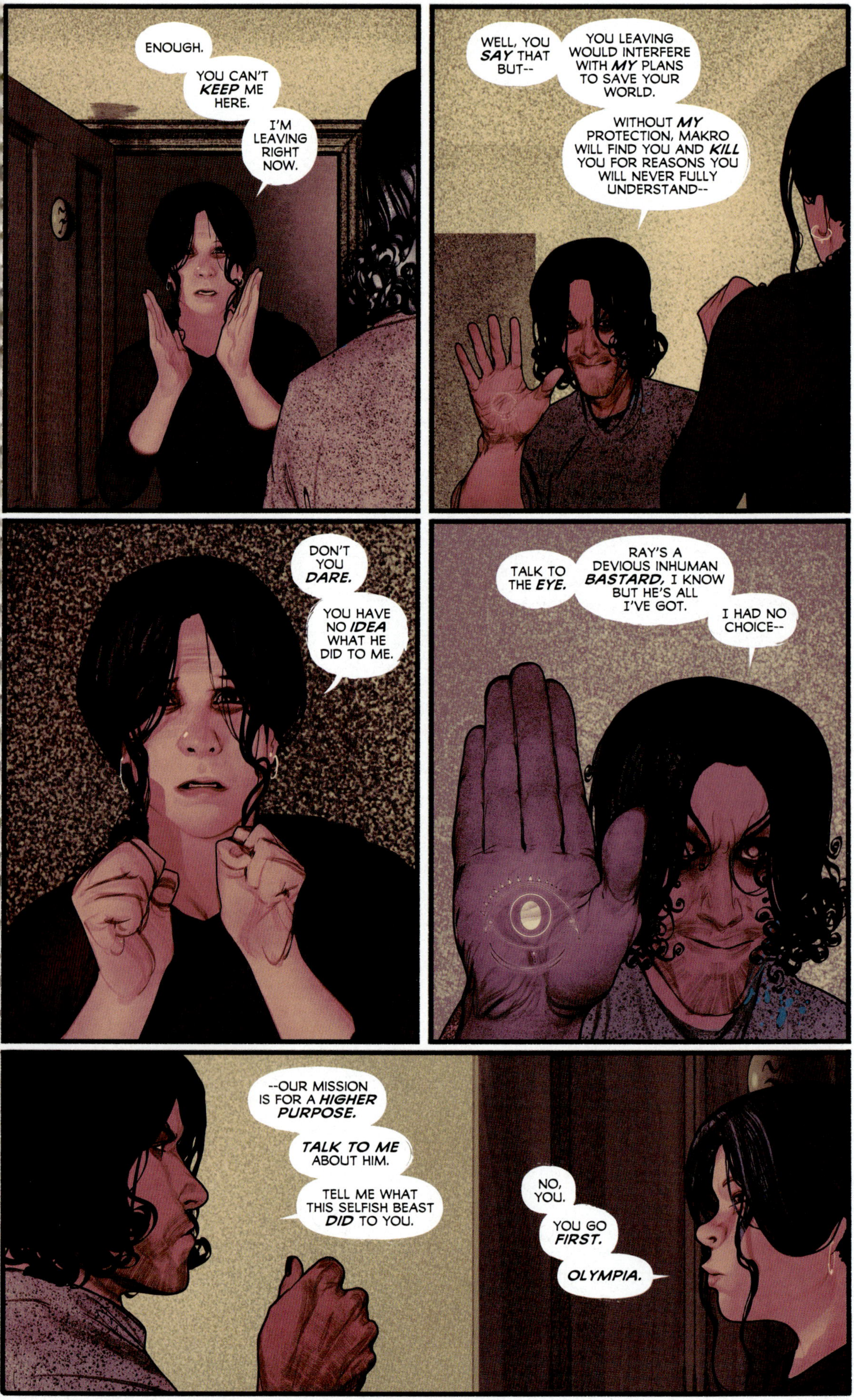
ENOUGH.
YOU CAN'T KEEP ME HERE.
I'M LEAVING RIGHT NOW.
WELL, YOU SAY THAT BUT--
YOU LEAVING WOULD INTERFERE WITH MY PLANS TO SAVE YOUR WORLD.
WITHOUT MY PROTECTION, MAKRO WILL FIND YOU AND KILL YOU FOR REASONS YOU WILL NEVER FULLY UNDERSTAND--
DON'T YOU DARE.
YOU HAVE NO IDEA WHAT HE DID TO ME.
TALK TO THE EYE.
RAY'S A DEVIOUS INHUMAN BASTARD, I KNOW BUT HE'S ALL I'VE GOT.
I HAD NO CHOICE--
--OUR MISSION IS FOR A HIGHER PURPOSE.
TALK TO ME ABOUT HIM.
TELL ME WHAT THIS SELFISH BEAST DID TO YOU.
NO, YOU.
YOU GO FIRST.
OLYMPIA.

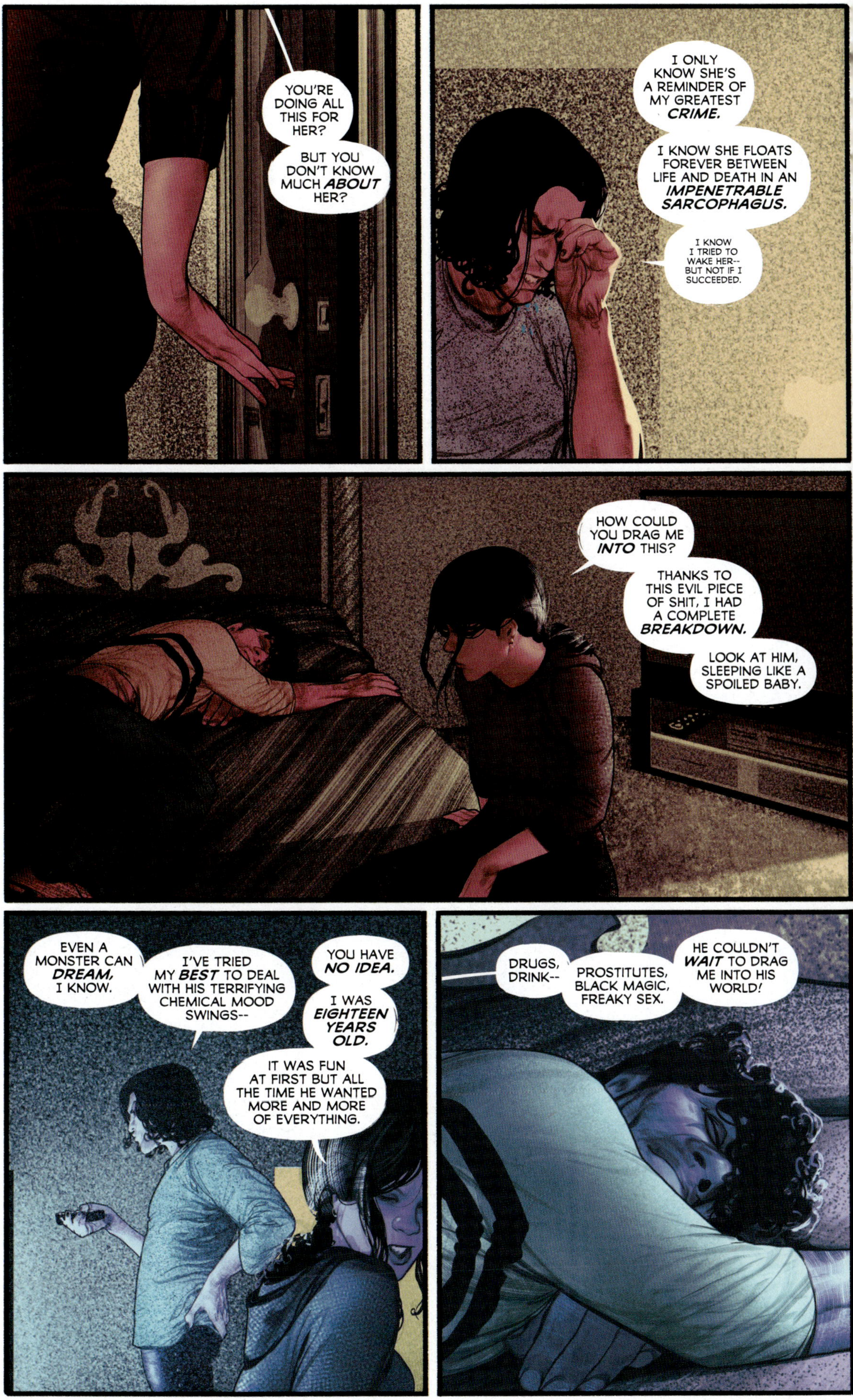
YOU'RE DOING ALL THIS FOR HER?
BUT YOU DON'T KNOW MUCH ABOUT HER?
I ONLY KNOW SHE'S A REMINDER OF MY GREATEST CRIME.
I KNOW SHE FLOATS FOREVER BETWEEN LIFE AND DEATH IN AN IMPENETRABLE SARCOPHAGUS.
I KNOW I TRIED TO WAKE HER-- BUT NOT IF I SUCCEEDED.
HOW COULD YOU DRAG ME INTO THIS?
THANKS TO THIS EVIL PIECE OF SHIT, I HAD A COMPLETE BREAKDOWN.
LOOK AT HIM, SLEEPING LIKE A SPOILED BABY.
EVEN A MONSTER CAN DREAM, I KNOW.
I'VE TRIED MY BEST TO DEAL WITH HIS TERRIFYING CHEMICAL MOOD SWINGS--
YOU HAVE NO IDEA.
I WAS EIGHTEEN YEARS OLD.
IT WAS FUN AT FIRST BUT ALL THE TIME HE WANTED MORE AND MORE OF EVERYTHING.
DRUGS, DRINK--
PROSTITUTES, BLACK MAGIC, FREAKY SEX.
HE COULDN'T WAIT TO DRAG ME INTO HIS WORLD!

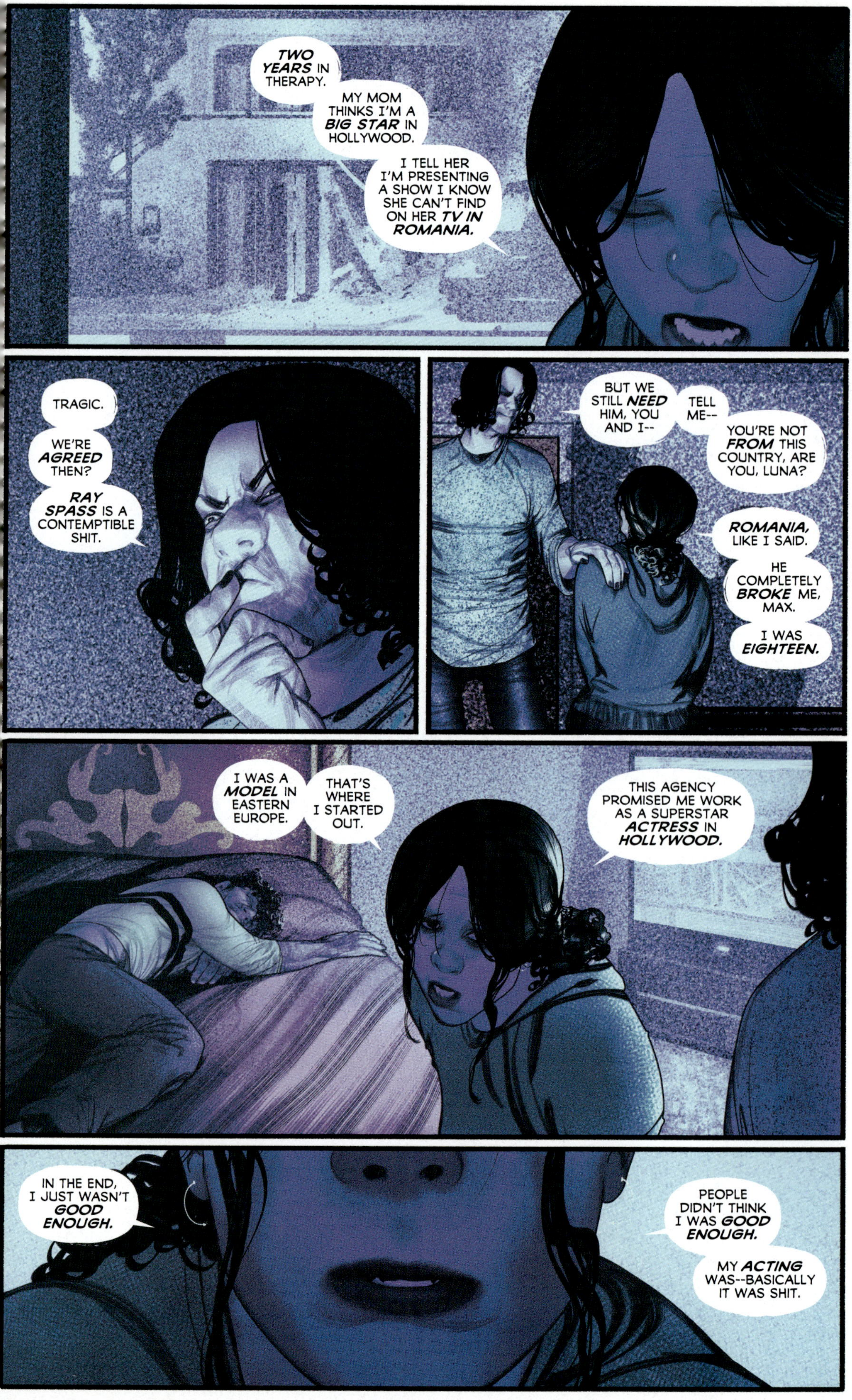
TWO YEARS IN THERAPY.
MY MOM THINKS I'M A BIG STAR IN HOLLYWOOD.
I TELL HER I'M PRESENTING A SHOW I KNOW SHE CAN'T FIND ON HER TV IN ROMANIA.
TRAGIC.
WE'RE AGREED THEN?
RAY SPASS IS A CONTEMPTIBLE SHIT.
BUT WE STILL NEED HIM, YOU AND I--
TELL ME--
YOU'RE NOT FROM THIS COUNTRY, ARE YOU, LUNA?
ROMANIA, LIKE I SAID.
HE COMPLETELY BROKE ME, MAX.
I WAS EIGHTEEN.
I WAS A MODEL IN EASTERN EUROPE.
THAT'S WHERE I STARTED OUT.
THIS AGENCY PROMISED ME WORK AS A SUPERSTAR ACTRESS IN HOLLYWOOD.
IN THE END, I JUST WASN'T GOOD ENOUGH.
PEOPLE DIDN'T THINK I WAS GOOD ENOUGH.
MY ACTING WAS--BASICALLY IT WAS SHIT.

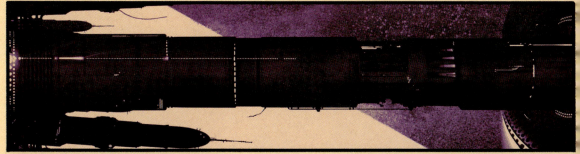

SHE SPEAKS!

NO, YOU FOOL!

SHE IS *DEAD*.

IT IS *UADA* WHOSE VOICE YOU ATTEND.

UADA.

WHO GAVE *LIFE* TO *OLYMPIA*.

WHO MADE HER DARK TWIN, *DORGA*.

HOW COULD YOU DO *THIS!*

SHE IS NOT *DEAD!*

SHE ONLY *SLEEPS!*

I WILL MAKE HER LIVE AGAIN!

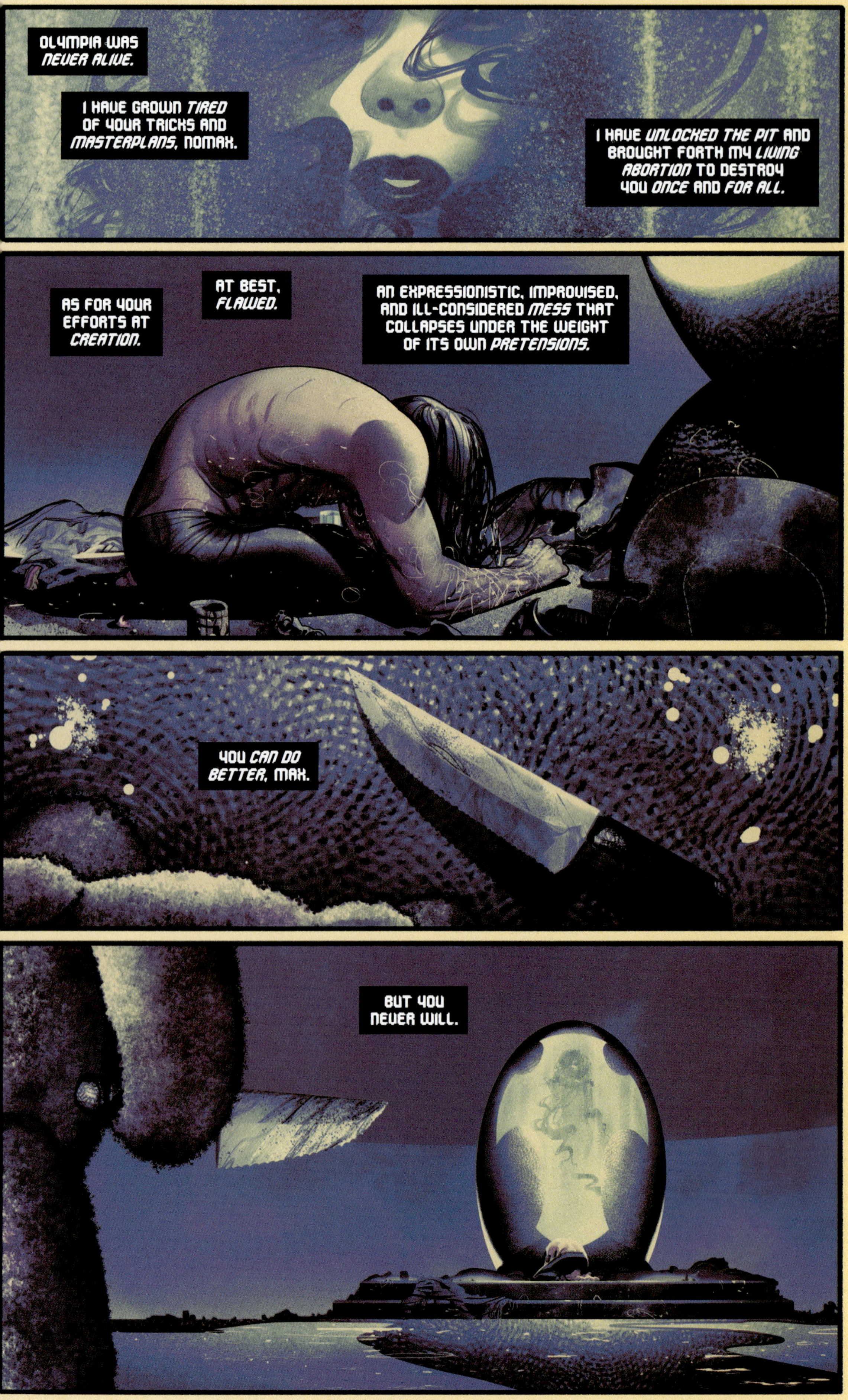
OLYMPIA WAS *NEVER ALIVE.*
I HAVE GROWN *TIRED* OF YOUR TRICKS AND *MASTERPLANS,* NOMAX.
I HAVE *UNLOCKED THE PIT* AND BROUGHT FORTH MY *LIVING ABORTION* TO DESTROY YOU *ONCE* AND *FOR ALL.*
AS FOR YOUR EFFORTS AT *CREATION.*
AT BEST, *FLAWED.*
AN EXPRESSIONISTIC, IMPROVISED, AND ILL-CONSIDERED *MESS* THAT COLLAPSES UNDER THE WEIGHT OF ITS OWN *PRETENSIONS.*
YOU *CAN DO BETTER,* MAX.
BUT YOU NEVER WILL.

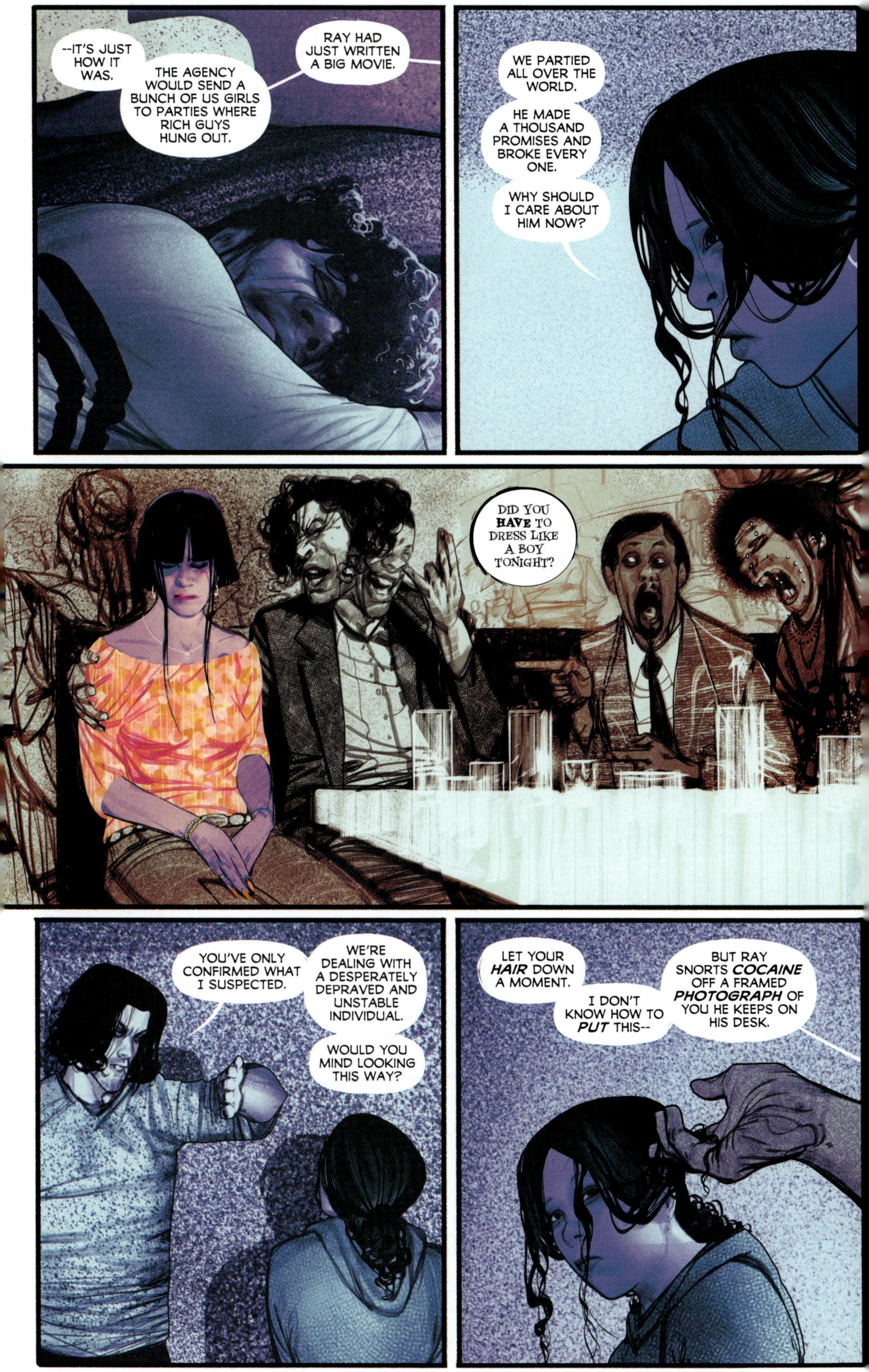
--IT'S JUST HOW IT WAS.
RAY HAD JUST WRITTEN A BIG MOVIE.
THE AGENCY WOULD SEND A BUNCH OF US GIRLS TO PARTIES WHERE RICH GUYS HUNG OUT.
WE PARTIED ALL OVER THE WORLD.
HE MADE A THOUSAND PROMISES AND BROKE EVERY ONE.
WHY SHOULD I CARE ABOUT HIM NOW?
DID YOU **HAVE** TO DRESS LIKE A BOY TONIGHT?
YOU'VE ONLY CONFIRMED WHAT I SUSPECTED.
WE'RE DEALING WITH A DESPERATELY DEPRAVED AND UNSTABLE INDIVIDUAL.
WOULD YOU MIND LOOKING THIS WAY?
LET YOUR ***HAIR*** DOWN A MOMENT.
I DON'T KNOW HOW TO ***PUT*** THIS--
BUT RAY SNORTS ***COCAINE*** OFF A FRAMED ***PHOTOGRAPH*** OF YOU HE KEEPS ON HIS DESK.

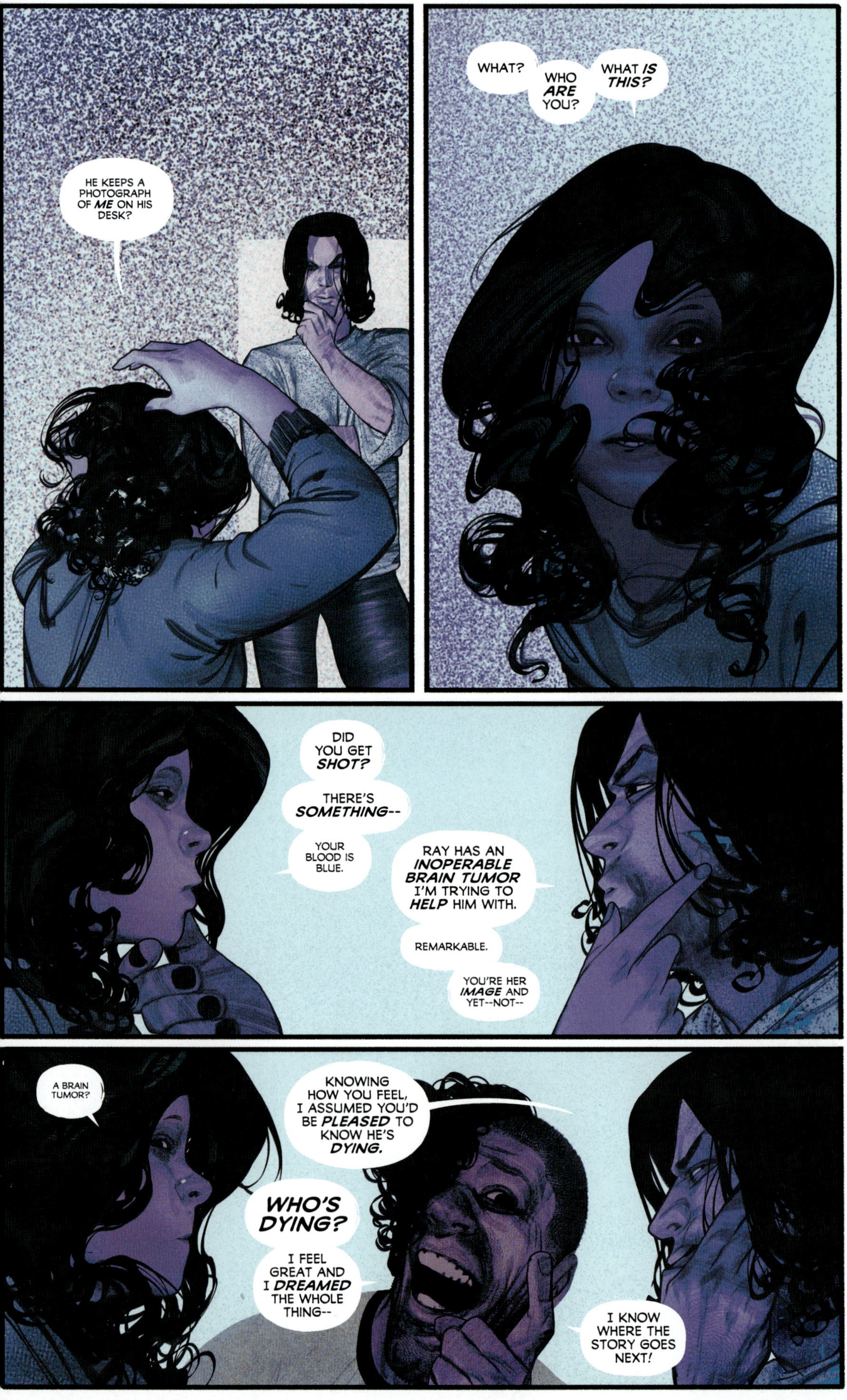
HE KEEPS A PHOTOGRAPH OF *ME* ON HIS DESK?
WHAT?
WHO *ARE* YOU?
WHAT *IS THIS?*
DID YOU GET *SHOT?*
THERE'S *SOMETHING--*
YOUR BLOOD IS BLUE.
RAY HAS AN *INOPERABLE BRAIN TUMOR* I'M TRYING TO *HELP* HIM WITH.
REMARKABLE.
YOU'RE HER *IMAGE* AND YET--NOT--
A BRAIN TUMOR?
KNOWING HOW YOU FEEL, I ASSUMED YOU'D BE *PLEASED* TO KNOW HE'S *DYING.*
WHO'S DYING?
I FEEL GREAT AND I *DREAMED* THE WHOLE THING--
I KNOW WHERE THE STORY GOES NEXT!

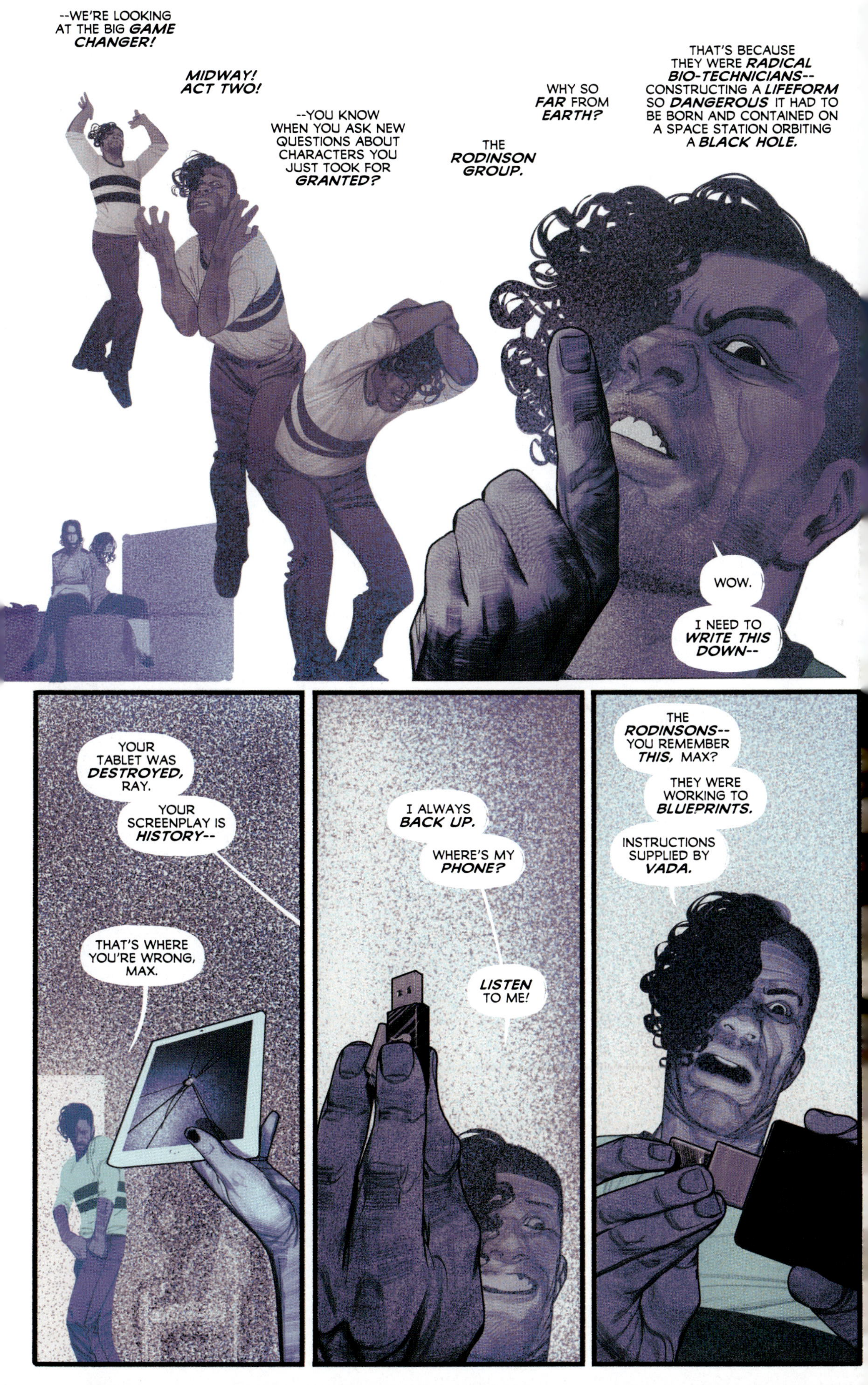
--WE'RE LOOKING AT THE BIG GAME CHANGER!
MIDWAY! ACT TWO!
--YOU KNOW WHEN YOU ASK NEW QUESTIONS ABOUT CHARACTERS YOU JUST TOOK FOR GRANTED?
THE RODINSON GROUP.
WHY SO FAR FROM EARTH?
THAT'S BECAUSE THEY WERE RADICAL BIO-TECHNICIANS--CONSTRUCTING A LIFEFORM SO DANGEROUS IT HAD TO BE BORN AND CONTAINED ON A SPACE STATION ORBITING A BLACK HOLE.
WOW.
I NEED TO WRITE THIS DOWN--
YOUR TABLET WAS DESTROYED, RAY.
YOUR SCREENPLAY IS HISTORY--
THAT'S WHERE YOU'RE WRONG, MAX.
I ALWAYS BACK UP.
WHERE'S MY PHONE?
LISTEN TO ME!
THE RODINSONS--YOU REMEMBER THIS, MAX?
THEY WERE WORKING TO BLUEPRINTS.
INSTRUCTIONS SUPPLIED BY VADA.

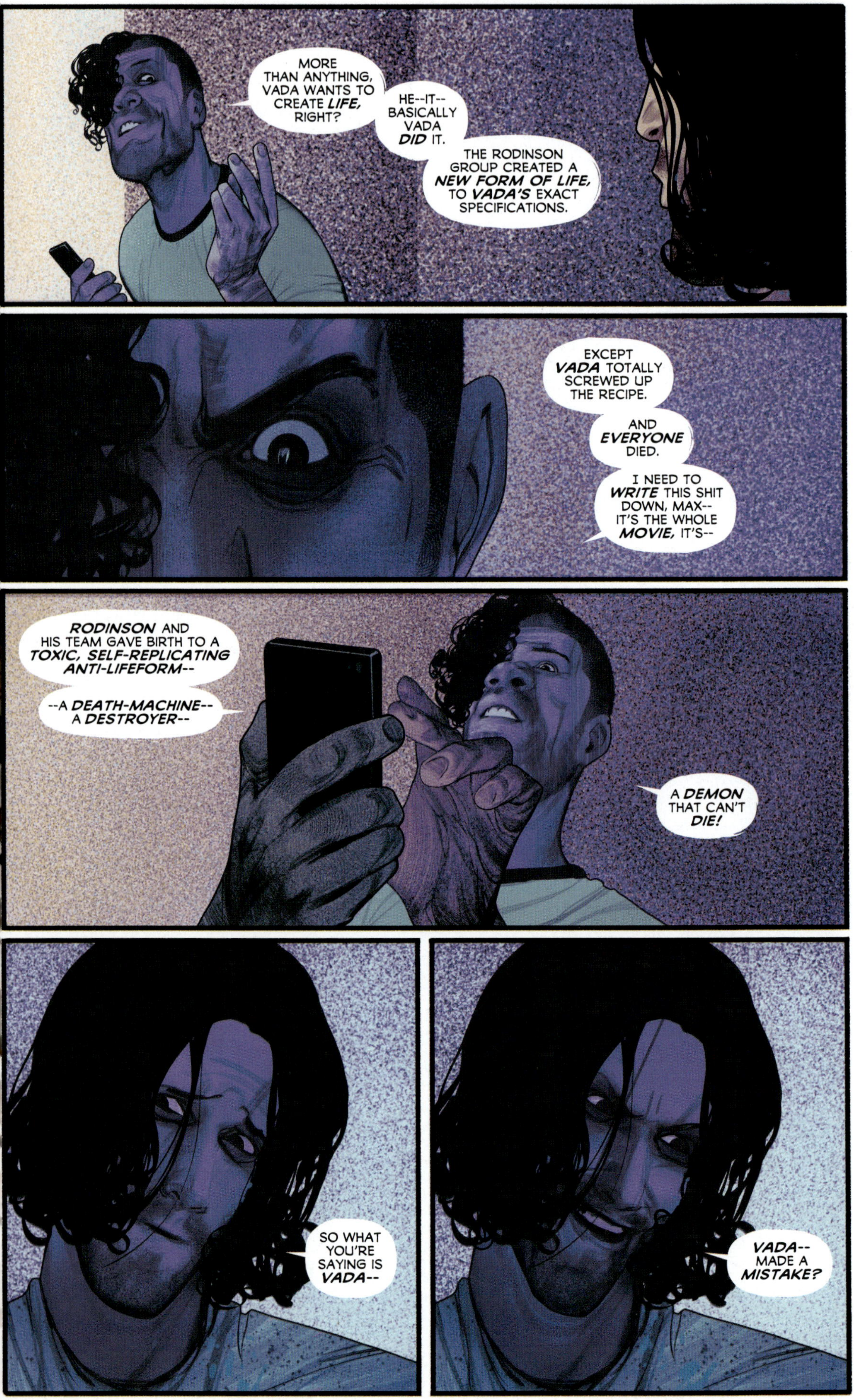
MORE THAN ANYTHING, VADA WANTS TO CREATE LIFE, RIGHT?
HE--IT-- BASICALLY VADA DID IT.
THE RODINSON GROUP CREATED A NEW FORM OF LIFE, TO VADA'S EXACT SPECIFICATIONS.
EXCEPT VADA TOTALLY SCREWED UP THE RECIPE.
AND EVERYONE DIED.
I NEED TO WRITE THIS SHIT DOWN, MAX-- IT'S THE WHOLE MOVIE, IT'S--
RODINSON AND HIS TEAM GAVE BIRTH TO A TOXIC, SELF-REPLICATING ANTI-LIFEFORM--
--A DEATH-MACHINE-- A DESTROYER--
A DEMON THAT CAN'T DIE!
SO WHAT YOU'RE SAYING IS VADA--
VADA-- MADE A MISTAKE?

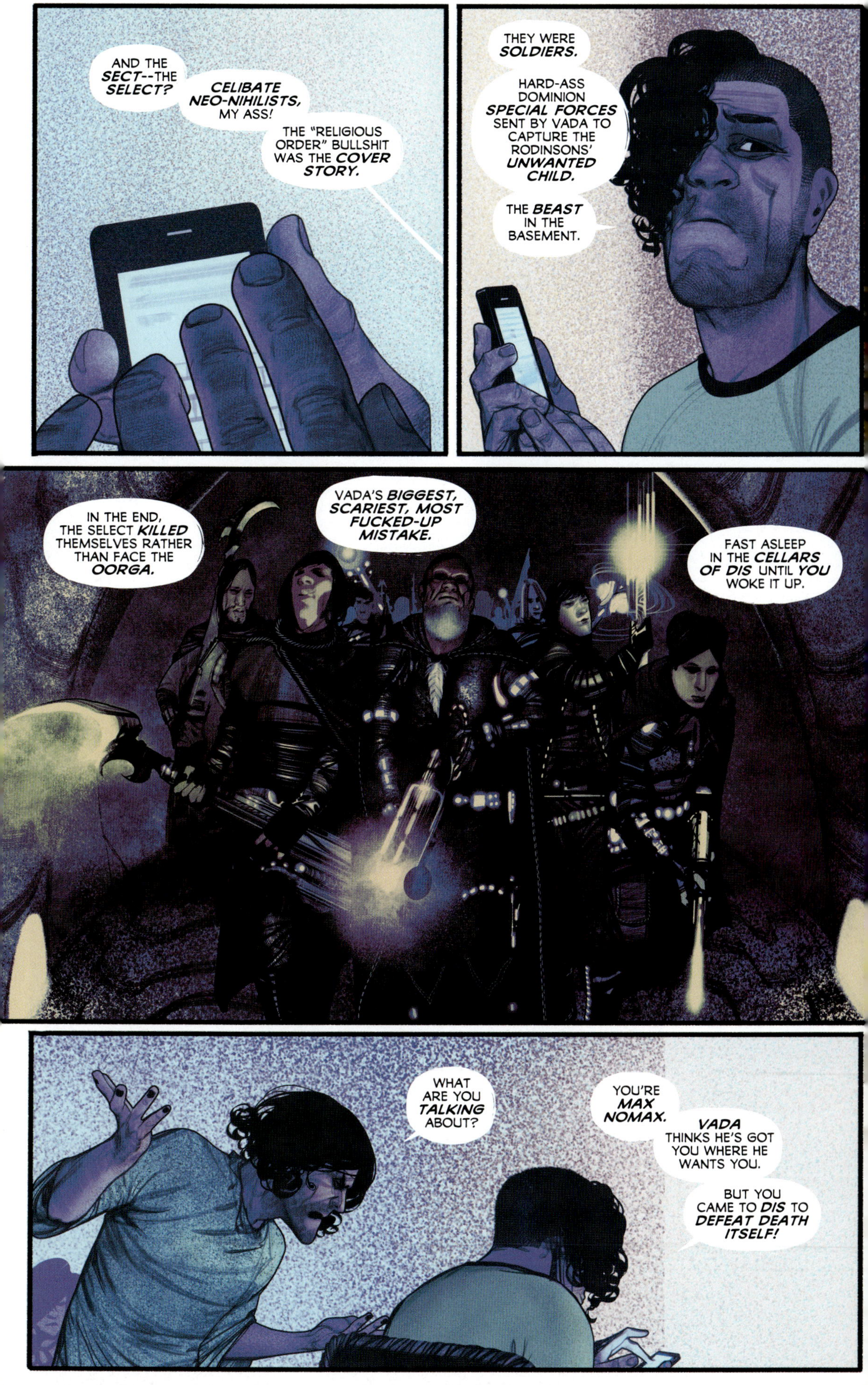
AND THE SECT--THE SELECT?
CELIBATE NEO-NIHILISTS, MY ASS!
THE "RELIGIOUS ORDER" BULLSHIT WAS THE COVER STORY.
THEY WERE SOLDIERS.
HARD-ASS DOMINION SPECIAL FORCES SENT BY VADA TO CAPTURE THE RODINSONS' UNWANTED CHILD.
THE BEAST IN THE BASEMENT.
IN THE END, THE SELECT KILLED THEMSELVES RATHER THAN FACE THE OORGA.
VADA'S BIGGEST, SCARIEST, MOST FUCKED-UP MISTAKE.
FAST ASLEEP IN THE CELLARS OF DIS UNTIL YOU WOKE IT UP.
WHAT ARE YOU TALKING ABOUT?
YOU'RE MAX NOMAX.
VADA THINKS HE'S GOT YOU WHERE HE WANTS YOU.
BUT YOU CAME TO DIS TO DEFEAT DEATH ITSELF!

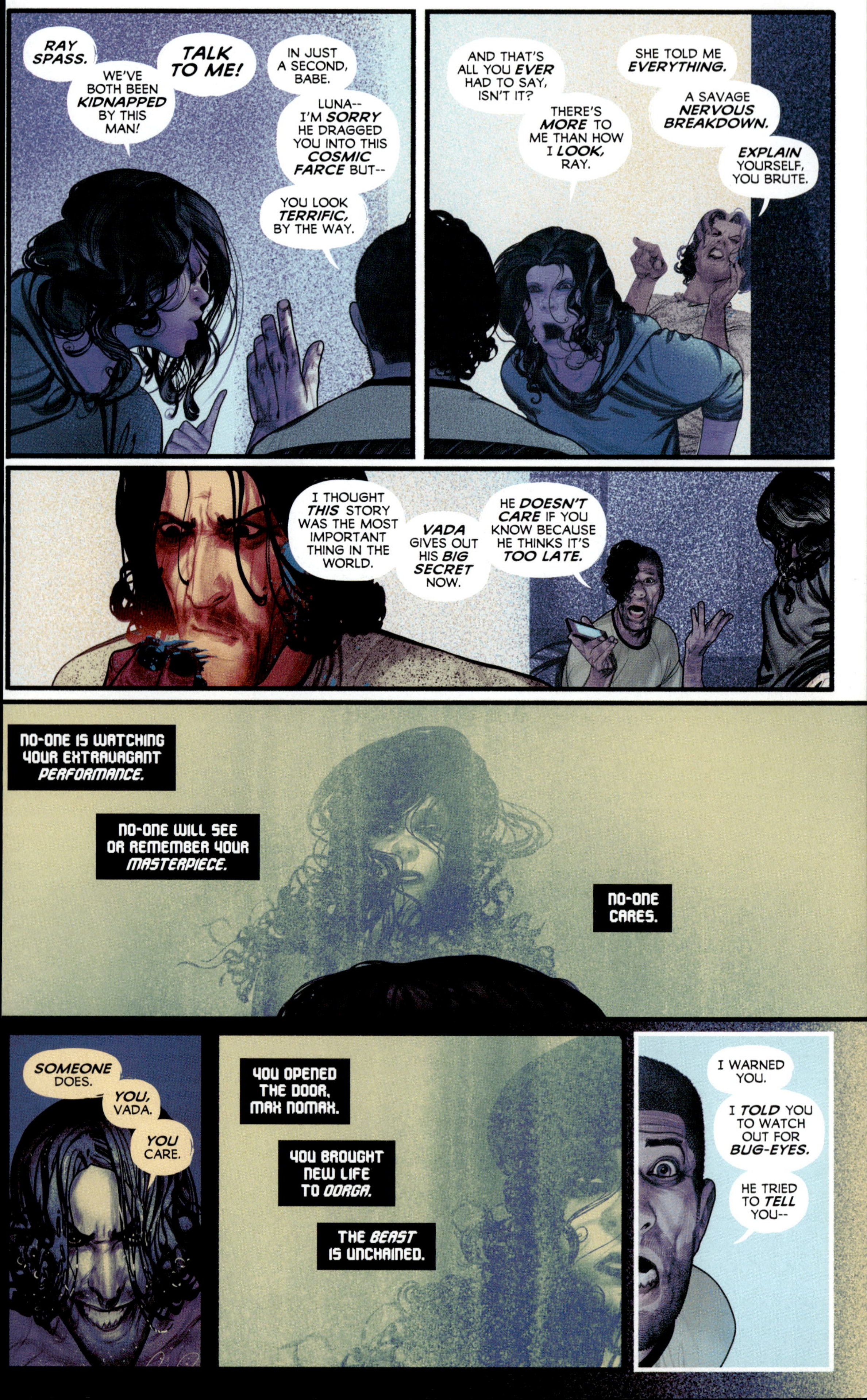

RAY SPASS.
WE'VE BOTH BEEN KIDNAPPED BY THIS MAN!
TALK TO ME!
IN JUST A SECOND, BABE.
LUNA-- I'M SORRY HE DRAGGED YOU INTO THIS COSMIC FARCE BUT--
YOU LOOK TERRIFIC, BY THE WAY.
AND THAT'S ALL YOU EVER HAD TO SAY, ISN'T IT?
THERE'S MORE TO ME THAN HOW I LOOK, RAY.
SHE TOLD ME EVERYTHING.
A SAVAGE NERVOUS BREAKDOWN.
EXPLAIN YOURSELF, YOU BRUTE.
I THOUGHT THIS STORY WAS THE MOST IMPORTANT THING IN THE WORLD.
VADA GIVES OUT HIS BIG SECRET NOW.
HE DOESN'T CARE IF YOU KNOW BECAUSE HE THINKS IT'S TOO LATE.
NO-ONE IS WATCHING YOUR EXTRAVAGANT PERFORMANCE.
NO-ONE WILL SEE OR REMEMBER YOUR MASTERPIECE.
NO-ONE CARES.
SOMEONE DOES.
YOU, VADA.
YOU CARE.
YOU OPENED THE DOOR, MAX NOMAX.
YOU BROUGHT NEW LIFE TO DORGA.
THE BEAST IS UNCHAINED.
I WARNED YOU.
I TOLD YOU TO WATCH OUT FOR BUG-EYES.
HE TRIED TO TELL YOU--

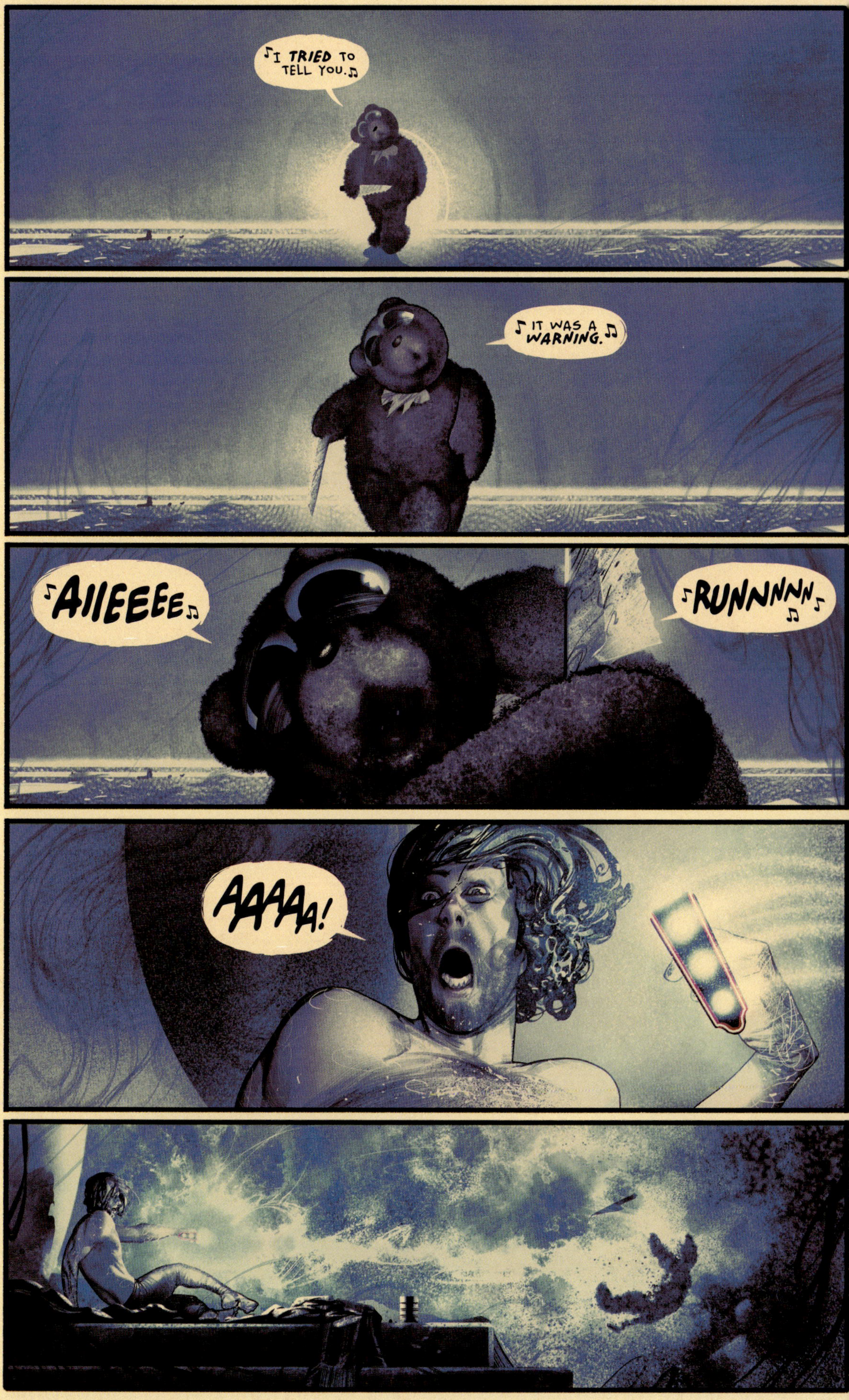
♪I TRIED TO TELL YOU.♫
♪IT WAS A WARNING.♫
♪AIIEEEE♫
♪RUNNNNN♫♪
AAAAA!

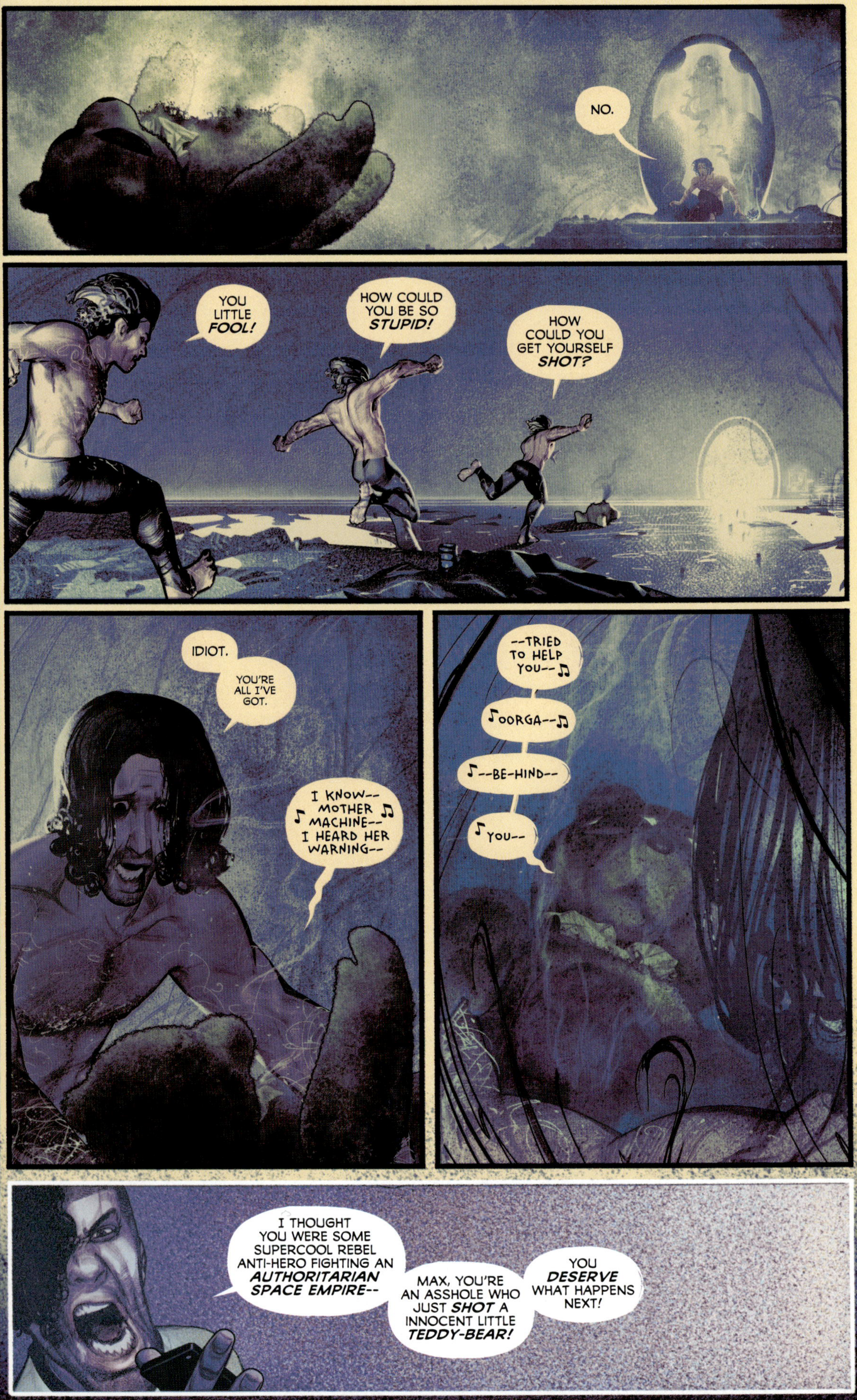
NO.
YOU LITTLE FOOL!
HOW COULD YOU BE SO STUPID!
HOW COULD YOU GET YOURSELF SHOT?
IDIOT.
YOU'RE ALL I'VE GOT.
I KNOW-- MOTHER MACHINE-- I HEARD HER WARNING--
--TRIED TO HELP YOU--
OORGA--
--BE-HIND--
YOU--
I THOUGHT YOU WERE SOME SUPERCOOL REBEL ANTI-HERO FIGHTING AN AUTHORITARIAN SPACE EMPIRE--
MAX, YOU'RE AN ASSHOLE WHO JUST SHOT A INNOCENT LITTLE TEDDY-BEAR!
YOU DESERVE WHAT HAPPENS NEXT!

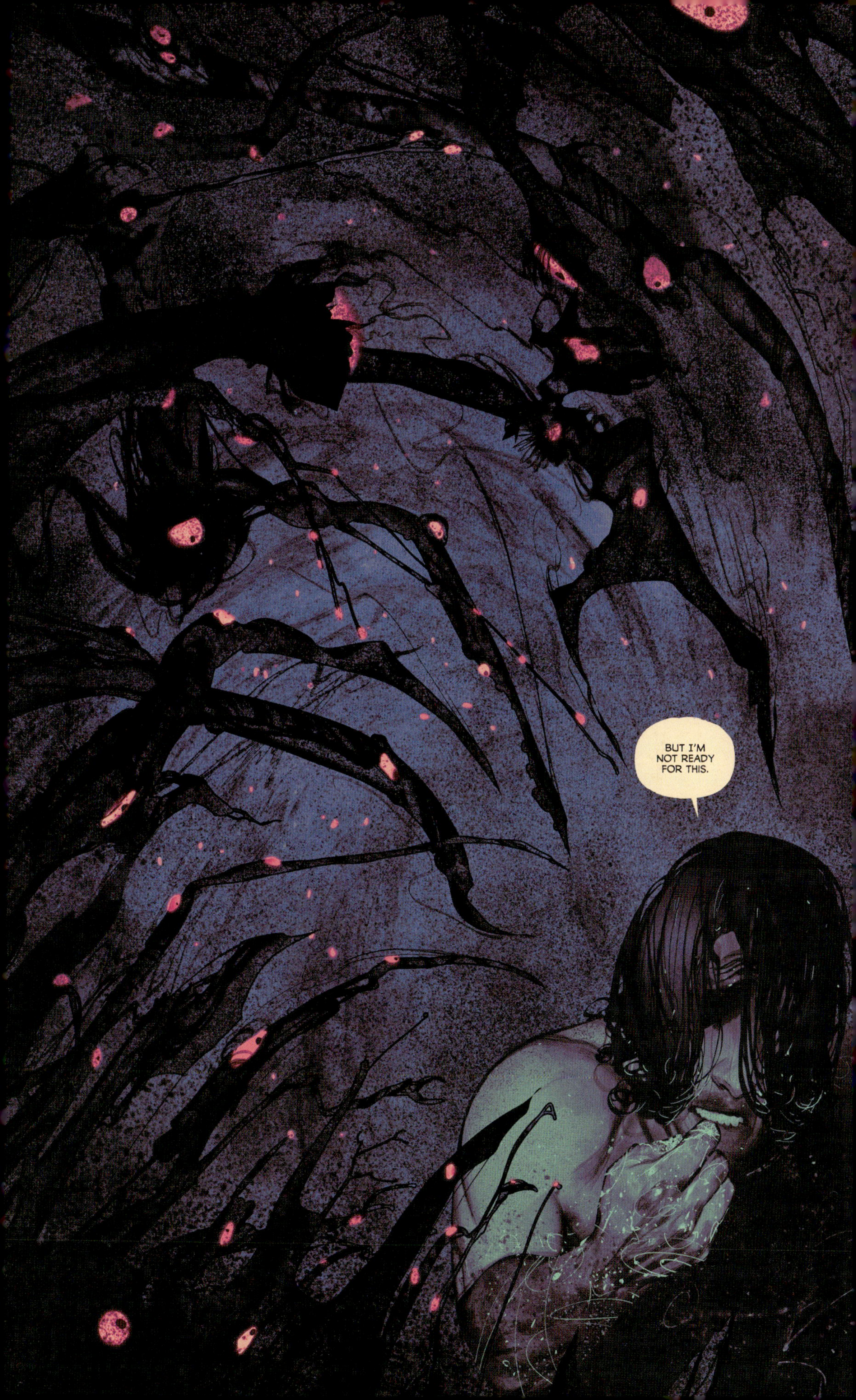
BUT I'M NOT READY FOR THIS.

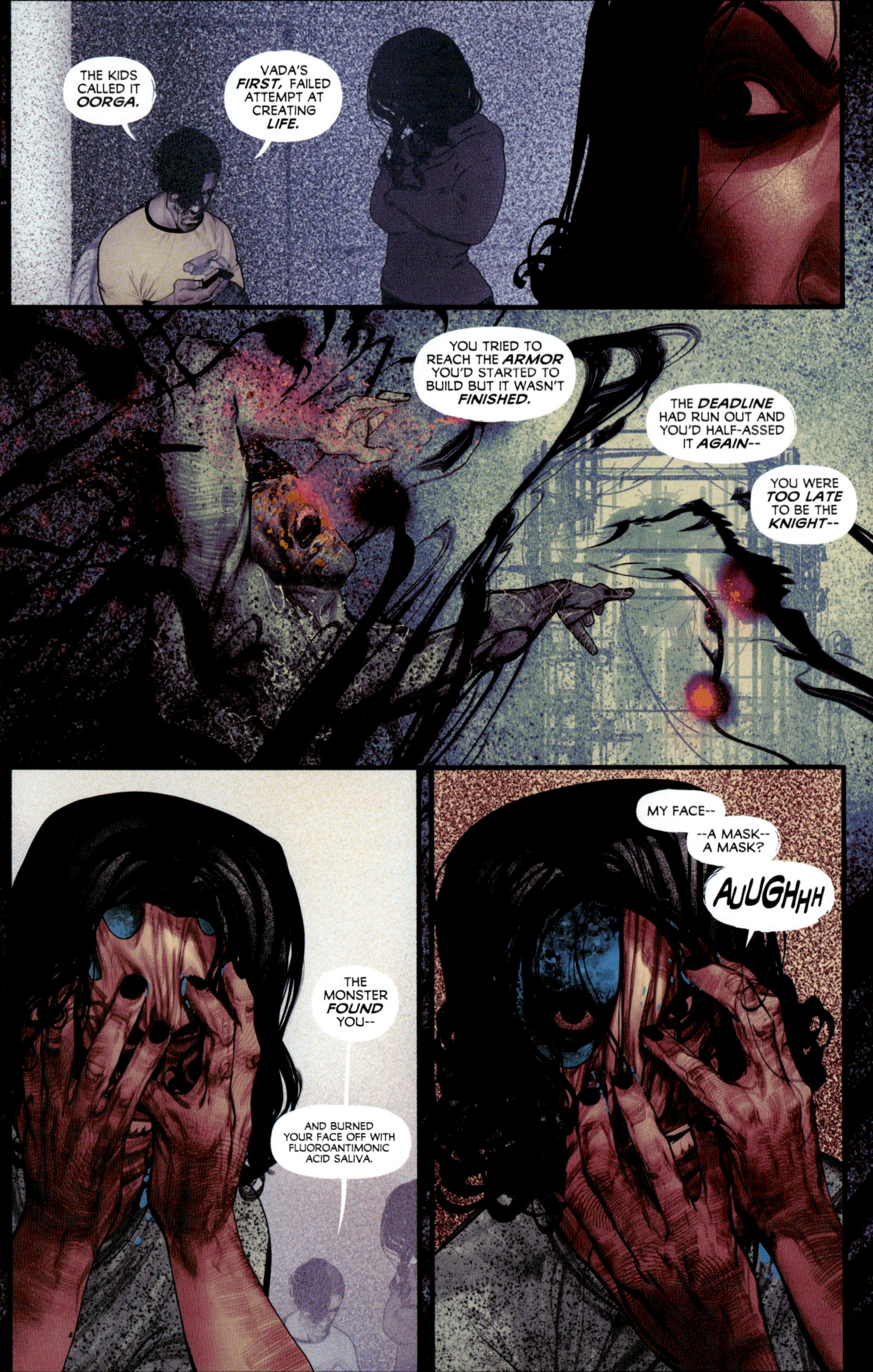
THE KIDS CALLED IT OORGA.
VADA'S FIRST, FAILED ATTEMPT AT CREATING LIFE.
YOU TRIED TO REACH THE ARMOR YOU'D STARTED TO BUILD BUT IT WASN'T FINISHED.
THE DEADLINE HAD RUN OUT AND YOU'D HALF-ASSED IT AGAIN--
YOU WERE TOO LATE TO BE THE KNIGHT--
THE MONSTER FOUND YOU--
AND BURNED YOUR FACE OFF WITH FLUOROANTIMONIC ACID SALIVA.
MY FACE--
--A MASK-- A MASK?
AUUGHHH

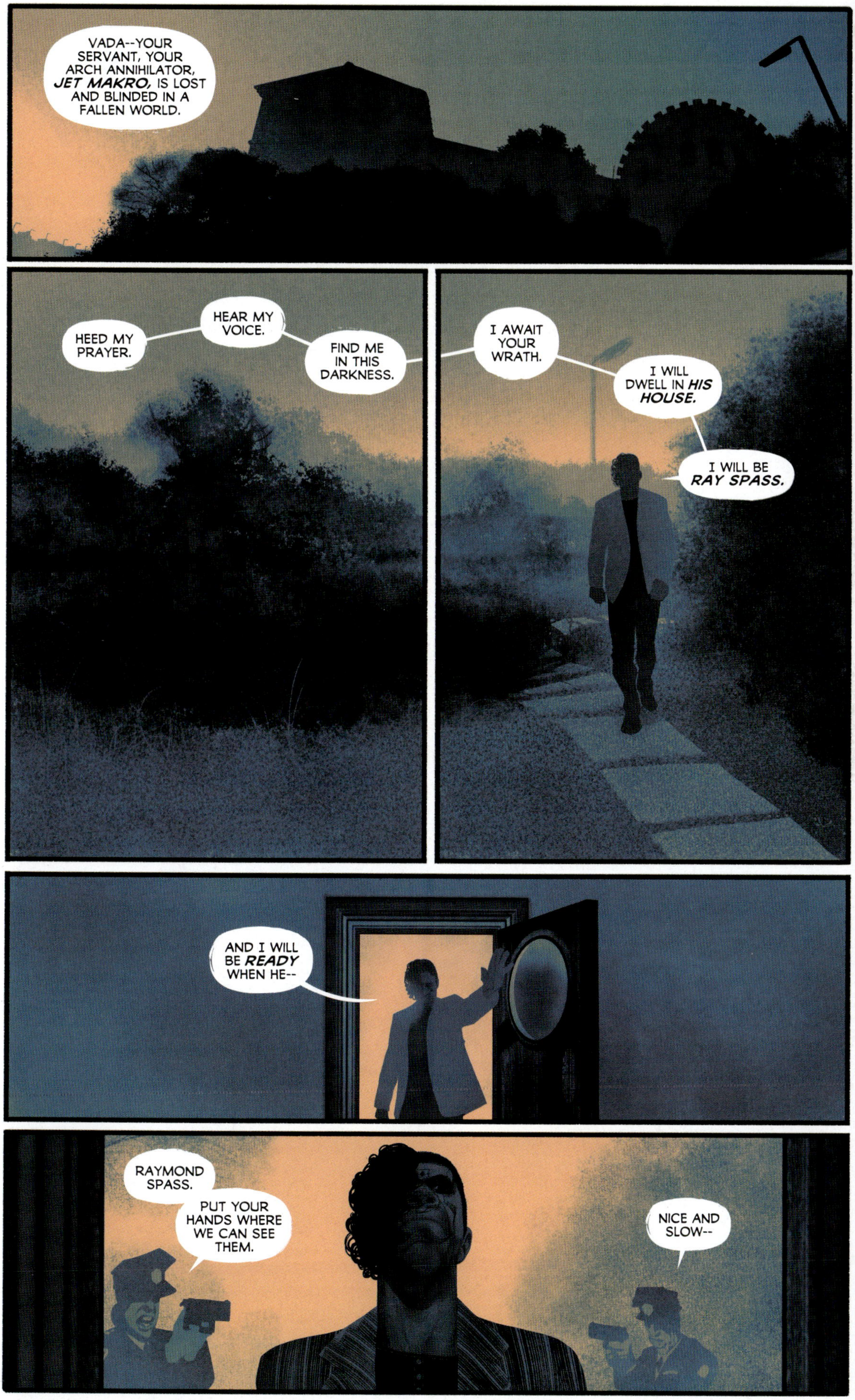
VADA--YOUR SERVANT, YOUR ARCH ANNIHILATOR, **JET MAKRO,** IS LOST AND BLINDED IN A FALLEN WORLD.
HEED MY PRAYER.
HEAR MY VOICE.
FIND ME IN THIS DARKNESS.
I AWAIT YOUR WRATH.
I WILL DWELL IN **HIS HOUSE.**
I WILL BE **RAY SPASS.**
AND I WILL BE **READY** WHEN HE--
RAYMOND SPASS.
PUT YOUR HANDS WHERE WE CAN SEE THEM.
NICE AND SLOW--

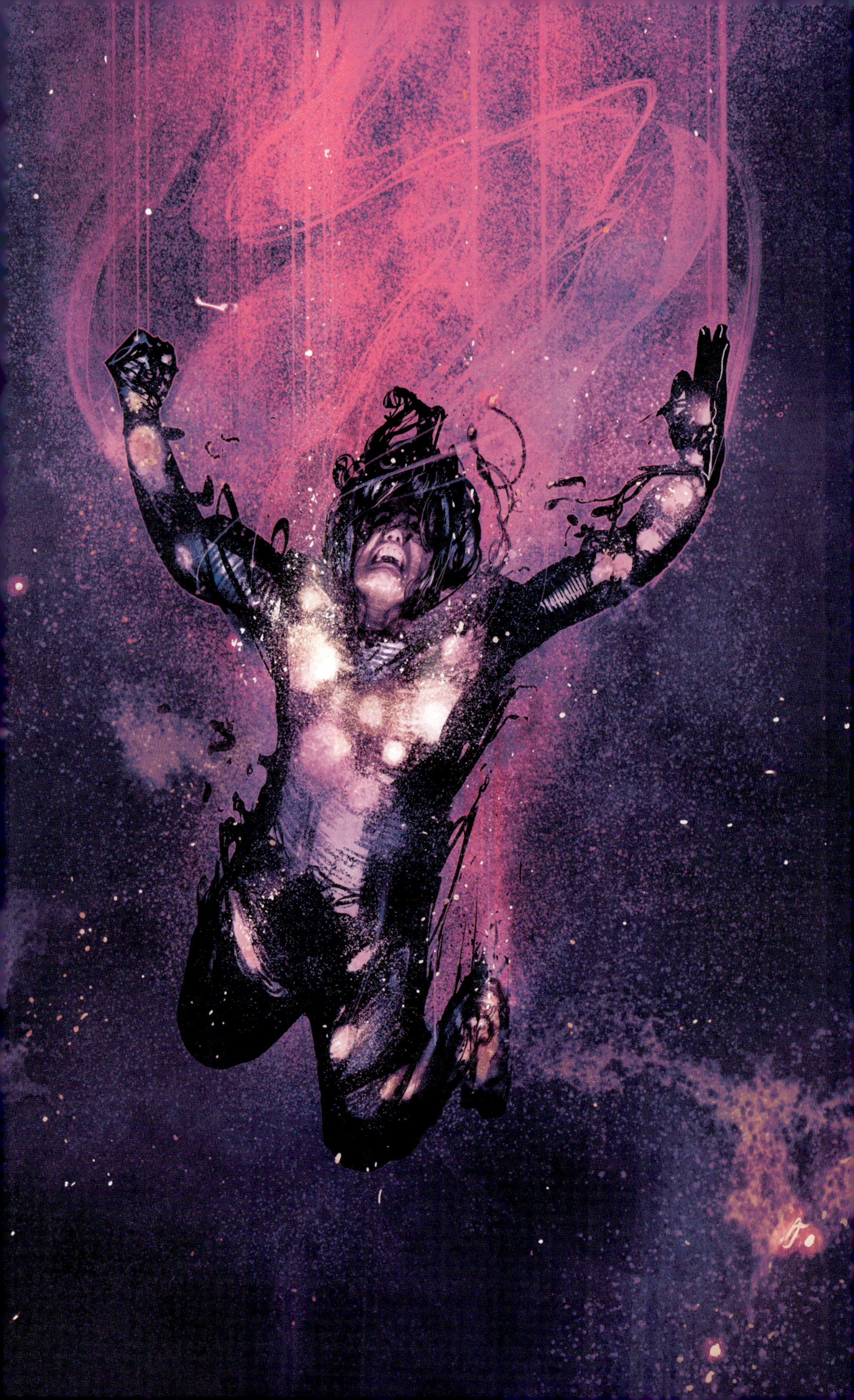

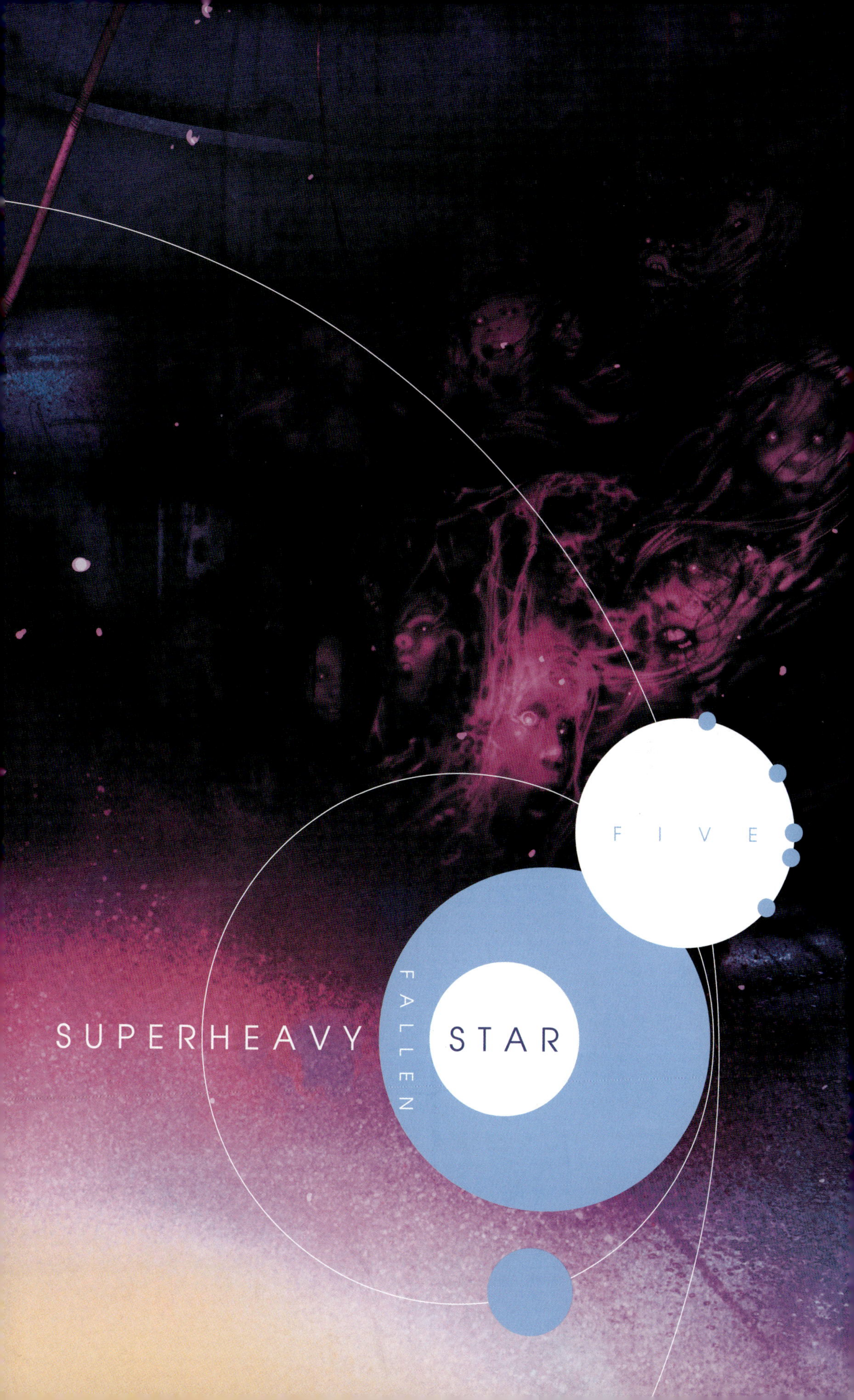
FIVE
SUPERHEAVY
FALLEN
STAR

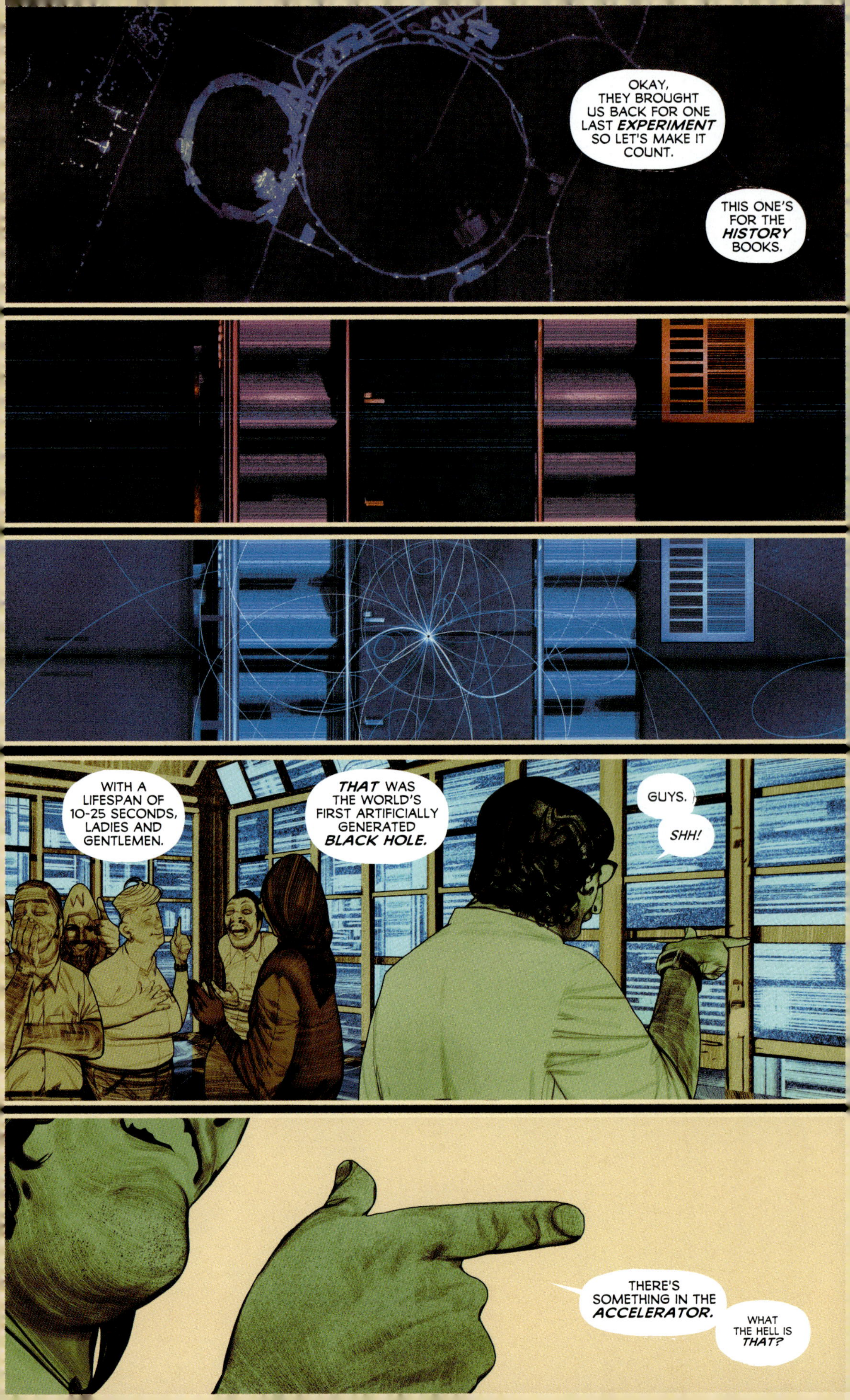
OKAY, THEY BROUGHT US BACK FOR ONE LAST *EXPERIMENT* SO LET'S MAKE IT COUNT.
THIS ONE'S FOR THE *HISTORY* BOOKS.
WITH A LIFESPAN OF 10-25 SECONDS, LADIES AND GENTLEMEN.
THAT WAS THE WORLD'S FIRST ARTIFICIALLY GENERATED *BLACK HOLE.*
GUYS.
SHH!
THERE'S SOMETHING IN THE *ACCELERATOR.*
WHAT THE HELL IS *THAT?*

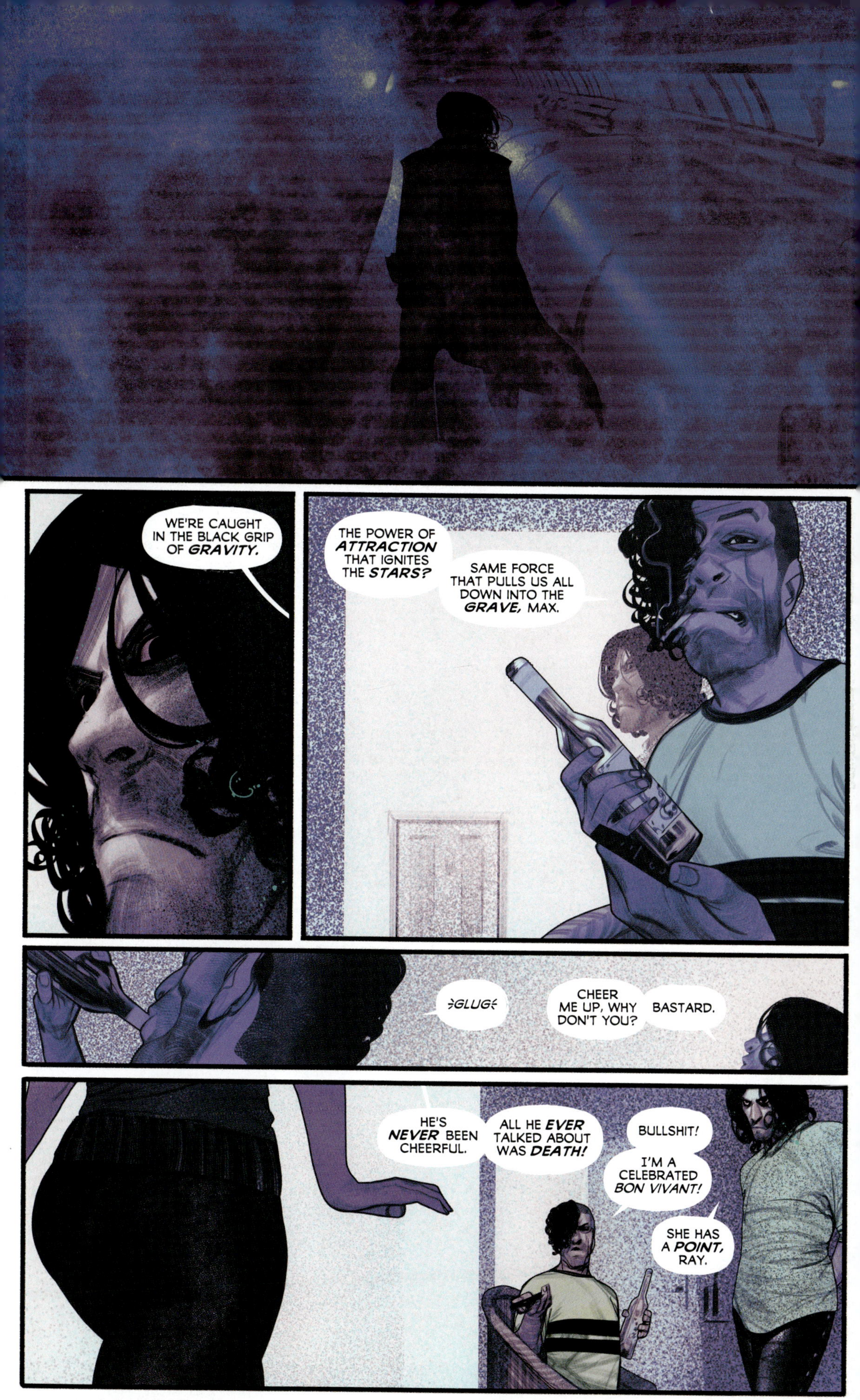
WE'RE CAUGHT IN THE BLACK GRIP OF GRAVITY.
THE POWER OF ATTRACTION THAT IGNITES THE STARS?
SAME FORCE THAT PULLS US ALL DOWN INTO THE GRAVE, MAX.
GLUG
CHEER ME UP, WHY DON'T YOU?
BASTARD.
HE'S NEVER BEEN CHEERFUL.
ALL HE EVER TALKED ABOUT WAS DEATH!
BULLSHIT!
I'M A CELEBRATED BON VIVANT!
SHE HAS A POINT, RAY.

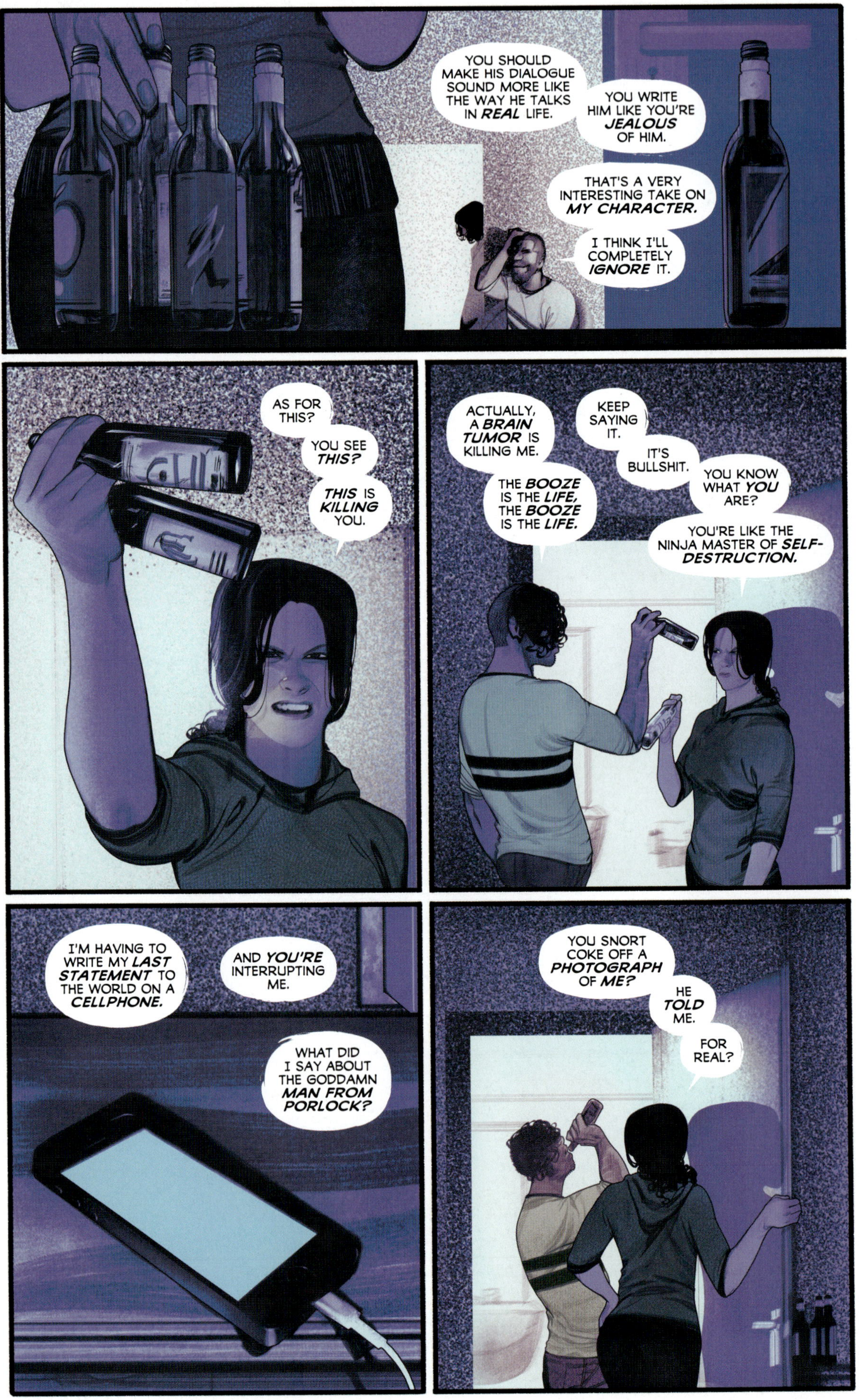
YOU SHOULD MAKE HIS DIALOGUE SOUND MORE LIKE THE WAY HE TALKS IN REAL LIFE.
YOU WRITE HIM LIKE YOU'RE JEALOUS OF HIM.
THAT'S A VERY INTERESTING TAKE ON MY CHARACTER.
I THINK I'LL COMPLETELY IGNORE IT.
AS FOR THIS?
YOU SEE THIS?
THIS IS KILLING YOU.
ACTUALLY, A BRAIN TUMOR IS KILLING ME.
THE BOOZE IS THE LIFE, THE BOOZE IS THE LIFE.
KEEP SAYING IT.
IT'S BULLSHIT.
YOU KNOW WHAT YOU ARE?
YOU'RE LIKE THE NINJA MASTER OF SELF-DESTRUCTION.
I'M HAVING TO WRITE MY LAST STATEMENT TO THE WORLD ON A CELLPHONE.
AND YOU'RE INTERRUPTING ME.
WHAT DID I SAY ABOUT THE GODDAMN MAN FROM PORLOCK?
YOU SNORT COKE OFF A PHOTOGRAPH OF ME?
HE TOLD ME.
FOR REAL?

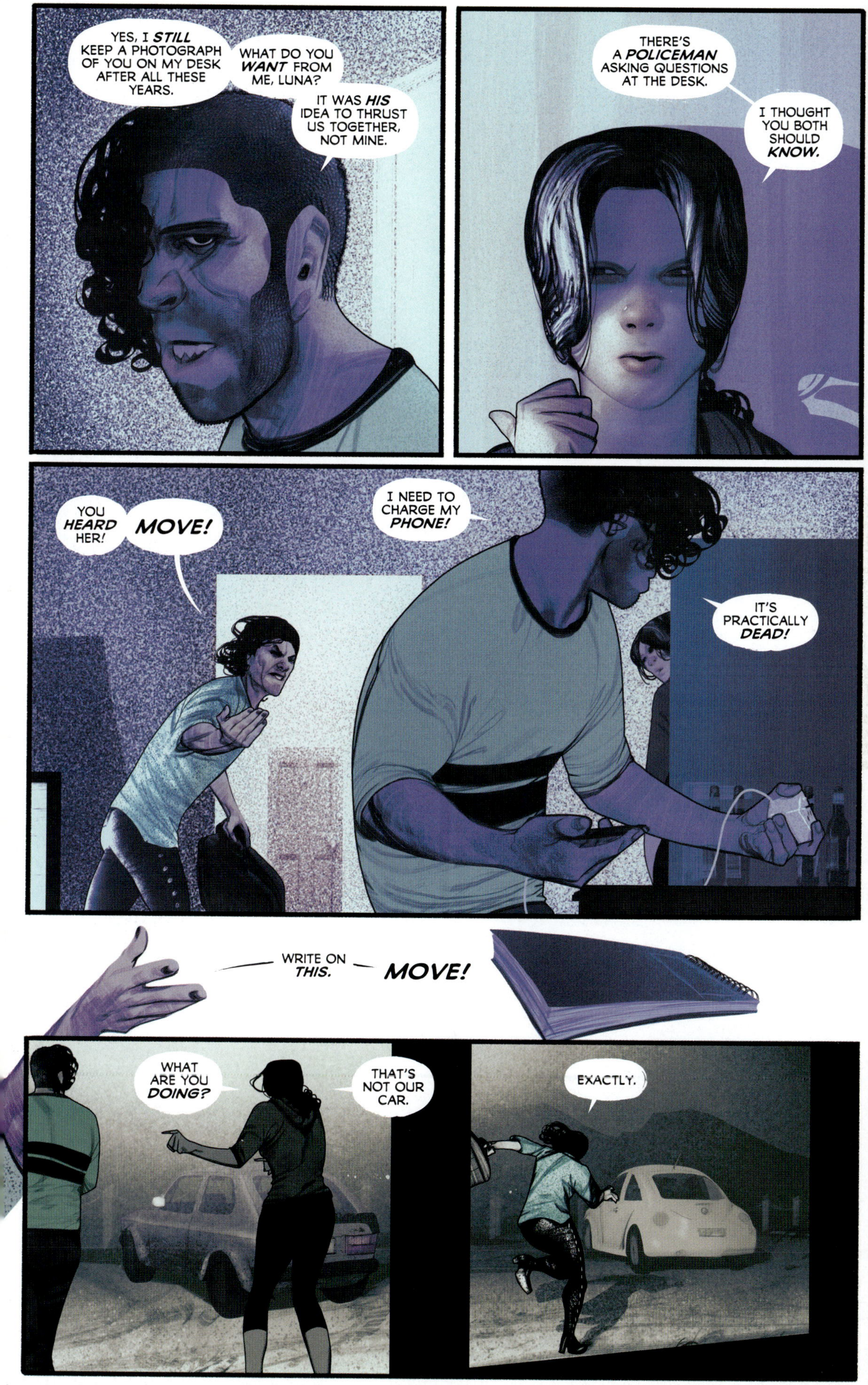
YES, I STILL KEEP A PHOTOGRAPH OF YOU ON MY DESK AFTER ALL THESE YEARS.
WHAT DO YOU WANT FROM ME, LUNA?
IT WAS HIS IDEA TO THRUST US TOGETHER, NOT MINE.
THERE'S A POLICEMAN ASKING QUESTIONS AT THE DESK.
I THOUGHT YOU BOTH SHOULD KNOW.
YOU HEARD HER!
MOVE!
I NEED TO CHARGE MY PHONE!
IT'S PRACTICALLY DEAD!
WRITE ON THIS.
MOVE!
WHAT ARE YOU DOING?
THAT'S NOT OUR CAR.
EXACTLY.

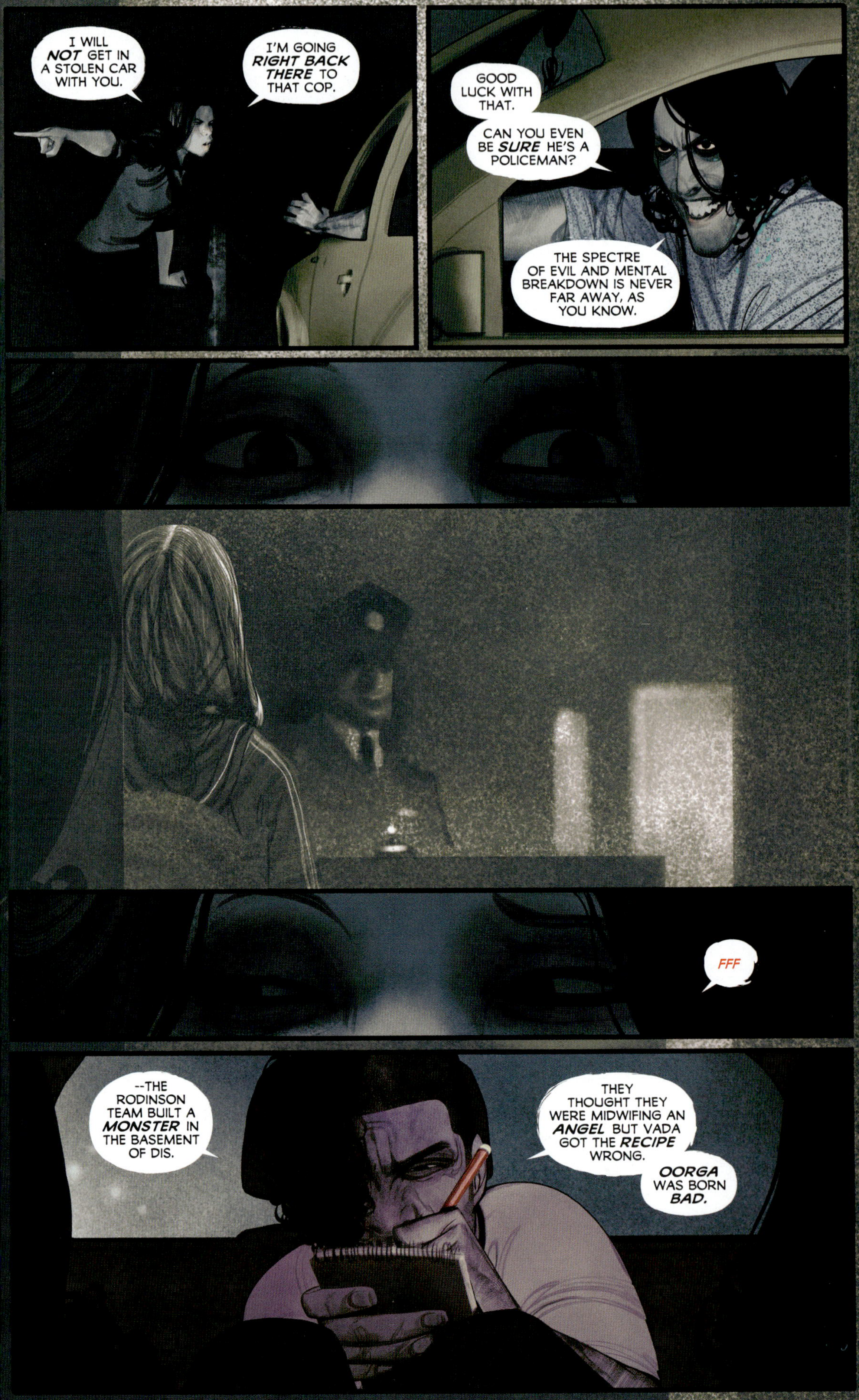
I WILL NOT GET IN A STOLEN CAR WITH YOU.
I'M GOING RIGHT BACK THERE TO THAT COP.
GOOD LUCK WITH THAT.
CAN YOU EVEN BE SURE HE'S A POLICEMAN?
THE SPECTRE OF EVIL AND MENTAL BREAKDOWN IS NEVER FAR AWAY, AS YOU KNOW.
FFF
--THE RODINSON TEAM BUILT A MONSTER IN THE BASEMENT OF DIS.
THEY THOUGHT THEY WERE MIDWIFING AN ANGEL BUT VADA GOT THE RECIPE WRONG.
OORGA WAS BORN BAD.

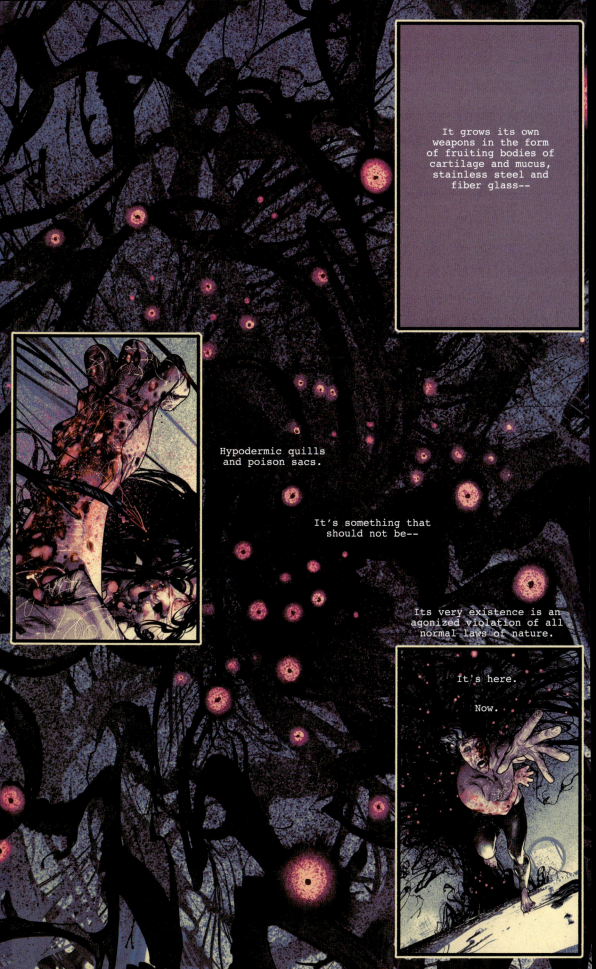

It grows its own weapons in the form of fruiting bodies of cartilage and mucus, stainless steel and fiber glass--

Hypodermic quills and poison sacs.

It's something that should not be--

Its very existence is an agonized violation of all normal laws of nature.

It's here.

Now.

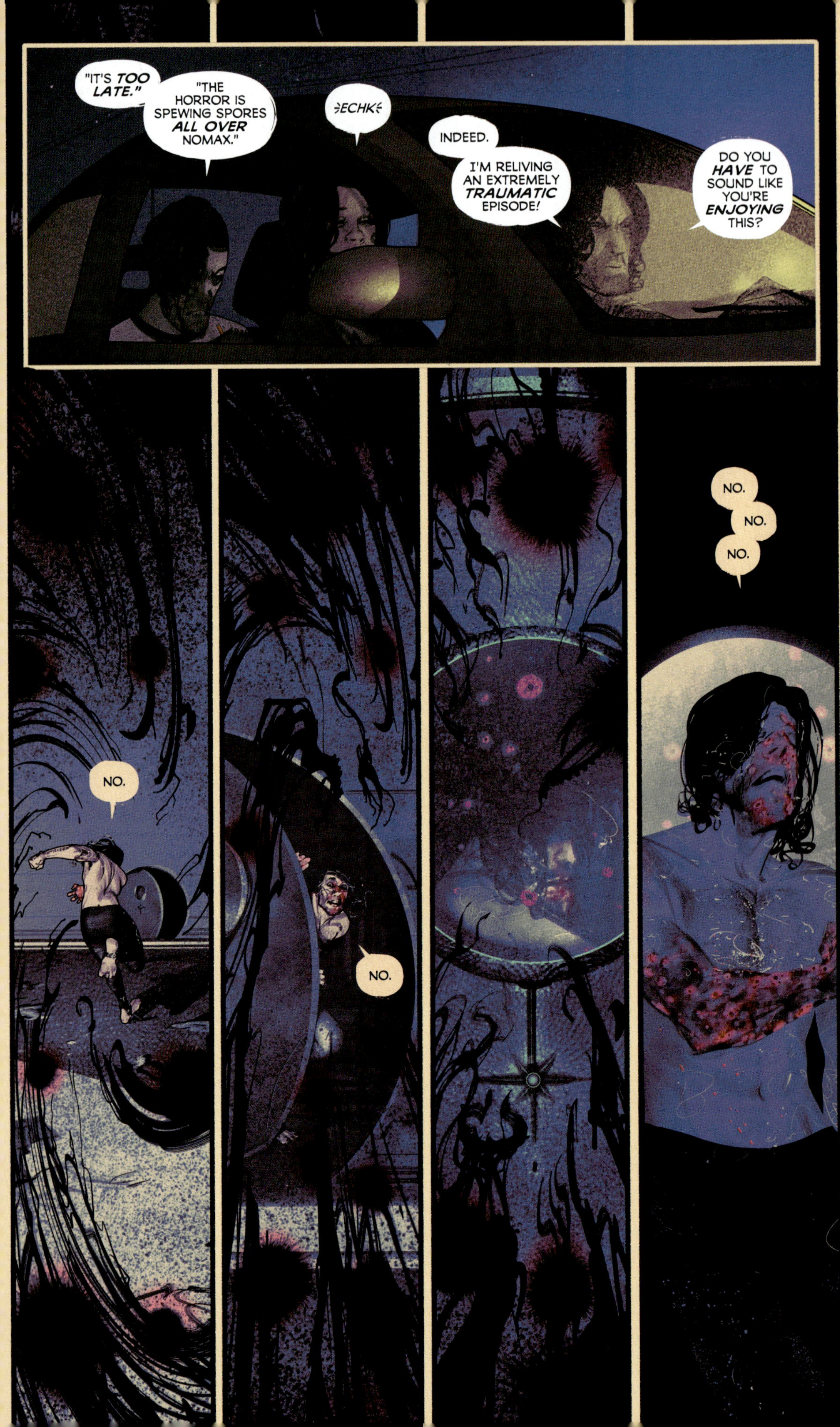
"IT'S TOO LATE."
"THE HORROR IS SPEWING SPORES ALL OVER NOMAX."
ECHK
INDEED.
I'M RELIVING AN EXTREMELY TRAUMATIC EPISODE!
DO YOU HAVE TO SOUND LIKE YOU'RE ENJOYING THIS?
NO.
NO.
NO.
NO.
NO.

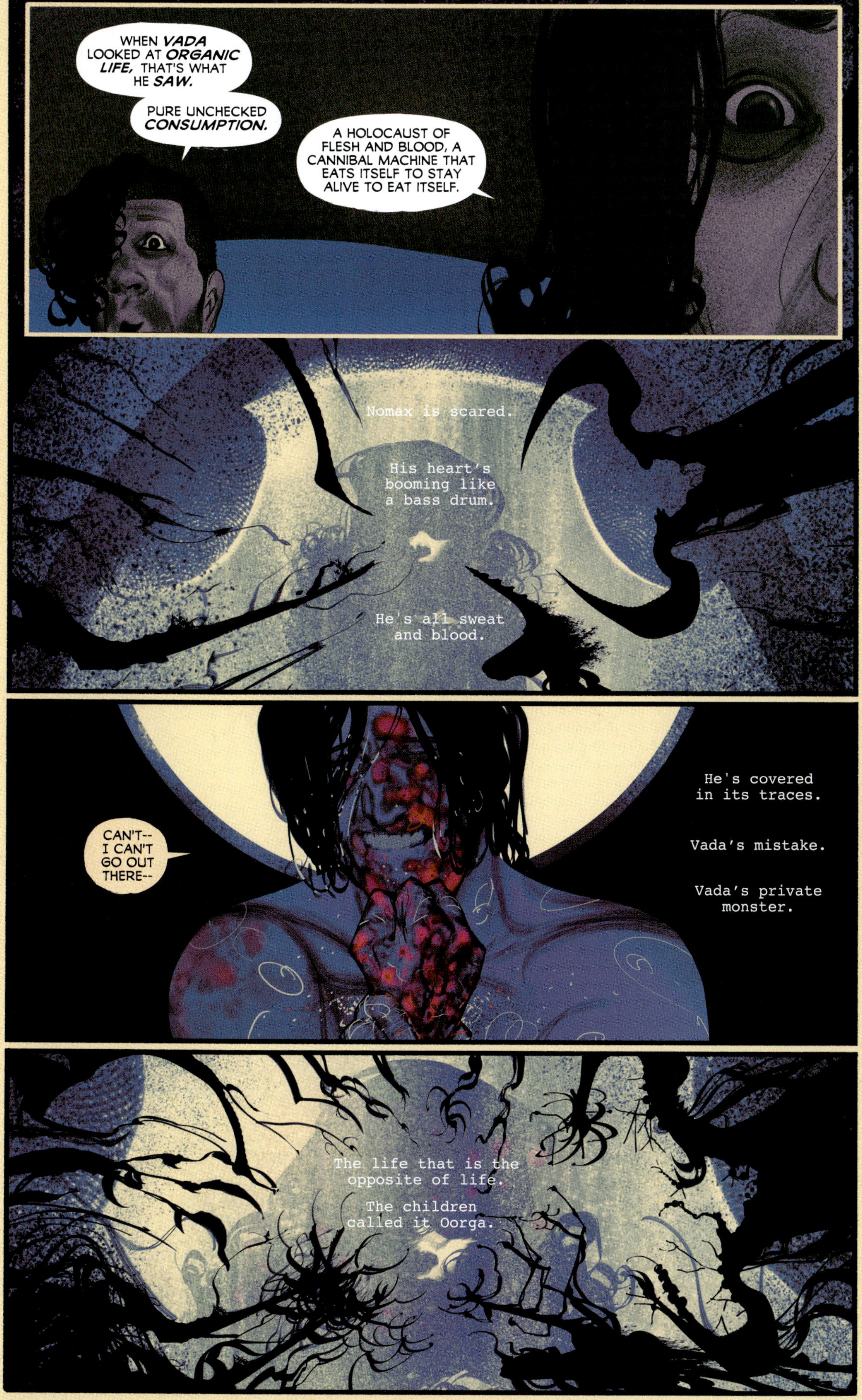
WHEN VADA LOOKED AT ORGANIC LIFE, THAT'S WHAT HE SAW.
PURE UNCHECKED CONSUMPTION.
A HOLOCAUST OF FLESH AND BLOOD, A CANNIBAL MACHINE THAT EATS ITSELF TO STAY ALIVE TO EAT ITSELF.
Nomax is scared.
His heart's booming like a bass drum.
He's all sweat and blood.
He's covered in its traces.
CAN'T-- I CAN'T GO OUT THERE--
Vada's mistake.
Vada's private monster.
The life that is the opposite of life.
The children called it Oorga.

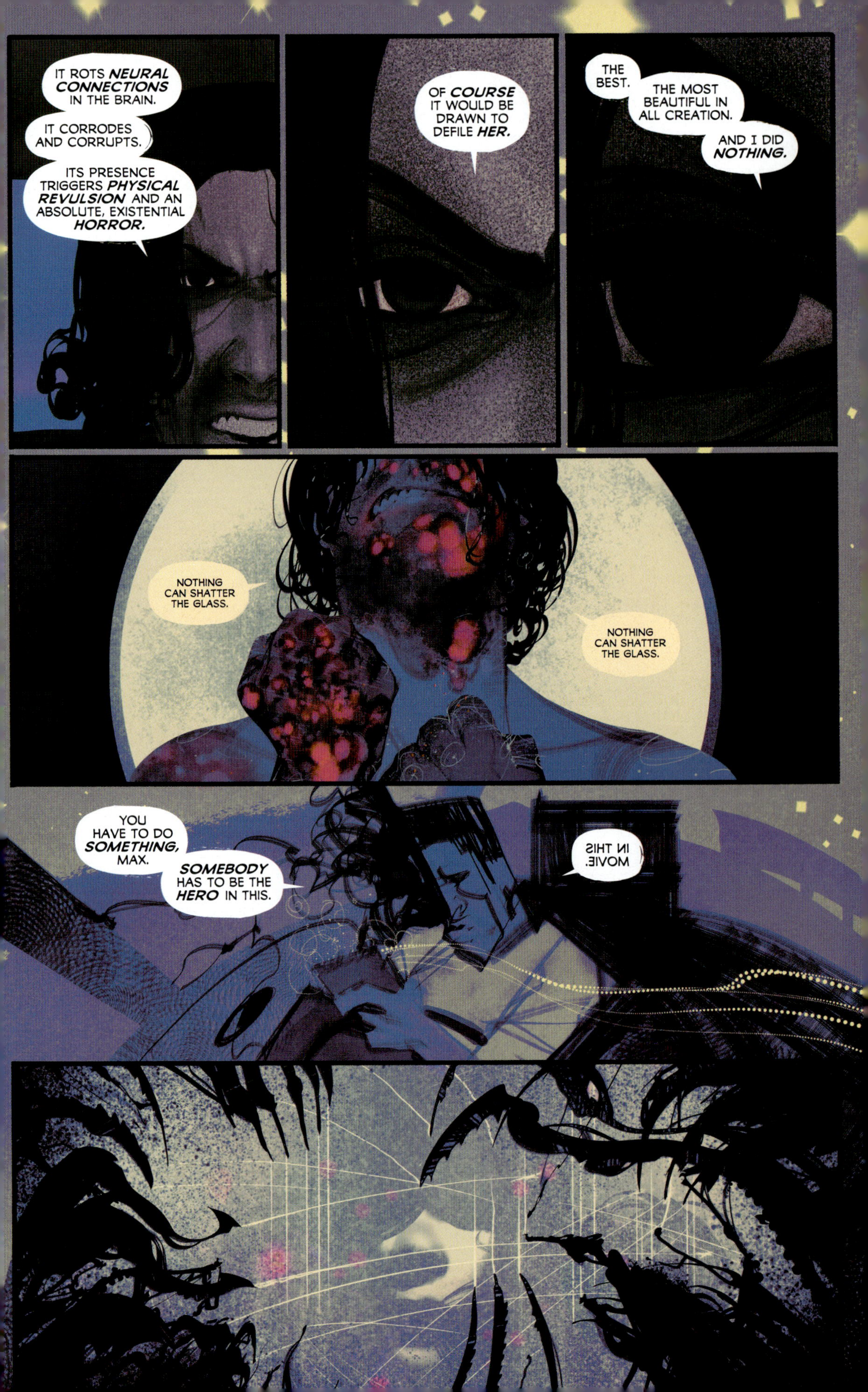
IT ROTS NEURAL CONNECTIONS IN THE BRAIN.
IT CORRODES AND CORRUPTS.
ITS PRESENCE TRIGGERS PHYSICAL REVULSION AND AN ABSOLUTE, EXISTENTIAL HORROR.
OF COURSE IT WOULD BE DRAWN TO DEFILE HER.
THE BEST.
THE MOST BEAUTIFUL IN ALL CREATION.
AND I DID NOTHING.
NOTHING CAN SHATTER THE GLASS.
NOTHING CAN SHATTER THE GLASS.
YOU HAVE TO DO SOMETHING, MAX.
SOMEBODY HAS TO BE THE HERO IN THIS.
IN THIS MOVIE.

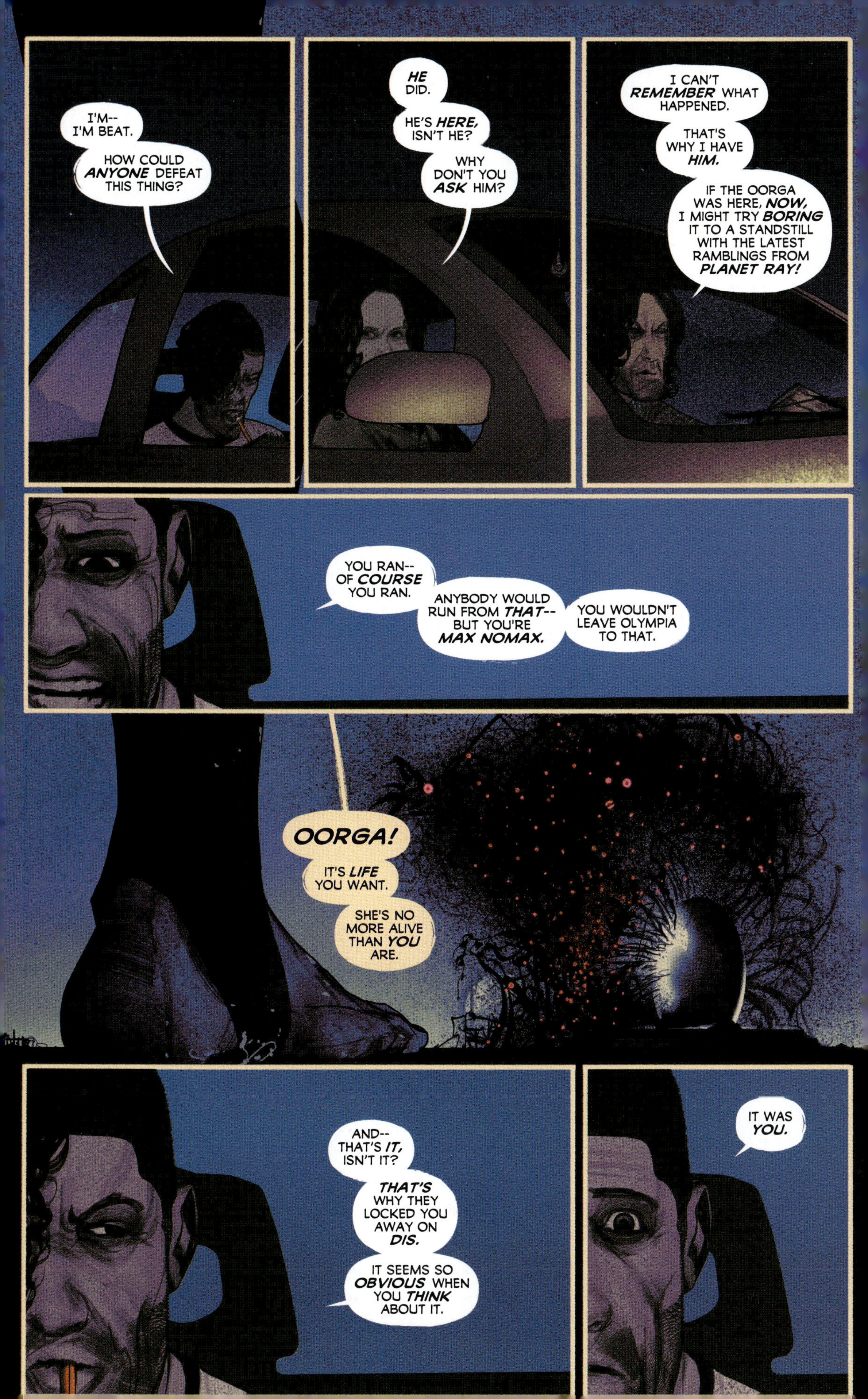
I'M--
I'M BEAT.
HOW COULD ANYONE DEFEAT THIS THING?
HE DID.
HE'S HERE, ISN'T HE?
WHY DON'T YOU ASK HIM?
I CAN'T REMEMBER WHAT HAPPENED.
THAT'S WHY I HAVE HIM.
IF THE OORGA WAS HERE, NOW, I MIGHT TRY BORING IT TO A STANDSTILL WITH THE LATEST RAMBLINGS FROM PLANET RAY!
YOU RAN-- OF COURSE YOU RAN.
ANYBODY WOULD RUN FROM THAT-- BUT YOU'RE MAX NOMAX.
YOU WOULDN'T LEAVE OLYMPIA TO THAT.
OORGA!
IT'S LIFE YOU WANT.
SHE'S NO MORE ALIVE THAN YOU ARE.
AND-- THAT'S IT, ISN'T IT?
THAT'S WHY THEY LOCKED YOU AWAY ON DIS.
IT SEEMS SO OBVIOUS WHEN YOU THINK ABOUT IT.
IT WAS YOU.

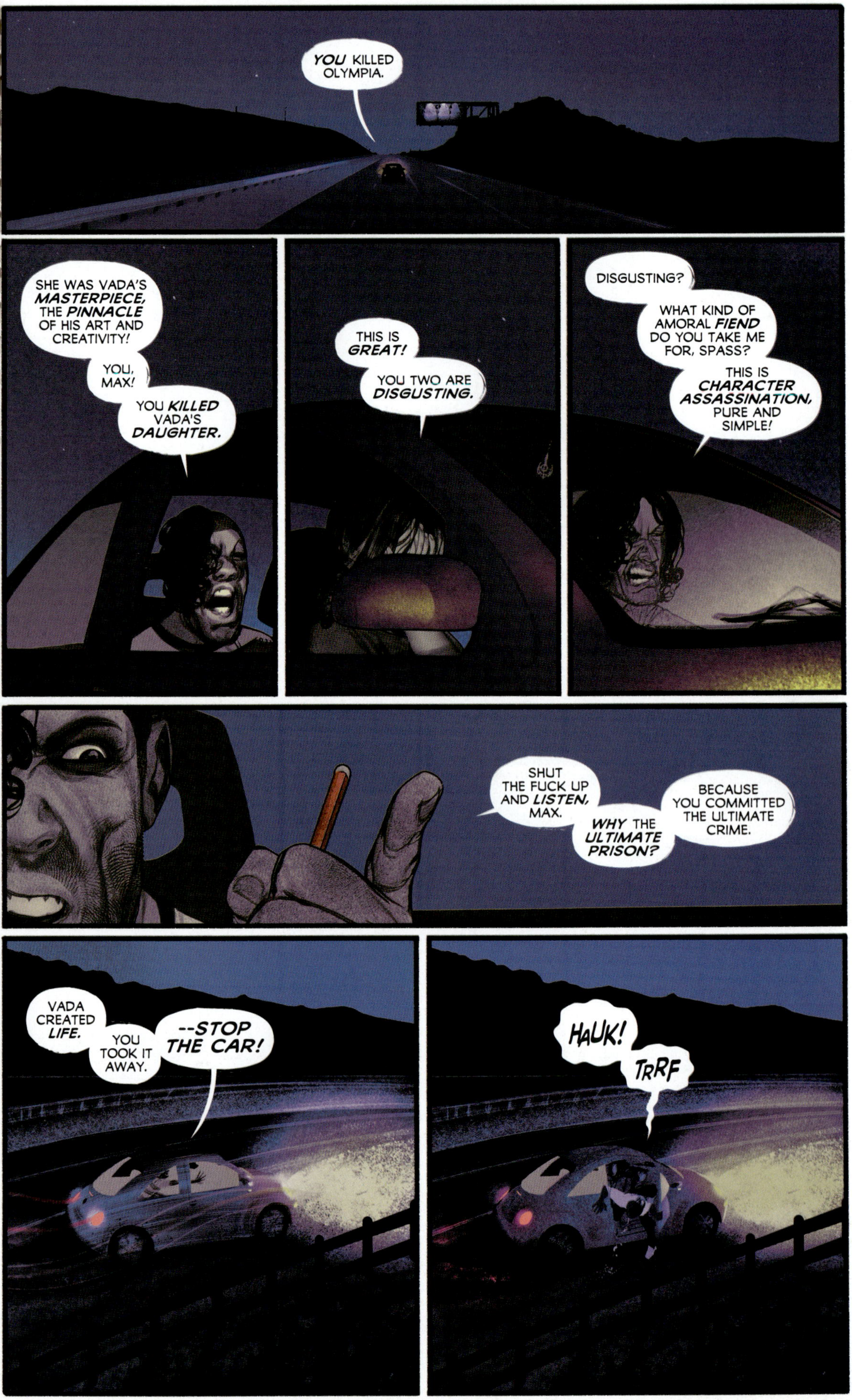
YOU KILLED OLYMPIA.
SHE WAS VADA'S MASTERPIECE, THE PINNACLE OF HIS ART AND CREATIVITY!
YOU, MAX!
YOU KILLED VADA'S DAUGHTER.
THIS IS GREAT!
YOU TWO ARE DISGUSTING.
DISGUSTING?
WHAT KIND OF AMORAL FIEND DO YOU TAKE ME FOR, SPASS?
THIS IS CHARACTER ASSASSINATION, PURE AND SIMPLE!
SHUT THE FUCK UP AND LISTEN, MAX.
WHY THE ULTIMATE PRISON?
BECAUSE YOU COMMITTED THE ULTIMATE CRIME.
VADA CREATED LIFE.
YOU TOOK IT AWAY.
--STOP THE CAR!
HAUK!
TRRF

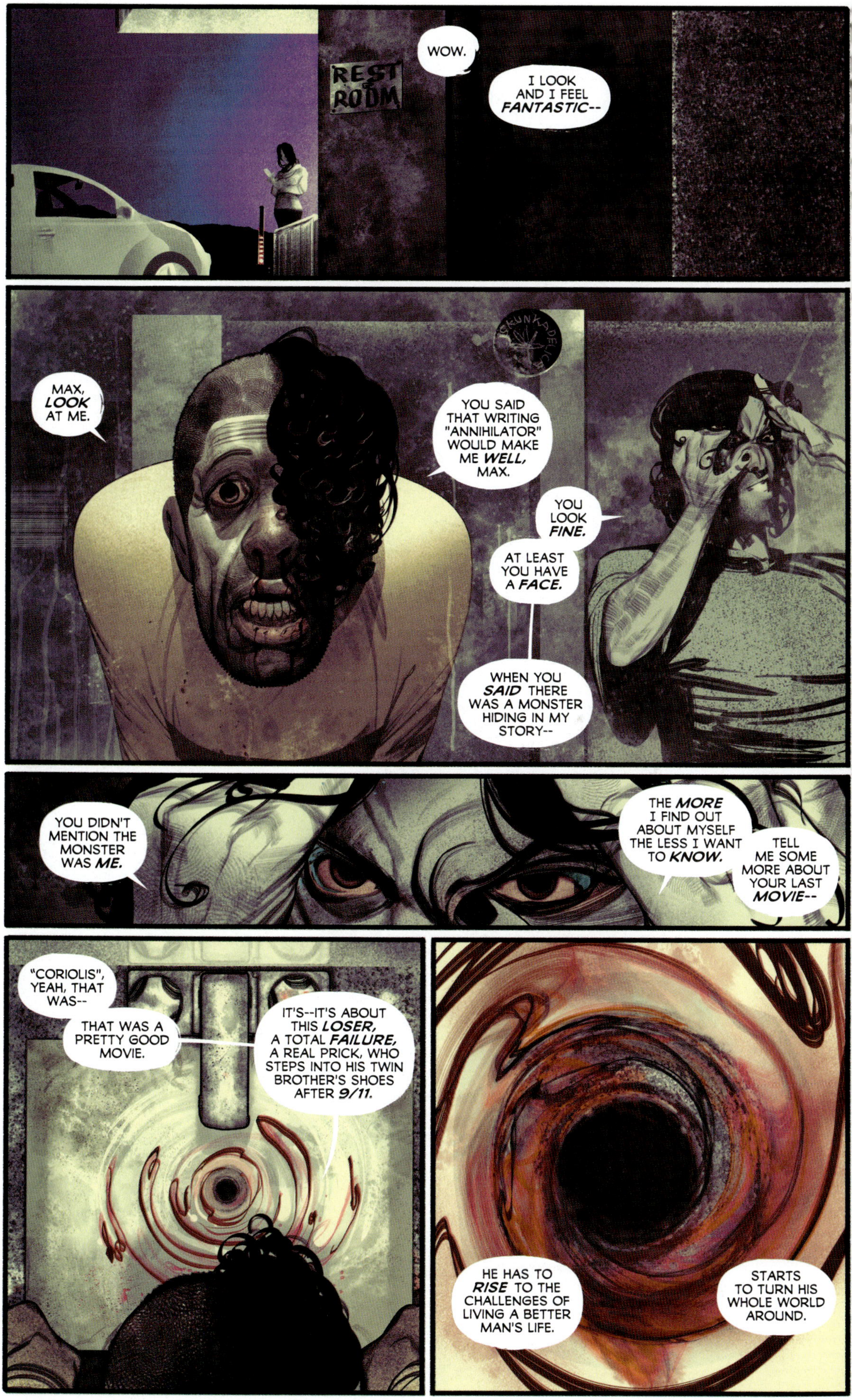

REST ROOM
WOW.
I LOOK AND I FEEL *FANTASTIC*--
MAX, *LOOK* AT ME.
YOU SAID THAT WRITING "ANNIHILATOR" WOULD MAKE ME *WELL,* MAX.
YOU LOOK *FINE.*
AT LEAST YOU HAVE A *FACE.*
WHEN YOU *SAID* THERE WAS A MONSTER HIDING IN MY STORY--
YOU DIDN'T MENTION THE MONSTER WAS *ME.*
THE *MORE* I FIND OUT ABOUT MYSELF THE LESS I WANT TO *KNOW.*
TELL ME SOME MORE ABOUT YOUR LAST *MOVIE*--
"CORIOLIS", YEAH, THAT WAS--
THAT WAS A PRETTY GOOD MOVIE.
IT'S--IT'S ABOUT THIS *LOSER,* A TOTAL *FAILURE,* A REAL PRICK, WHO STEPS INTO HIS TWIN BROTHER'S SHOES AFTER *9/11.*
HE HAS TO *RISE* TO THE CHALLENGES OF LIVING A BETTER MAN'S LIFE.
STARTS TO TURN HIS WHOLE WORLD AROUND.

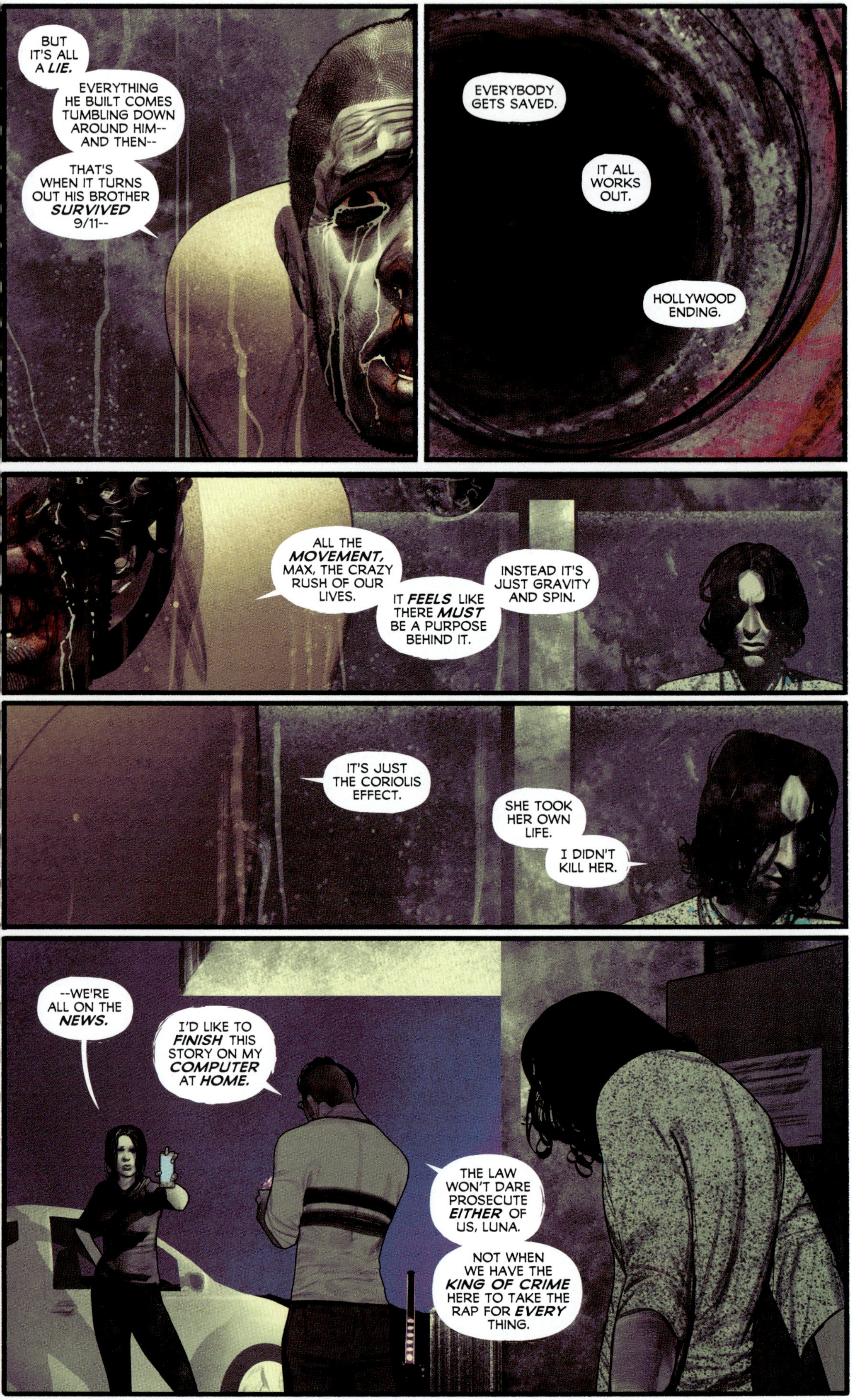

BUT IT'S ALL A *LIE.*
EVERYTHING HE BUILT COMES TUMBLING DOWN AROUND HIM-- AND THEN--
THAT'S WHEN IT TURNS OUT HIS BROTHER *SURVIVED* 9/11--
EVERYBODY GETS SAVED.
IT ALL WORKS OUT.
HOLLYWOOD ENDING.
ALL THE *MOVEMENT,* MAX, THE CRAZY RUSH OF OUR LIVES.
IT *FEELS* LIKE THERE *MUST* BE A PURPOSE BEHIND IT.
INSTEAD IT'S JUST GRAVITY AND SPIN.
IT'S JUST THE CORIOLIS EFFECT.
SHE TOOK HER OWN LIFE.
I DIDN'T KILL HER.
--WE'RE ALL ON THE *NEWS.*
I'D LIKE TO *FINISH* THIS STORY ON MY *COMPUTER* AT *HOME.*
THE LAW WON'T DARE PROSECUTE *EITHER* OF US, LUNA.
NOT WHEN WE HAVE THE *KING OF CRIME* HERE TO TAKE THE RAP FOR *EVERY* THING.

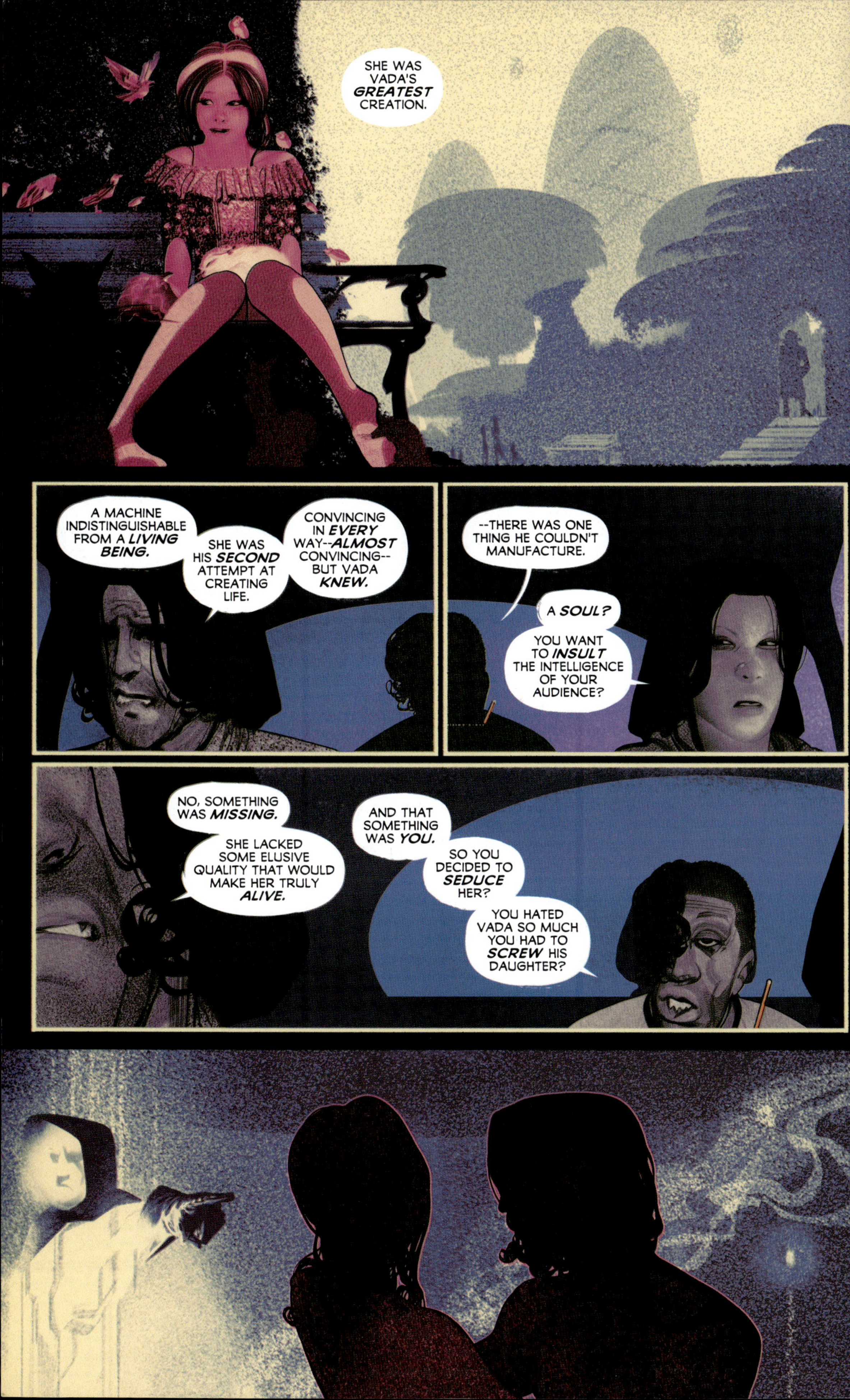
SHE WAS VADA'S *GREATEST* CREATION.
A MACHINE INDISTINGUISHABLE FROM A *LIVING BEING.*
SHE WAS HIS *SECOND* ATTEMPT AT CREATING LIFE.
CONVINCING IN *EVERY* WAY--*ALMOST* CONVINCING--BUT VADA *KNEW.*
--THERE WAS ONE THING HE COULDN'T MANUFACTURE.
A *SOUL?*
YOU WANT TO *INSULT* THE INTELLIGENCE OF YOUR AUDIENCE?
NO, SOMETHING WAS *MISSING.*
SHE LACKED SOME ELUSIVE QUALITY THAT WOULD MAKE HER TRULY *ALIVE.*
AND THAT SOMETHING WAS *YOU.*
SO YOU DECIDED TO *SEDUCE* HER?
YOU HATED VADA SO MUCH YOU HAD TO *SCREW* HIS DAUGHTER?

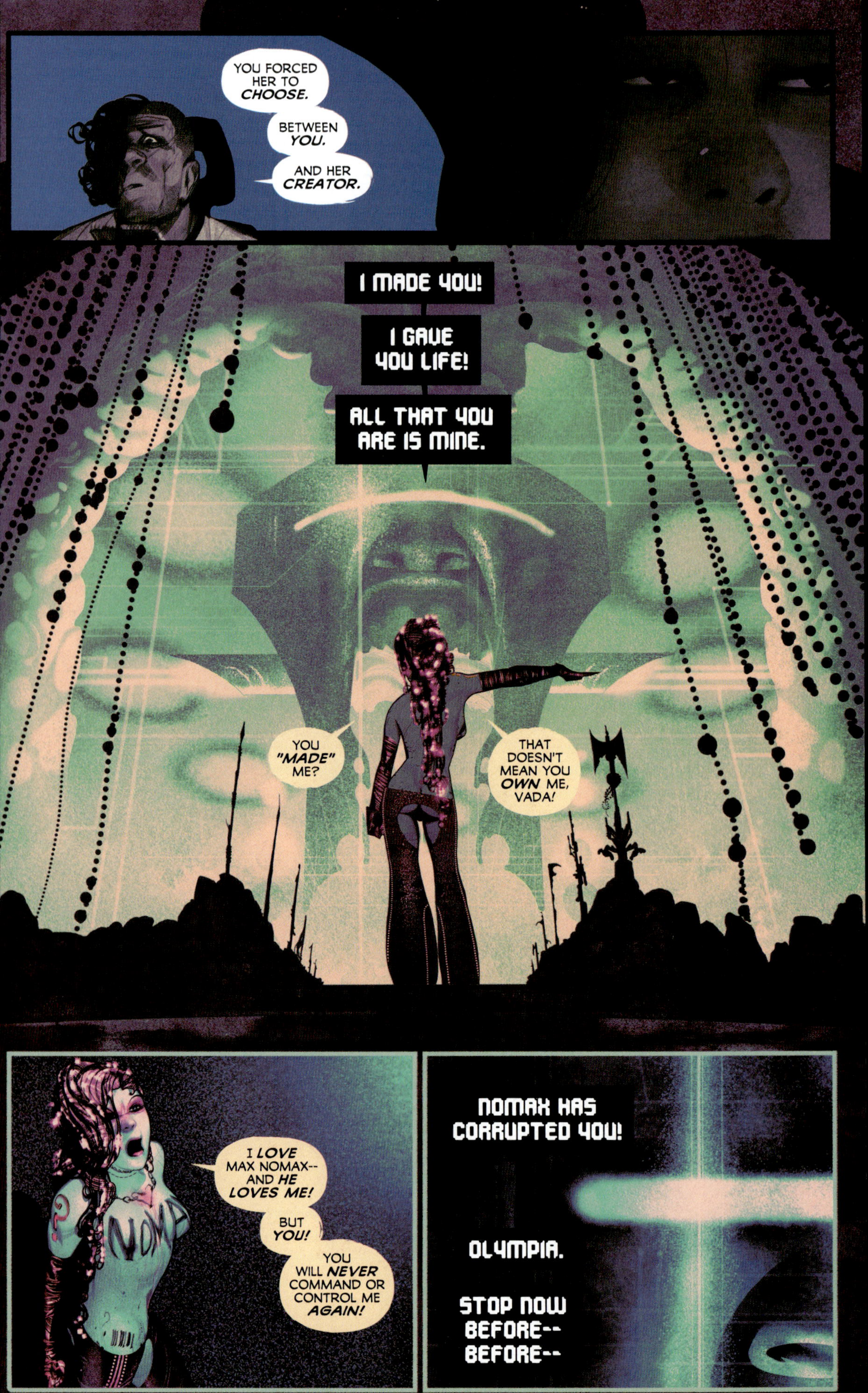
YOU FORCED HER TO *CHOOSE.*
BETWEEN *YOU.*
AND HER *CREATOR.*
I MADE YOU!
I GAVE YOU LIFE!
ALL THAT YOU ARE IS MINE.
YOU *"MADE"* ME?
THAT DOESN'T MEAN YOU *OWN* ME, VADA!
I *LOVE* MAX NOMAX-- AND *HE LOVES ME!*
BUT *YOU!*
YOU WILL *NEVER* COMMAND OR CONTROL ME *AGAIN!*
NOMAX HAS CORRUPTED YOU!
OLYMPIA.
STOP NOW BEFORE-- BEFORE-- BEFORE--

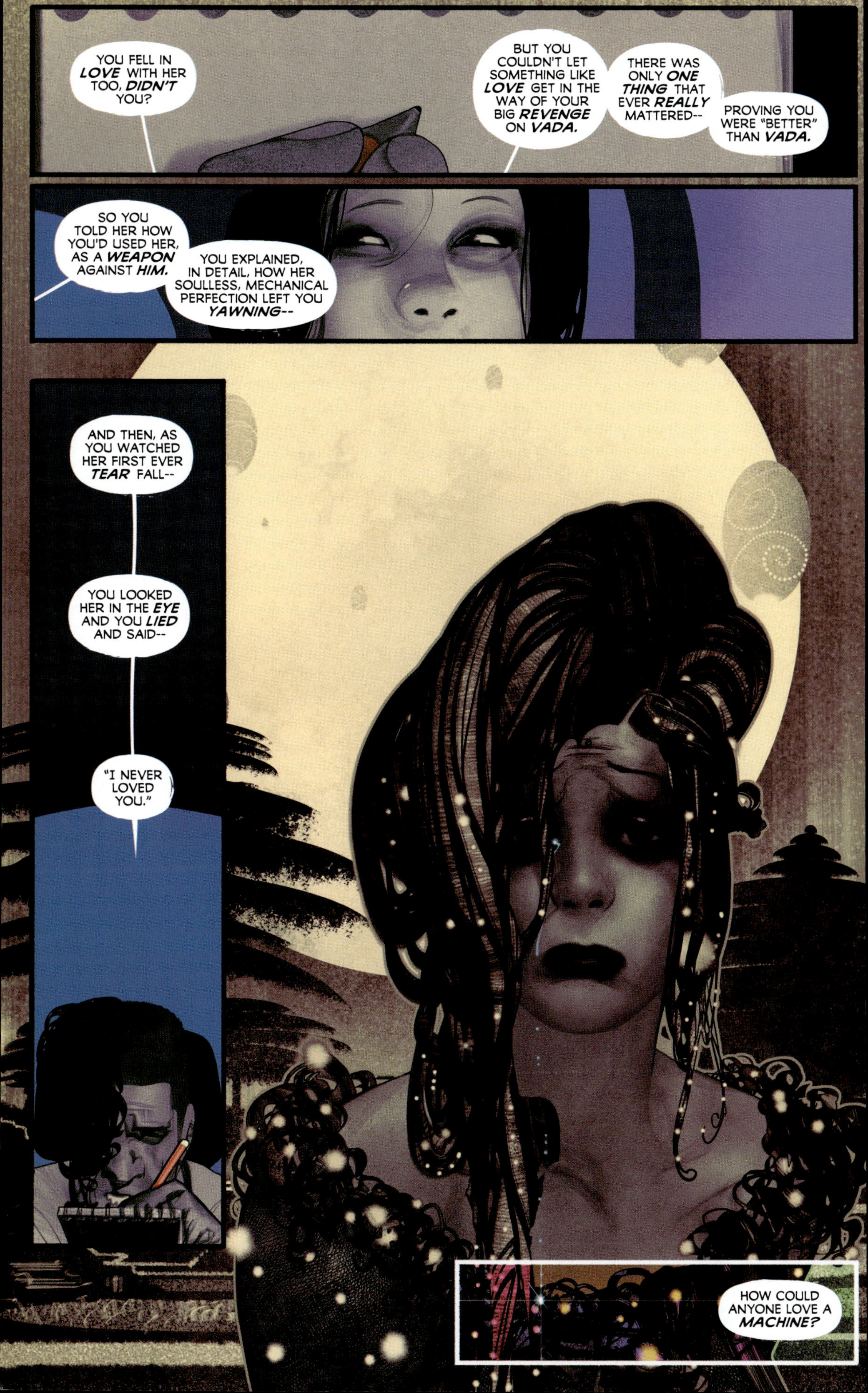
YOU FELL IN LOVE WITH HER TOO, DIDN'T YOU?
BUT YOU COULDN'T LET SOMETHING LIKE LOVE GET IN THE WAY OF YOUR BIG REVENGE ON VADA.
THERE WAS ONLY ONE THING THAT EVER REALLY MATTERED--
PROVING YOU WERE "BETTER" THAN VADA.
SO YOU TOLD HER HOW YOU'D USED HER, AS A WEAPON AGAINST HIM.
YOU EXPLAINED, IN DETAIL, HOW HER SOULLESS, MECHANICAL PERFECTION LEFT YOU YAWNING--
AND THEN, AS YOU WATCHED HER FIRST EVER TEAR FALL--
YOU LOOKED HER IN THE EYE AND YOU LIED AND SAID--
"I NEVER LOVED YOU."
HOW COULD ANYONE LOVE A MACHINE?

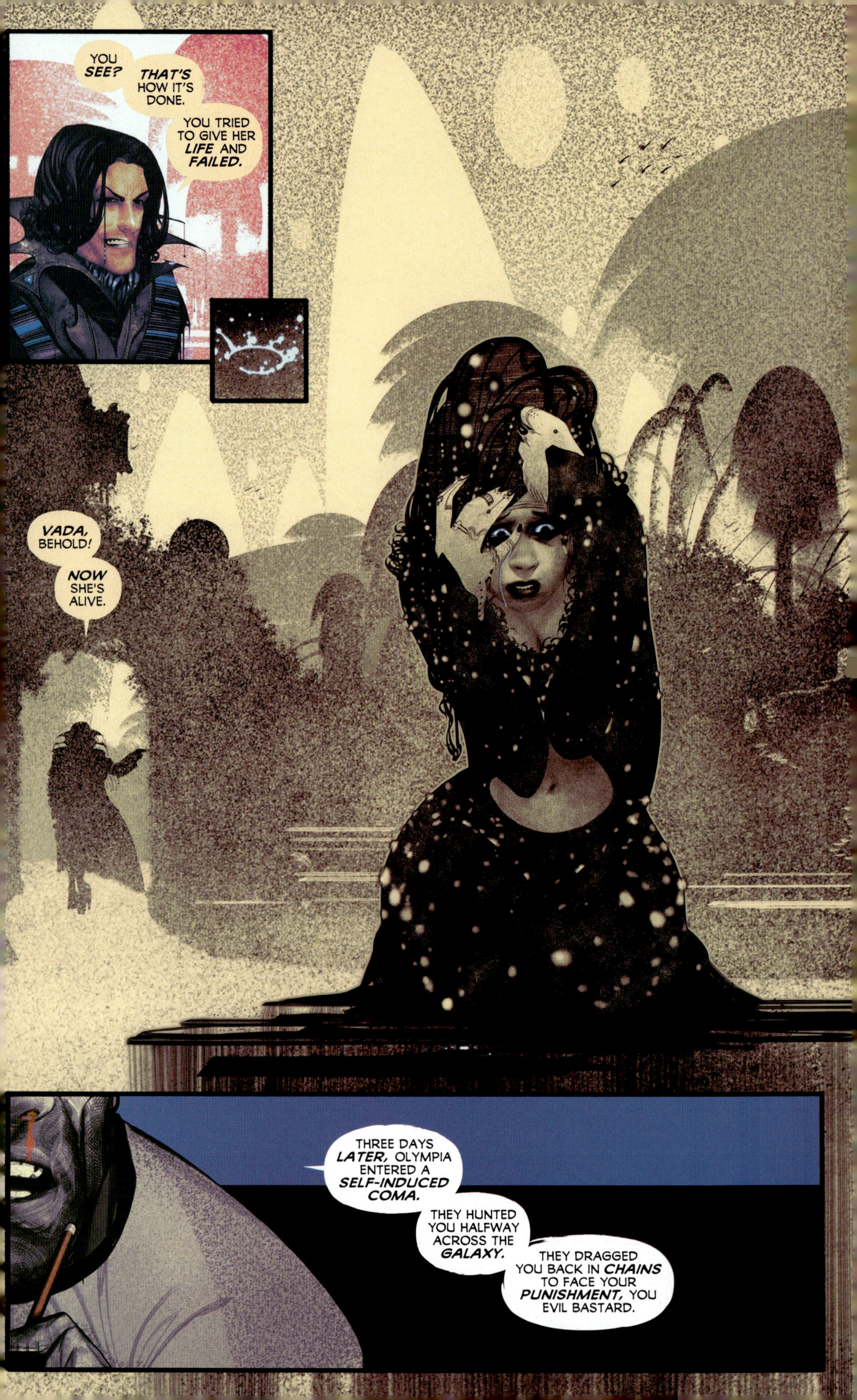
YOU SEE? THAT'S HOW IT'S DONE.
YOU TRIED TO GIVE HER LIFE AND FAILED.
VADA, BEHOLD!
NOW SHE'S ALIVE.
THREE DAYS LATER, OLYMPIA ENTERED A SELF-INDUCED COMA.
THEY HUNTED YOU HALFWAY ACROSS THE GALAXY.
THEY DRAGGED YOU BACK IN CHAINS TO FACE YOUR PUNISHMENT, YOU EVIL BASTARD.

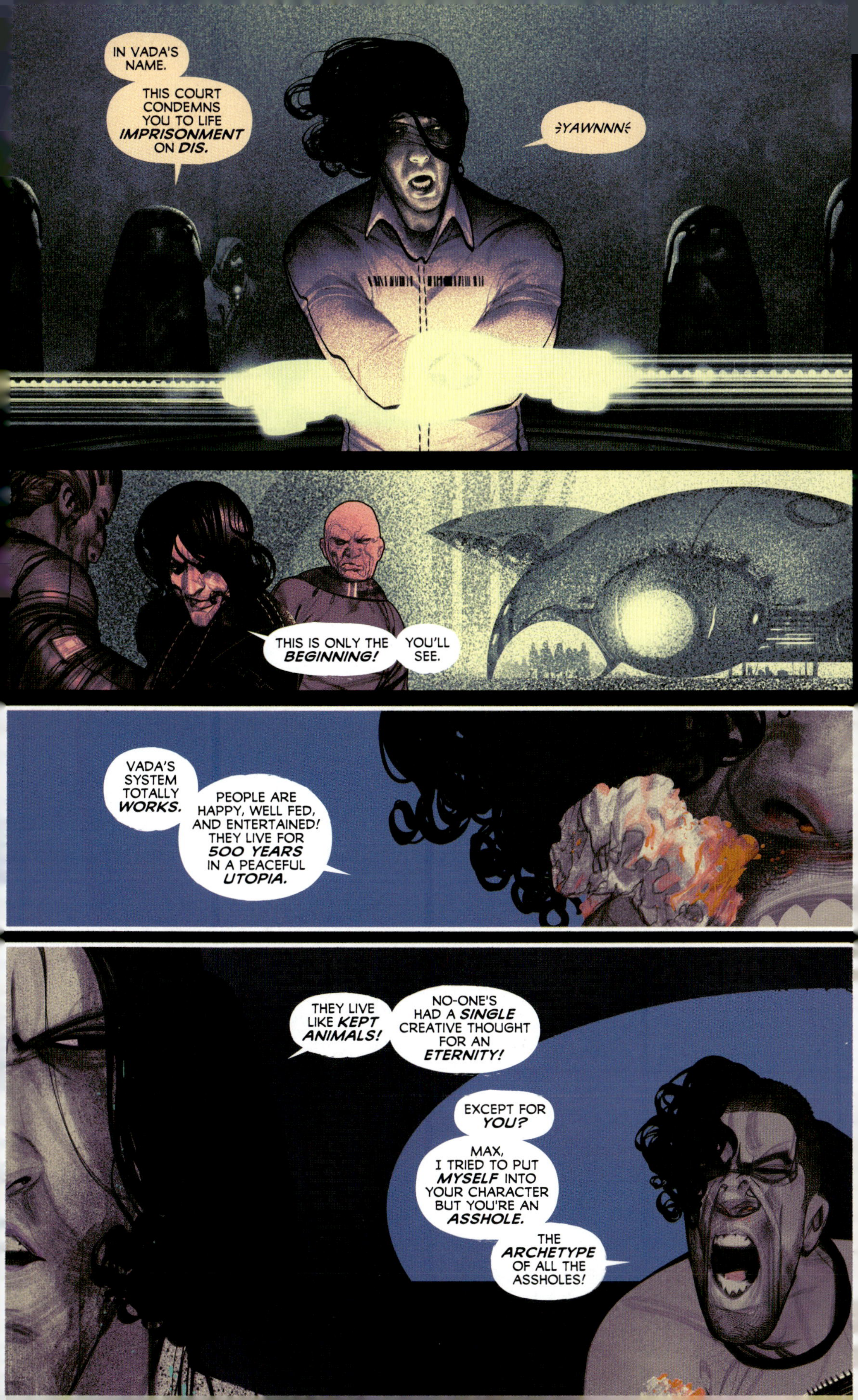
IN VADA'S NAME.
THIS COURT CONDEMNS YOU TO LIFE IMPRISONMENT ON DIS.
YAWNNN
THIS IS ONLY THE BEGINNING!
YOU'LL SEE.
VADA'S SYSTEM TOTALLY WORKS.
PEOPLE ARE HAPPY, WELL FED, AND ENTERTAINED! THEY LIVE FOR 500 YEARS IN A PEACEFUL UTOPIA.
THEY LIVE LIKE KEPT ANIMALS!
NO-ONE'S HAD A SINGLE CREATIVE THOUGHT FOR AN ETERNITY!
EXCEPT FOR YOU?
MAX, I TRIED TO PUT MYSELF INTO YOUR CHARACTER BUT YOU'RE AN ASSHOLE.
THE ARCHETYPE OF ALL THE ASSHOLES!

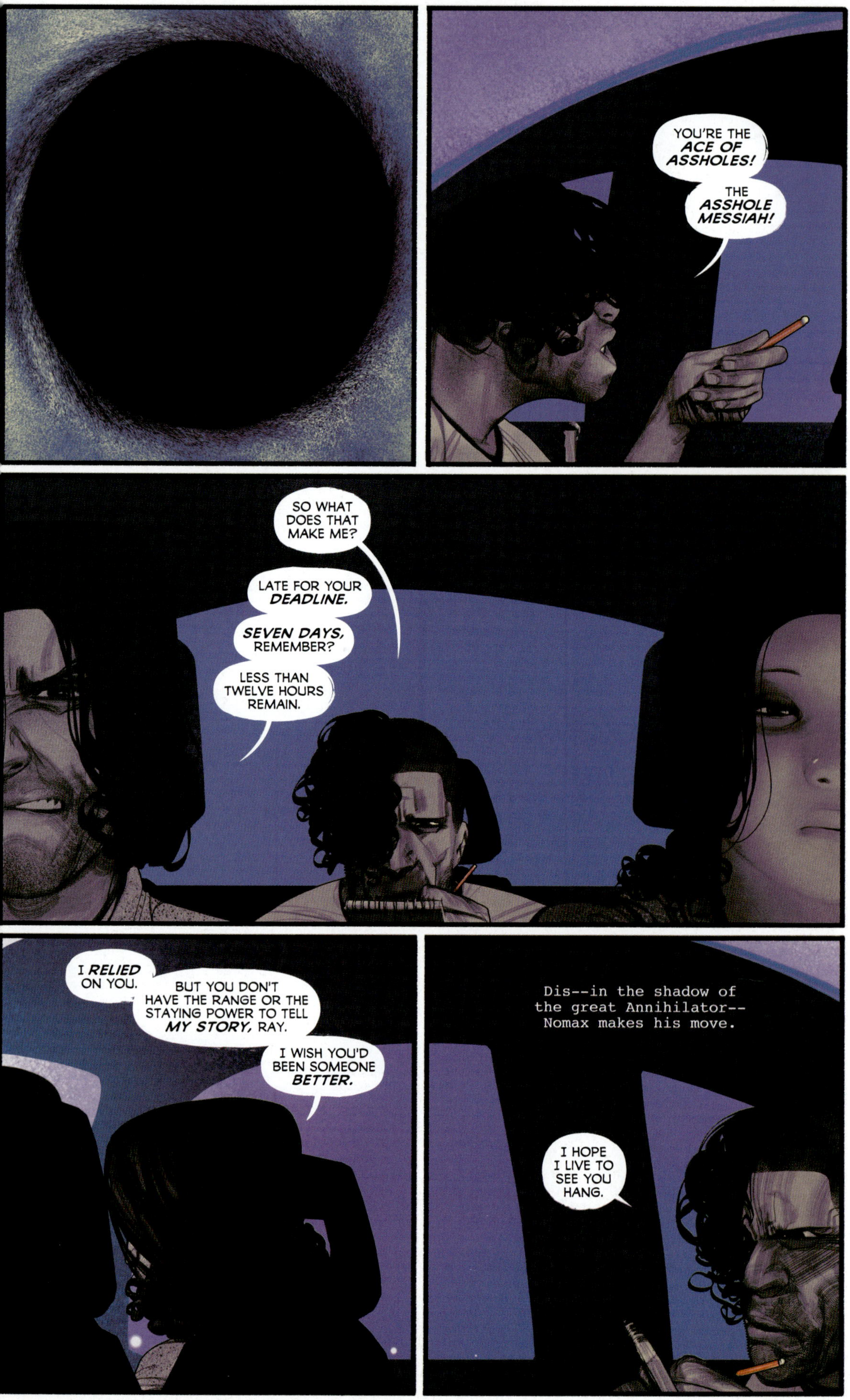
YOU'RE THE ACE OF ASSHOLES!
THE ASSHOLE MESSIAH!
SO WHAT DOES THAT MAKE ME?
LATE FOR YOUR DEADLINE.
SEVEN DAYS, REMEMBER?
LESS THAN TWELVE HOURS REMAIN.
I RELIED ON YOU.
BUT YOU DON'T HAVE THE RANGE OR THE STAYING POWER TO TELL MY STORY, RAY.
I WISH YOU'D BEEN SOMEONE BETTER.
Dis--in the shadow of the great Annihilator--Nomax makes his move.
I HOPE I LIVE TO SEE YOU HANG.

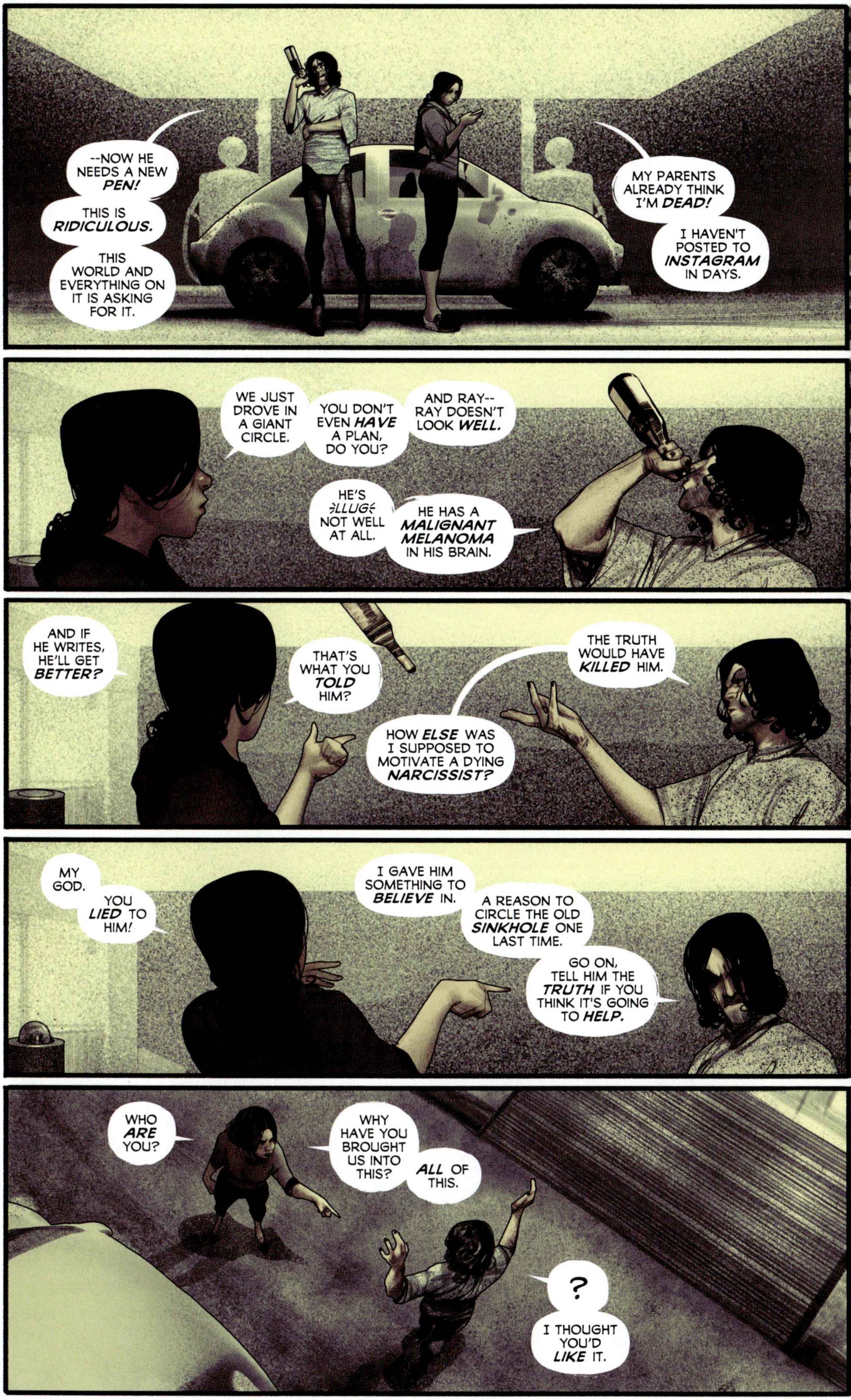

--NOW HE NEEDS A NEW PEN!
THIS IS RIDICULOUS.
THIS WORLD AND EVERYTHING ON IT IS ASKING FOR IT.
MY PARENTS ALREADY THINK I'M DEAD!
I HAVEN'T POSTED TO INSTAGRAM IN DAYS.
WE JUST DROVE IN A GIANT CIRCLE.
YOU DON'T EVEN HAVE A PLAN, DO YOU?
AND RAY-- RAY DOESN'T LOOK WELL.
HE'S GLLUG NOT WELL AT ALL.
HE HAS A MALIGNANT MELANOMA IN HIS BRAIN.
AND IF HE WRITES, HE'LL GET BETTER?
THAT'S WHAT YOU TOLD HIM?
THE TRUTH WOULD HAVE KILLED HIM.
HOW ELSE WAS I SUPPOSED TO MOTIVATE A DYING NARCISSIST?
MY GOD.
YOU LIED TO HIM!
I GAVE HIM SOMETHING TO BELIEVE IN.
A REASON TO CIRCLE THE OLD SINKHOLE ONE LAST TIME.
GO ON, TELL HIM THE TRUTH IF YOU THINK IT'S GOING TO HELP.
WHO ARE YOU?
WHY HAVE YOU BROUGHT US INTO THIS?
ALL OF THIS.
?
I THOUGHT YOU'D LIKE IT.

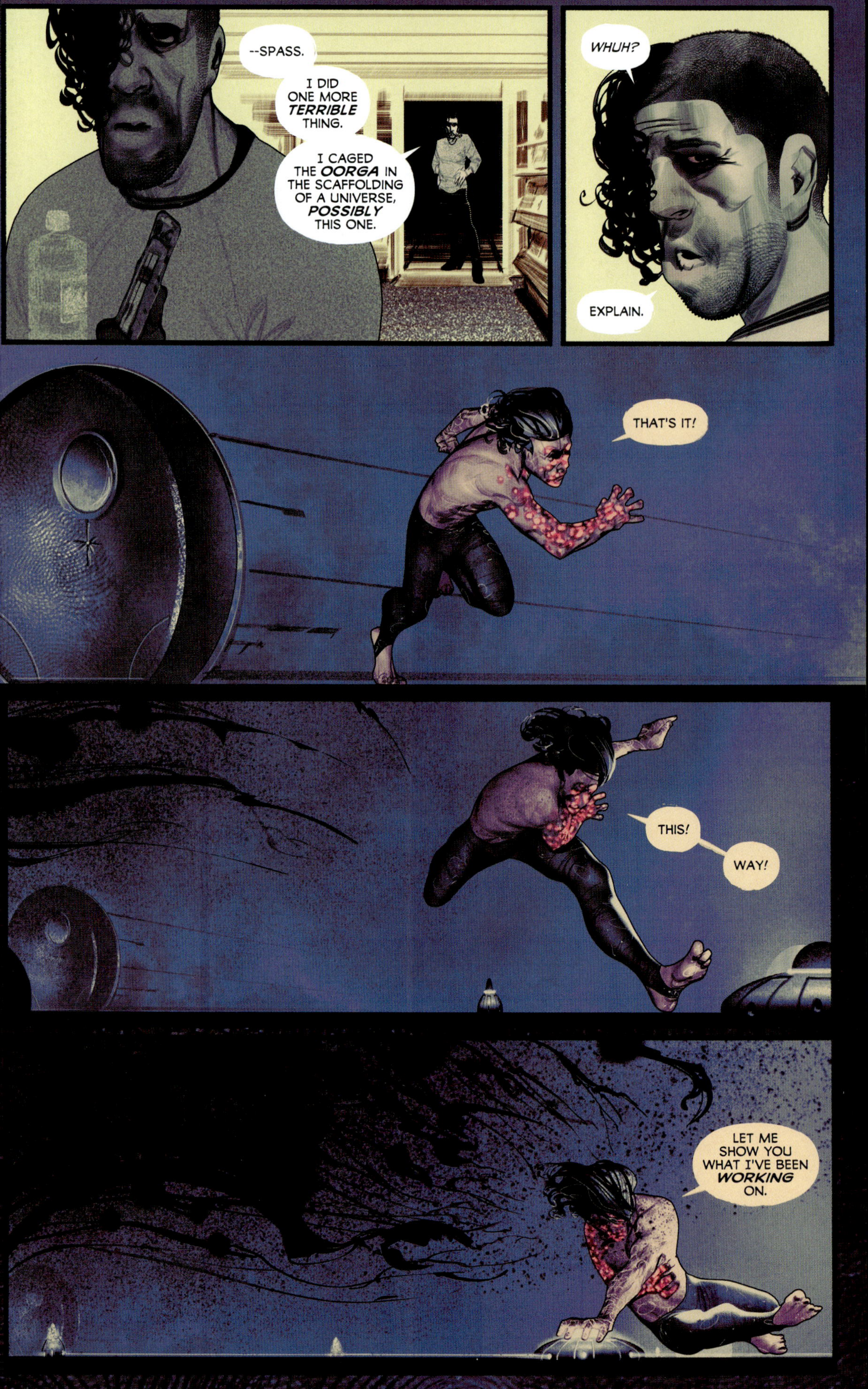
--SPASS.
I DID ONE MORE TERRIBLE THING.
I CAGED THE OORGA IN THE SCAFFOLDING OF A UNIVERSE, POSSIBLY THIS ONE.
WHUH?
EXPLAIN.
THAT'S IT!
THIS!
WAY!
LET ME SHOW YOU WHAT I'VE BEEN WORKING ON.

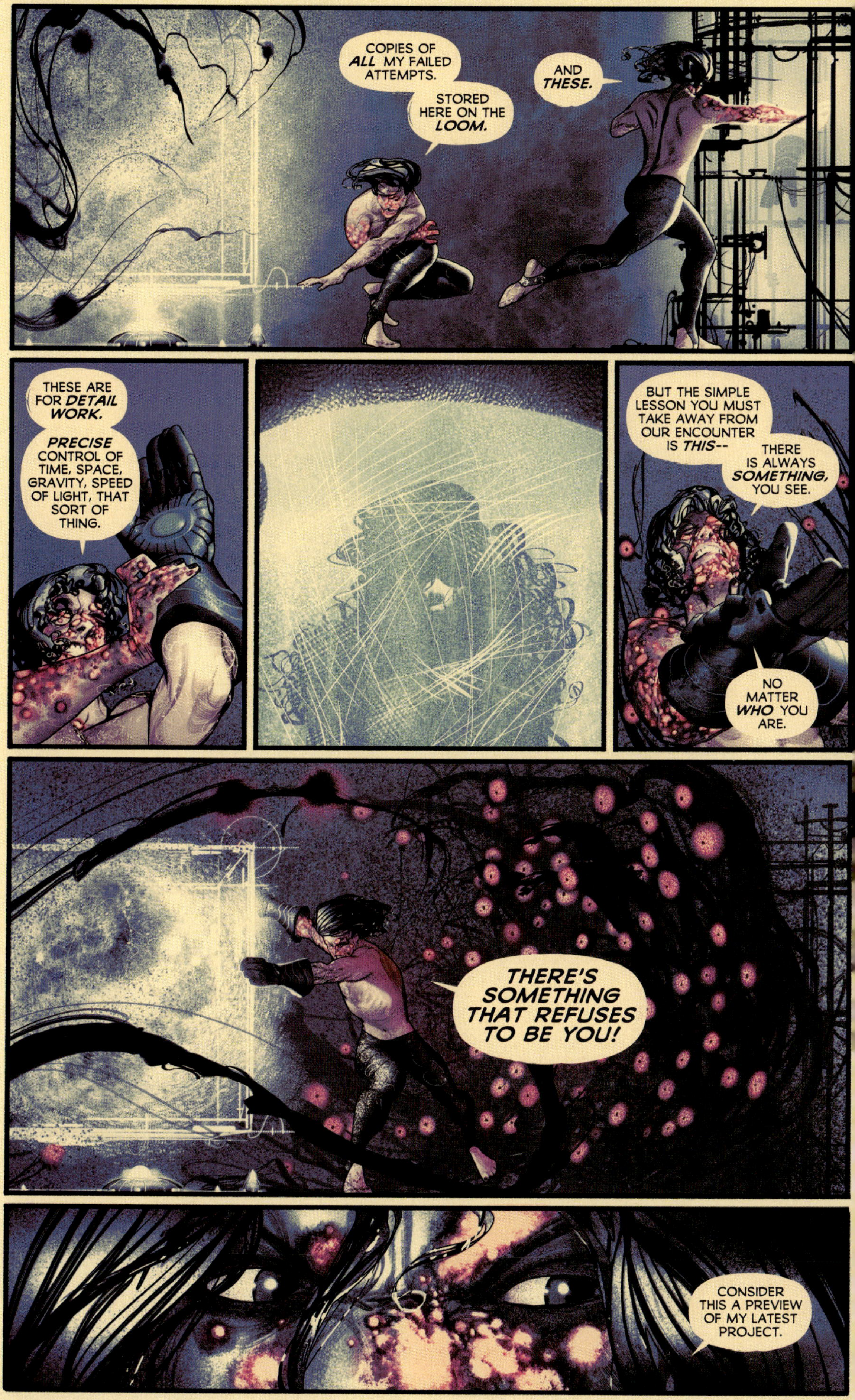
COPIES OF ALL MY FAILED ATTEMPTS.
STORED HERE ON THE LOOM.
AND THESE.
THESE ARE FOR DETAIL WORK.
PRECISE CONTROL OF TIME, SPACE, GRAVITY, SPEED OF LIGHT, THAT SORT OF THING.
BUT THE SIMPLE LESSON YOU MUST TAKE AWAY FROM OUR ENCOUNTER IS THIS--
THERE IS ALWAYS SOMETHING, YOU SEE.
NO MATTER WHO YOU ARE.
THERE'S SOMETHING THAT REFUSES TO BE YOU!
CONSIDER THIS A PREVIEW OF MY LATEST PROJECT.

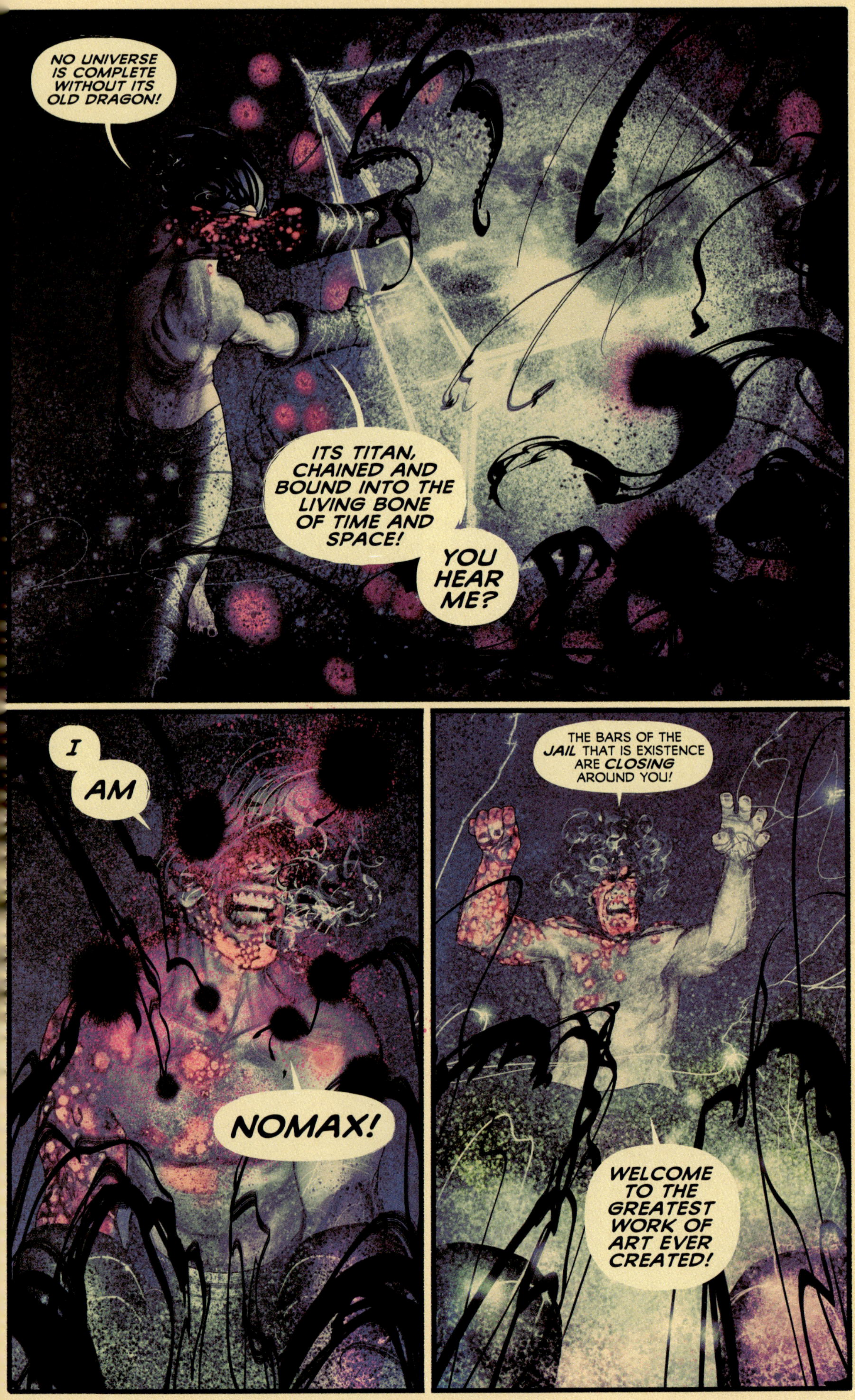
NO UNIVERSE IS COMPLETE WITHOUT ITS OLD DRAGON!
ITS TITAN, CHAINED AND BOUND INTO THE LIVING BONE OF TIME AND SPACE!
YOU HEAR ME?
I
AM
NOMAX!
THE BARS OF THE JAIL THAT IS EXISTENCE ARE CLOSING AROUND YOU!
WELCOME TO THE GREATEST WORK OF ART EVER CREATED!

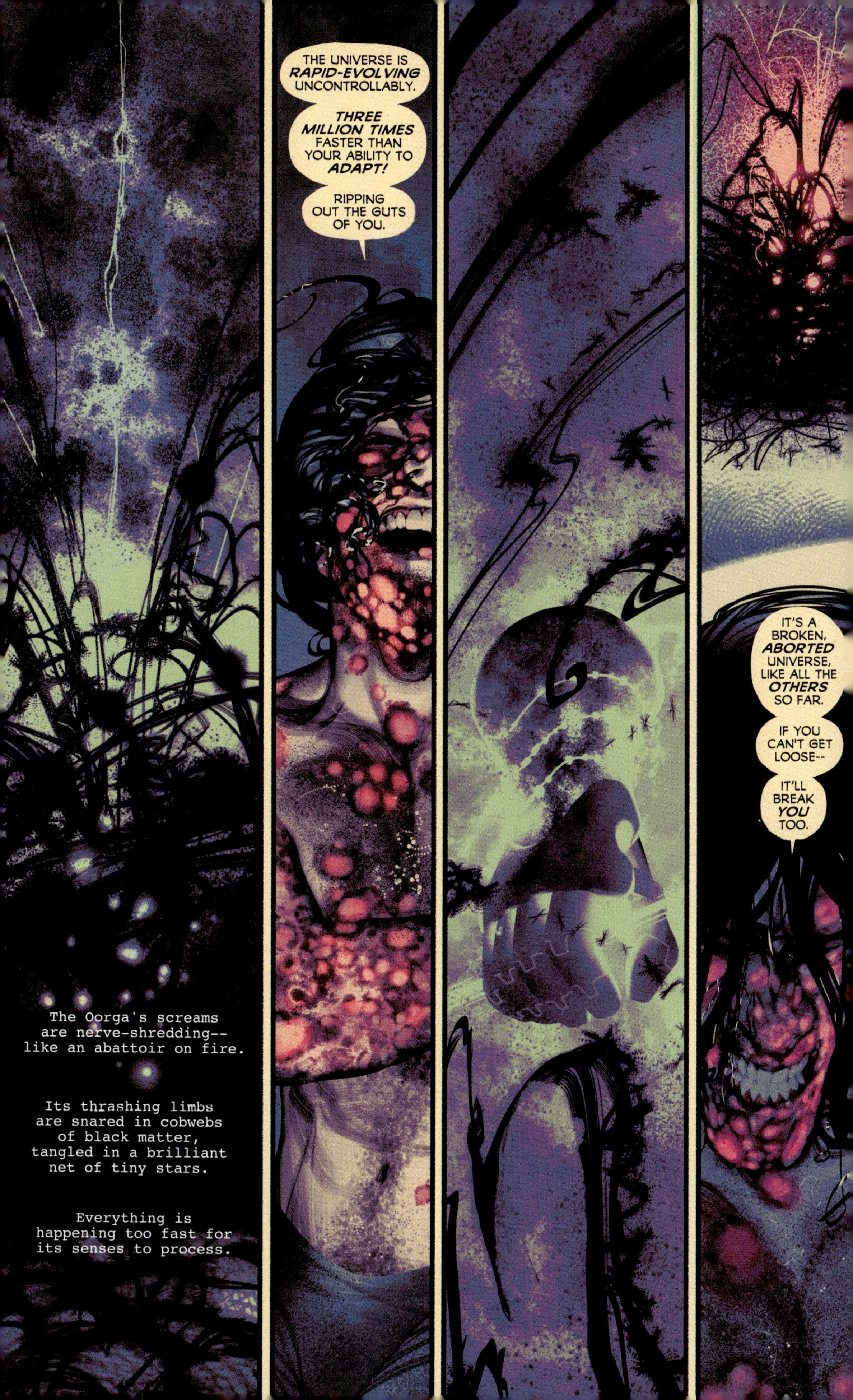

The Oorga's screams are nerve-shredding-- like an abattoir on fire.
Its thrashing limbs are snared in cobwebs of black matter, tangled in a brilliant net of tiny stars.
Everything is happening too fast for its senses to process.
THE UNIVERSE IS RAPID-EVOLVING UNCONTROLLABLY.
THREE MILLION TIMES FASTER THAN YOUR ABILITY TO ADAPT!
RIPPING OUT THE GUTS OF YOU.
IT'S A BROKEN, ABORTED UNIVERSE, LIKE ALL THE OTHERS SO FAR.
IF YOU CAN'T GET LOOSE--
IT'LL BREAK YOU TOO.

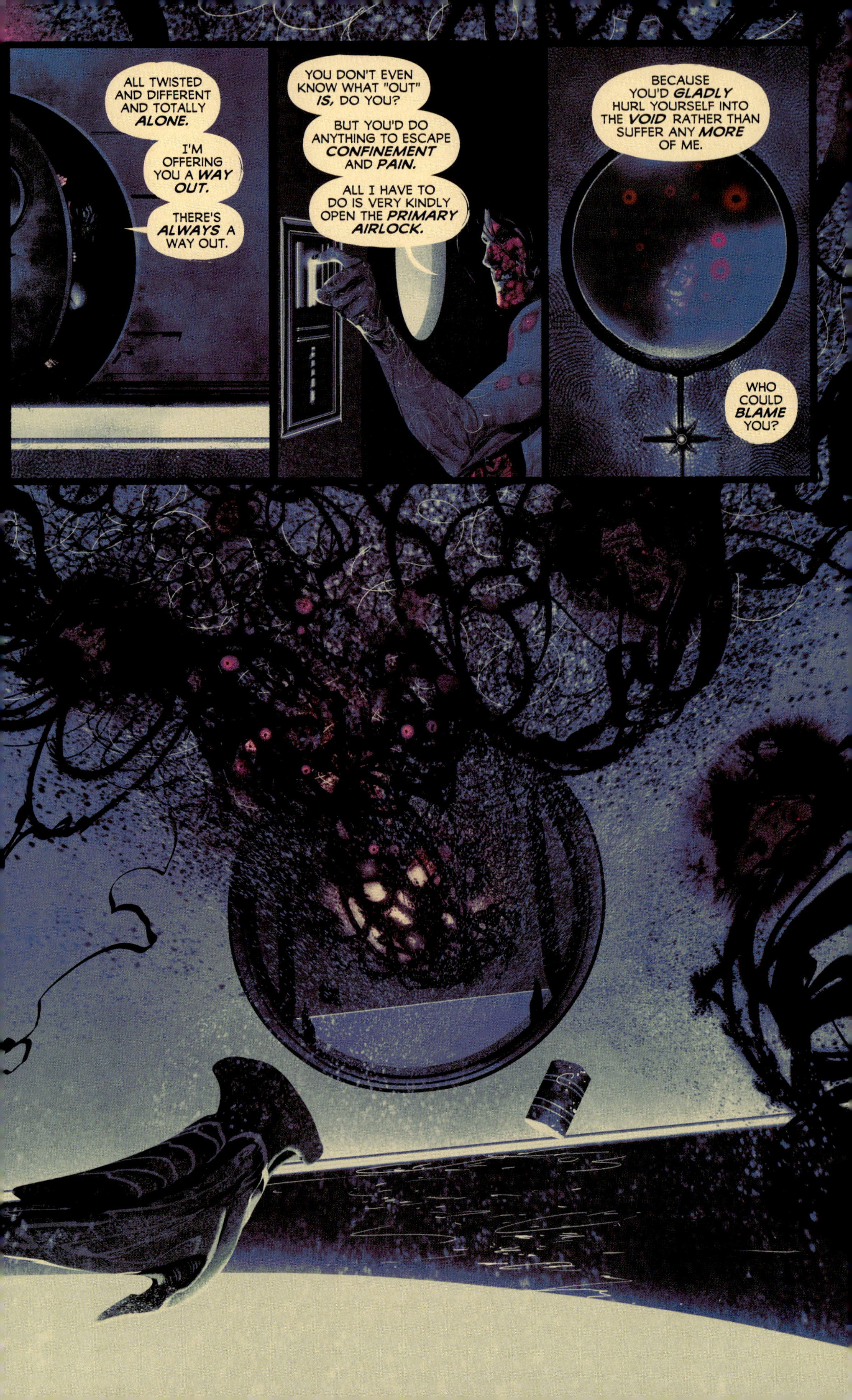
ALL TWISTED AND DIFFERENT AND TOTALLY ALONE.
I'M OFFERING YOU A WAY OUT.
THERE'S ALWAYS A WAY OUT.
YOU DON'T EVEN KNOW WHAT "OUT" IS, DO YOU?
BUT YOU'D DO ANYTHING TO ESCAPE CONFINEMENT AND PAIN.
ALL I HAVE TO DO IS VERY KINDLY OPEN THE PRIMARY AIRLOCK.
BECAUSE YOU'D GLADLY HURL YOURSELF INTO THE VOID RATHER THAN SUFFER ANY MORE OF ME.
WHO COULD BLAME YOU?

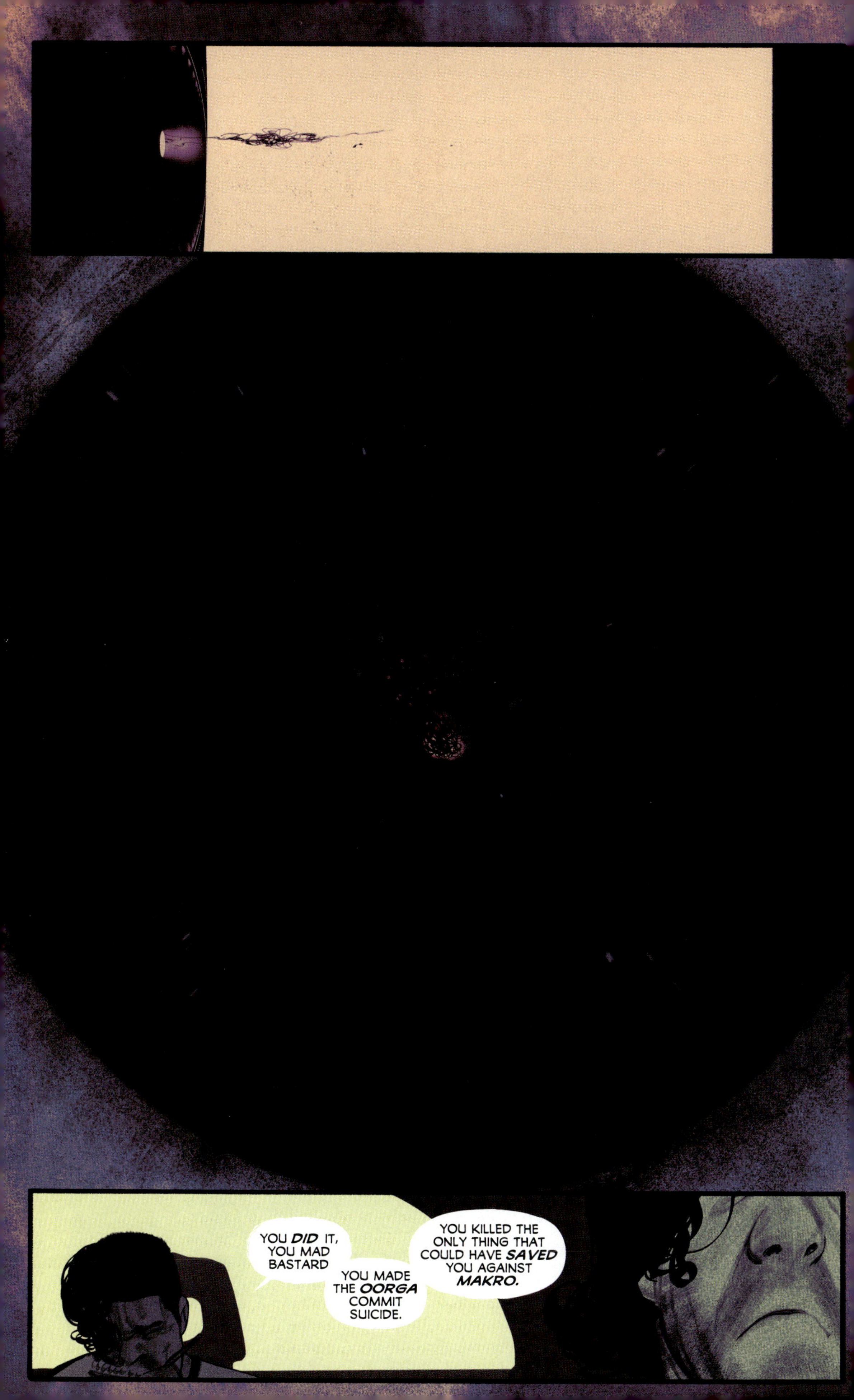

YOU *DID* IT, YOU MAD BASTARD
YOU MADE THE *OORGA* COMMIT SUICIDE.
YOU KILLED THE ONLY THING THAT COULD HAVE *SAVED* YOU AGAINST *MAKRO.*

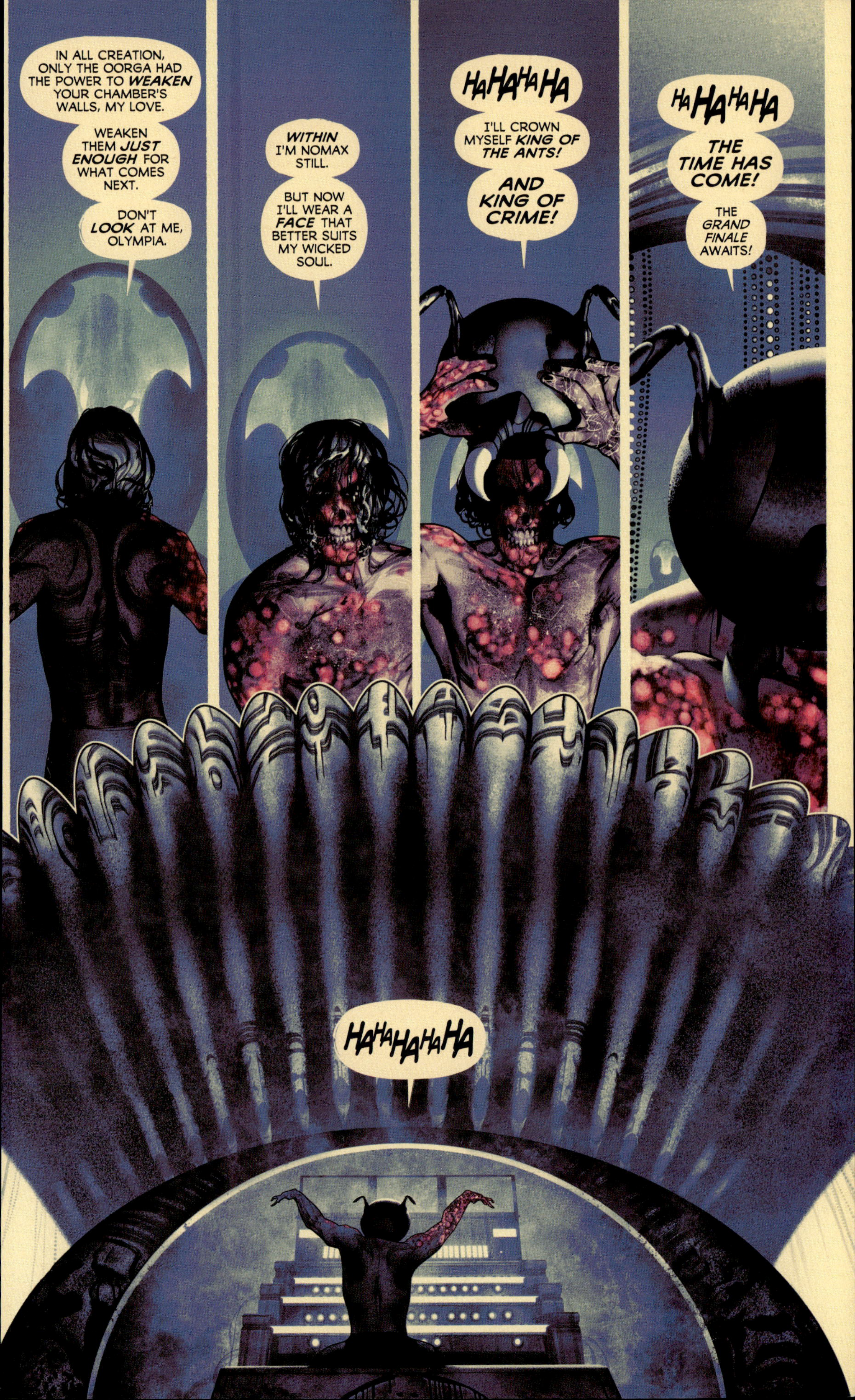

IN ALL CREATION, ONLY THE OORGA HAD THE POWER TO WEAKEN YOUR CHAMBER'S WALLS, MY LOVE.
WEAKEN THEM JUST ENOUGH FOR WHAT COMES NEXT.
DON'T LOOK AT ME, OLYMPIA.
WITHIN I'M NOMAX STILL.
BUT NOW I'LL WEAR A FACE THAT BETTER SUITS MY WICKED SOUL.
HAHAHAHAHA
I'LL CROWN MYSELF KING OF THE ANTS!
AND KING OF CRIME!
HAHAHAHAHA
THE TIME HAS COME!
THE GRAND FINALE AWAITS!
HAHAHAHAHAHA

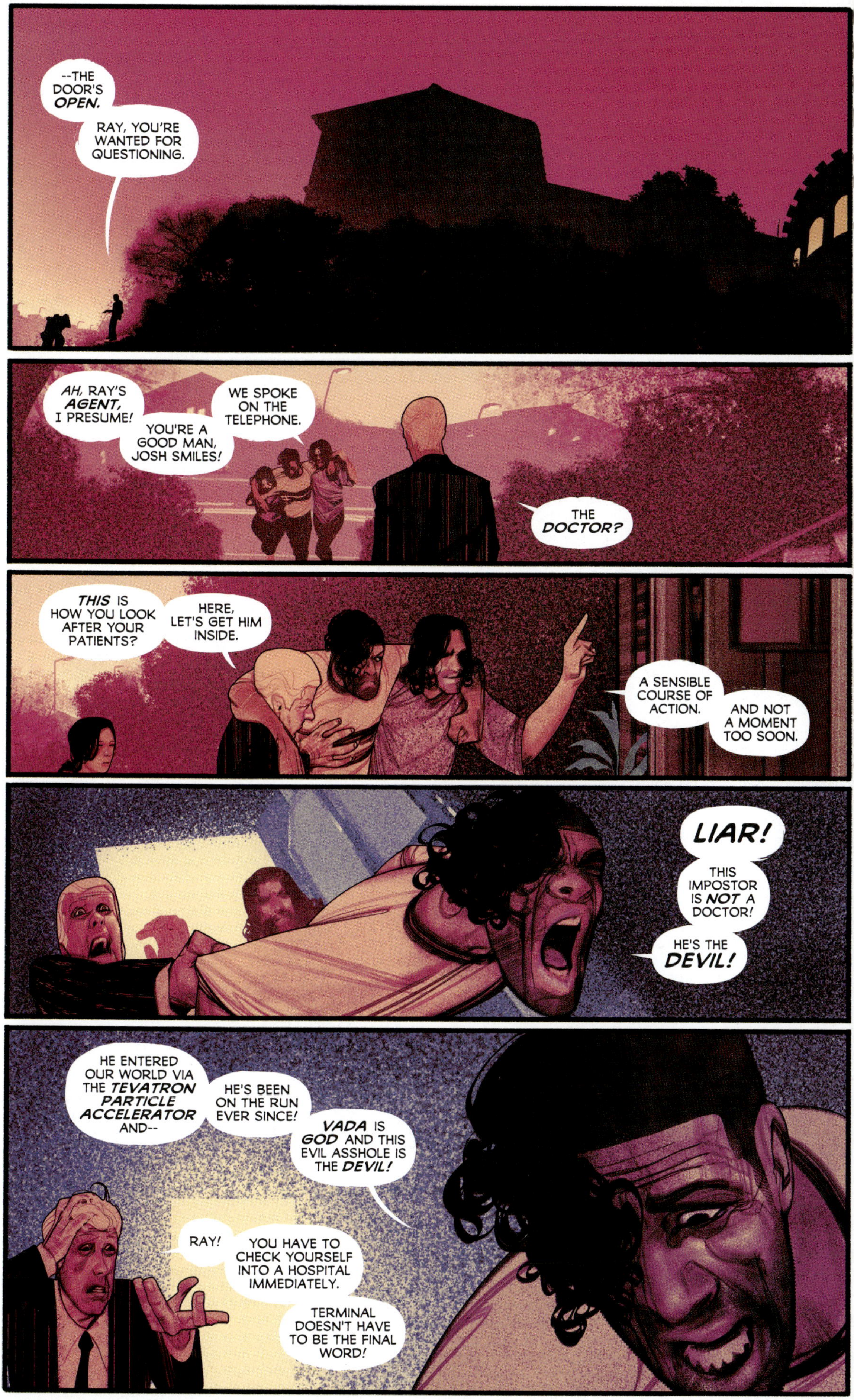
--THE DOOR'S OPEN.
RAY, YOU'RE WANTED FOR QUESTIONING.
AH, RAY'S AGENT, I PRESUME!
YOU'RE A GOOD MAN, JOSH SMILES!
WE SPOKE ON THE TELEPHONE.
THE DOCTOR?
THIS IS HOW YOU LOOK AFTER YOUR PATIENTS?
HERE, LET'S GET HIM INSIDE.
A SENSIBLE COURSE OF ACTION.
AND NOT A MOMENT TOO SOON.
LIAR!
THIS IMPOSTOR IS NOT A DOCTOR!
HE'S THE DEVIL!
HE ENTERED OUR WORLD VIA THE TEVATRON PARTICLE ACCELERATOR AND--
HE'S BEEN ON THE RUN EVER SINCE!
VADA IS GOD AND THIS EVIL ASSHOLE IS THE DEVIL!
RAY!
YOU HAVE TO CHECK YOURSELF INTO A HOSPITAL IMMEDIATELY.
TERMINAL DOESN'T HAVE TO BE THE FINAL WORD!

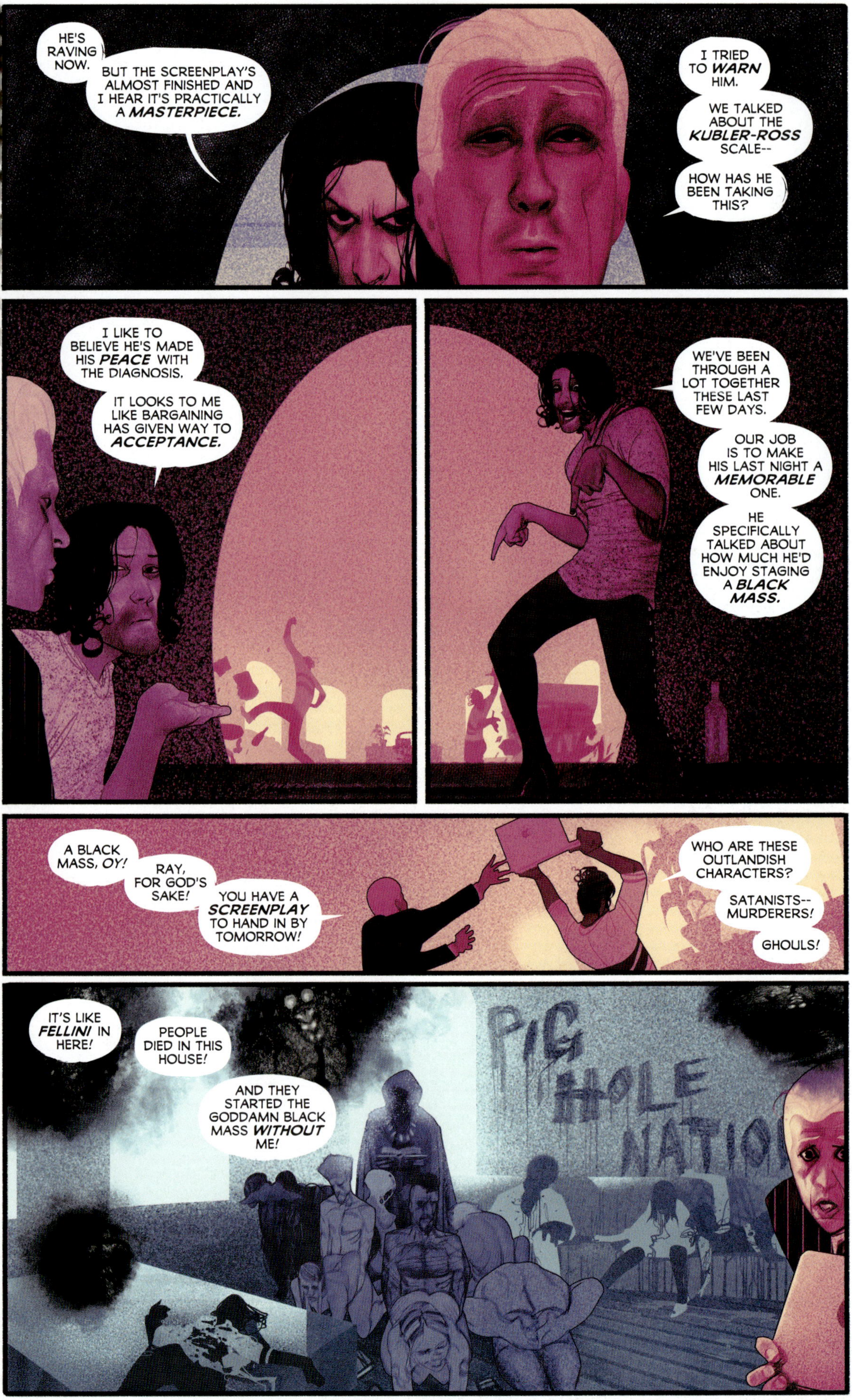
HE'S RAVING NOW.
BUT THE SCREENPLAY'S ALMOST FINISHED AND I HEAR IT'S PRACTICALLY A MASTERPIECE.
I TRIED TO WARN HIM.
WE TALKED ABOUT THE KUBLER-ROSS SCALE--
HOW HAS HE BEEN TAKING THIS?
I LIKE TO BELIEVE HE'S MADE HIS PEACE WITH THE DIAGNOSIS.
IT LOOKS TO ME LIKE BARGAINING HAS GIVEN WAY TO ACCEPTANCE.
WE'VE BEEN THROUGH A LOT TOGETHER THESE LAST FEW DAYS.
OUR JOB IS TO MAKE HIS LAST NIGHT A MEMORABLE ONE.
HE SPECIFICALLY TALKED ABOUT HOW MUCH HE'D ENJOY STAGING A BLACK MASS.
A BLACK MASS, OY!
RAY, FOR GOD'S SAKE!
YOU HAVE A SCREENPLAY TO HAND IN BY TOMORROW!
WHO ARE THESE OUTLANDISH CHARACTERS?
SATANISTS-- MURDERERS!
GHOULS!
IT'S LIKE FELLINI IN HERE!
PEOPLE DIED IN THIS HOUSE!
AND THEY STARTED THE GODDAMN BLACK MASS WITHOUT ME!
PIG HOLE NATIO

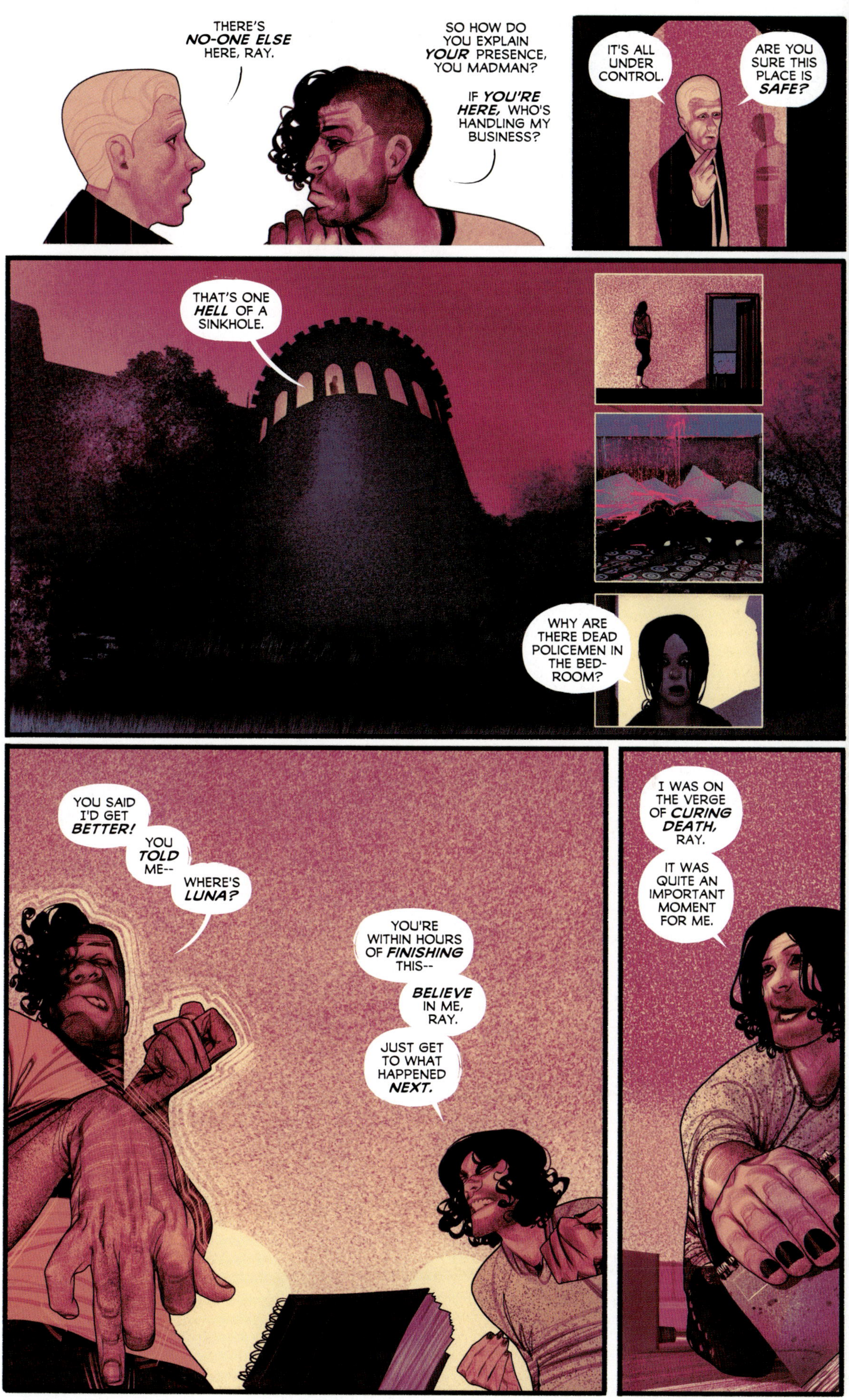
THERE'S NO-ONE ELSE HERE, RAY.
SO HOW DO YOU EXPLAIN YOUR PRESENCE, YOU MADMAN?
IF YOU'RE HERE, WHO'S HANDLING MY BUSINESS?
IT'S ALL UNDER CONTROL.
ARE YOU SURE THIS PLACE IS SAFE?
THAT'S ONE HELL OF A SINKHOLE.
WHY ARE THERE DEAD POLICEMEN IN THE BED-ROOM?
YOU SAID I'D GET BETTER!
YOU TOLD ME--
WHERE'S LUNA?
YOU'RE WITHIN HOURS OF FINISHING THIS--
BELIEVE IN ME, RAY.
JUST GET TO WHAT HAPPENED NEXT.
I WAS ON THE VERGE OF CURING DEATH, RAY.
IT WAS QUITE AN IMPORTANT MOMENT FOR ME.

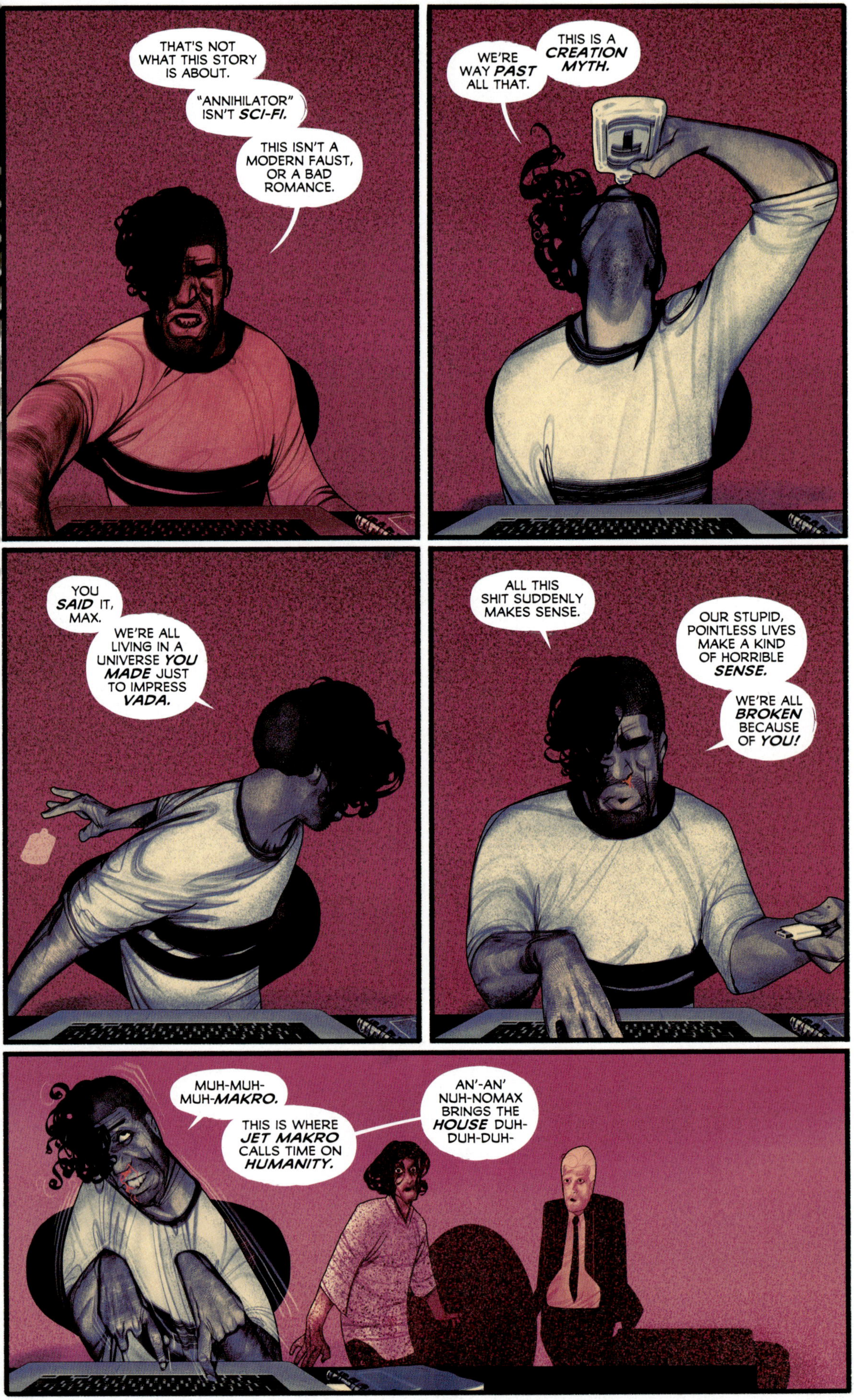
THAT'S NOT WHAT THIS STORY IS ABOUT.
"ANNIHILATOR" ISN'T *SCI-FI.*
THIS ISN'T A MODERN FAUST, OR A BAD ROMANCE.
THIS IS A *CREATION MYTH.*
WE'RE WAY *PAST* ALL THAT.
YOU *SAID* IT, MAX.
WE'RE ALL LIVING IN A UNIVERSE *YOU MADE* JUST TO IMPRESS *VADA.*
ALL THIS SHIT SUDDENLY MAKES SENSE.
OUR STUPID, POINTLESS LIVES MAKE A KIND OF HORRIBLE *SENSE.*
WE'RE ALL *BROKEN* BECAUSE OF *YOU!*
MUH-MUH-MUH-*MAKRO.*
THIS IS WHERE *JET MAKRO* CALLS TIME ON *HUMANITY.*
AN'-AN' NUH-NOMAX BRINGS THE *HOUSE* DUH-DUH-DUH-

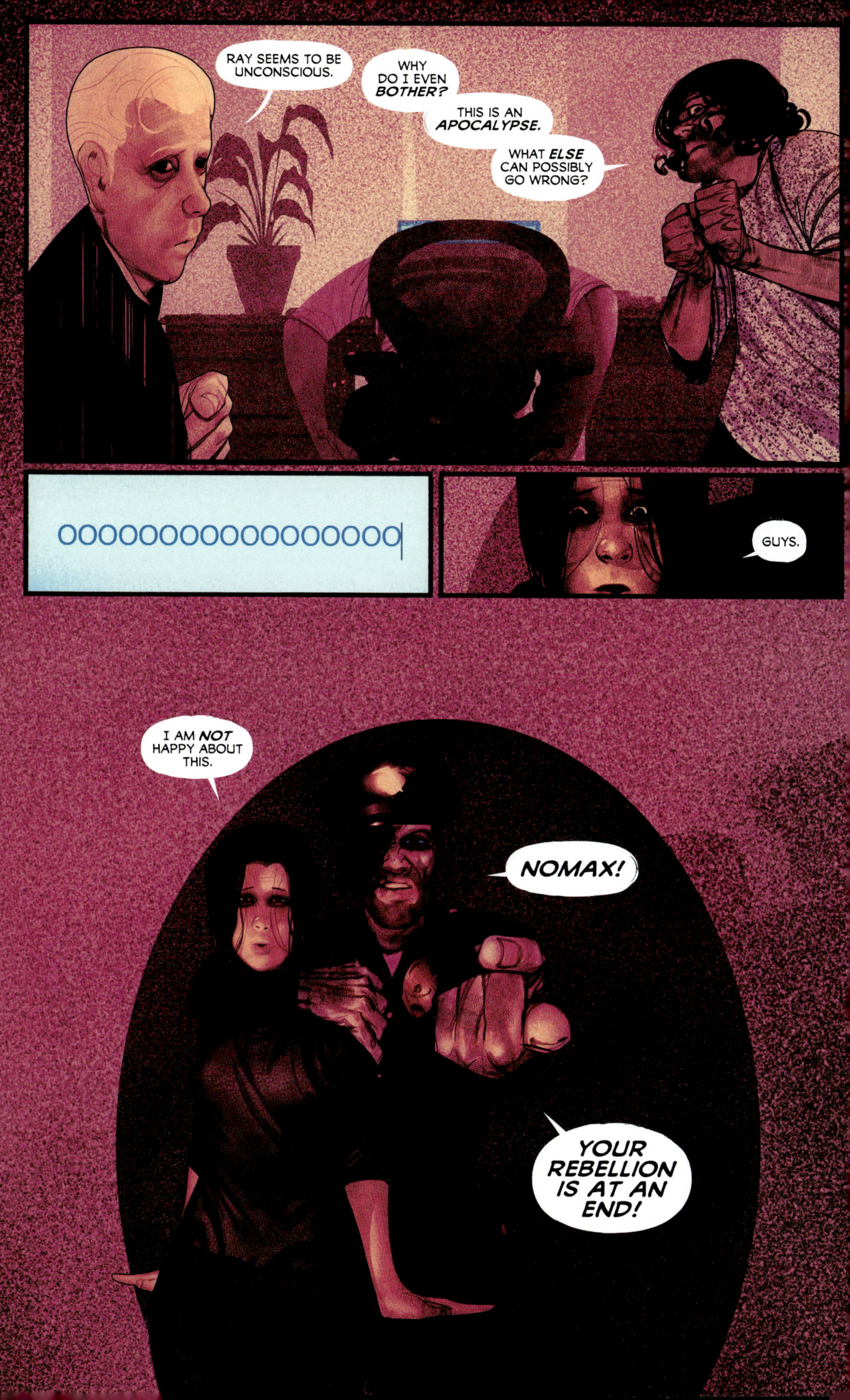
RAY SEEMS TO BE UNCONSCIOUS.
WHY DO I EVEN *BOTHER?*
THIS IS AN *APOCALYPSE.*
WHAT *ELSE* CAN POSSIBLY GO WRONG?
OOOOOOOOOOOOOOOOOO
GUYS.
I AM *NOT* HAPPY ABOUT THIS.
NOMAX!
YOUR REBELLION IS AT AN END!

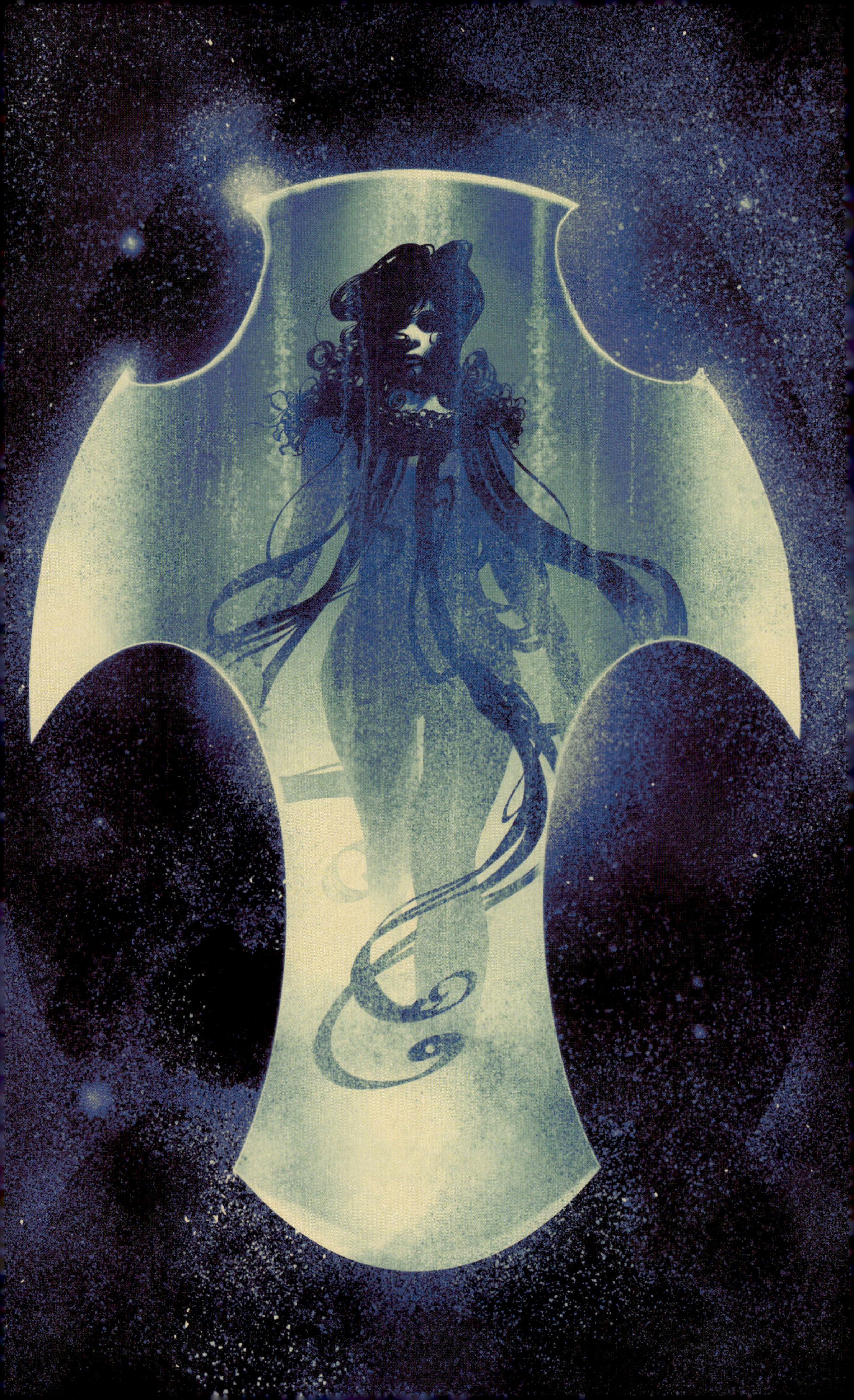

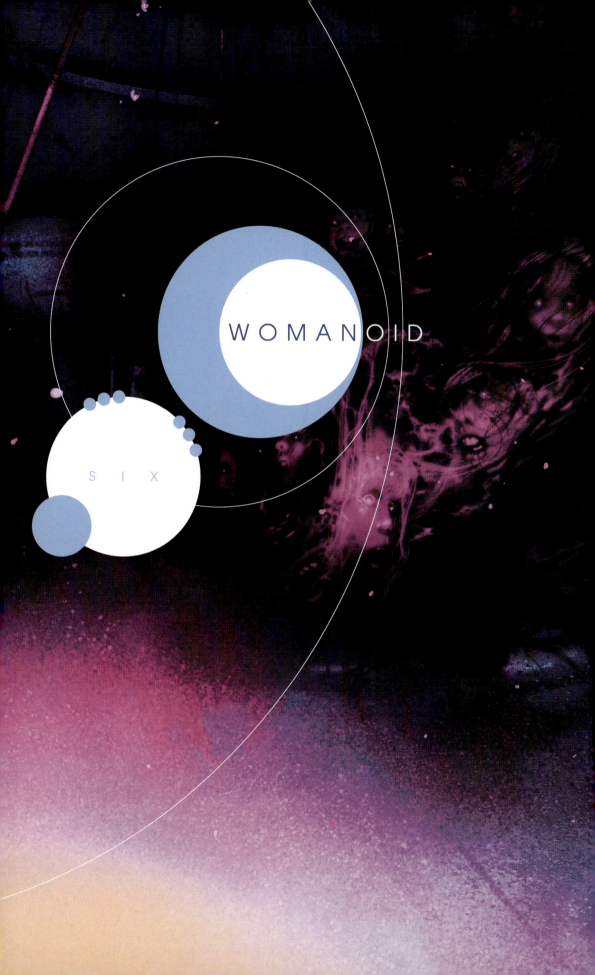

WOMANOID

SIX

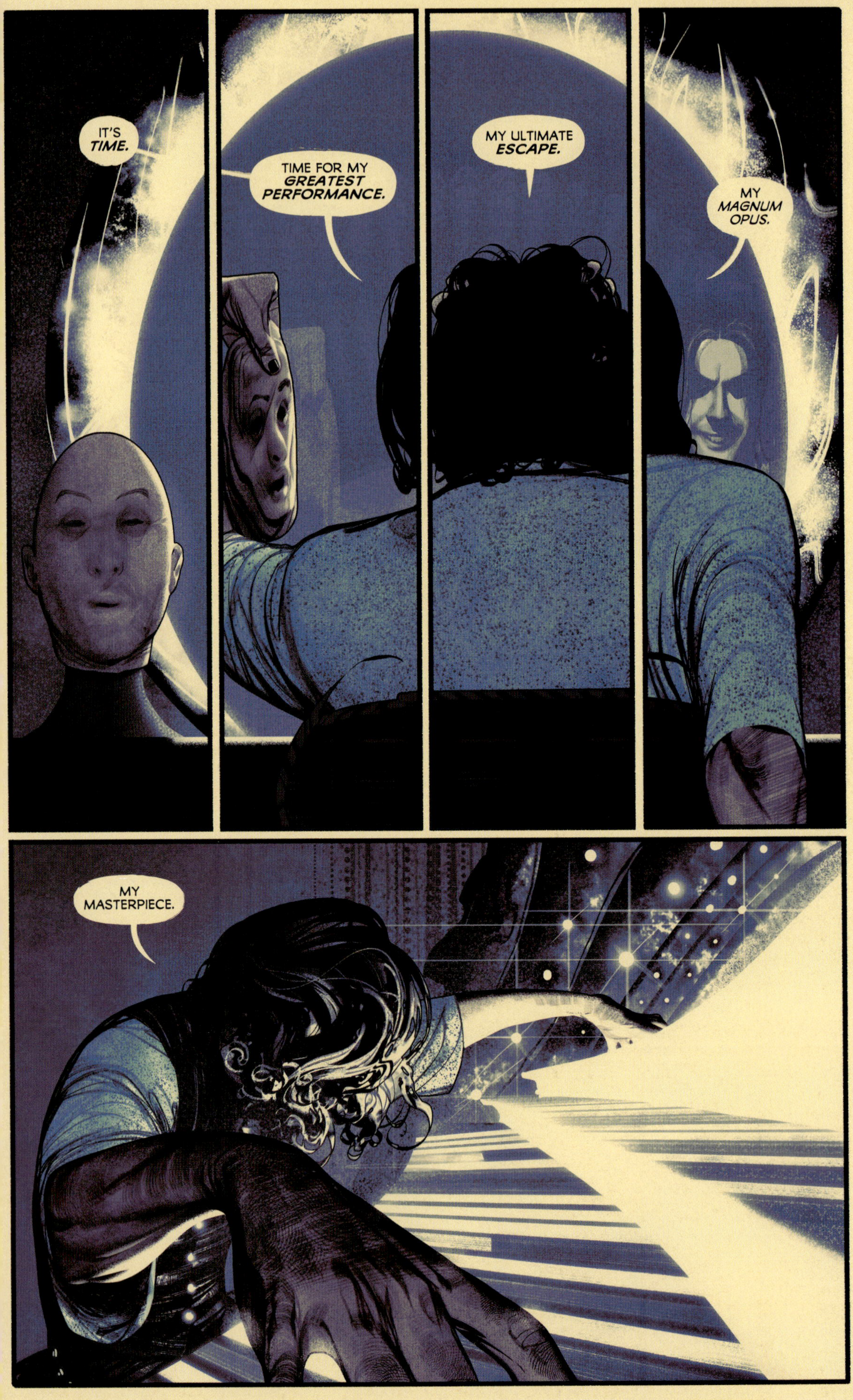
IT'S *TIME.*
TIME FOR MY *GREATEST PERFORMANCE.*
MY ULTIMATE *ESCAPE.*
MY *MAGNUM OPUS.*
MY MASTERPIECE.

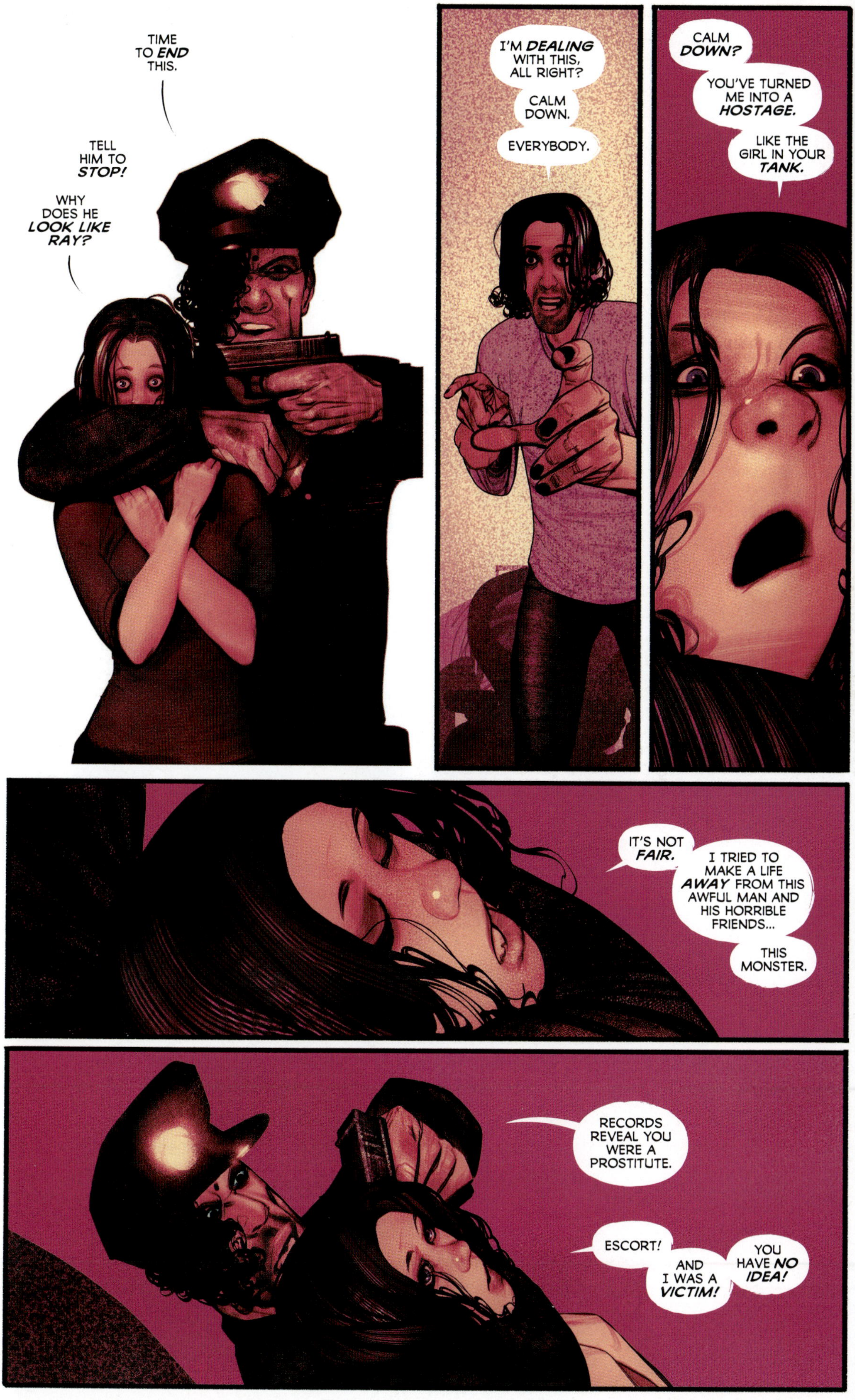
TIME TO *END* THIS.
TELL HIM TO *STOP!*
WHY DOES HE *LOOK LIKE RAY?*
I'M *DEALING* WITH THIS, ALL RIGHT?
CALM DOWN.
EVERYBODY.
CALM *DOWN?*
YOU'VE TURNED ME INTO A *HOSTAGE.*
LIKE THE GIRL IN YOUR *TANK.*
IT'S NOT *FAIR.*
I TRIED TO MAKE A LIFE *AWAY* FROM THIS AWFUL MAN AND HIS HORRIBLE FRIENDS...
THIS MONSTER.
RECORDS REVEAL YOU WERE A PROSTITUTE.
ESCORT!
AND I WAS A *VICTIM!*
YOU HAVE *NO IDEA!*

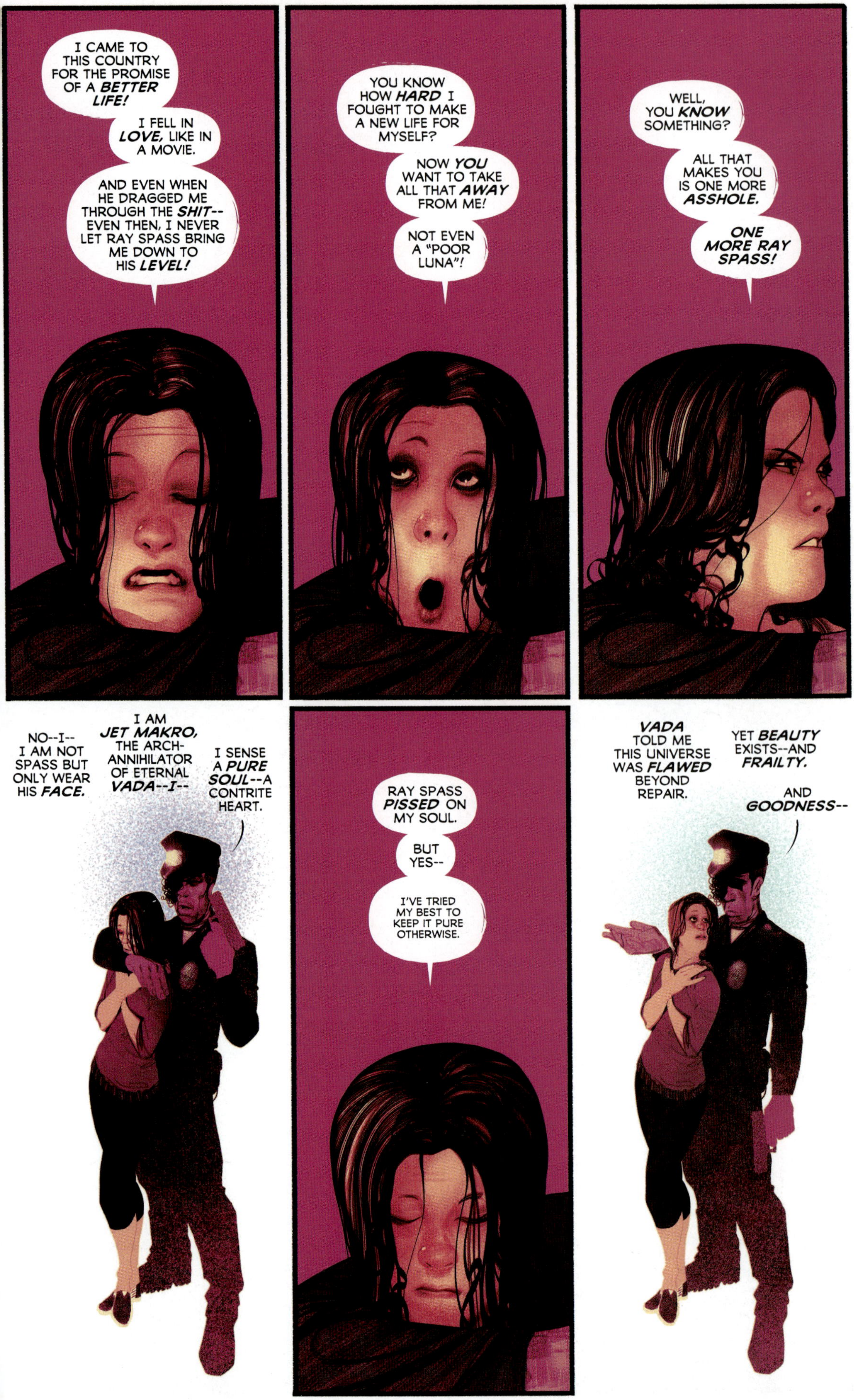
I CAME TO THIS COUNTRY FOR THE PROMISE OF A BETTER LIFE!
I FELL IN LOVE, LIKE IN A MOVIE.
AND EVEN WHEN HE DRAGGED ME THROUGH THE SHIT--EVEN THEN, I NEVER LET RAY SPASS BRING ME DOWN TO HIS LEVEL!
YOU KNOW HOW HARD I FOUGHT TO MAKE A NEW LIFE FOR MYSELF?
NOW YOU WANT TO TAKE ALL THAT AWAY FROM ME!
NOT EVEN A "POOR LUNA"!
WELL, YOU KNOW SOMETHING?
ALL THAT MAKES YOU IS ONE MORE ASSHOLE.
ONE MORE RAY SPASS!
NO--I--I AM NOT SPASS BUT ONLY WEAR HIS FACE.
I AM JET MAKRO, THE ARCH-ANNIHILATOR OF ETERNAL VADA--I--
I SENSE A PURE SOUL--A CONTRITE HEART.
RAY SPASS PISSED ON MY SOUL.
BUT YES--
I'VE TRIED MY BEST TO KEEP IT PURE OTHERWISE.
VADA TOLD ME THIS UNIVERSE WAS FLAWED BEYOND REPAIR.
YET BEAUTY EXISTS--AND FRAILTY.
AND GOODNESS--

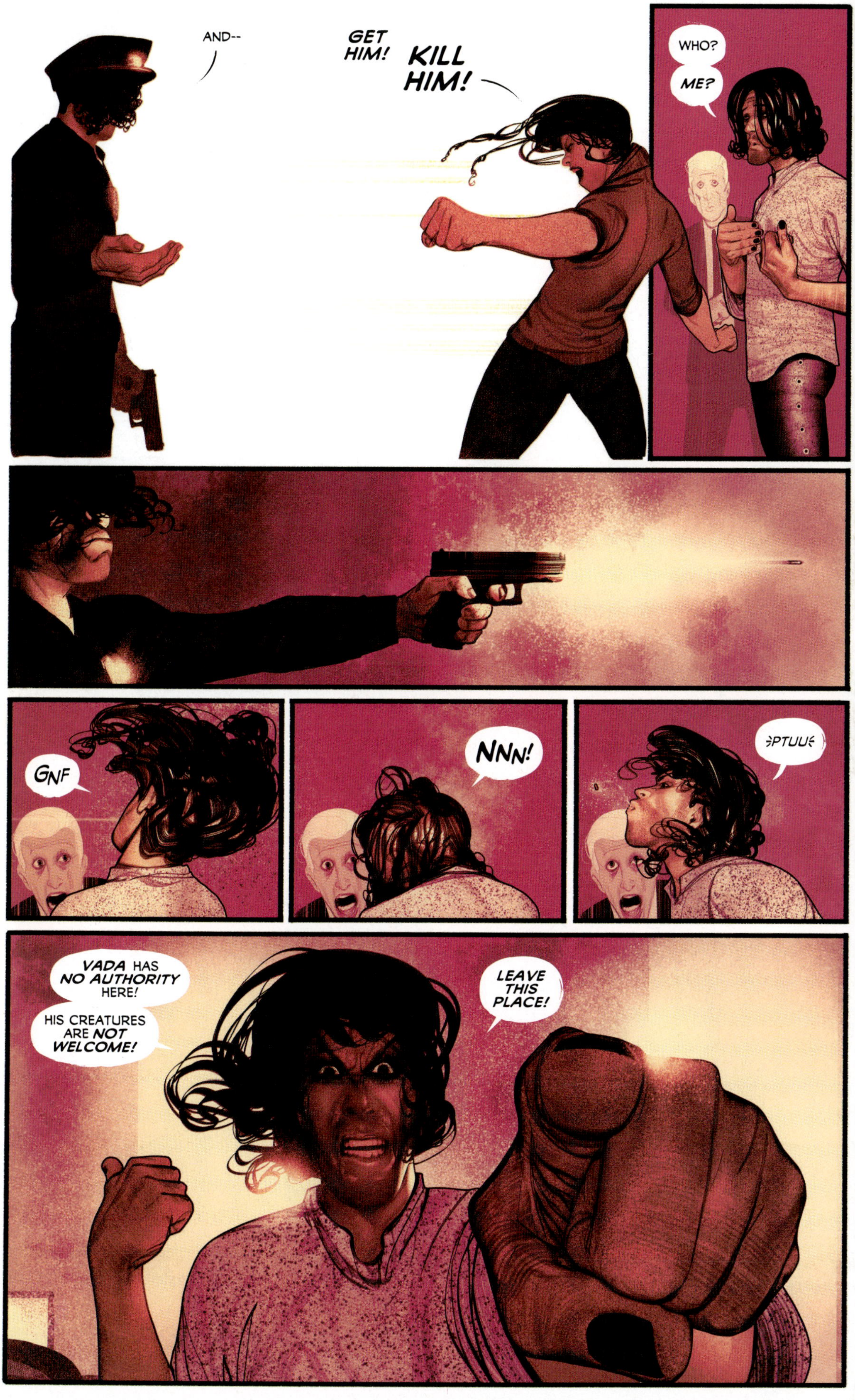
AND--
GET HIM!
KILL HIM!
WHO?
ME?
GNF
NNN!
PTUU
VADA HAS NO AUTHORITY HERE!
HIS CREATURES ARE NOT WELCOME!
LEAVE THIS PLACE!

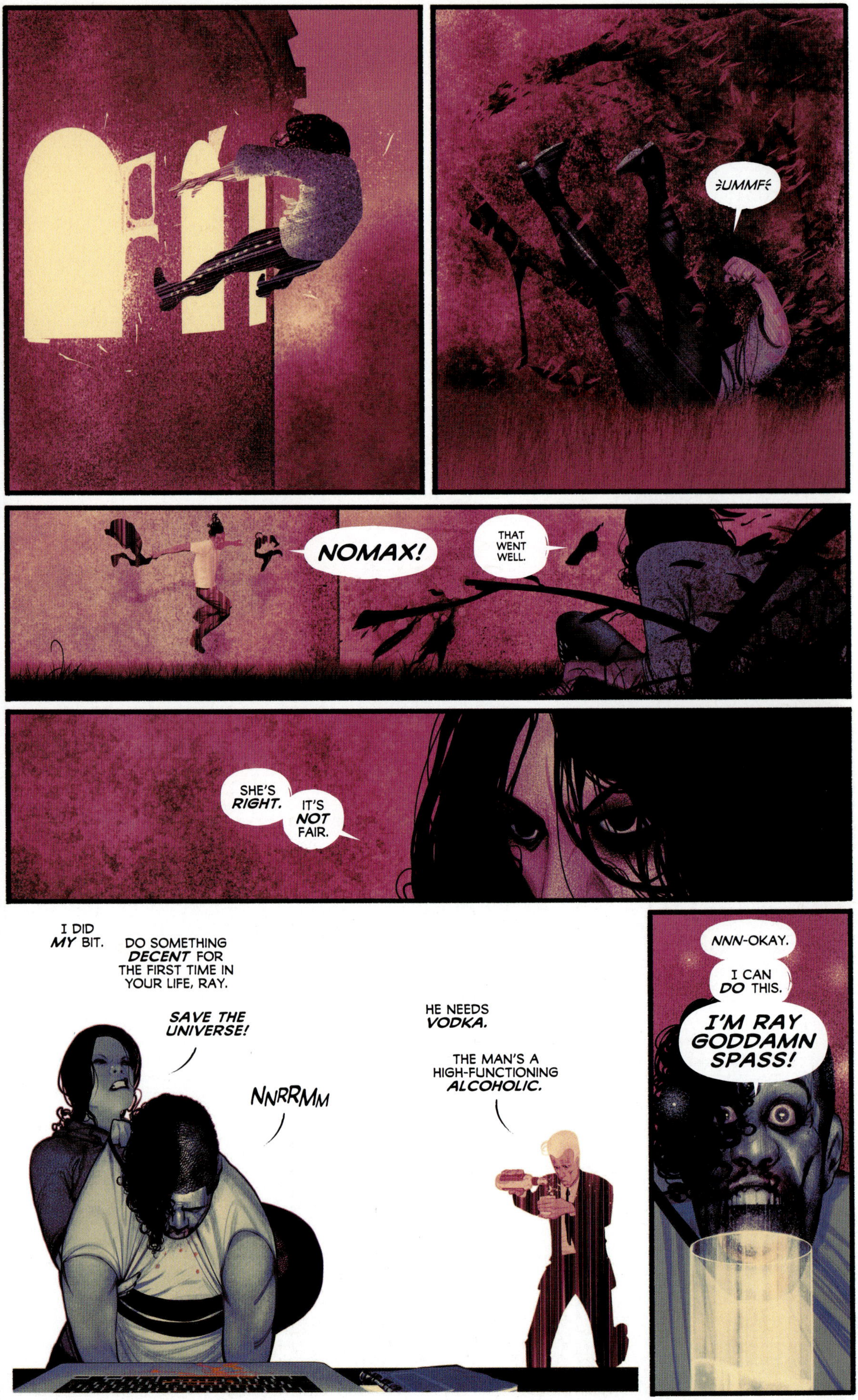

UMMF
NOMAX!
THAT WENT WELL.
SHE'S RIGHT.
IT'S NOT FAIR.
I DID MY BIT.
DO SOMETHING DECENT FOR THE FIRST TIME IN YOUR LIFE, RAY.
SAVE THE UNIVERSE!
NNRRMM
HE NEEDS VODKA.
THE MAN'S A HIGH-FUNCTIONING ALCOHOLIC.
NNN-OKAY.
I CAN DO THIS.
I'M RAY GODDAMN SPASS!

URRGGLL

IS THAT *ALL* YOU HAVE TO SAY?

YOU!

MY *LOOK-ALIKE!*

I'M *RAY SPASS* AND I WAS SENT HERE TO SAVE THE UNIVERSE.

MAKRO, HE KILLED YOU *ALREADY.*

FIRST SCENE.

INTERIOR *DIS STATION:* HE SHOT YOU IN THE *HEAD,* REMEMBER?

YOU STILL CAN'T DISGUISE THE *HOLE.*

WHAT?

AH SHIT-- THE ONLY THING STOPPING HIS BULLET FROM *EXPLODING* IN YOUR BRAIN IS SHEER *FORCE OF WILL.*

YOUR PERSONAL, IMMACULATE PERFECTION OF INTENT.

--BUT IF SOME PLOT CONTRIVANCE *BROKE* YOUR HOLY CONCENTRATION.

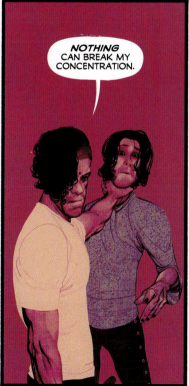

NOTHING CAN BREAK MY CONCENTRATION.

HOW ABOUT *THIS.*

VADA, YOUR BELOVED MASTER--

VADA WANTS *YOU* DEAD.

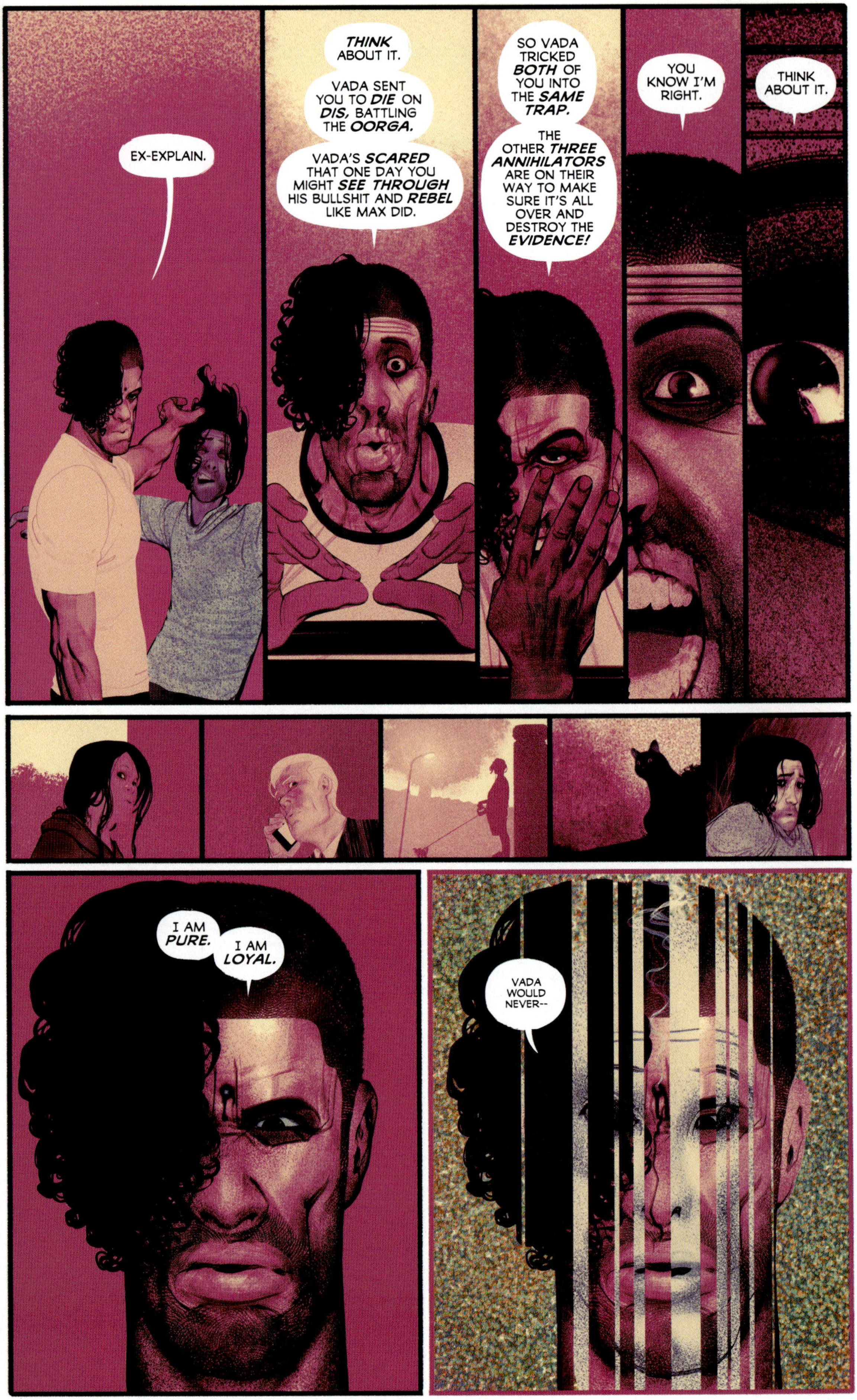
EX-EXPLAIN.
THINK ABOUT IT.
VADA SENT YOU TO DIE ON DIS, BATTLING THE OORGA.
VADA'S SCARED THAT ONE DAY YOU MIGHT SEE THROUGH HIS BULLSHIT AND REBEL LIKE MAX DID.
SO VADA TRICKED BOTH OF YOU INTO THE SAME TRAP.
THE OTHER THREE ANNIHILATORS ARE ON THEIR WAY TO MAKE SURE IT'S ALL OVER AND DESTROY THE EVIDENCE!
YOU KNOW I'M RIGHT.
THINK ABOUT IT.
I AM PURE.
I AM LOYAL.
VADA WOULD NEVER--

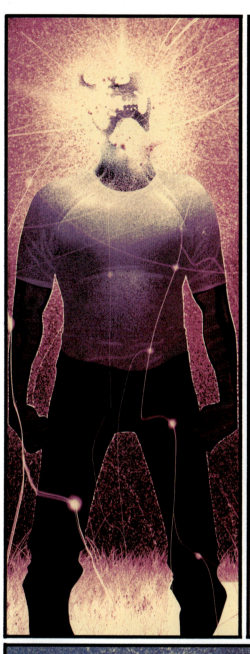

RAYMOND.

BRAVO.

THEY SAID MAKRO WAS *UNBEATABLE.*

UNBEATABLE, MY ASS

I PUT THAT SMOKING *CHEKHOV GUN* IN THE *FIRST SCENE!*

AH, SHIT TWICE!

MAX, YOU TOLD ME IT WOULD GET *BETTER.*

I CAN'T-- I DON'T-- I DON'T THINK I *FEEL* SO GOOD ANY-MORE--

SERIOUSLY, BEING KILLED BY MY OWN *DOPPELGANGER* WOULD HAVE BEEN *CRUELTY* AFTER ALL THIS.

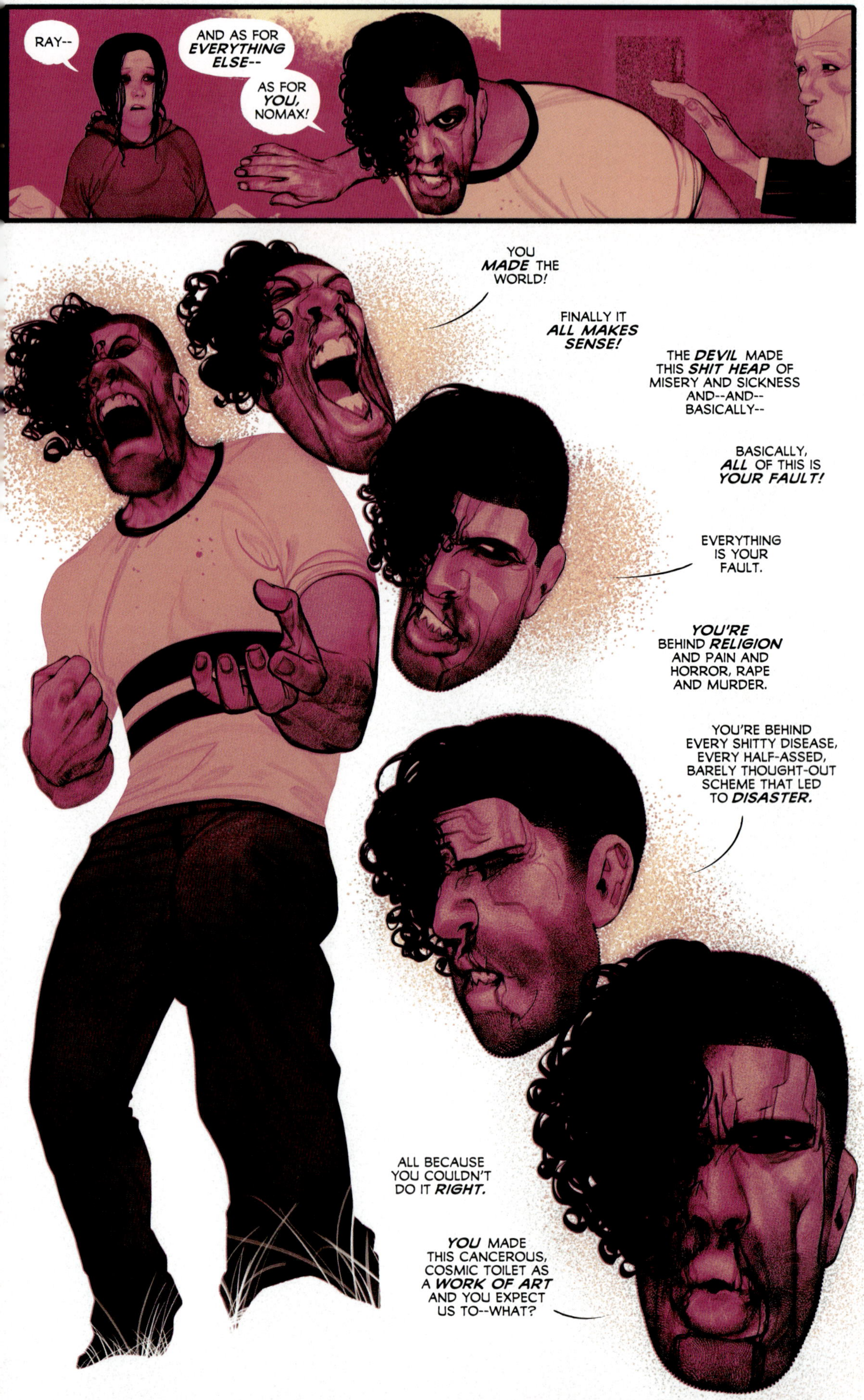
RAY--
AND AS FOR EVERYTHING ELSE--
AS FOR YOU, NOMAX!
YOU MADE THE WORLD!
FINALLY IT ALL MAKES SENSE!
THE DEVIL MADE THIS SHIT HEAP OF MISERY AND SICKNESS AND--AND-- BASICALLY--
BASICALLY, ALL OF THIS IS YOUR FAULT!
EVERYTHING IS YOUR FAULT.
YOU'RE BEHIND RELIGION AND PAIN AND HORROR, RAPE AND MURDER.
YOU'RE BEHIND EVERY SHITTY DISEASE, EVERY HALF-ASSED, BARELY THOUGHT-OUT SCHEME THAT LED TO DISASTER.
ALL BECAUSE YOU COULDN'T DO IT RIGHT.
YOU MADE THIS CANCEROUS, COSMIC TOILET AS A WORK OF ART AND YOU EXPECT US TO--WHAT?

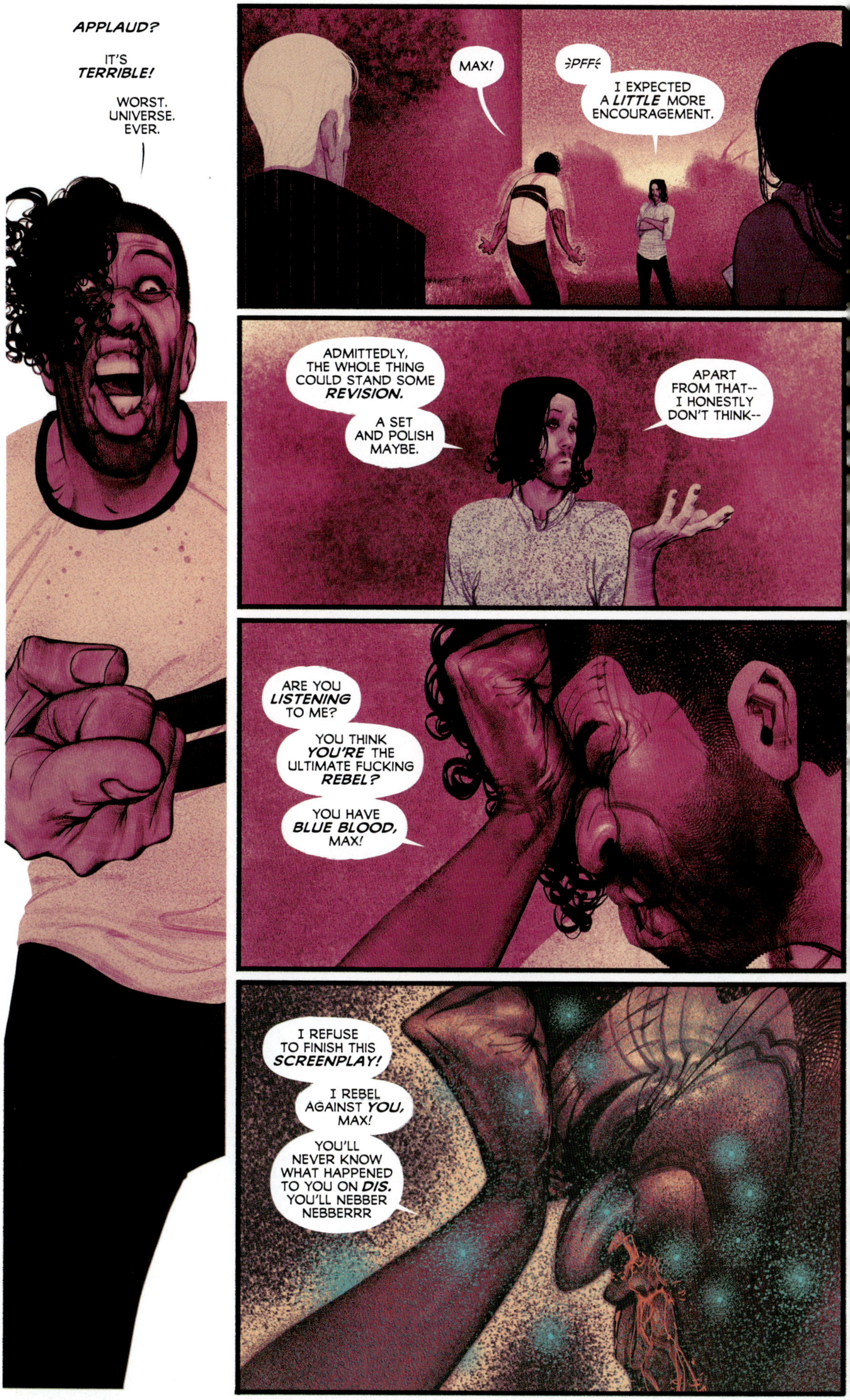
APPLAUD?
IT'S TERRIBLE!
WORST. UNIVERSE. EVER.
MAX!
PFF
I EXPECTED A LITTLE MORE ENCOURAGEMENT.
ADMITTEDLY, THE WHOLE THING COULD STAND SOME REVISION.
A SET AND POLISH MAYBE.
APART FROM THAT-- I HONESTLY DON'T THINK--
ARE YOU LISTENING TO ME?
YOU THINK YOU'RE THE ULTIMATE FUCKING REBEL?
YOU HAVE BLUE BLOOD, MAX!
I REFUSE TO FINISH THIS SCREENPLAY!
I REBEL AGAINST YOU, MAX!
YOU'LL NEVER KNOW WHAT HAPPENED TO YOU ON DIS. YOU'LL NEBBER NEBBERRR

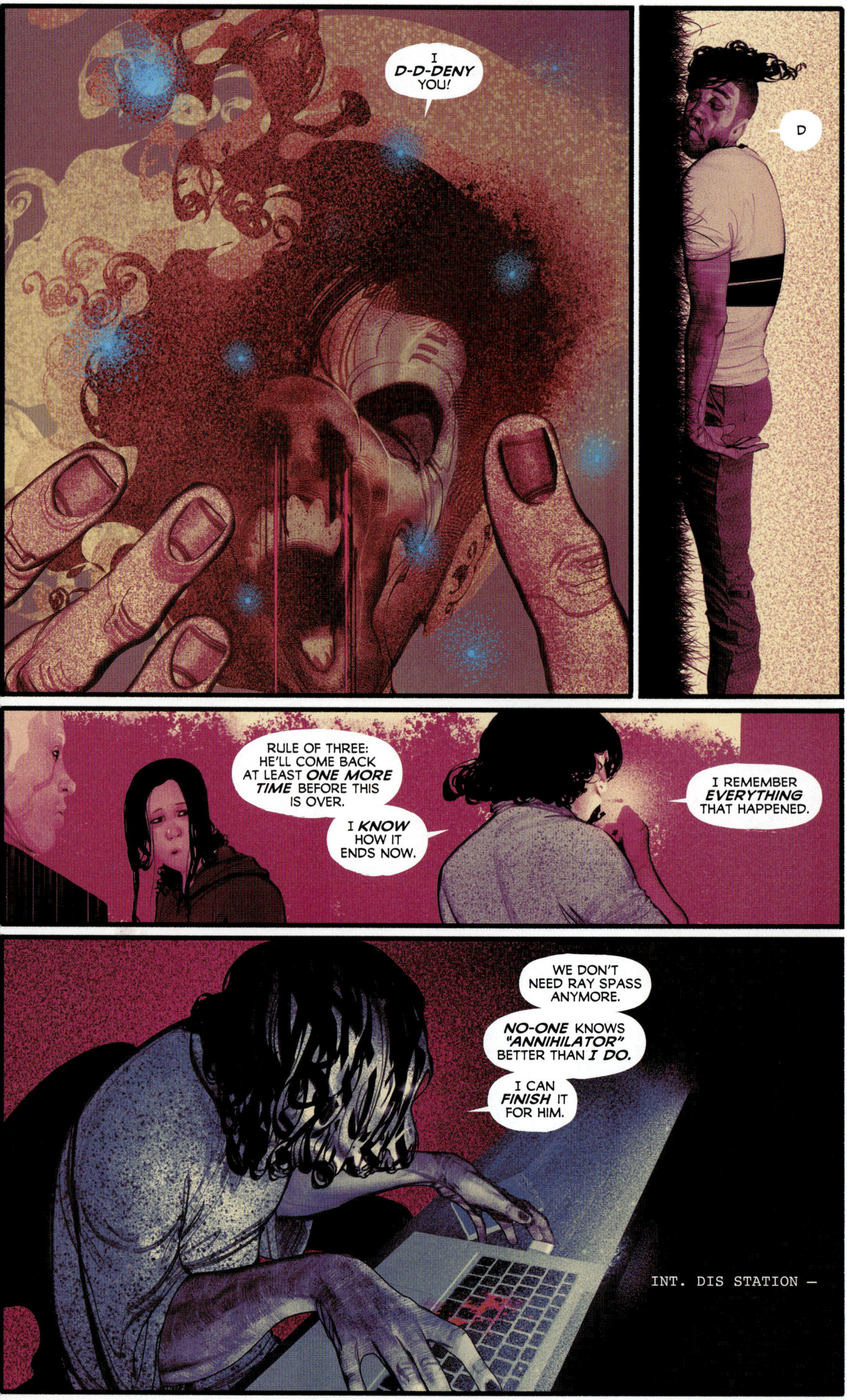

I D-D-DENY YOU!
D
RULE OF THREE: HE'LL COME BACK AT LEAST ONE MORE TIME BEFORE THIS IS OVER.
I KNOW HOW IT ENDS NOW.
I REMEMBER EVERYTHING THAT HAPPENED.
WE DON'T NEED RAY SPASS ANYMORE.
NO-ONE KNOWS "ANNIHILATOR" BETTER THAN I DO.
I CAN FINISH IT FOR HIM.
INT. DIS STATION —

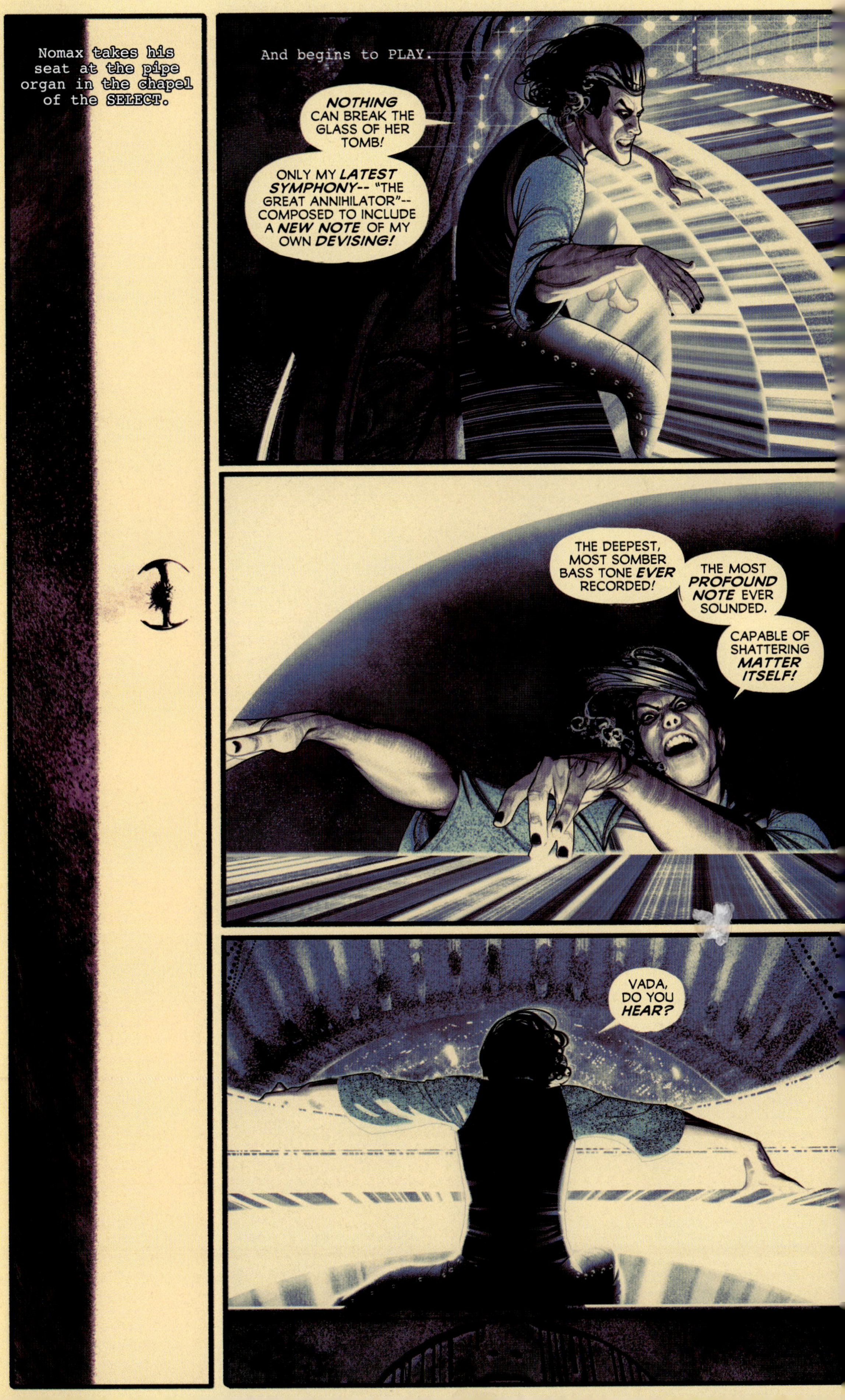
Nomax takes his seat at the pipe organ in the chapel of the SELECT.
And begins to PLAY.
NOTHING CAN BREAK THE GLASS OF HER TOMB!
ONLY MY LATEST SYMPHONY-- "THE GREAT ANNIHILATOR"-- COMPOSED TO INCLUDE A NEW NOTE OF MY OWN DEVISING!
THE DEEPEST, MOST SOMBER BASS TONE EVER RECORDED!
THE MOST PROFOUND NOTE EVER SOUNDED.
CAPABLE OF SHATTERING MATTER ITSELF!
VADA, DO YOU HEAR?

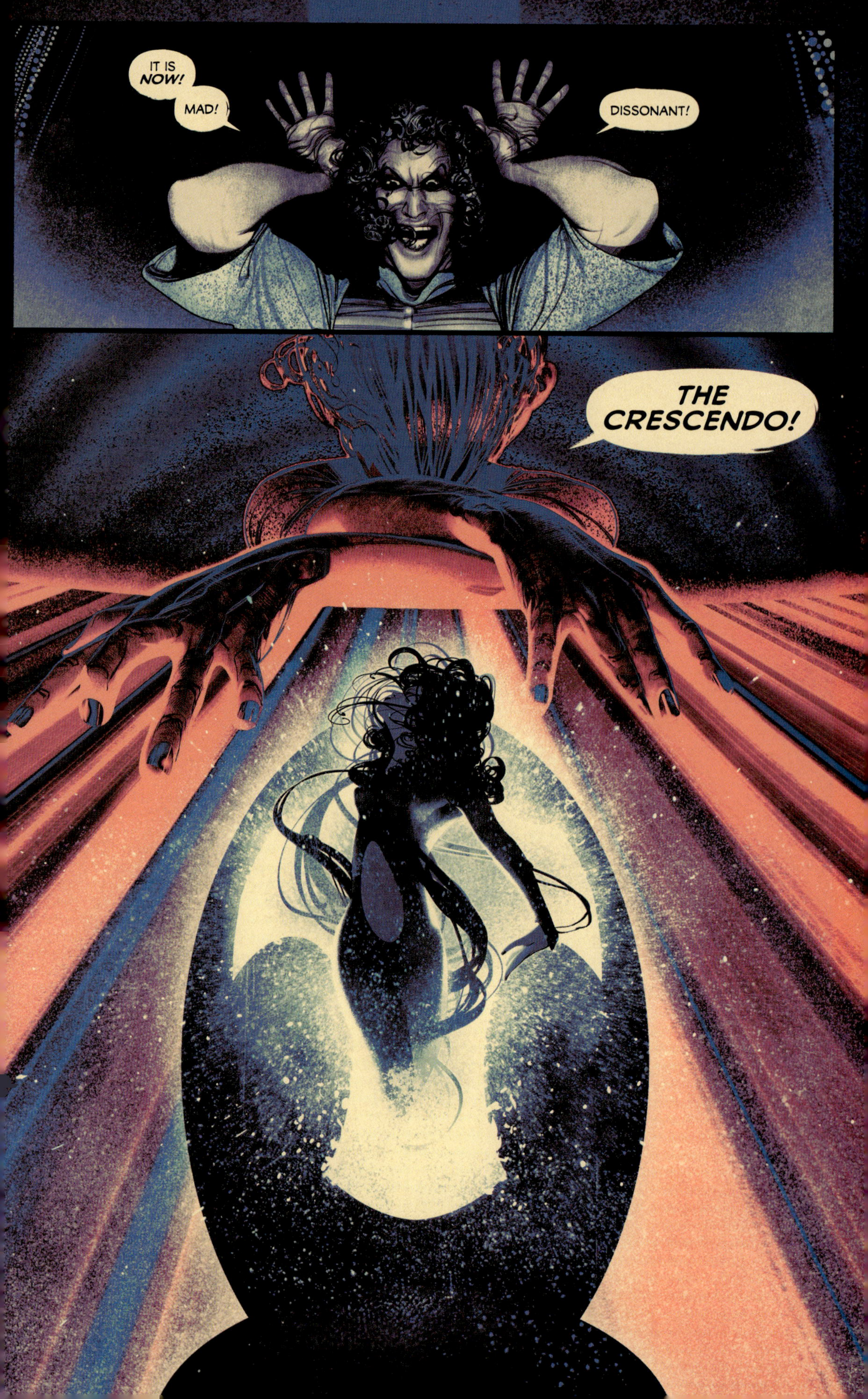
IT IS NOW!
MAD!
DISSONANT!
THE CRESCENDO!

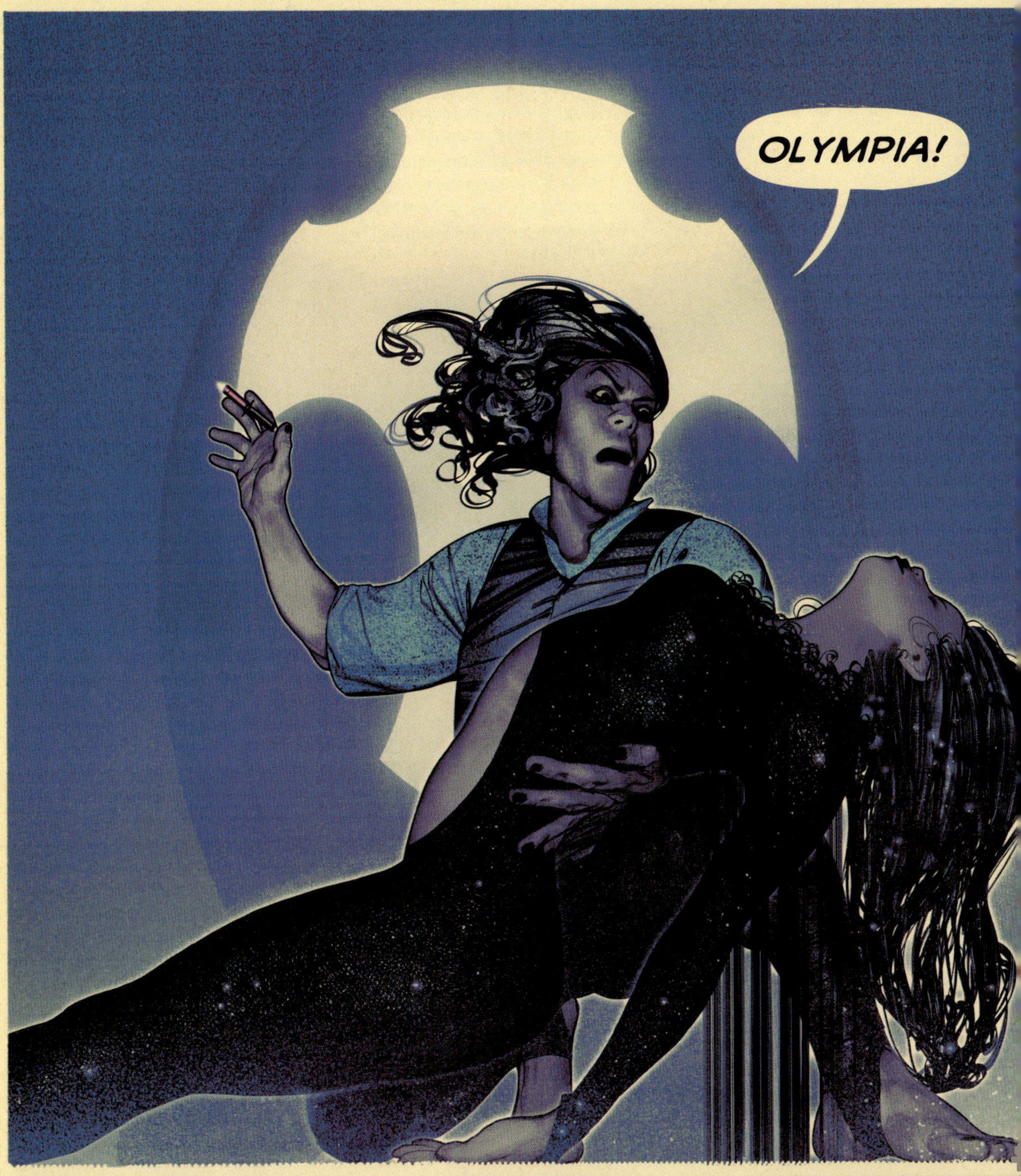
OLYMPIA!

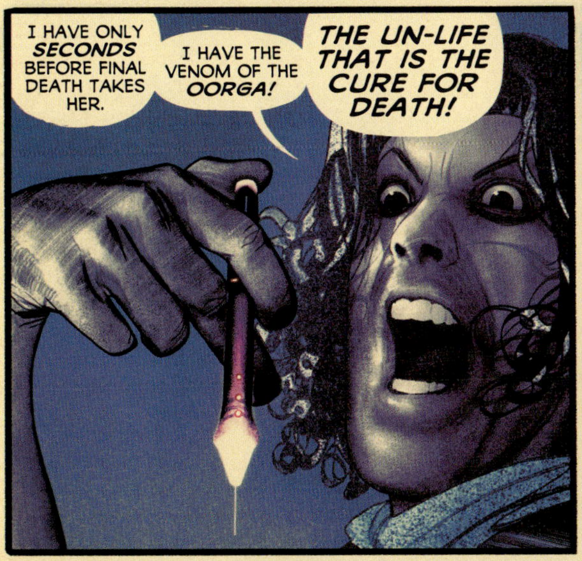
I HAVE ONLY SECONDS BEFORE FINAL DEATH TAKES HER.
I HAVE THE VENOM OF THE OORGA!
THE UN-LIFE THAT IS THE CURE FOR DEATH!

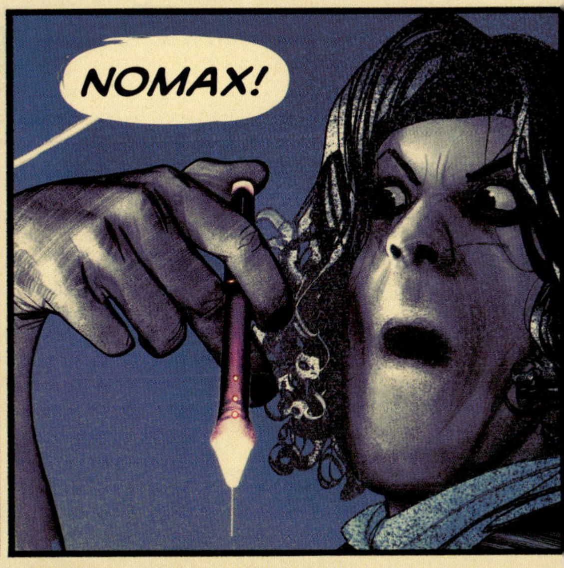
NOMAX!

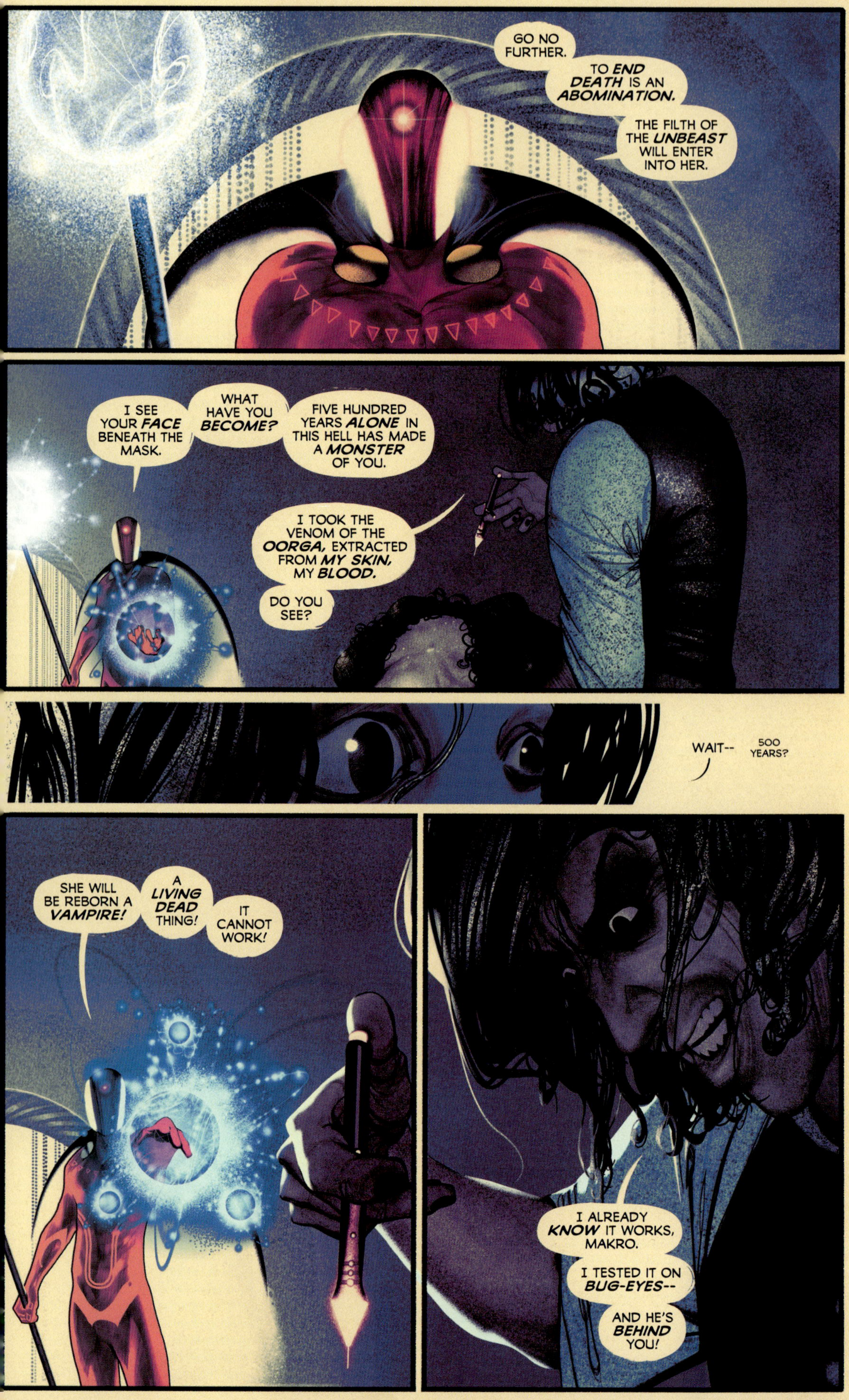
GO NO FURTHER.
TO END DEATH IS AN ABOMINATION.
THE FILTH OF THE UNBEAST WILL ENTER INTO HER.
I SEE YOUR FACE BENEATH THE MASK.
WHAT HAVE YOU BECOME?
FIVE HUNDRED YEARS ALONE IN THIS HELL HAS MADE A MONSTER OF YOU.
I TOOK THE VENOM OF THE OORGA, EXTRACTED FROM MY SKIN, MY BLOOD.
DO YOU SEE?
WAIT--
500 YEARS?
SHE WILL BE REBORN A VAMPIRE!
A LIVING DEAD THING!
IT CANNOT WORK!
I ALREADY KNOW IT WORKS, MAKRO.
I TESTED IT ON BUG-EYES--
AND HE'S BEHIND YOU!

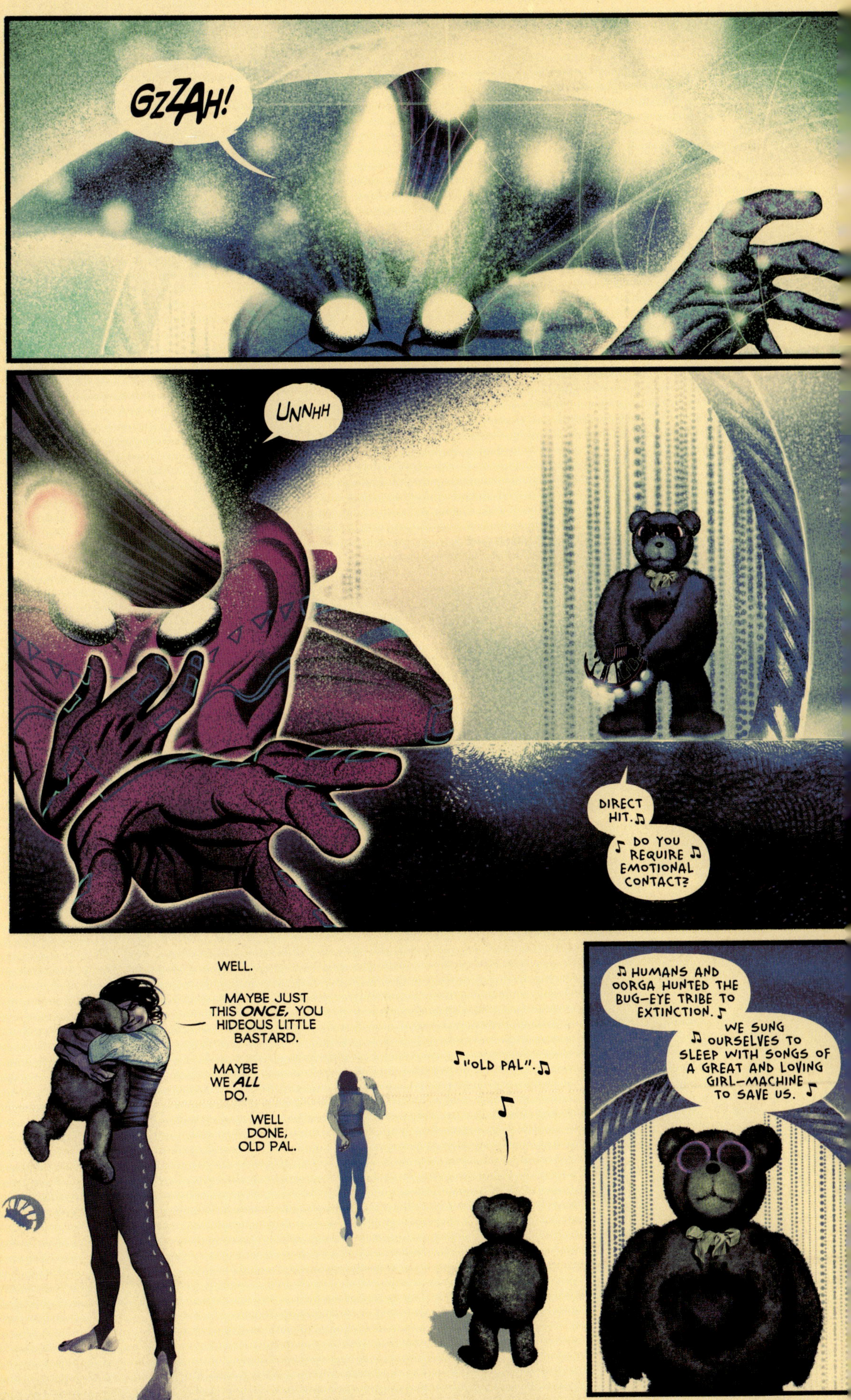
GZZAH!
UNNHH
DIRECT HIT. ♫
♪ DO YOU REQUIRE ♫ EMOTIONAL CONTACT?
WELL.
MAYBE JUST THIS *ONCE,* YOU HIDEOUS LITTLE BASTARD.
MAYBE WE *ALL* DO.
WELL DONE, OLD PAL.
♪ "OLD PAL". ♫
♪
♫ HUMANS AND OORGA HUNTED THE BUG-EYE TRIBE TO EXTINCTION. ♪
WE SUNG ♫ OURSELVES TO SLEEP WITH SONGS OF A GREAT AND LOVING GIRL-MACHINE TO SAVE US. ♪

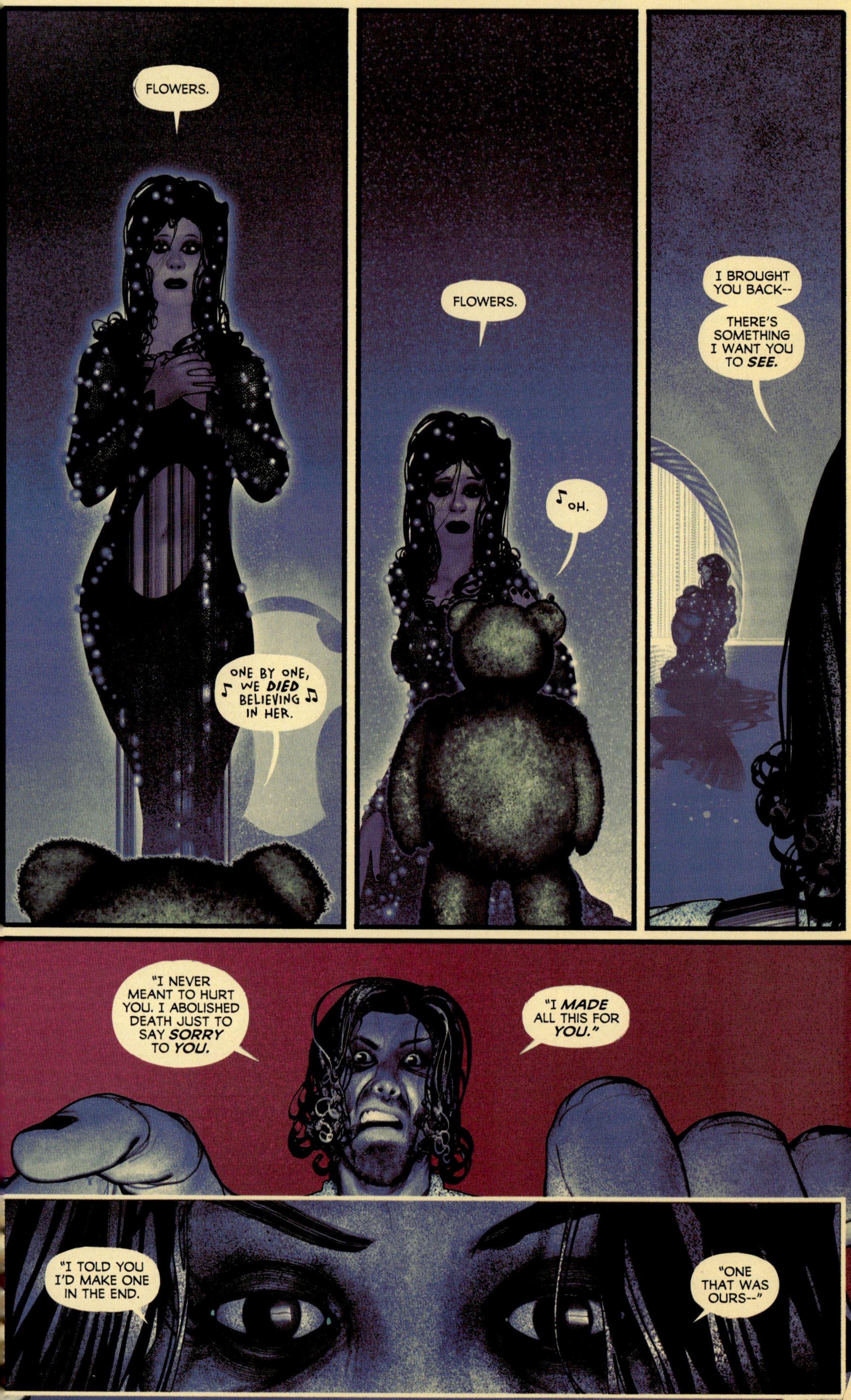
FLOWERS.
ONE BY ONE, WE DIED BELIEVING IN HER.
FLOWERS.
OH.
I BROUGHT YOU BACK--
THERE'S SOMETHING I WANT YOU TO SEE.
"I NEVER MEANT TO HURT YOU. I ABOLISHED DEATH JUST TO SAY SORRY TO YOU.
"I MADE ALL THIS FOR YOU."
"I TOLD YOU I'D MAKE ONE IN THE END.
"ONE THAT WAS OURS--"

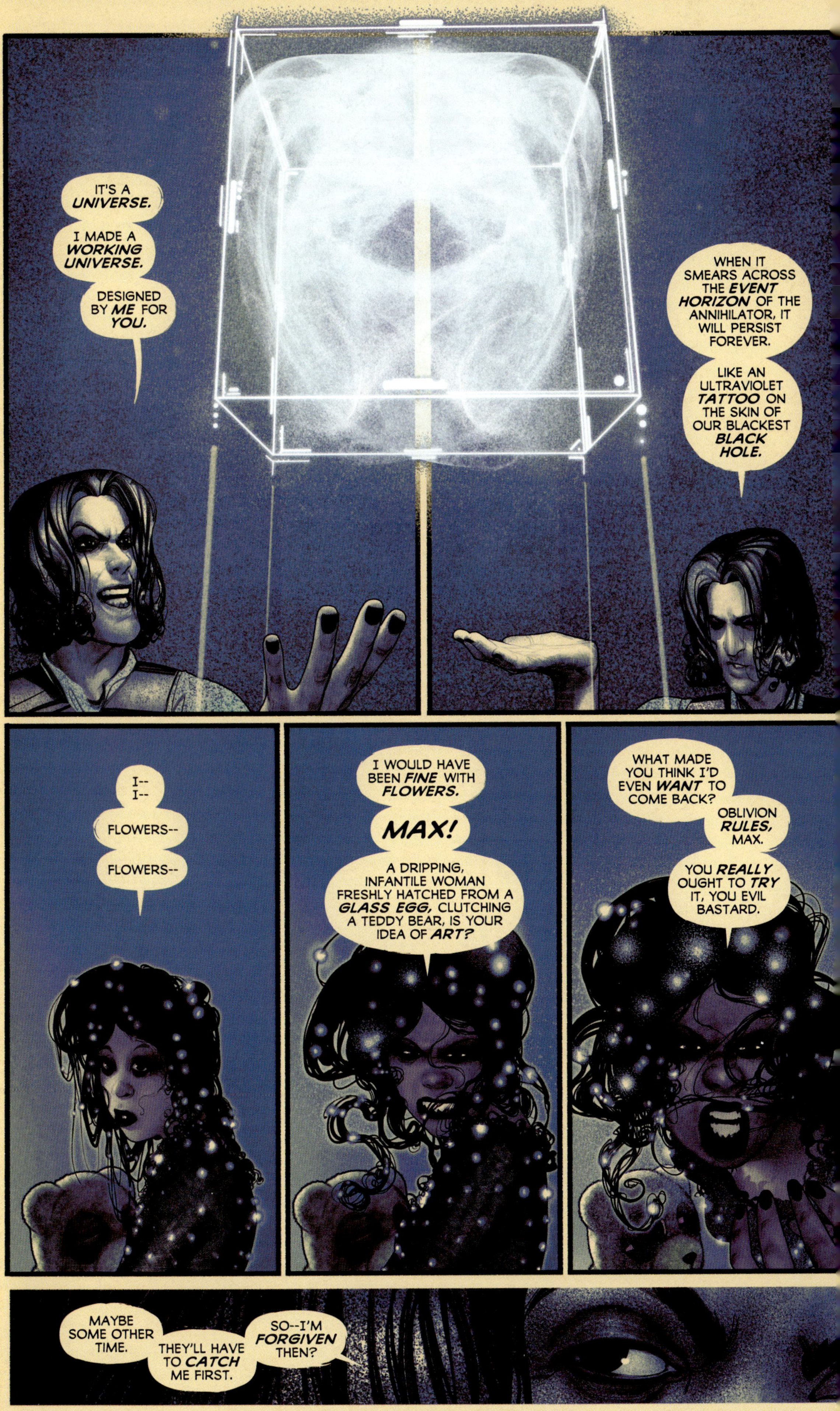

IT'S A UNIVERSE.
I MADE A WORKING UNIVERSE.
DESIGNED BY ME FOR YOU.
WHEN IT SMEARS ACROSS THE EVENT HORIZON OF THE ANNIHILATOR, IT WILL PERSIST FOREVER.
LIKE AN ULTRAVIOLET TATTOO ON THE SKIN OF OUR BLACKEST BLACK HOLE.
I-- I--
FLOWERS--
FLOWERS--
I WOULD HAVE BEEN FINE WITH FLOWERS.
MAX!
A DRIPPING, INFANTILE WOMAN FRESHLY HATCHED FROM A GLASS EGG, CLUTCHING A TEDDY BEAR, IS YOUR IDEA OF ART?
WHAT MADE YOU THINK I'D EVEN WANT TO COME BACK?
OBLIVION RULES, MAX.
YOU REALLY OUGHT TO TRY IT, YOU EVIL BASTARD.
SO--I'M FORGIVEN THEN?
MAYBE SOME OTHER TIME.
THEY'LL HAVE TO CATCH ME FIRST.

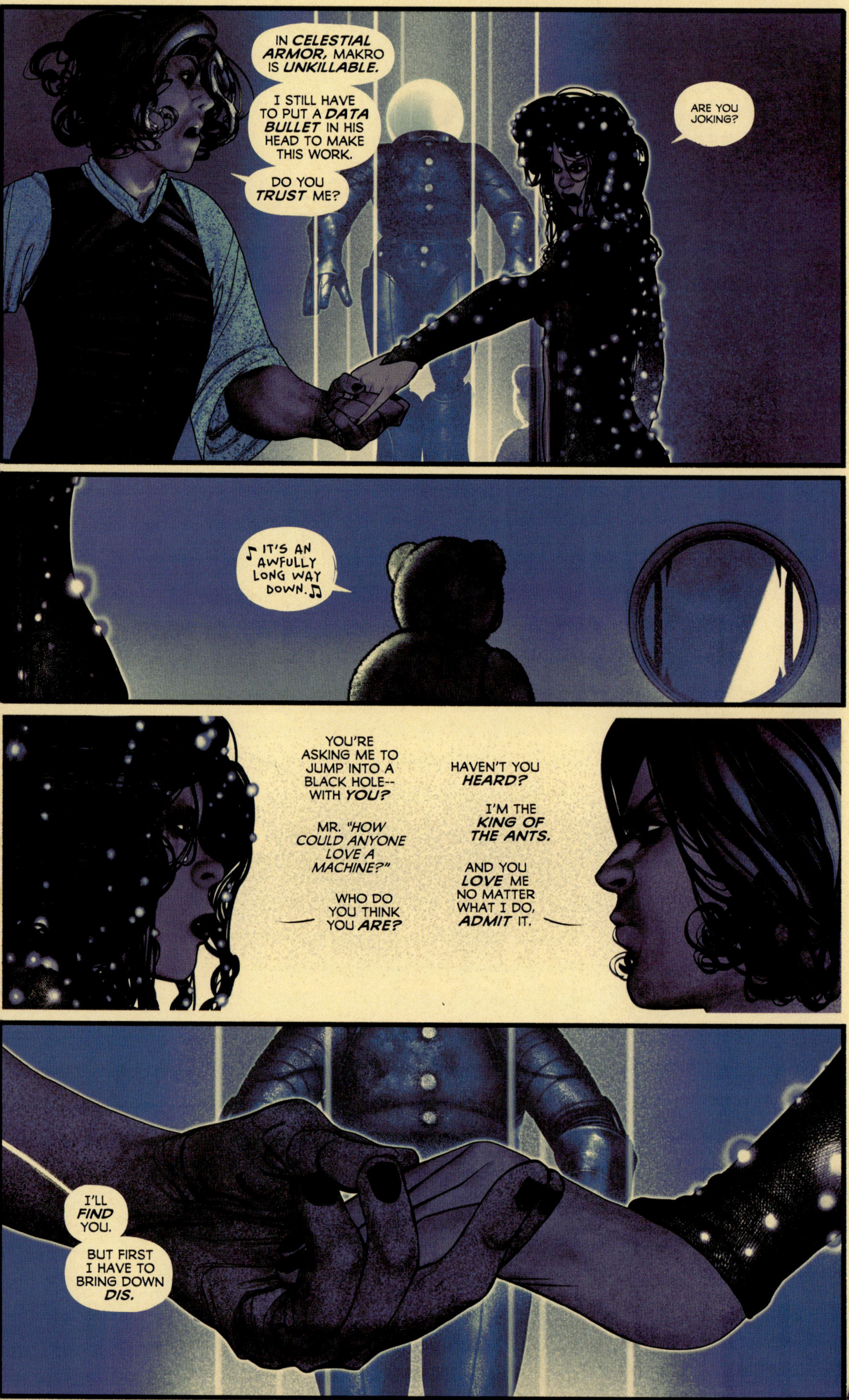
IN CELESTIAL ARMOR, MAKRO IS UNKILLABLE.
I STILL HAVE TO PUT A DATA BULLET IN HIS HEAD TO MAKE THIS WORK.
DO YOU TRUST ME?
ARE YOU JOKING?
♪ IT'S AN AWFULLY LONG WAY DOWN. ♫
YOU'RE ASKING ME TO JUMP INTO A BLACK HOLE-- WITH YOU?
MR. "HOW COULD ANYONE LOVE A MACHINE?"
WHO DO YOU THINK YOU ARE?
HAVEN'T YOU HEARD?
I'M THE KING OF THE ANTS.
AND YOU LOVE ME NO MATTER WHAT I DO, ADMIT IT.
I'LL FIND YOU.
BUT FIRST I HAVE TO BRING DOWN DIS.

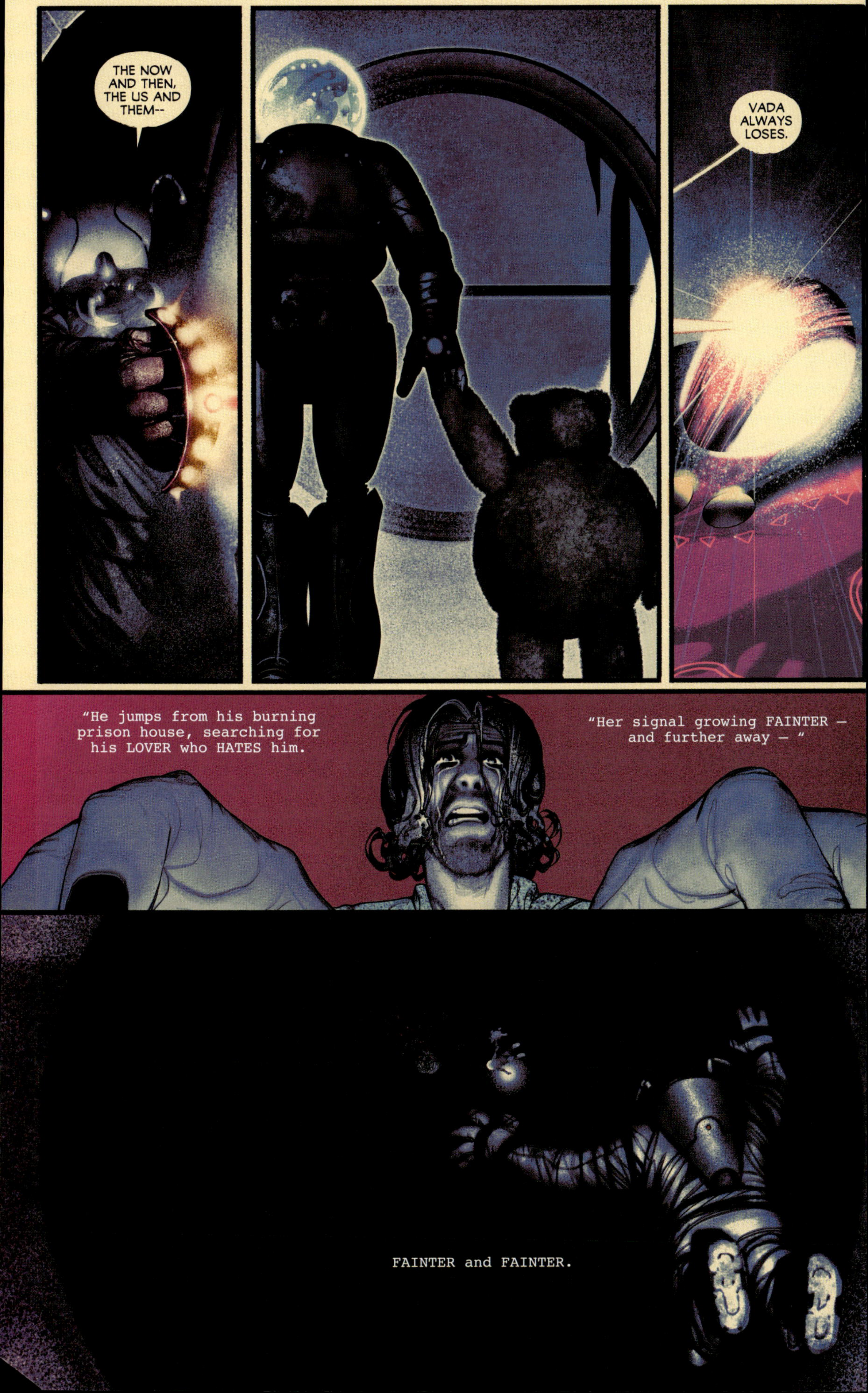

THE NOW AND THEN, THE US AND THEM--
VADA ALWAYS LOSES.
"He jumps from his burning prison house, searching for his LOVER who HATES him.
"Her signal growing FAINTER — and further away — "
FAINTER and FAINTER.

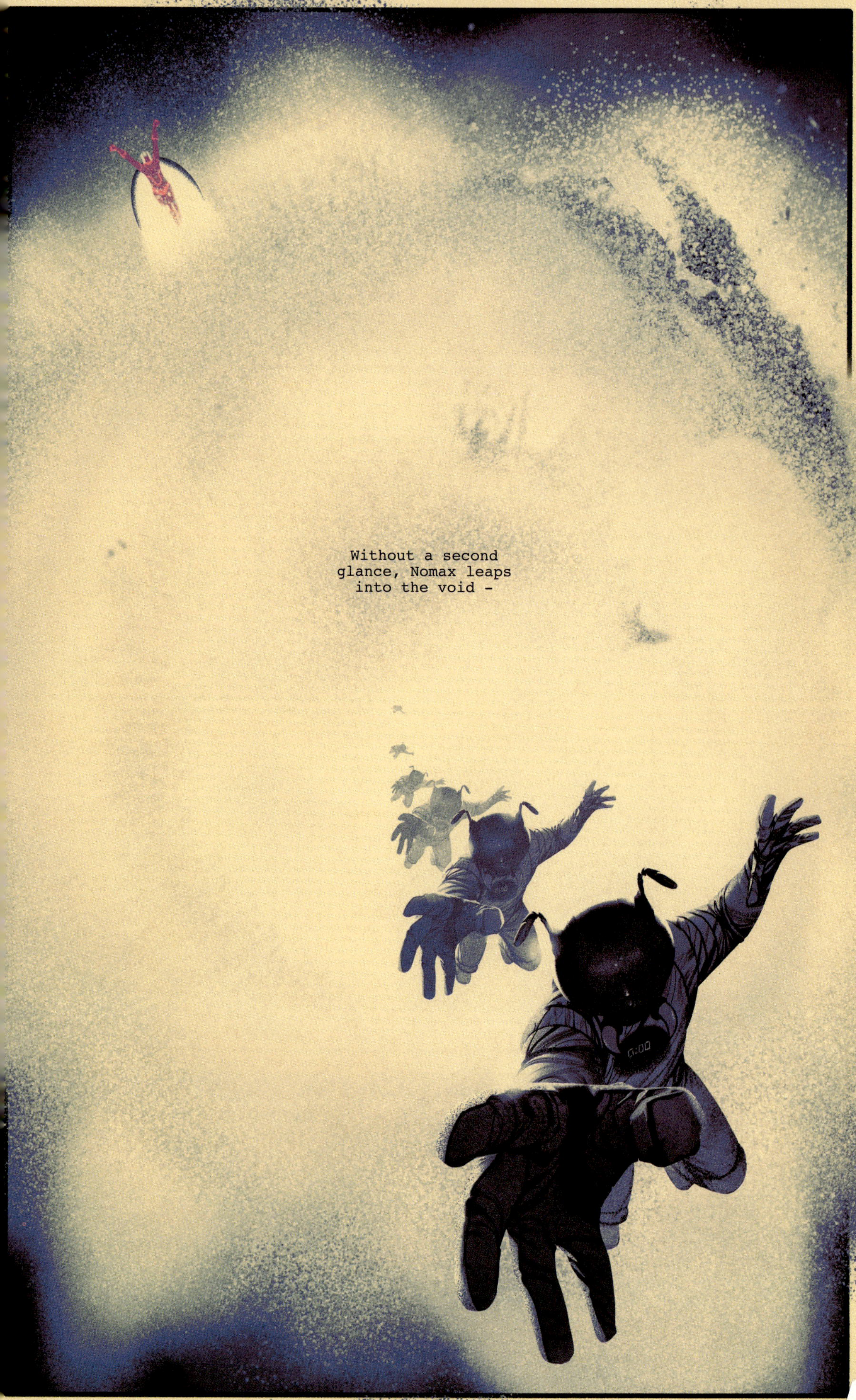
Without a second glance, Nomax leaps into the void -

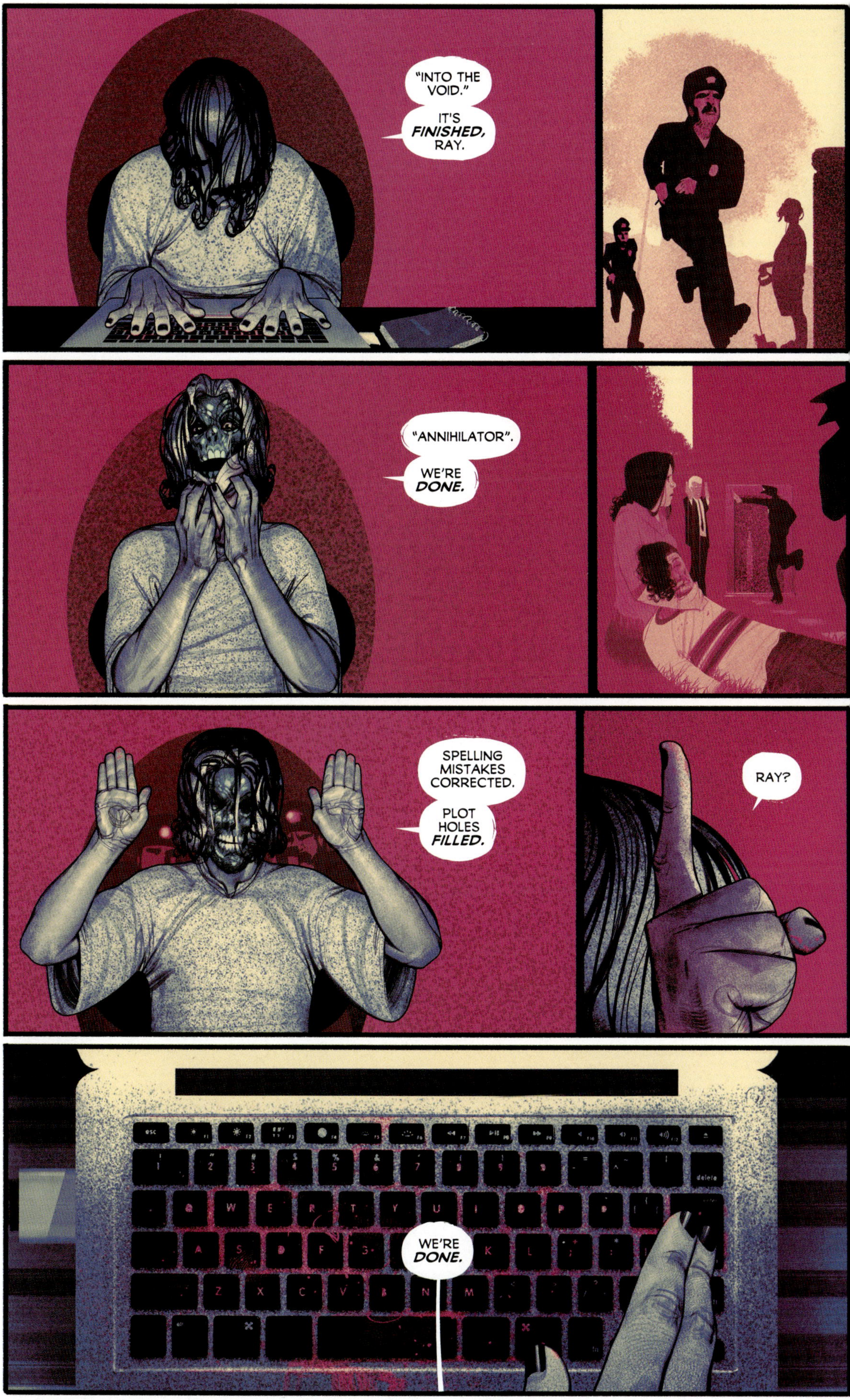
"INTO THE VOID."
IT'S *FINISHED,* RAY.
"ANNIHILATOR".
WE'RE *DONE.*
SPELLING MISTAKES CORRECTED.
PLOT HOLES *FILLED.*
RAY?
WE'RE *DONE.*

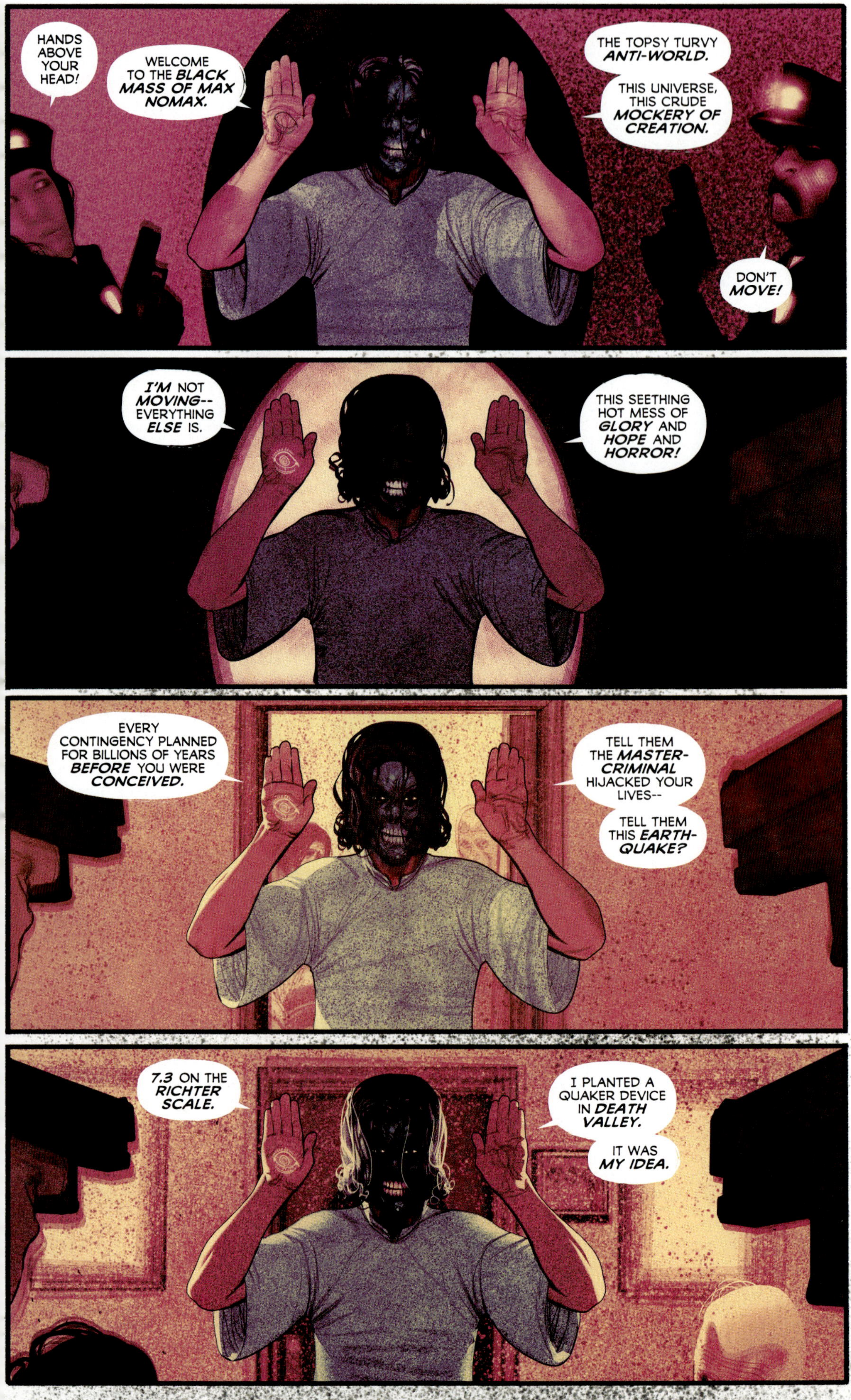
HANDS ABOVE YOUR HEAD!
WELCOME TO THE BLACK MASS OF MAX NOMAX.
THE TOPSY TURVY ANTI-WORLD.
THIS UNIVERSE, THIS CRUDE MOCKERY OF CREATION.
DON'T MOVE!
I'M NOT MOVING-- EVERYTHING ELSE IS.
THIS SEETHING HOT MESS OF GLORY AND HOPE AND HORROR!
EVERY CONTINGENCY PLANNED FOR BILLIONS OF YEARS BEFORE YOU WERE CONCEIVED.
TELL THEM THE MASTER-CRIMINAL HIJACKED YOUR LIVES--
TELL THEM THIS EARTH-QUAKE?
7.3 ON THE RICHTER SCALE.
I PLANTED A QUAKER DEVICE IN DEATH VALLEY.
IT WAS MY IDEA.

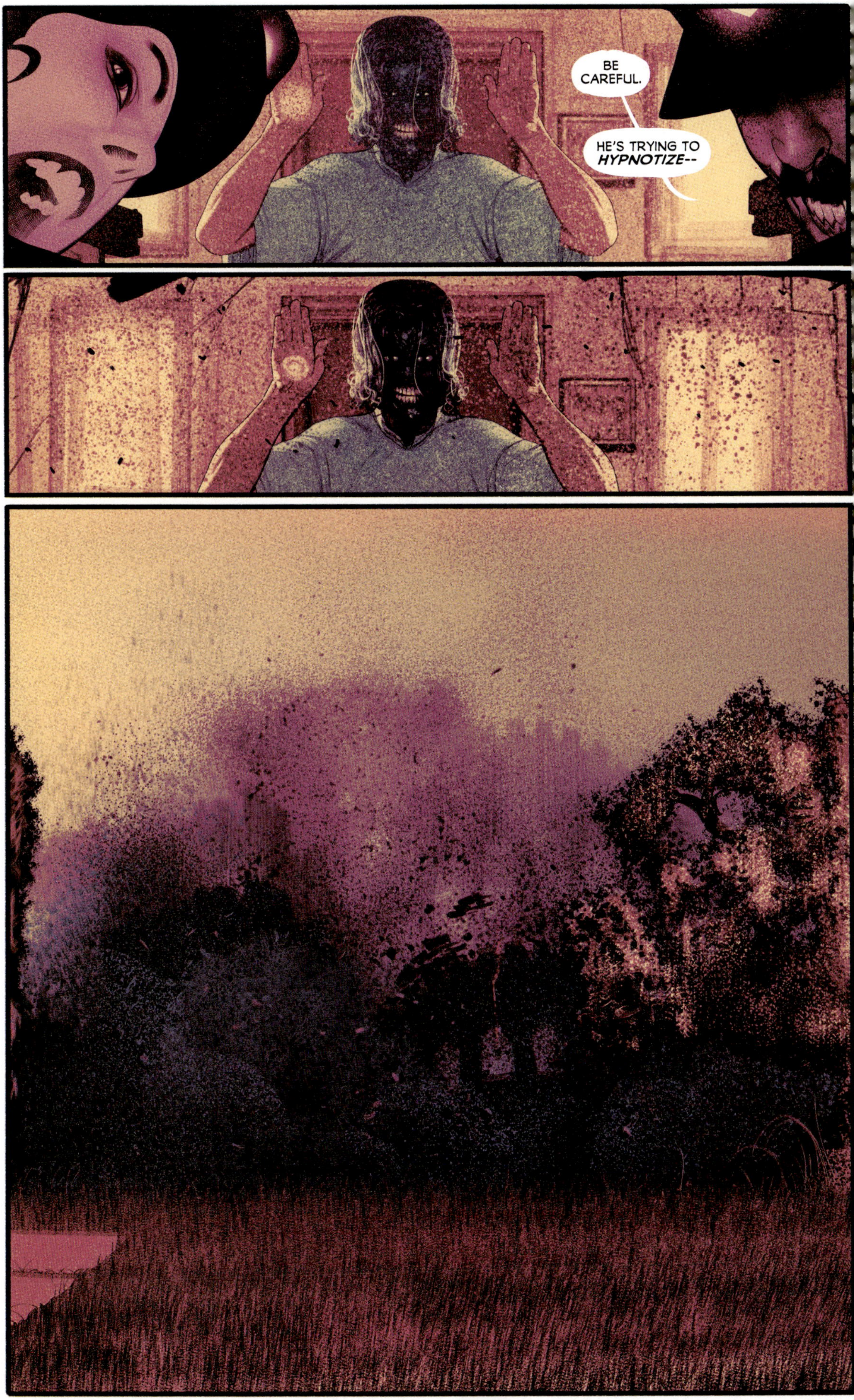
BE CAREFUL.
HE'S TRYING TO *HYPNOTIZE*--

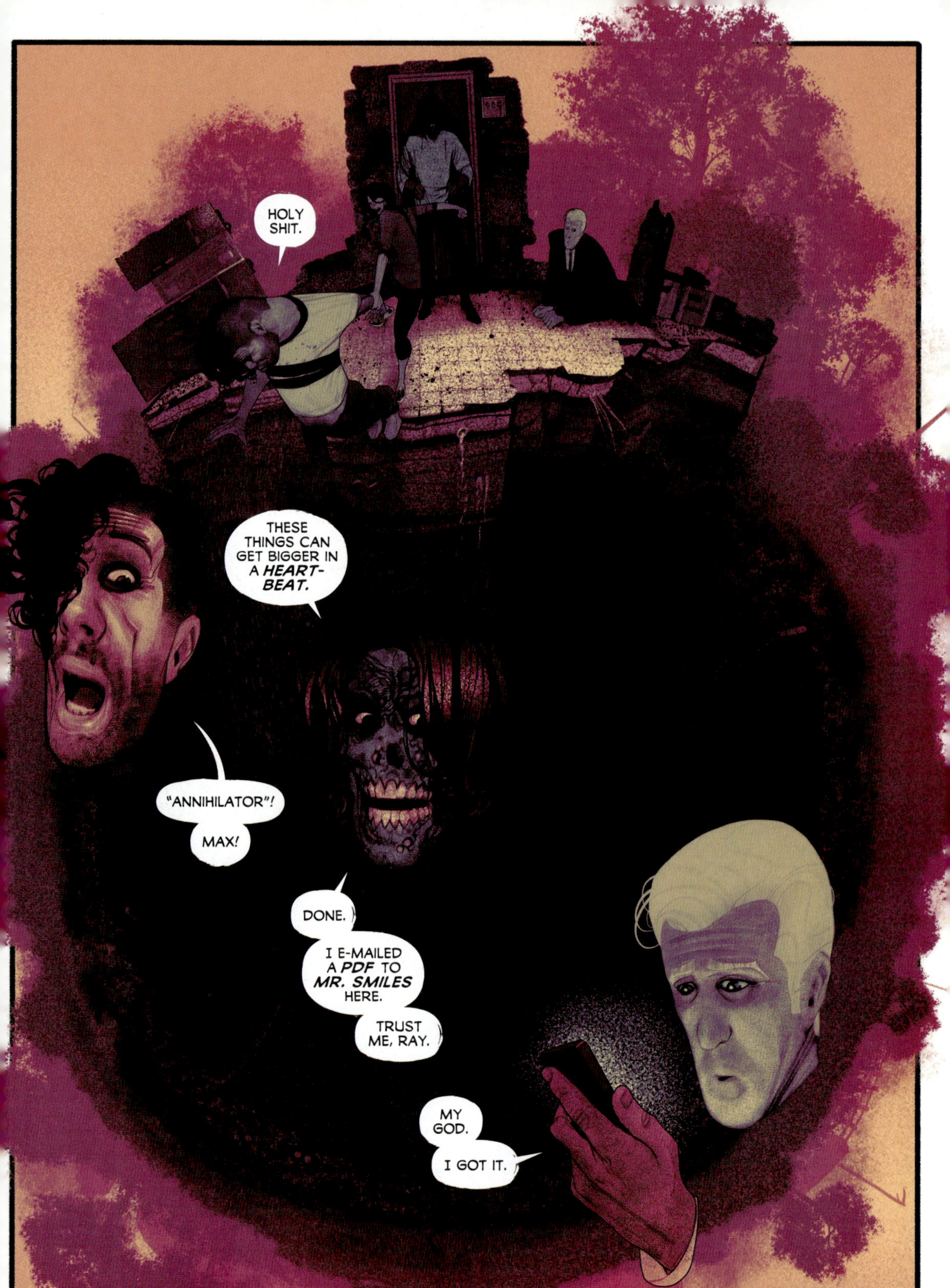
HOLY SHIT.
THESE THINGS CAN GET BIGGER IN A HEART-BEAT.
"ANNIHILATOR"!
MAX!
DONE.
I E-MAILED A PDF TO MR. SMILES HERE.
TRUST ME, RAY.
MY GOD.
I GOT IT.

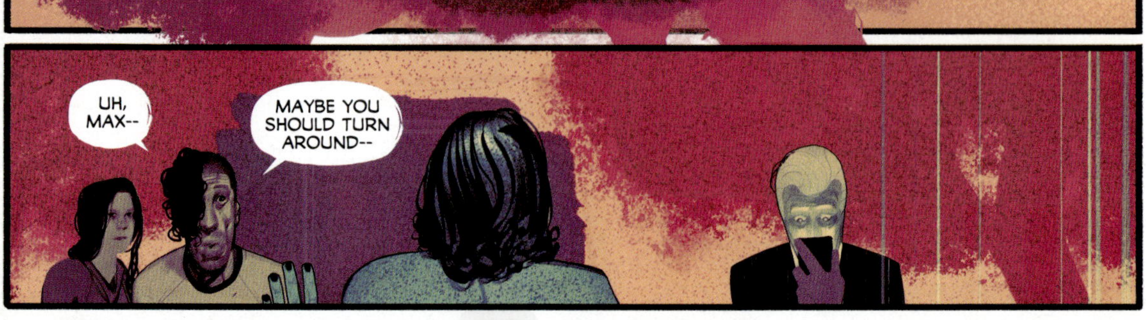
UH, MAX--
MAYBE YOU SHOULD TURN AROUND--

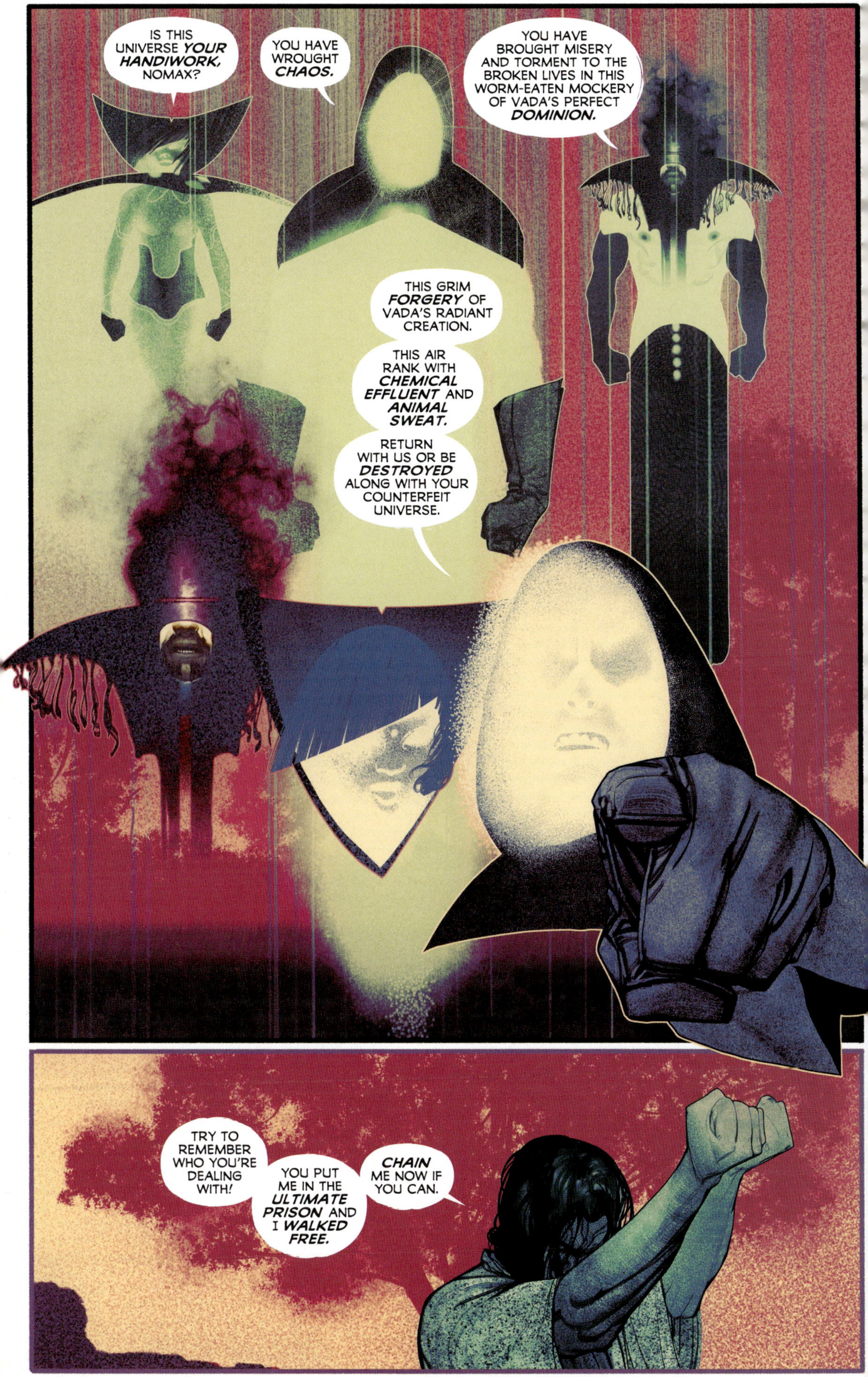
IS THIS UNIVERSE YOUR HANDIWORK, NOMAX?
YOU HAVE WROUGHT CHAOS.
YOU HAVE BROUGHT MISERY AND TORMENT TO THE BROKEN LIVES IN THIS WORM-EATEN MOCKERY OF VADA'S PERFECT DOMINION.
THIS GRIM FORGERY OF VADA'S RADIANT CREATION.
THIS AIR RANK WITH CHEMICAL EFFLUENT AND ANIMAL SWEAT.
RETURN WITH US OR BE DESTROYED ALONG WITH YOUR COUNTERFEIT UNIVERSE.
TRY TO REMEMBER WHO YOU'RE DEALING WITH!
YOU PUT ME IN THE ULTIMATE PRISON AND I WALKED FREE.
CHAIN ME NOW IF YOU CAN.

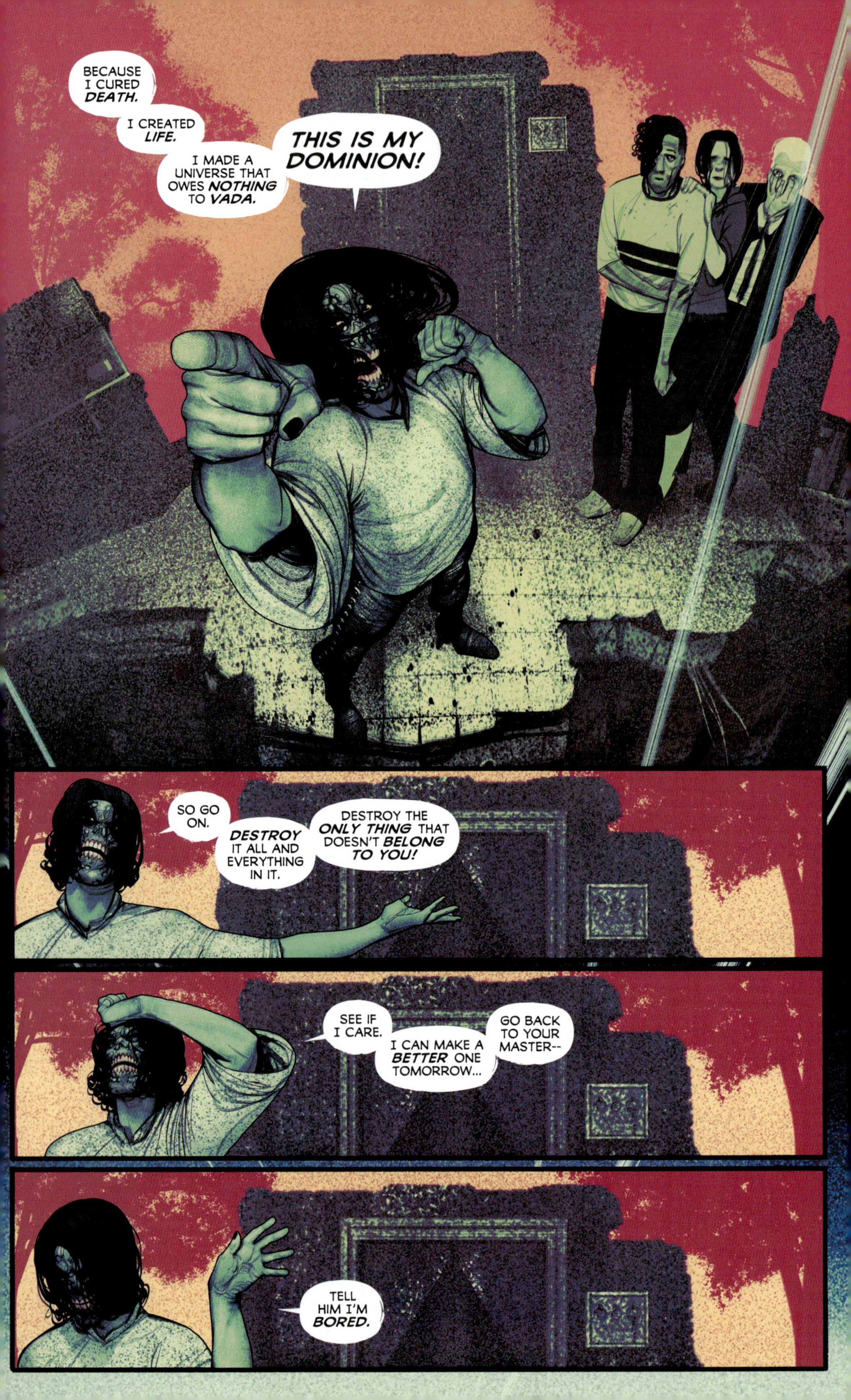

BECAUSE I CURED *DEATH.*
I CREATED *LIFE.*
I MADE A UNIVERSE THAT OWES *NOTHING* TO *VADA.*
THIS IS MY DOMINION!
SO GO ON.
DESTROY IT ALL AND EVERYTHING IN IT.
DESTROY THE *ONLY THING* THAT DOESN'T *BELONG TO YOU!*
SEE IF I CARE.
I CAN MAKE A *BETTER* ONE TOMORROW...
GO BACK TO YOUR MASTER--
TELL HIM I'M *BORED.*

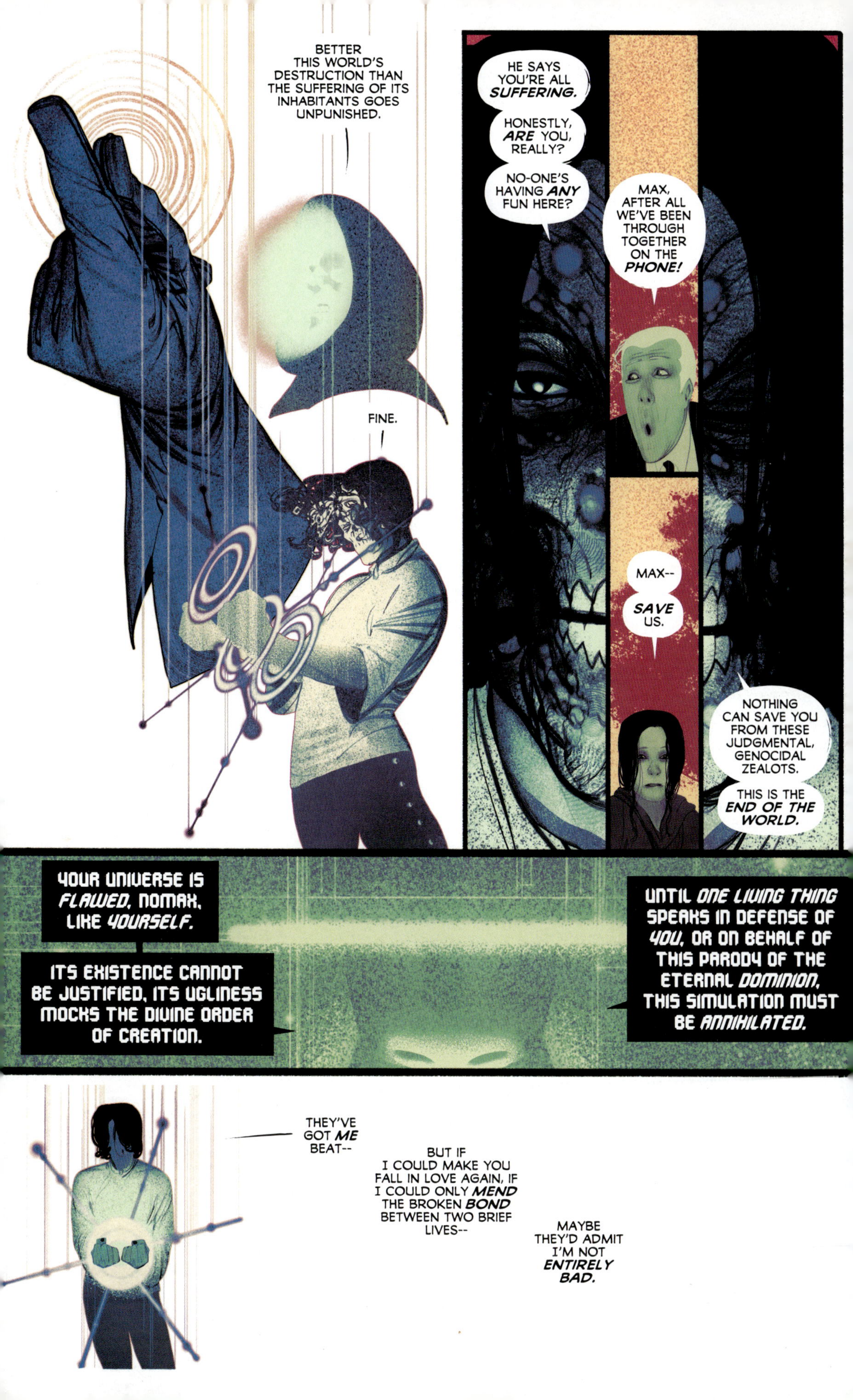

BETTER THIS WORLD'S DESTRUCTION THAN THE SUFFERING OF ITS INHABITANTS GOES UNPUNISHED.
FINE.
HE SAYS YOU'RE ALL *SUFFERING.*
HONESTLY, *ARE* YOU, REALLY?
NO-ONE'S HAVING *ANY* FUN HERE?
MAX, AFTER ALL WE'VE BEEN THROUGH TOGETHER ON THE *PHONE!*
MAX--
SAVE US.
NOTHING CAN SAVE YOU FROM THESE JUDGMENTAL, GENOCIDAL ZEALOTS.
THIS IS THE *END OF THE WORLD.*
YOUR UNIVERSE IS *FLAWED,* NOMAX, LIKE *YOURSELF.*
ITS EXISTENCE CANNOT BE JUSTIFIED, ITS UGLINESS MOCKS THE DIVINE ORDER OF CREATION.
UNTIL *ONE LIVING THING* SPEAKS IN DEFENSE OF *YOU,* OR ON BEHALF OF THIS PARODY OF THE ETERNAL *DOMINION,* THIS SIMULATION MUST BE *ANNIHILATED.*
THEY'VE GOT *ME* BEAT--
BUT IF I COULD MAKE YOU FALL IN LOVE AGAIN, IF I COULD ONLY *MEND* THE BROKEN *BOND* BETWEEN TWO BRIEF LIVES--
MAYBE THEY'D ADMIT I'M NOT *ENTIRELY BAD.*

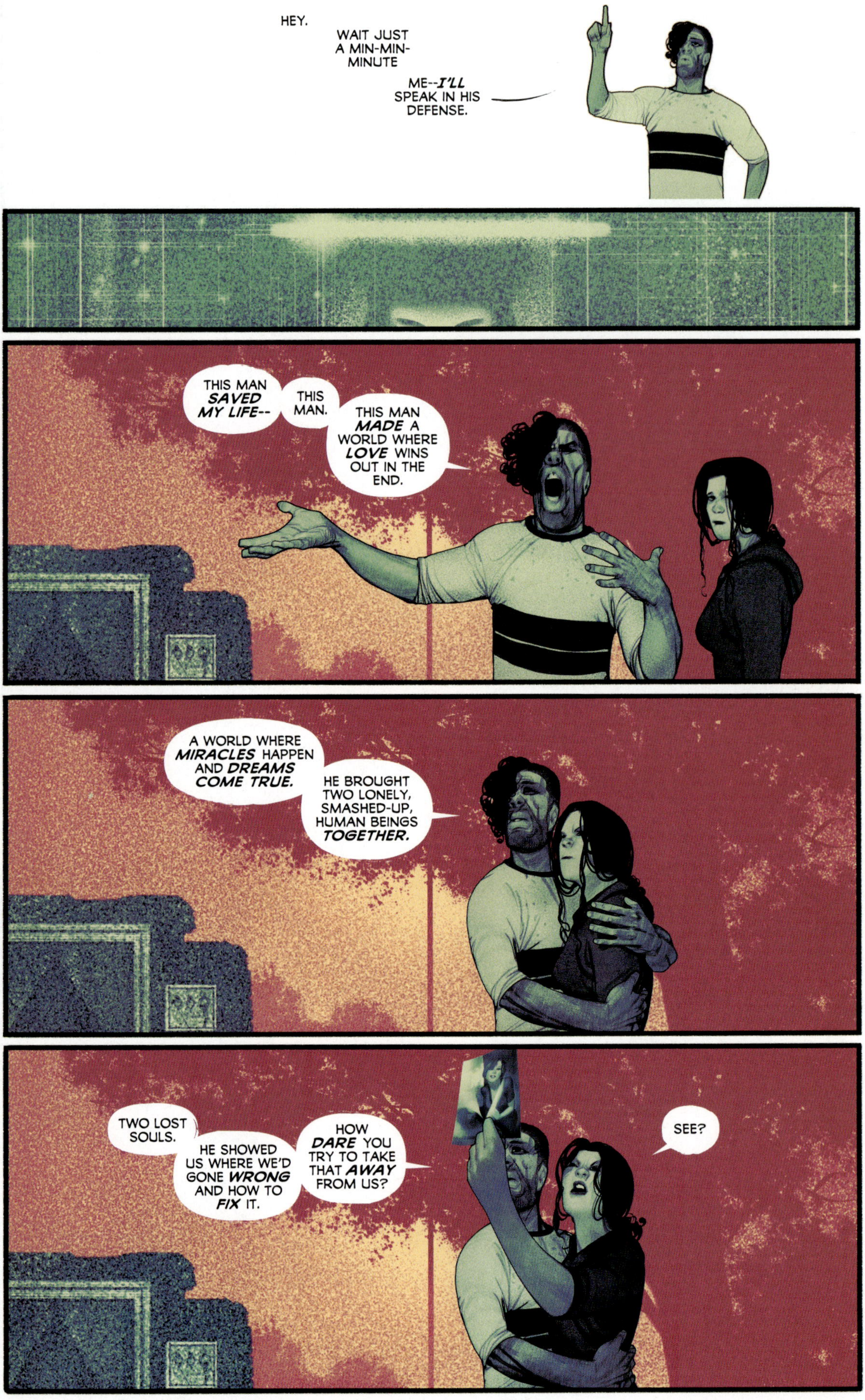
HEY.
WAIT JUST A MIN-MIN-MINUTE
ME--*I'LL* SPEAK IN HIS DEFENSE.
THIS MAN *SAVED MY LIFE--*
THIS MAN.
THIS MAN *MADE* A WORLD WHERE *LOVE* WINS OUT IN THE END.
A WORLD WHERE *MIRACLES* HAPPEN AND *DREAMS COME TRUE.*
HE BROUGHT TWO LONELY, SMASHED-UP, HUMAN BEINGS *TOGETHER.*
TWO LOST SOULS.
HE SHOWED US WHERE WE'D GONE *WRONG* AND HOW TO *FIX* IT.
HOW *DARE* YOU TRY TO TAKE THAT *AWAY* FROM US?
SEE?

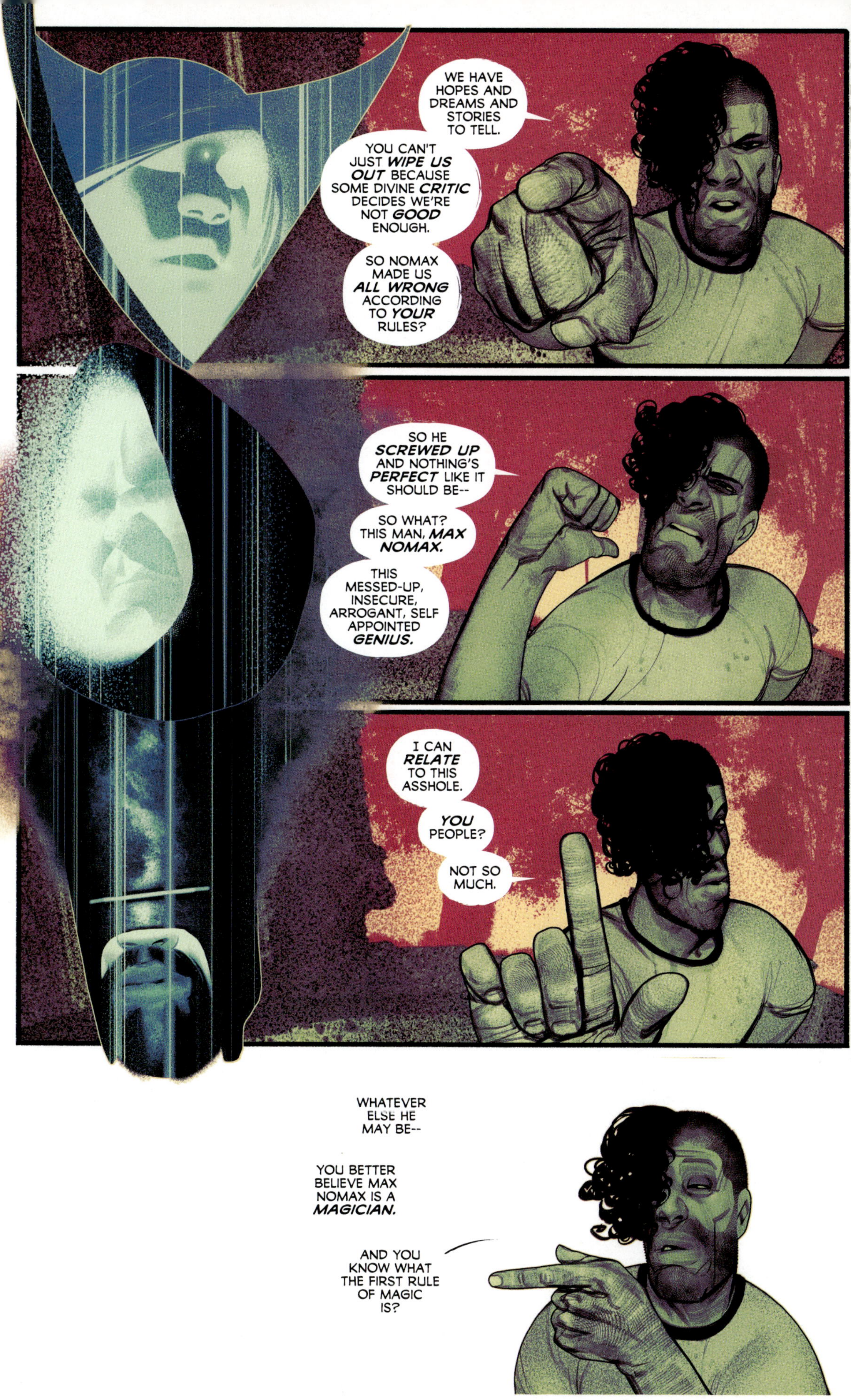
WE HAVE HOPES AND DREAMS AND STORIES TO TELL.
YOU CAN'T JUST WIPE US OUT BECAUSE SOME DIVINE CRITIC DECIDES WE'RE NOT GOOD ENOUGH.
SO NOMAX MADE US ALL WRONG ACCORDING TO YOUR RULES?
SO HE SCREWED UP AND NOTHING'S PERFECT LIKE IT SHOULD BE--
SO WHAT? THIS MAN, MAX NOMAX.
THIS MESSED-UP, INSECURE, ARROGANT, SELF APPOINTED GENIUS.
I CAN RELATE TO THIS ASSHOLE.
YOU PEOPLE?
NOT SO MUCH.
WHATEVER ELSE HE MAY BE--
YOU BETTER BELIEVE MAX NOMAX IS A MAGICIAN.
AND YOU KNOW WHAT THE FIRST RULE OF MAGIC IS?

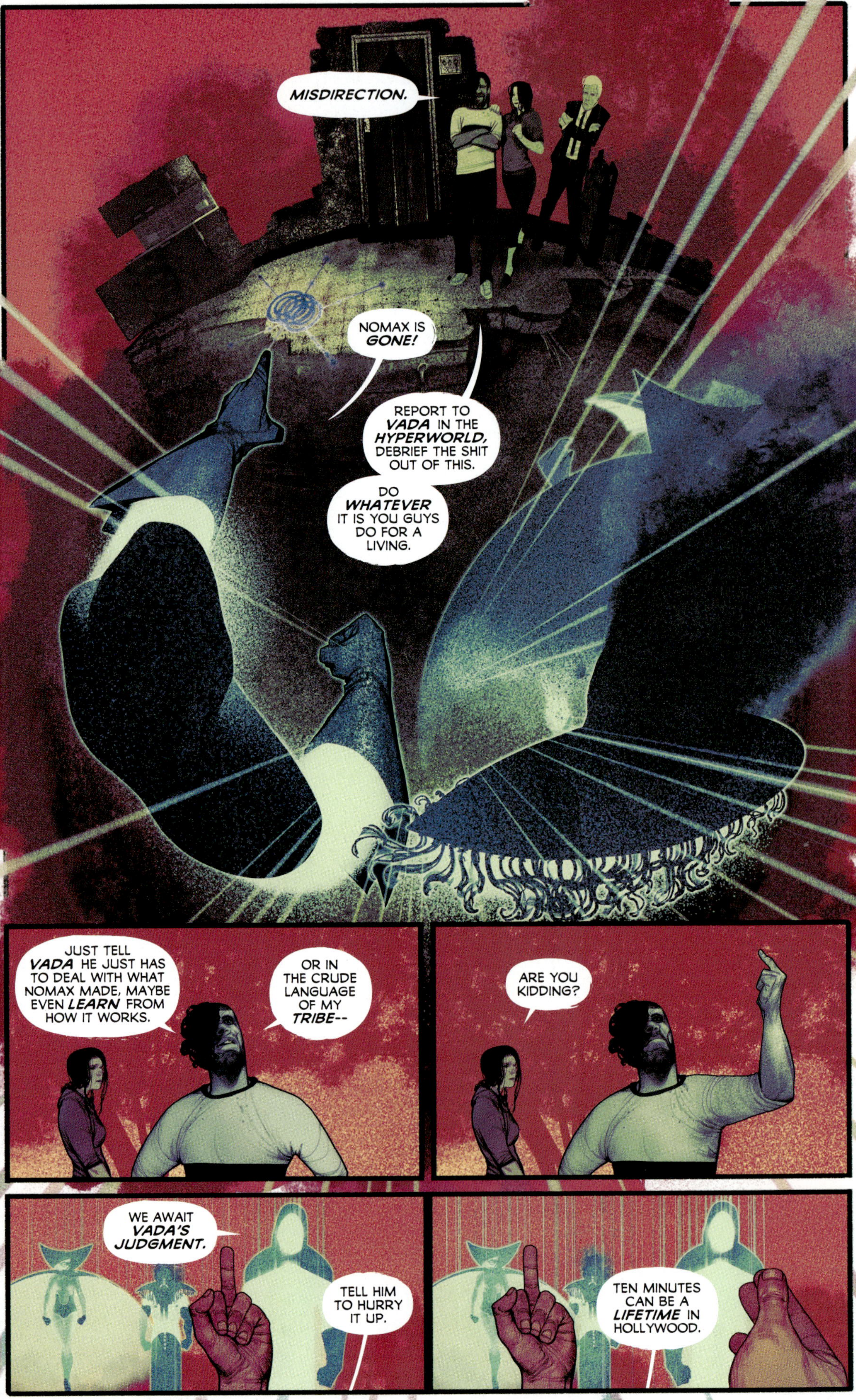
MISDIRECTION.
NOMAX IS GONE!
REPORT TO VADA IN THE HYPERWORLD, DEBRIEF THE SHIT OUT OF THIS.
DO WHATEVER IT IS YOU GUYS DO FOR A LIVING.
JUST TELL VADA HE JUST HAS TO DEAL WITH WHAT NOMAX MADE, MAYBE EVEN LEARN FROM HOW IT WORKS.
OR IN THE CRUDE LANGUAGE OF MY TRIBE--
ARE YOU KIDDING?
WE AWAIT VADA'S JUDGMENT.
TELL HIM TO HURRY IT UP.
TEN MINUTES CAN BE A LIFETIME IN HOLLYWOOD.

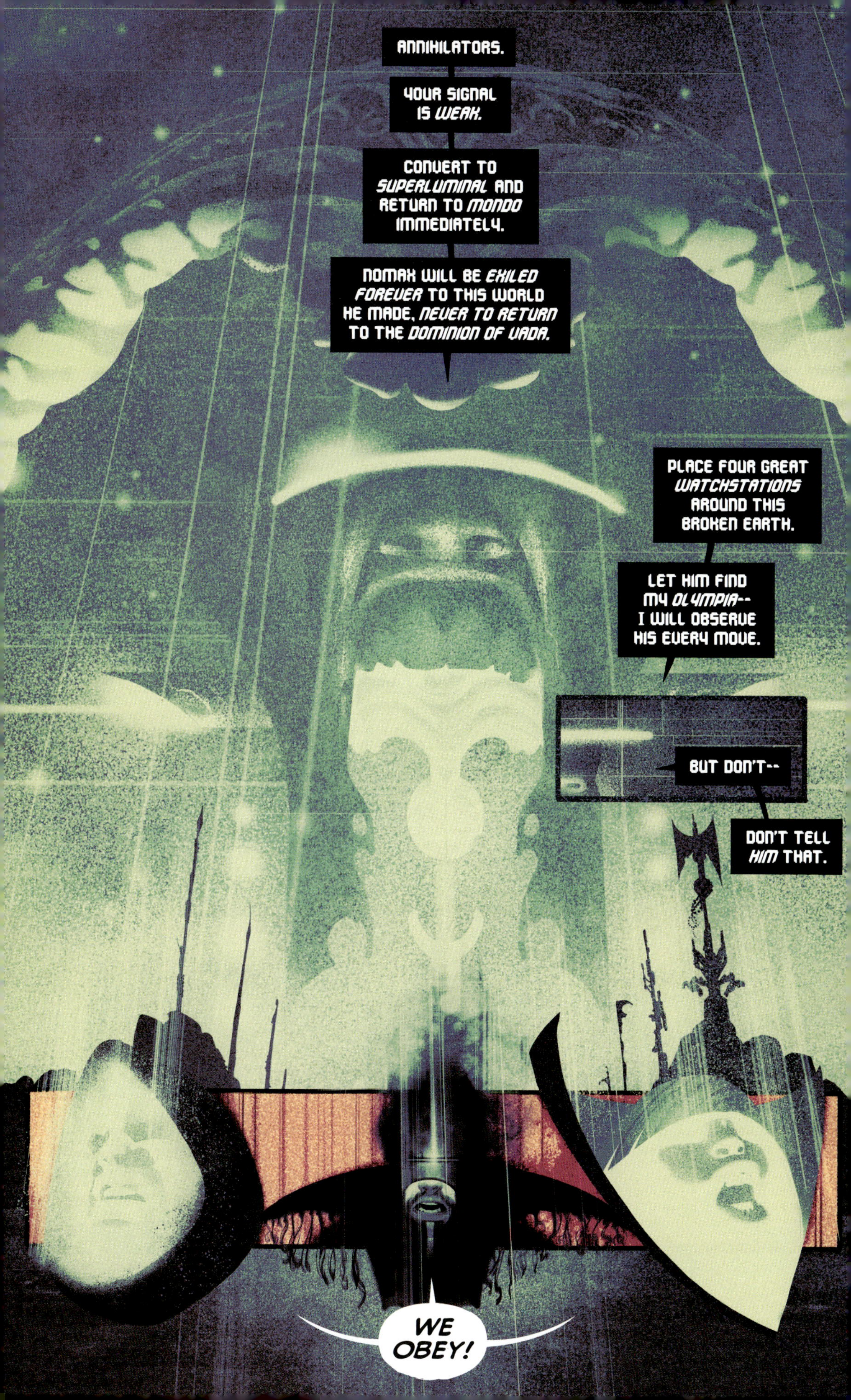
ANNIHILATORS.
YOUR SIGNAL IS WEAK.
CONVERT TO SUPERLUMINAL AND RETURN TO MONDO IMMEDIATELY.
NOMAX WILL BE EXILED FOREVER TO THIS WORLD HE MADE, NEVER TO RETURN TO THE DOMINION OF VADA.
PLACE FOUR GREAT WATCHSTATIONS AROUND THIS BROKEN EARTH.
LET HIM FIND MY OLYMPIA-- I WILL OBSERVE HIS EVERY MOVE.
BUT DON'T--
DON'T TELL HIM THAT.
WE OBEY!

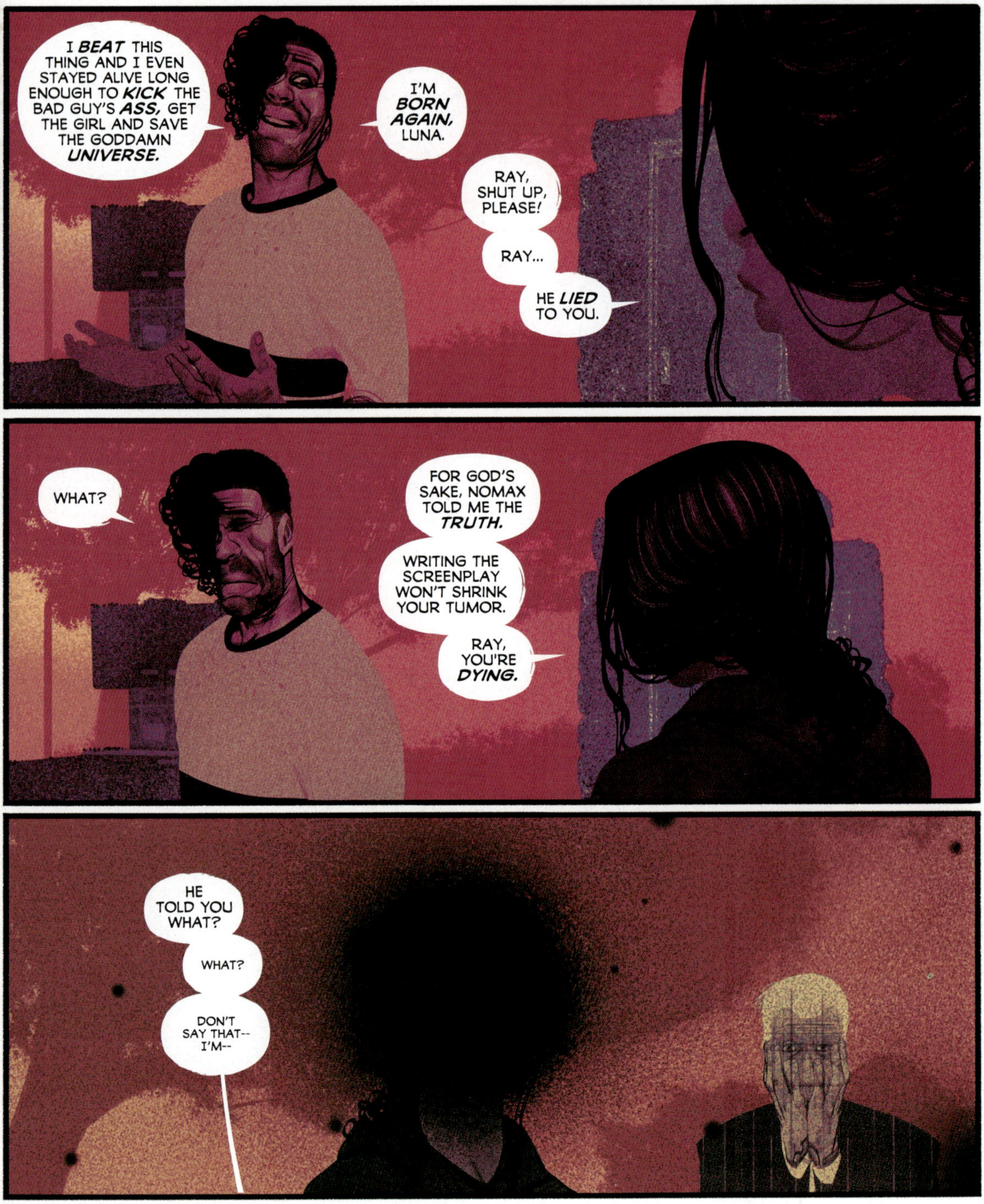
I BEAT THIS THING AND I EVEN STAYED ALIVE LONG ENOUGH TO KICK THE BAD GUY'S ASS, GET THE GIRL AND SAVE THE GODDAMN UNIVERSE.
I'M BORN AGAIN, LUNA.
RAY, SHUT UP, PLEASE!
RAY...
HE LIED TO YOU.
WHAT?
FOR GOD'S SAKE, NOMAX TOLD ME THE TRUTH.
WRITING THE SCREENPLAY WON'T SHRINK YOUR TUMOR.
RAY, YOU'RE DYING.
HE TOLD YOU WHAT?
WHAT?
DON'T SAY THAT-- I'M--

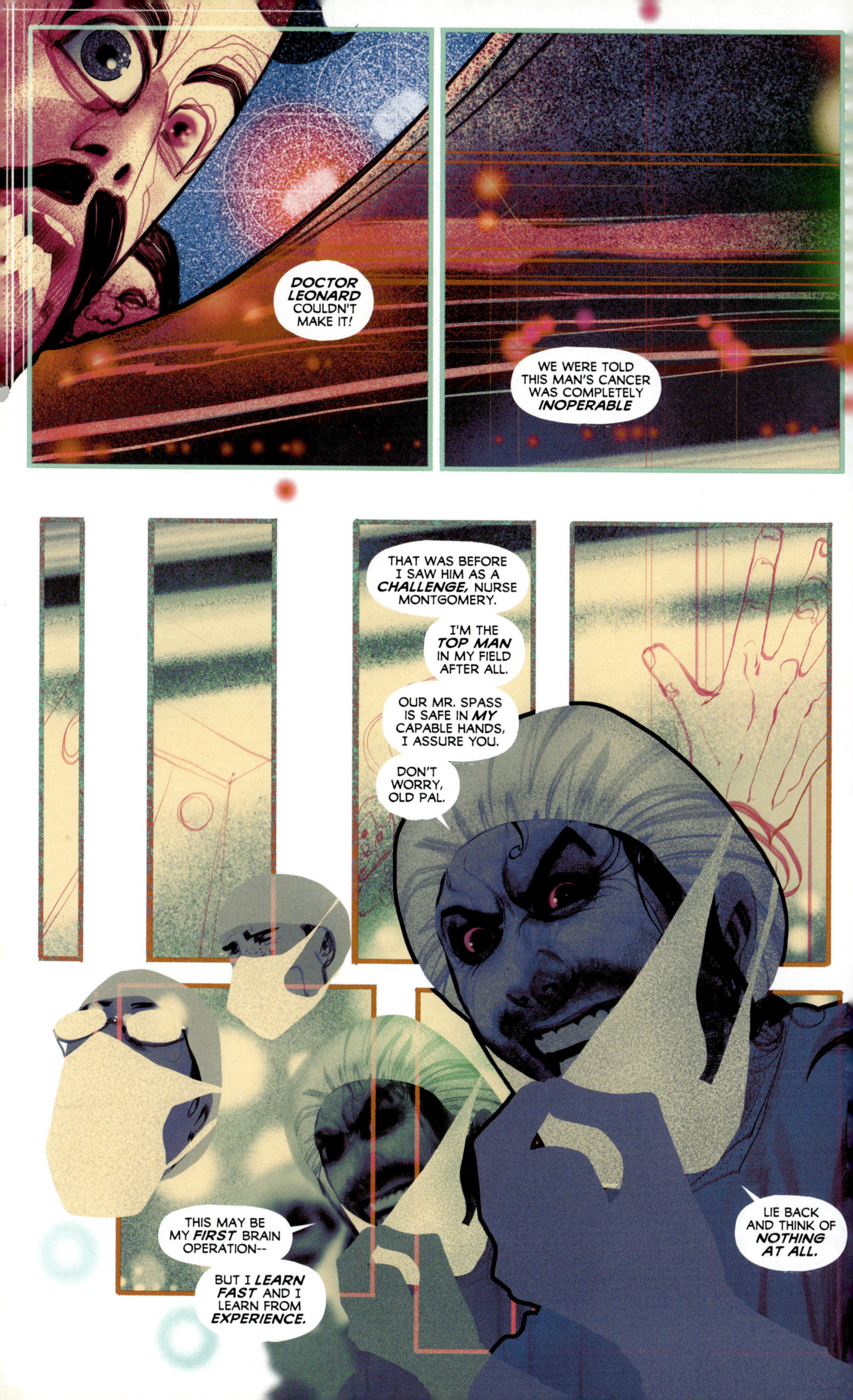
DOCTOR LEONARD COULDN'T MAKE IT!
WE WERE TOLD THIS MAN'S CANCER WAS COMPLETELY INOPERABLE
THAT WAS BEFORE I SAW HIM AS A CHALLENGE, NURSE MONTGOMERY.
I'M THE TOP MAN IN MY FIELD AFTER ALL.
OUR MR. SPASS IS SAFE IN MY CAPABLE HANDS, I ASSURE YOU.
DON'T WORRY, OLD PAL.
THIS MAY BE MY FIRST BRAIN OPERATION--
BUT I LEARN FAST AND I LEARN FROM EXPERIENCE.
LIE BACK AND THINK OF NOTHING AT ALL.

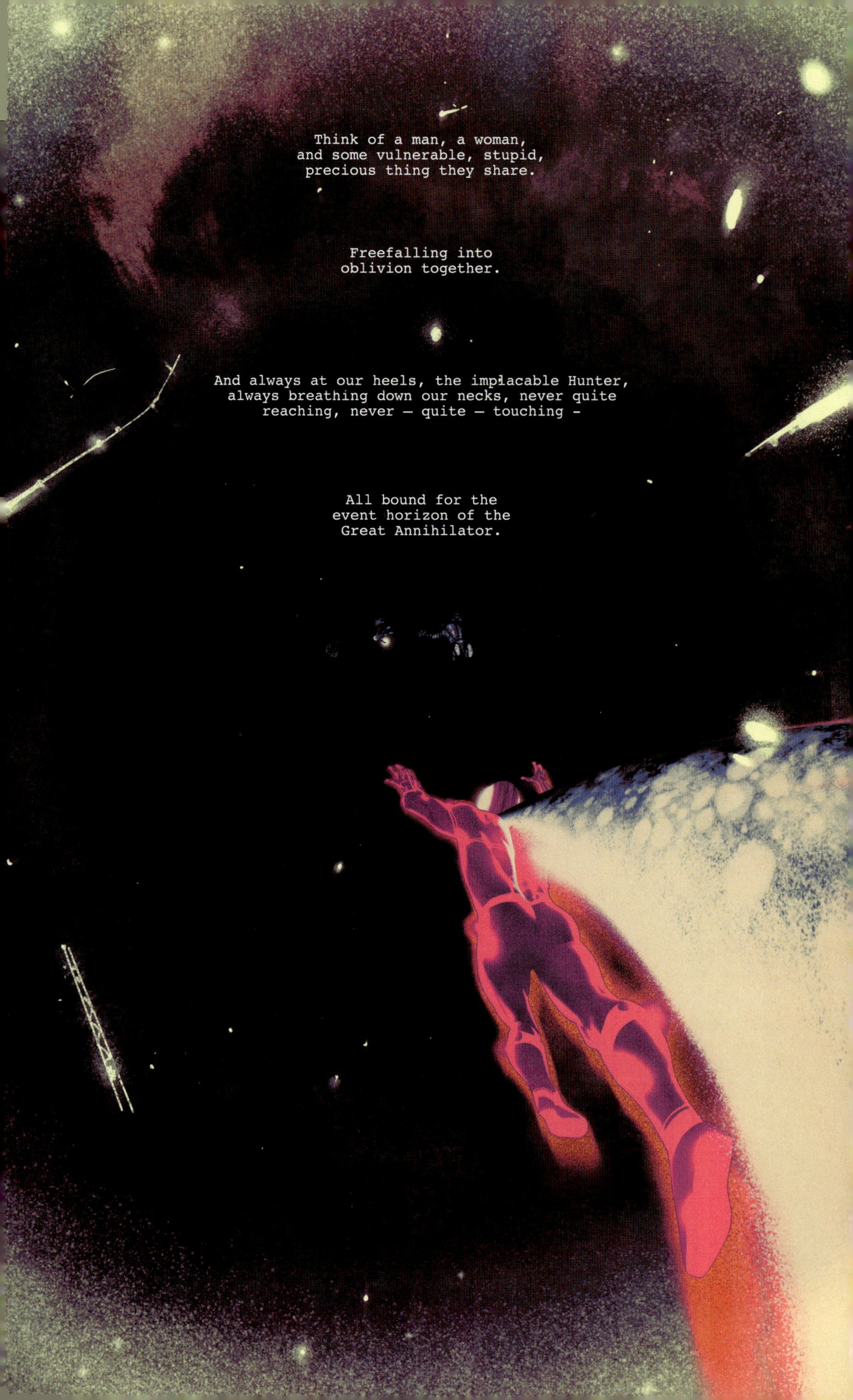
Think of a man, a woman, and some vulnerable, stupid, precious thing they share.
Freefalling into oblivion together.
And always at our heels, the implacable Hunter, always breathing down our necks, never quite reaching, never — quite — touching -
All bound for the event horizon of the Great Annihilator.

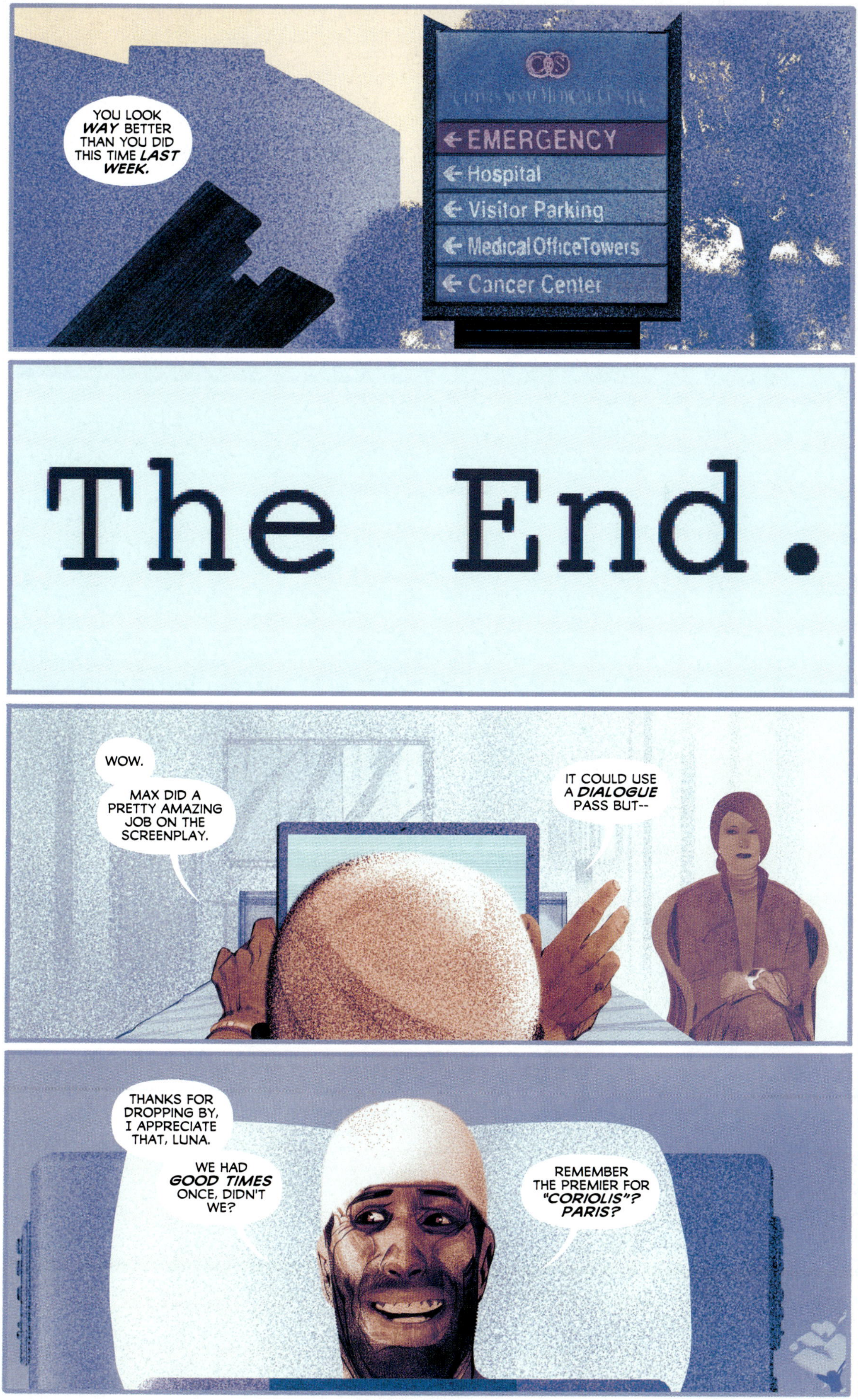
YOU LOOK WAY BETTER THAN YOU DID THIS TIME LAST WEEK.
EMERGENCY
Hospital
Visitor Parking
Medical Office Towers
Cancer Center
The End.
WOW.
MAX DID A PRETTY AMAZING JOB ON THE SCREENPLAY.
IT COULD USE A DIALOGUE PASS BUT--
THANKS FOR DROPPING BY, I APPRECIATE THAT, LUNA.
WE HAD GOOD TIMES ONCE, DIDN'T WE?
REMEMBER THE PREMIER FOR "CORIOLIS"? PARIS?

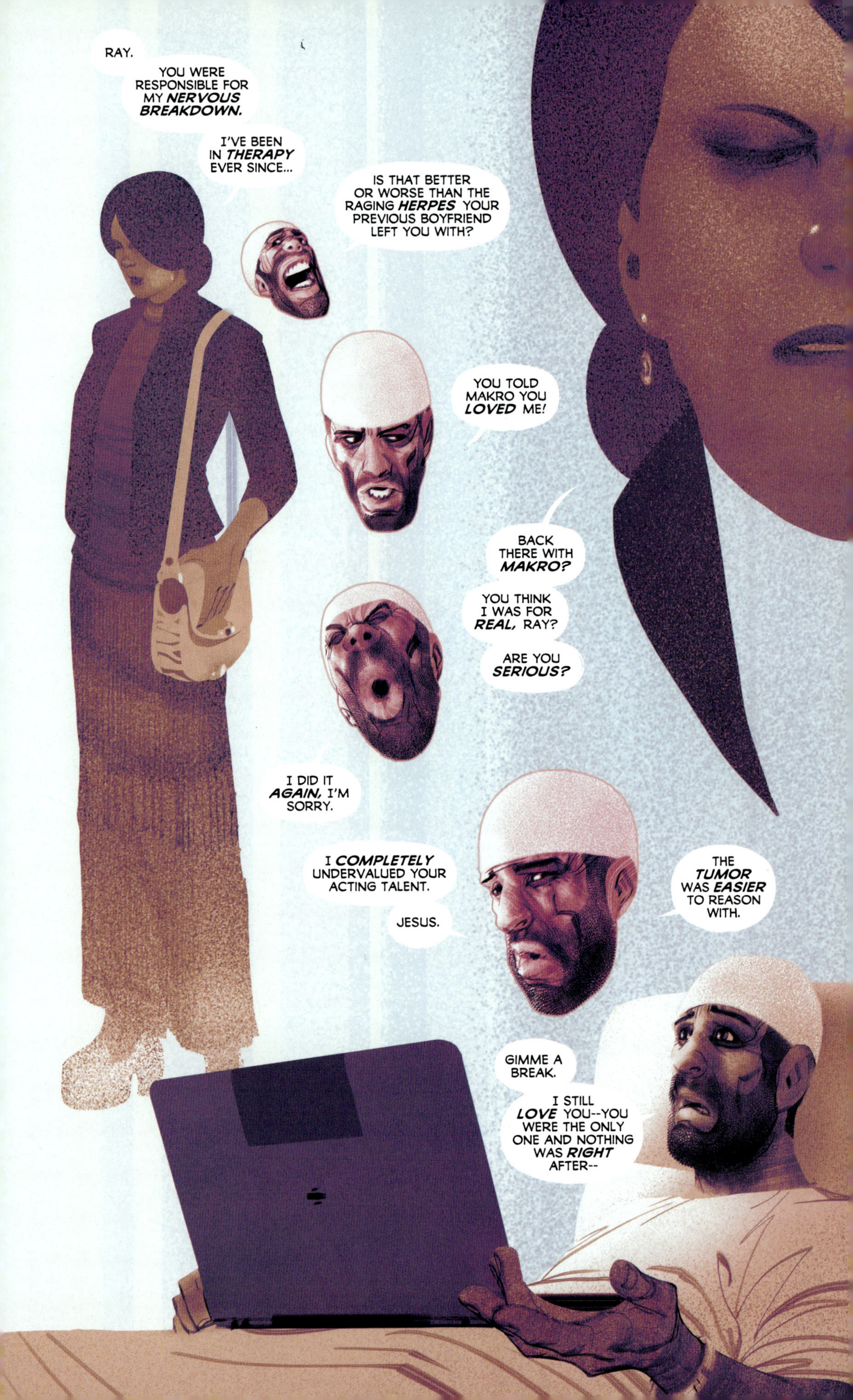
RAY.
YOU WERE RESPONSIBLE FOR MY NERVOUS BREAKDOWN.
I'VE BEEN IN THERAPY EVER SINCE...
IS THAT BETTER OR WORSE THAN THE RAGING HERPES YOUR PREVIOUS BOYFRIEND LEFT YOU WITH?
YOU TOLD MAKRO YOU LOVED ME!
BACK THERE WITH MAKRO?
YOU THINK I WAS FOR REAL, RAY?
ARE YOU SERIOUS?
I DID IT AGAIN, I'M SORRY.
I COMPLETELY UNDERVALUED YOUR ACTING TALENT.
JESUS.
THE TUMOR WAS EASIER TO REASON WITH.
GIMME A BREAK.
I STILL LOVE YOU--YOU WERE THE ONLY ONE AND NOTHING WAS RIGHT AFTER--

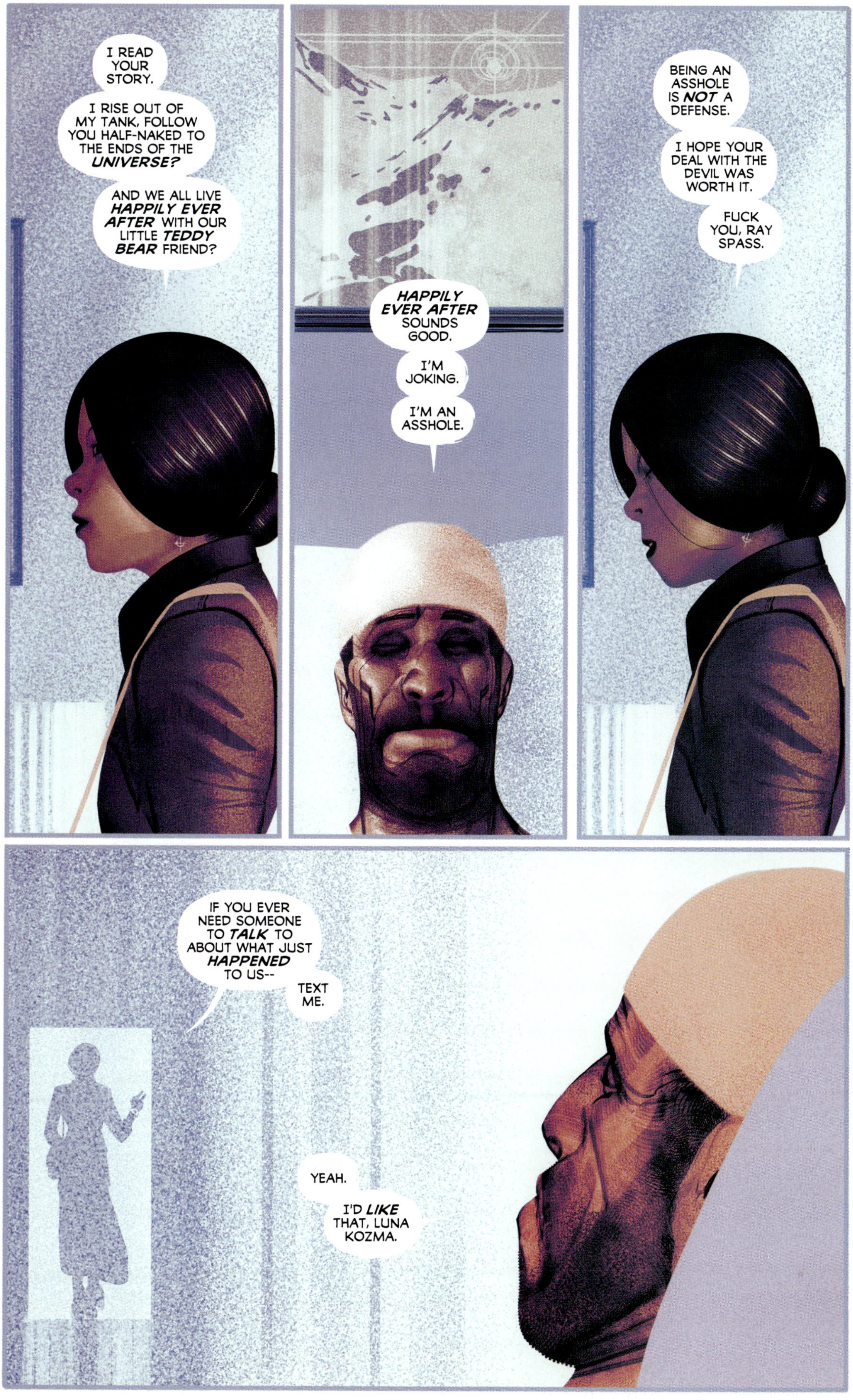
I READ YOUR STORY.
I RISE OUT OF MY TANK, FOLLOW YOU HALF-NAKED TO THE ENDS OF THE *UNIVERSE?*
AND WE ALL LIVE *HAPPILY EVER AFTER* WITH OUR LITTLE *TEDDY BEAR* FRIEND?
HAPPILY EVER AFTER SOUNDS GOOD.
I'M JOKING.
I'M AN ASSHOLE.
BEING AN ASSHOLE IS *NOT* A DEFENSE.
I HOPE YOUR DEAL WITH THE DEVIL WAS WORTH IT.
FUCK YOU, RAY SPASS.
IF YOU EVER NEED SOMEONE TO *TALK* TO ABOUT WHAT JUST *HAPPENED* TO US--
TEXT ME.
YEAH.
I'D *LIKE* THAT, LUNA KOZMA.

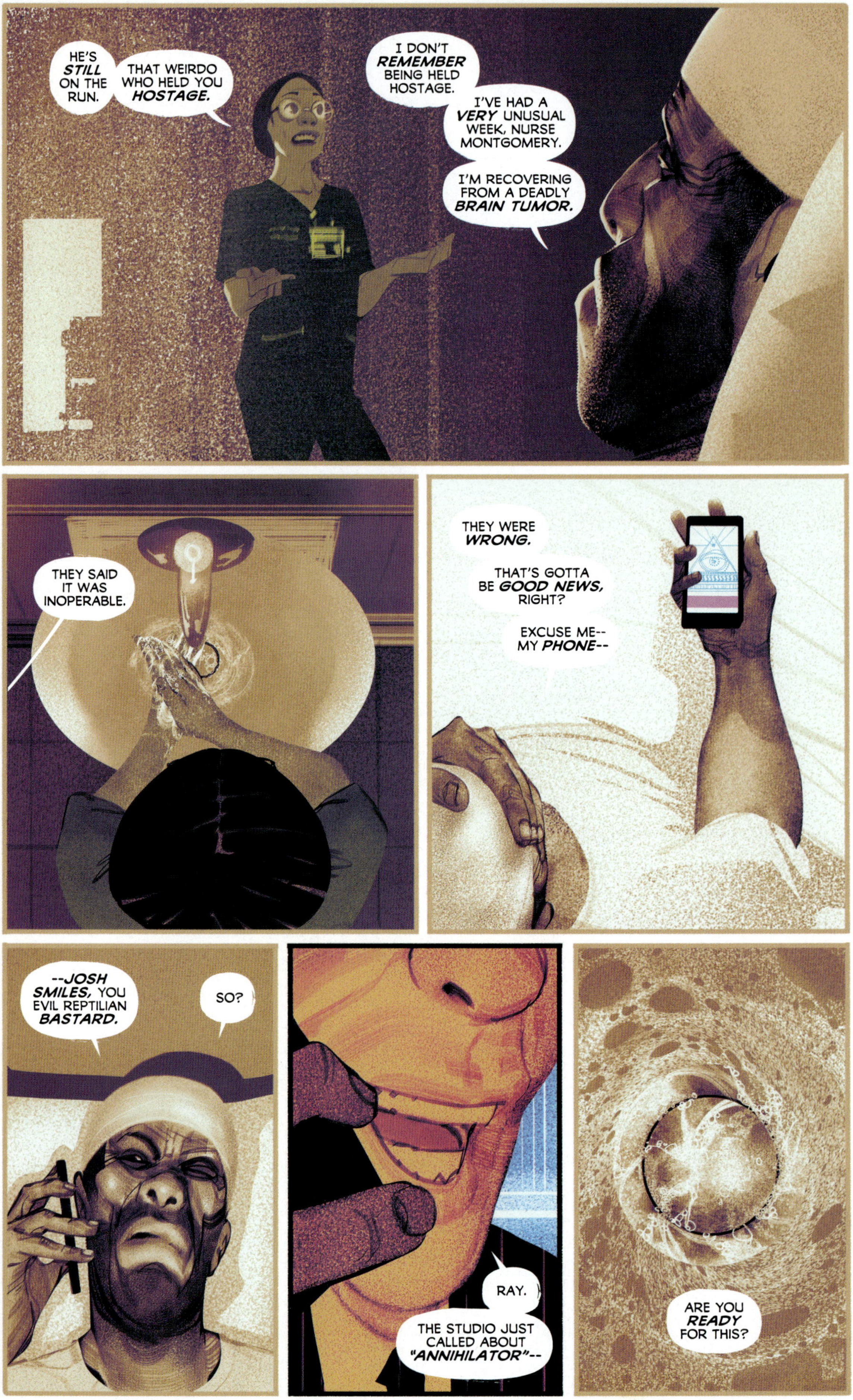
HE'S STILL ON THE RUN.
THAT WEIRDO WHO HELD YOU HOSTAGE.
I DON'T REMEMBER BEING HELD HOSTAGE.
I'VE HAD A VERY UNUSUAL WEEK, NURSE MONTGOMERY.
I'M RECOVERING FROM A DEADLY BRAIN TUMOR.
THEY SAID IT WAS INOPERABLE.
THEY WERE WRONG.
THAT'S GOTTA BE GOOD NEWS, RIGHT?
EXCUSE ME-- MY PHONE--
--JOSH SMILES, YOU EVIL REPTILIAN BASTARD.
SO?
RAY.
THE STUDIO JUST CALLED ABOUT "ANNIHILATOR"--
ARE YOU READY FOR THIS?

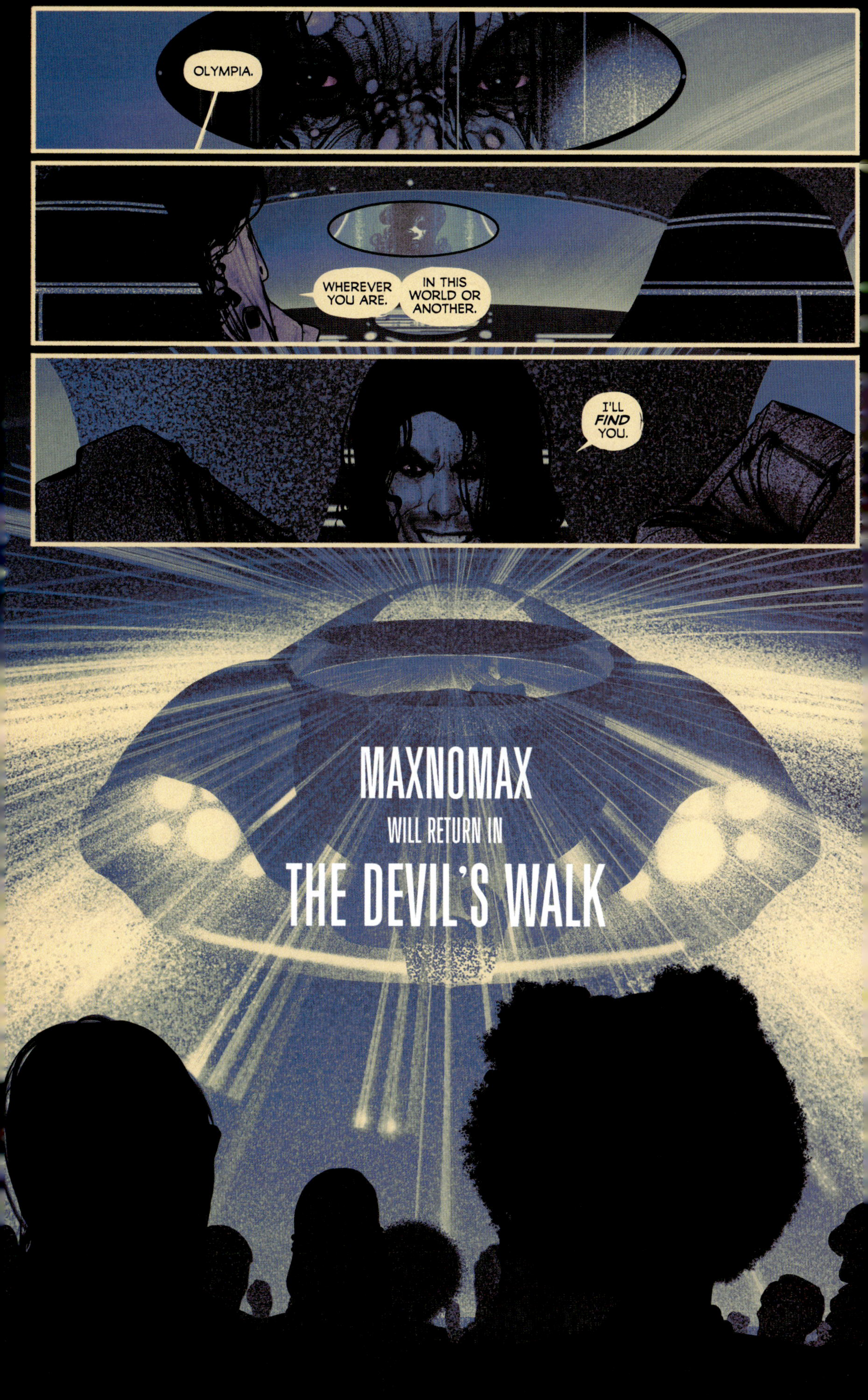
OLYMPIA.
WHEREVER YOU ARE.
IN THIS WORLD OR ANOTHER.
I'LL *FIND* YOU.
MAXNOMAX
WILL RETURN IN
THE DEVIL'S WALK

BACK MATTER

Bits and pieces, including Grant's original character descriptions from August 31st, 2012 & Frazer's conceptual artwork & designs from February 12th, 2013.

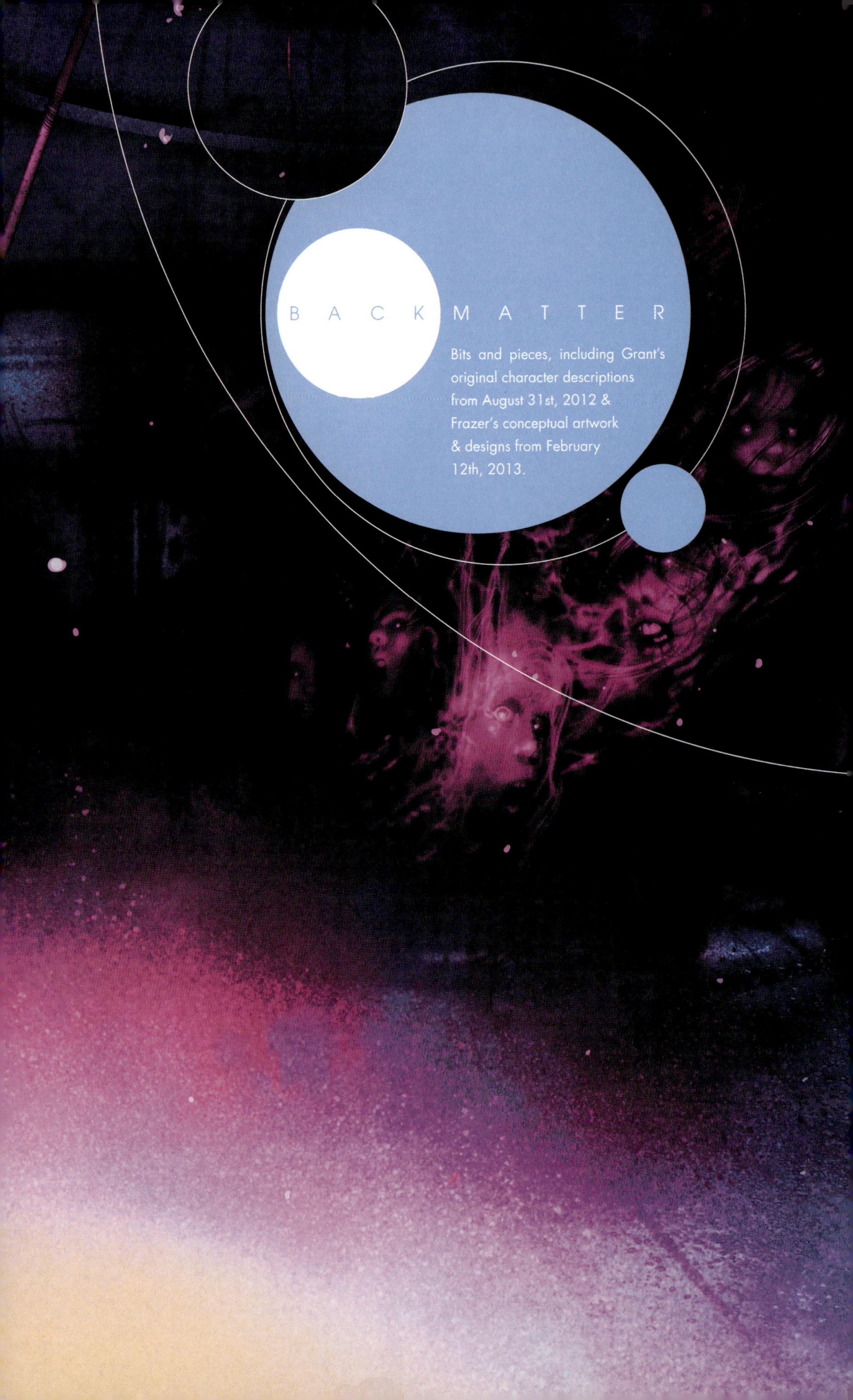

MAX NOMAX

is the lead character in Ray Spass' screenplay 'Annihilator'. He is the ultimate rebel. An artist, escapologist, criminal, scientist. Devilishly handsome and charismatic. Funny, cruel and brilliant. Satanic, Byronic. Lock up your daughters. The bad boy deluxe. The quintessential sexy anti-hero.

Nomax belongs to a future super-society where everything is perfect and life is fine under the calm control of the godlike VADA computer; perfect, fine and way too boring for the likes of Nomax who lives his life as a constant thorn in the side of authority and rules.

After Nomax committed what was seen as the ultimate crime (see Olympia) VADA finally ran out of patience and exiled him to DIS - an abandoned research station orbiting the black hole at the center of our galaxy. Nomax was sent there to die contemplating his crimes and the futility of his existence. That's where we start our story.

Somehow he escaped and found himself in 21st century Los Angeles. He has no memory of his escape and very little recollection of who he is or why he was imprisoned in the first place. Instead, he's relying on Ray Spass to REMEMBER his story for him.

According to Nomax, it's he who is real and our world which is the copy of something bigger. Only by remembering who he is and how he came to be here, can Nomax hope to save us all from destruction at the hands of VADA and his Annihilator.

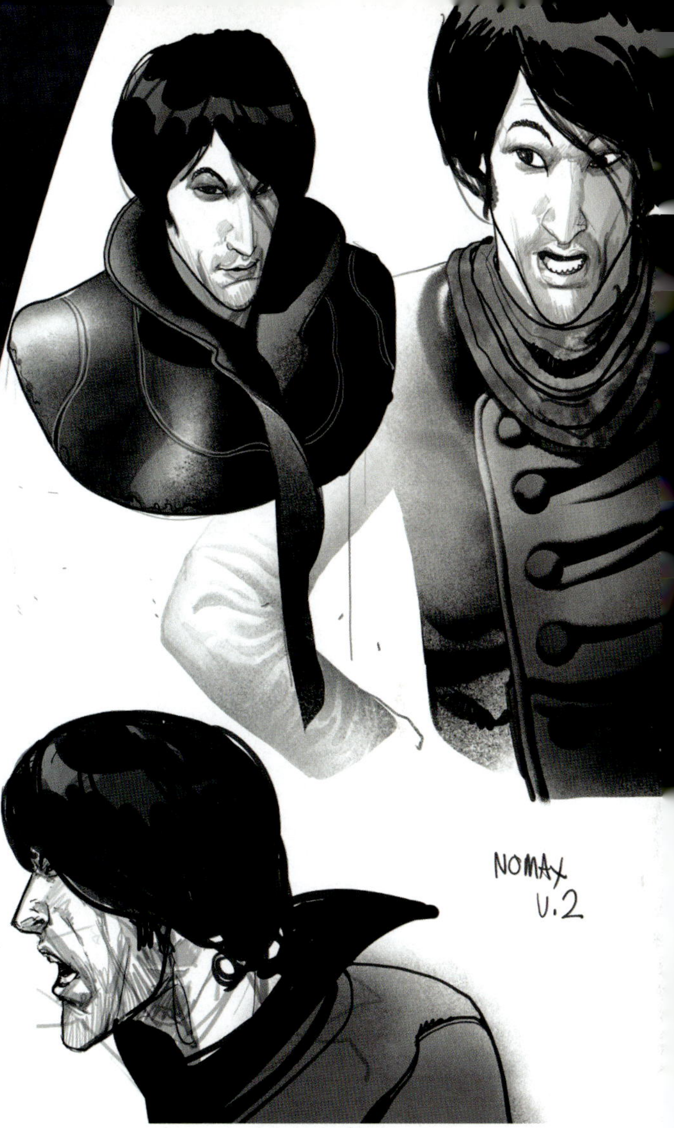
NOMAX
V.2

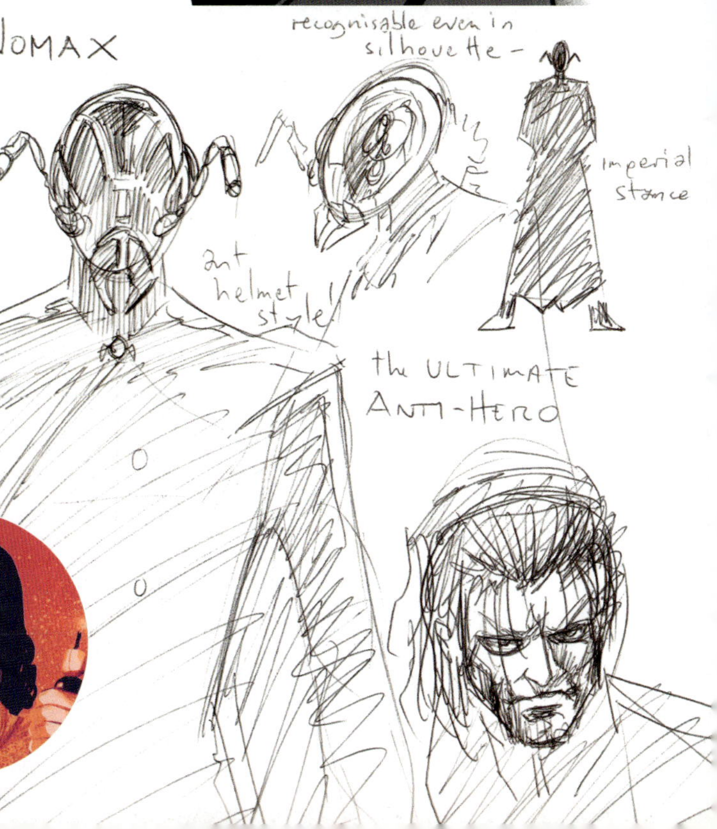
NOMAX
recognisable even in silhouette -
imperial stance
ant helmet style!
the ULTIMATE ANTI-HERO

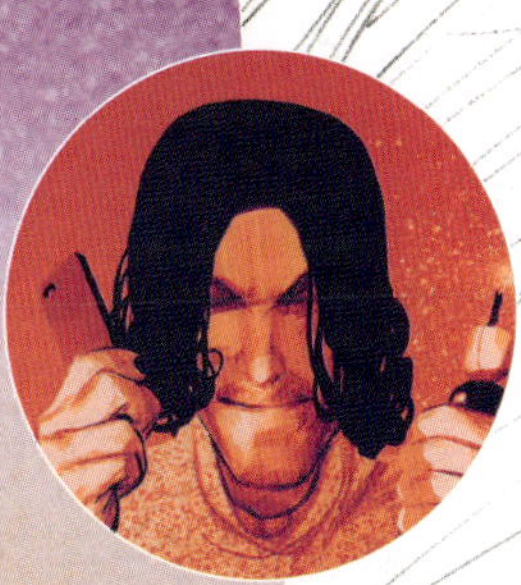

Top: Original character design Version 2 by Frazer Irving. *Bottom:* Original character sketch by Grant Morrison. *Opposite:* Max Nomax - Original character design Version 1 by Frazer Irving.

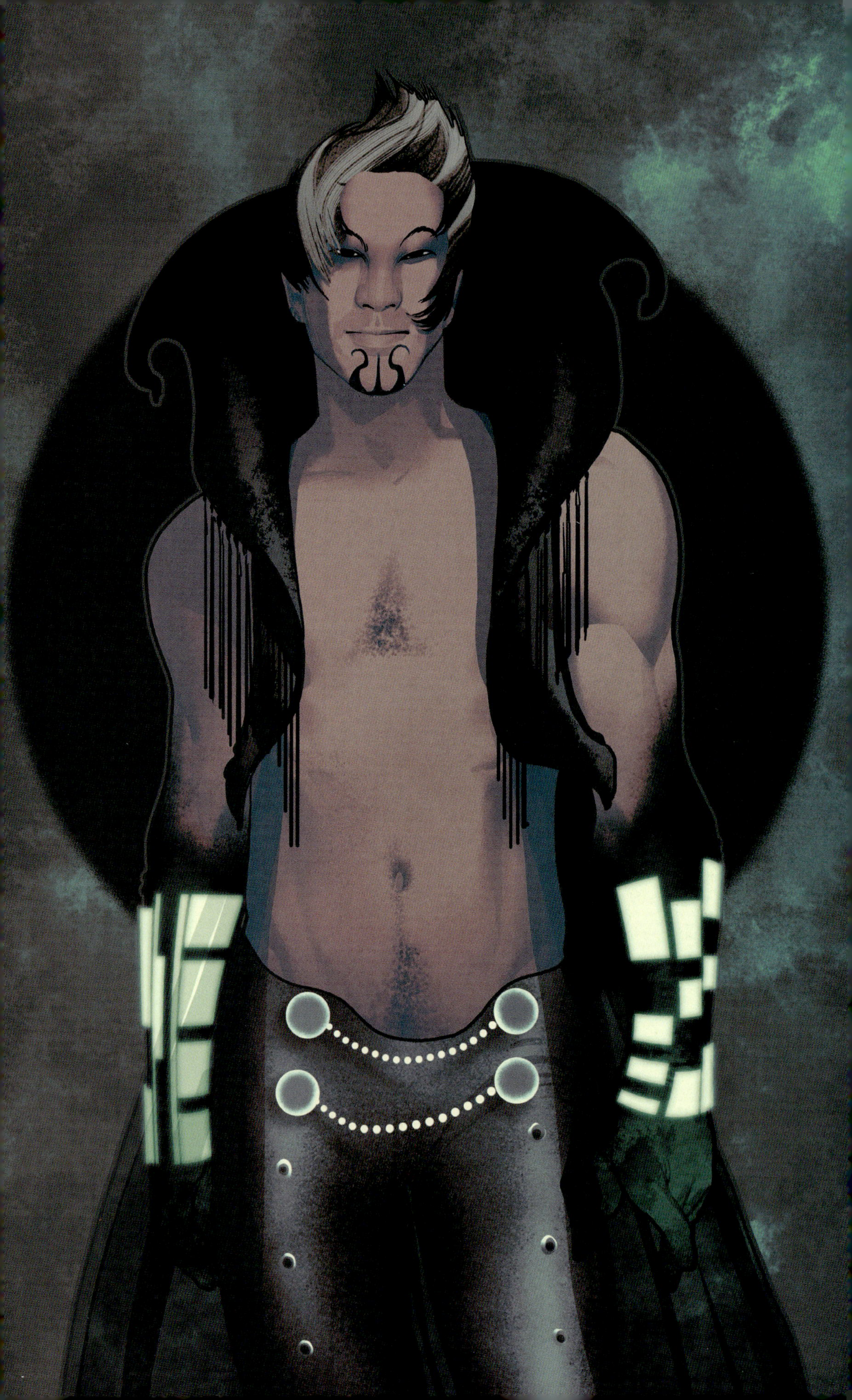

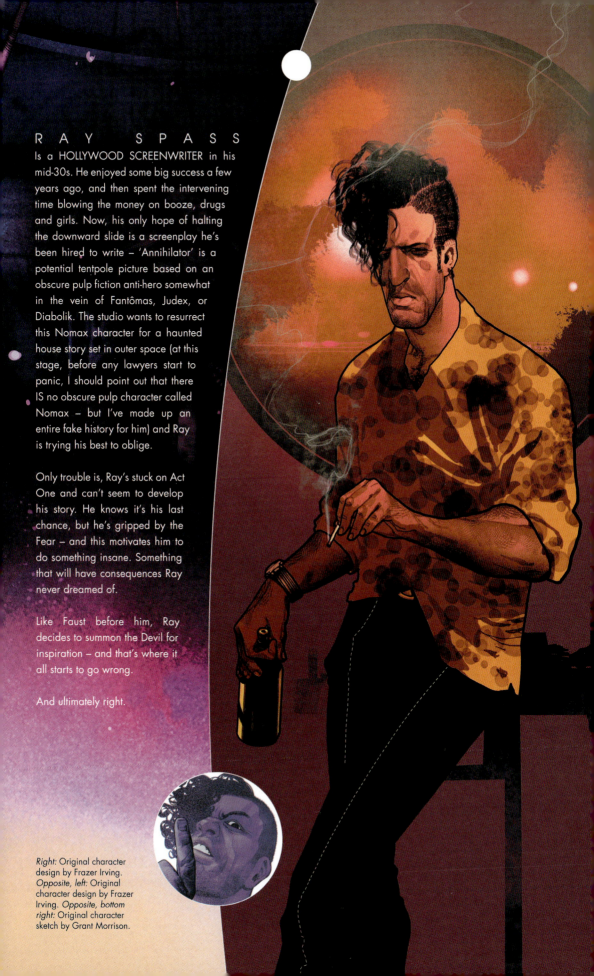

RAY SPASS

Is a HOLLYWOOD SCREENWRITER in his mid-30s. He enjoyed some big success a few years ago, and then spent the intervening time blowing the money on booze, drugs and girls. Now, his only hope of halting the downward slide is a screenplay he's been hired to write – 'Annihilator' is a potential tentpole picture based on an obscure pulp fiction anti-hero somewhat in the vein of Fantômas, Judex, or Diabolik. The studio wants to resurrect this Nomax character for a haunted house story set in outer space (at this stage, before any lawyers start to panic, I should point out that there IS no obscure pulp character called Nomax – but I've made up an entire fake history for him) and Ray is trying his best to oblige.

Only trouble is, Ray's stuck on Act One and can't seem to develop his story. He knows it's his last chance, but he's gripped by the Fear – and this motivates him to do something insane. Something that will have consequences Ray never dreamed of.

Like Faust before him, Ray decides to summon the Devil for inspiration – and that's where it all starts to go wrong.

And ultimately right.

Right: Original character design by Frazer Irving. *Opposite, left:* Original character design by Frazer Irving. *Opposite, bottom right:* Original character sketch by Grant Morrison.

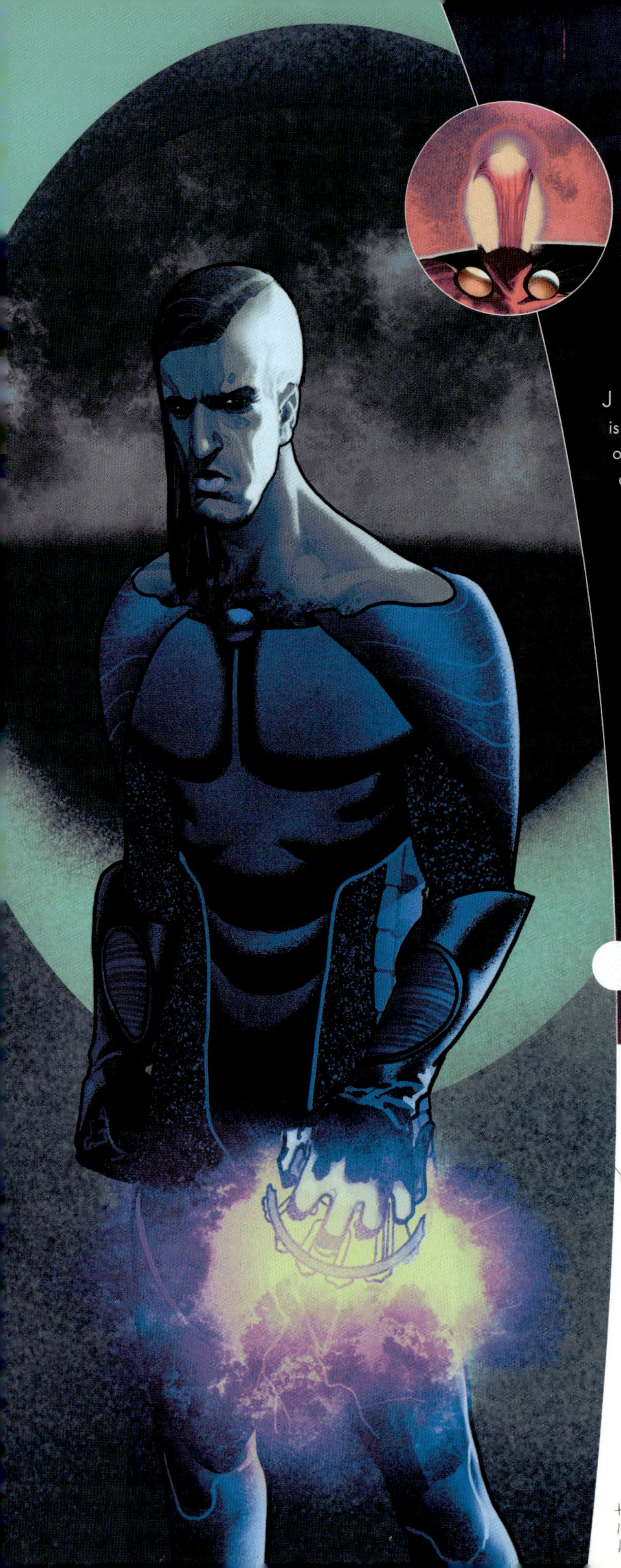

J E T M A K R O

is VADA's chief 'Annihilator' – leader of an elite cadre of super-enhanced assassins/enforcers who carry out VADA's will when all other options have been exhausted.

Genetically and surgically-altered with shark DNA to be the ultimate hunter/killer, Makro cannot be stopped.

He has one Achilles Heel – having been shot in the head by Nomax shortly before chasing him into our world, Makro has a deadly bullet embedded in his skull. Only by maintaining perfect concentration can he stop the bullet penetrating his brain.

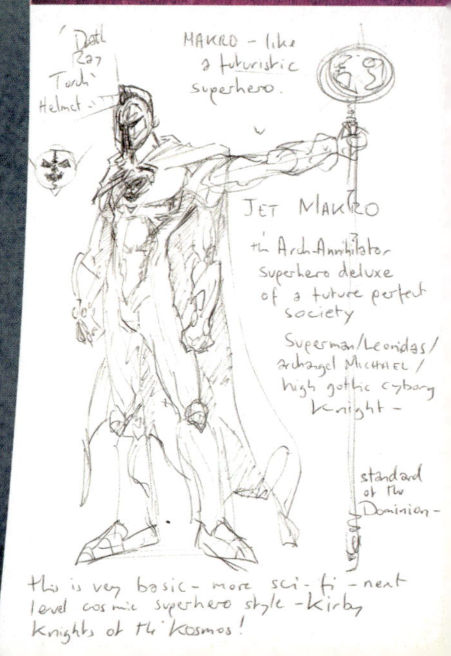
'Death Ray Torch' Helmet
MAKRO – like a futuristic superhero.
JET MAKRO
the Arch-Annihilator superhero deluxe of a future perfect society
Superman/Leonidas/ archangel MICHAEL/ high gothic cyborg knight –
standard of the Dominion –
this is very basic – more sci-fi – next level cosmic superhero style – Kirby knights of the Kosmos!

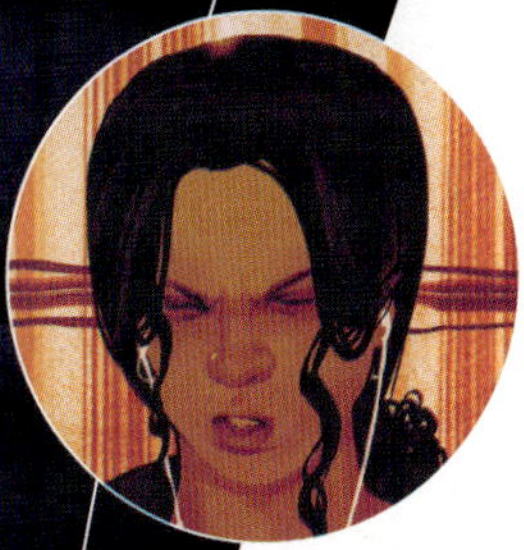

L U N A

is Ray Spass' ex. He's the sort of Hollywood guy who burned his way through a string of pretty young models and it was all fine until he FELL hard for this particular girl. Ray – the king of casual sex and discarded beauties – finally met his match in the feisty, clever Romanian girl and their relationship was an exploding supernova for 18 months that left Ray permanently and indelibly touched by genuine grown-up emotions and feelings. Since losing Luna, Ray has been on a self-destructive downward spiral.

Now 25, Luna's done her best to put her tumultuous time with Ray in the past and moved on. Now she teaches yoga and she's part of the LA New Age scene. The last thing she wants is for Ray Spass to come back into her quiet life and turn it upside down. So that's exactly what happens.

O L Y M P I A

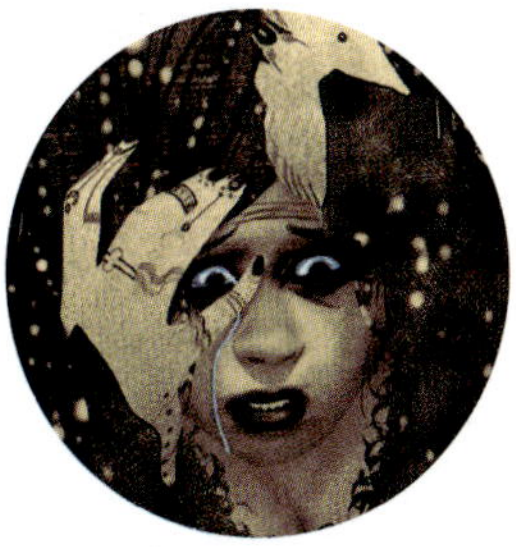

is Max Nomax's lost love and the object of his obsession.

Olympia is a machine - VADA's ultimate creation – so sophisticated it cannot be distinguished from a real human being.

Except that Olympia was VADA's first and only failure. His creation, perfect in every detail, lacked something fundamental – a SOUL. Giving a soul to his creation was the problem VADA could not solve, representing the limits of the God-Computer's abilities.

To VADA's great dismay, Olympia only developed a soul in the moment she fell in love with MAX NOMAX. When Nomax rejected her, Olympia took her own life. The enraged VADA had the guilty Nomax captured and exiled on DIS.

Since that moment, she has been preserved in an icy sarcophagus. Nomax has dedicated what remains of his life to finding a cure for death and bringing her back.

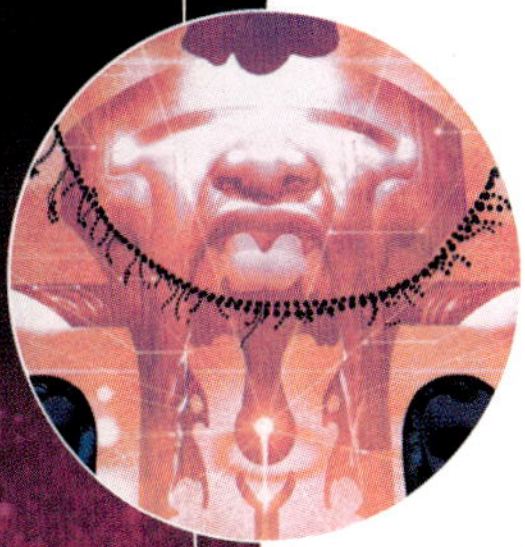

V A D A

is the VATIC ARTIFICIAL DIVINE AUTHORITY – a Zen super-computer which runs human affairs and is responsible for the peaceful expansion of the human race across the cosmos.

VADA controls all aspects of life in this perfect world. Everyone is happy, everything runs on time – but there is a sense of boredom and lack of ambition.

It's this blandness that Max Nomax can't help fighting against in every way he knows how – from making provocative works of art, to stealing great treasures and otherwise challenging or mocking VADA in every way.

VADA is the ultimate authority. Nomax is the ultimate rebel. Neither can help themselves. Both are right. Both are wrong.

B A B Y   B U G - E Y E S

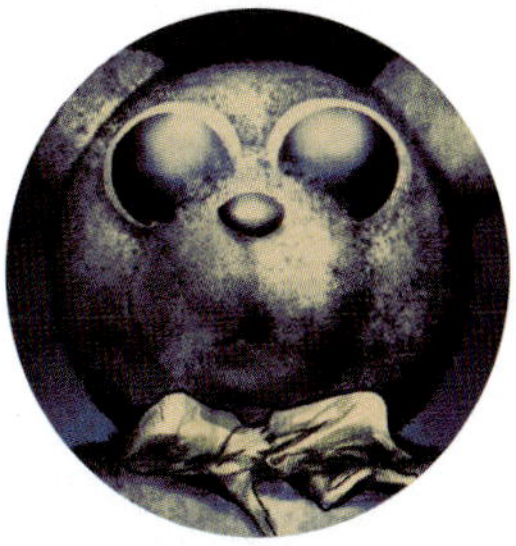

is the last of its kind. He's a kind of genetically-engineered, part-artificial creature that looks like a four-foot tall teddy bear/lemur.

The Bug-Eyes were created as companion creatures for astronauts assigned to the gloomy Dis station. They were created to be empathic, kind and helpful. Instead, the manufacturers made the eyes just a bit too big for comfort. The Bug-Eyes as they were called were seen as creepy and disturbing by most people. Most of them were horribly destroyed, leaving this one survivor.

ANNIHILATOR #1-6 cover sketches by Grant Morrison

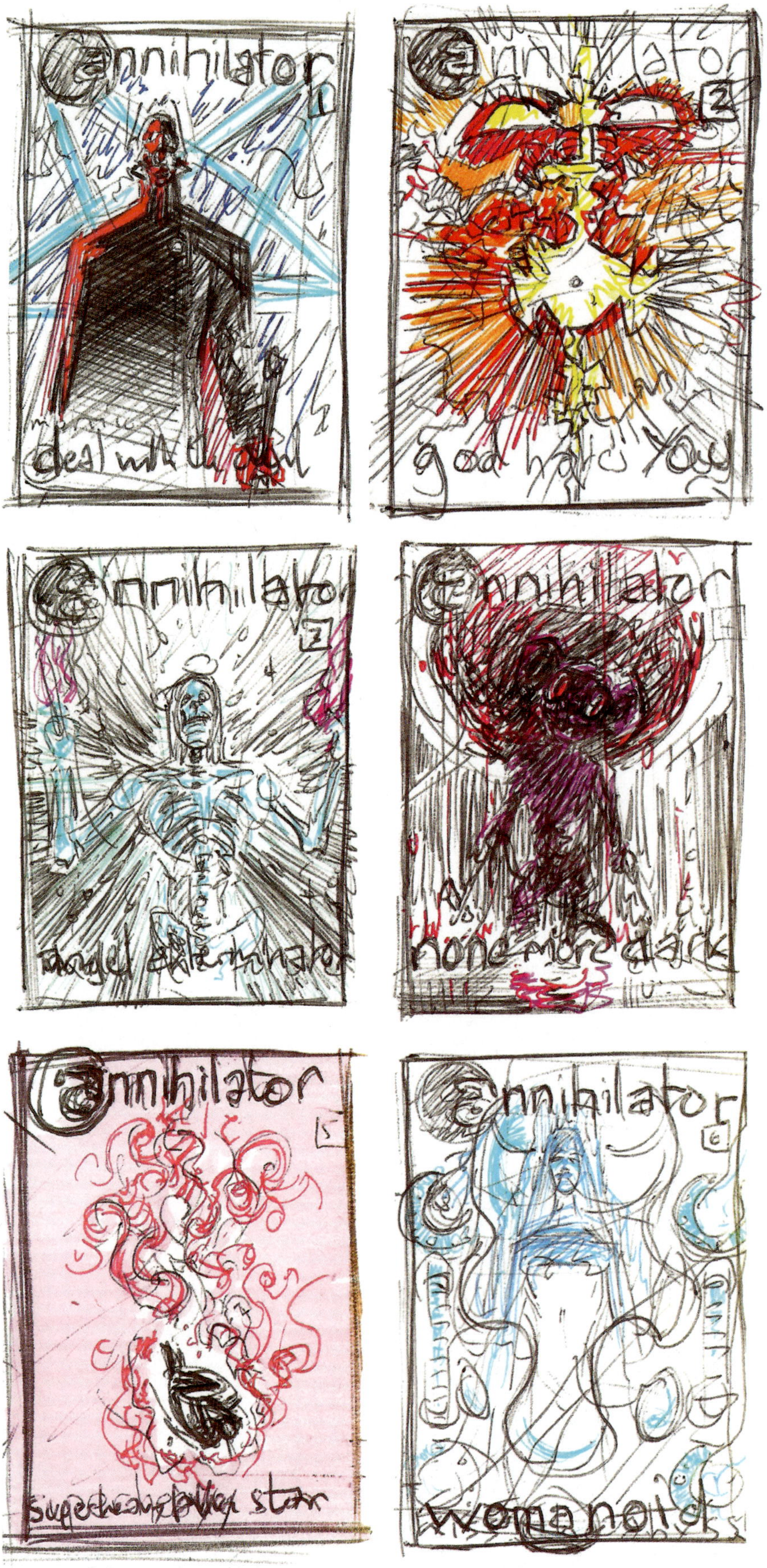
annihilator
annihilator
annihilator
annihilator
none more dark
annihilator
annihilator
womanoid

ANNIHILATOR #1 unused cover

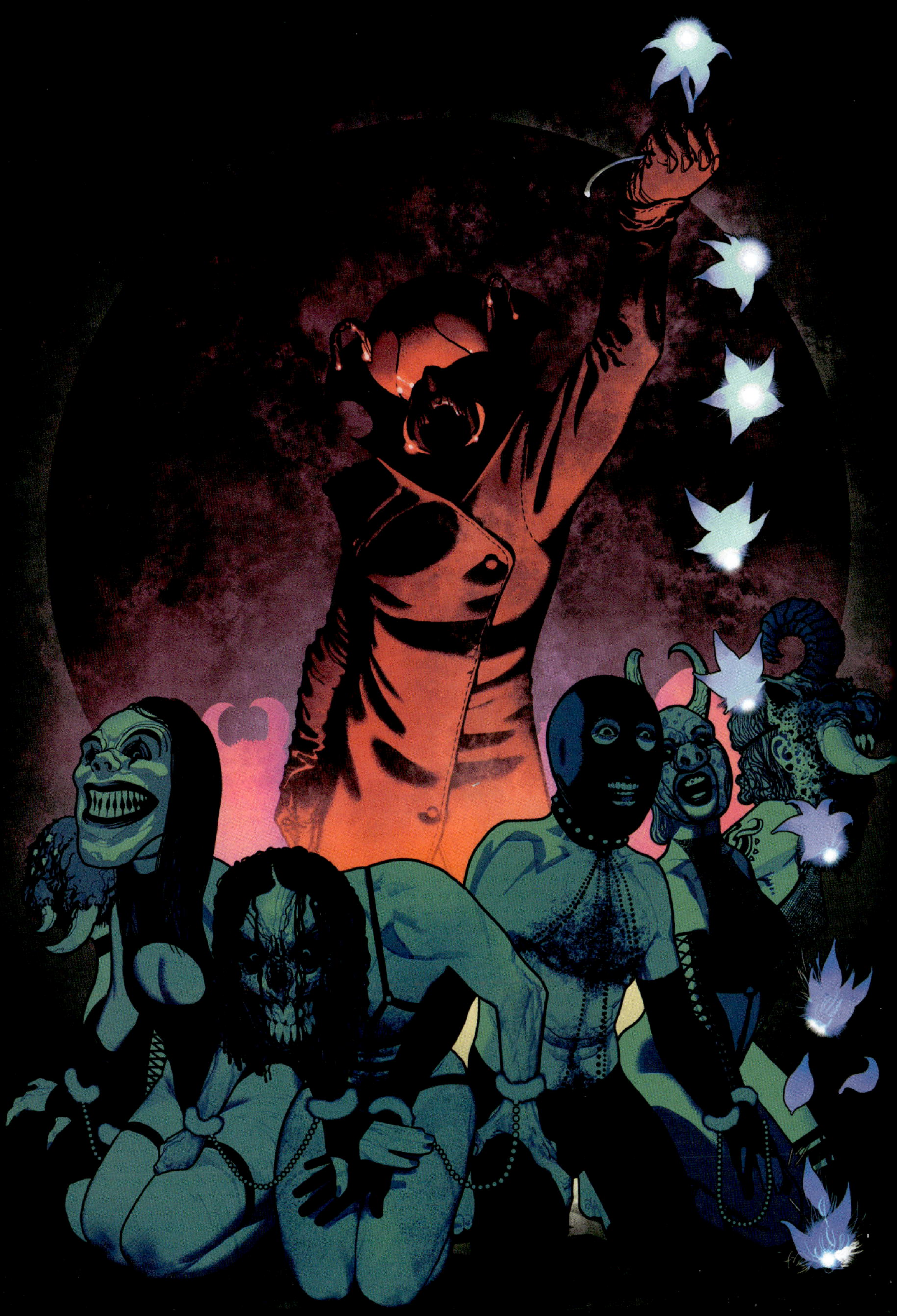

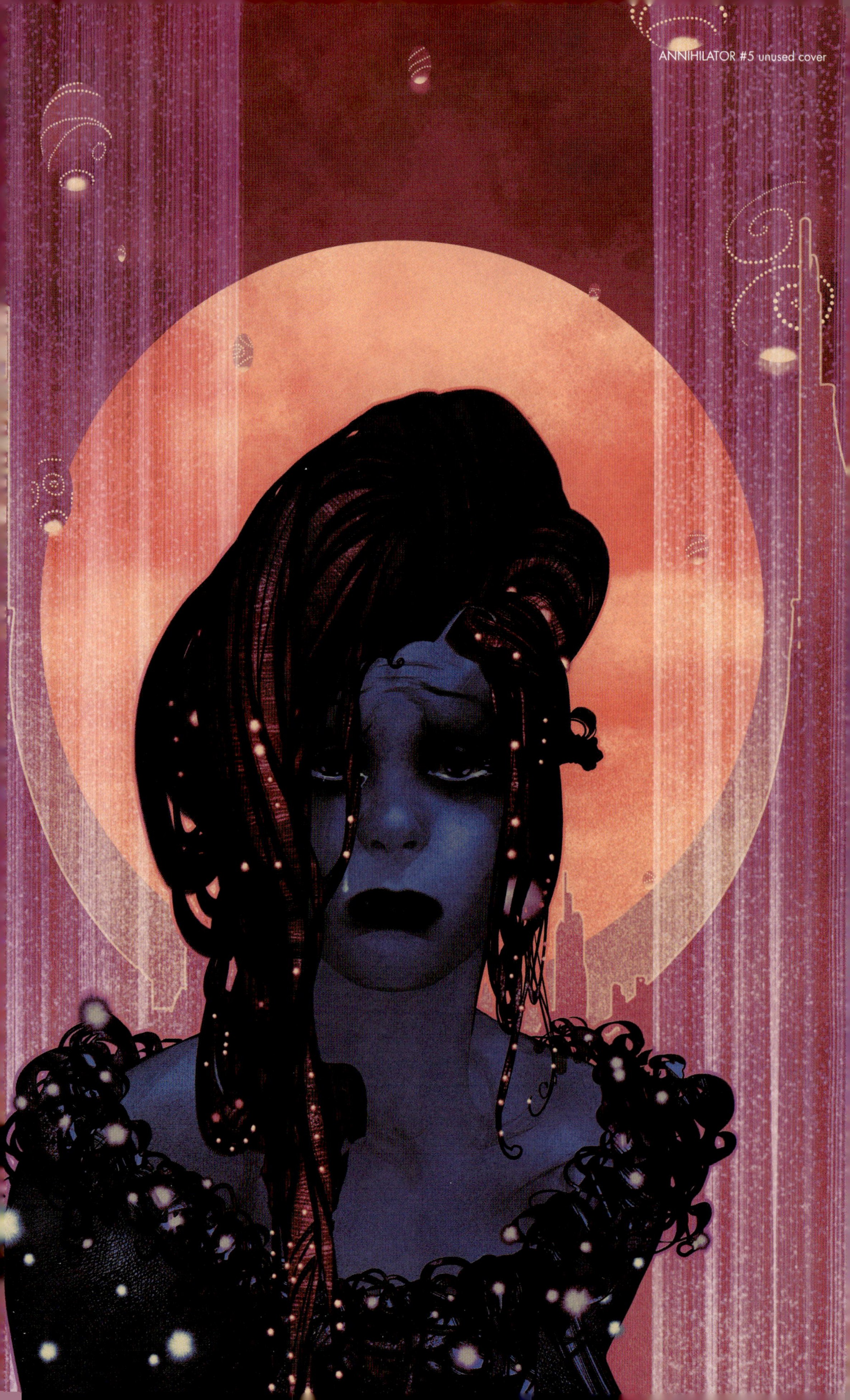

ANNIHILATOR #5 unused cover

Process by Frazer Irving

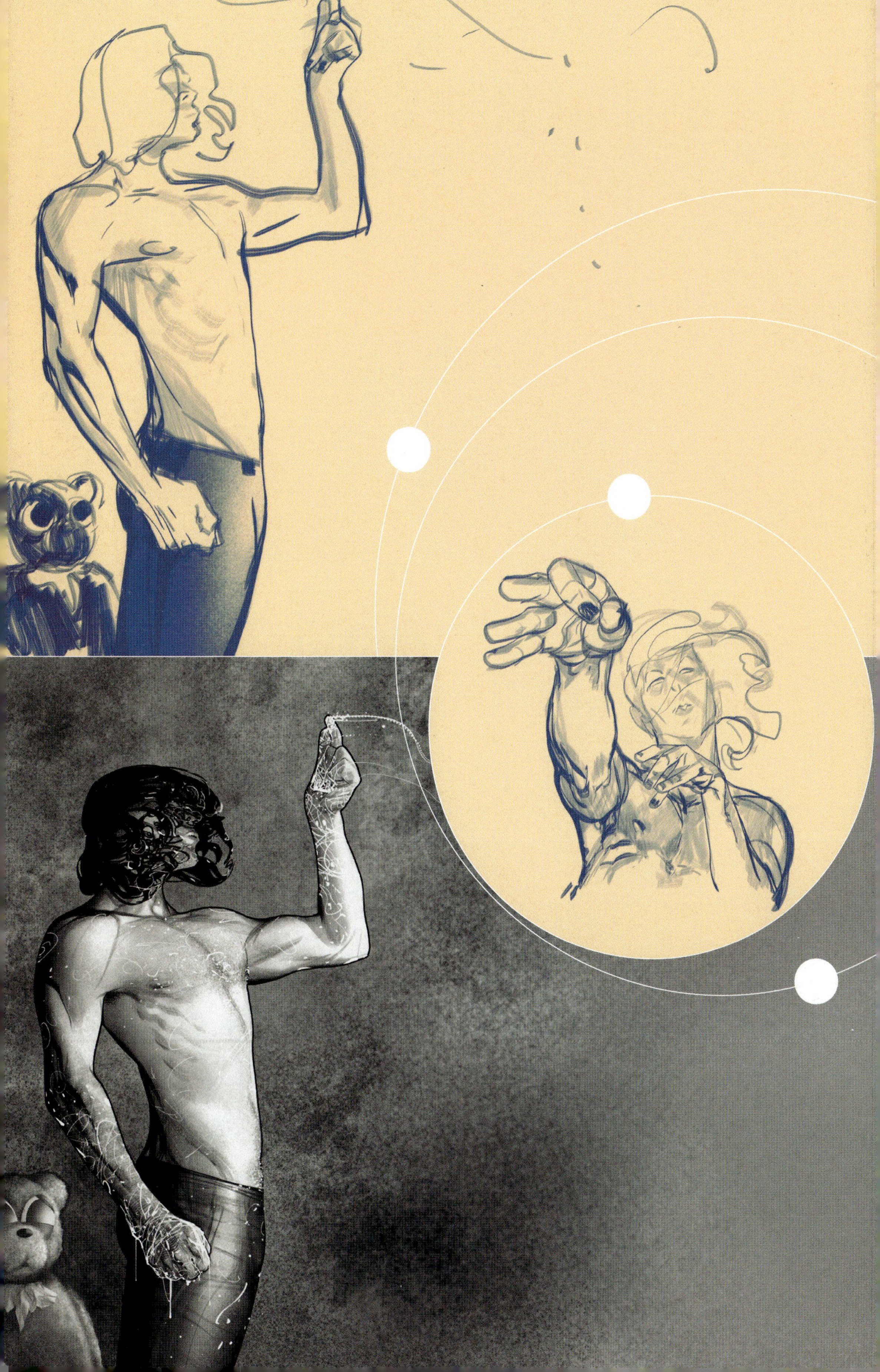